Haiti

the Bradt Travel Guide

Paul Clammer

edition 1

www.bradtguides.com

Bradt Travel Guides Ltd, UK
The Globe Pequot Press Inc, USA

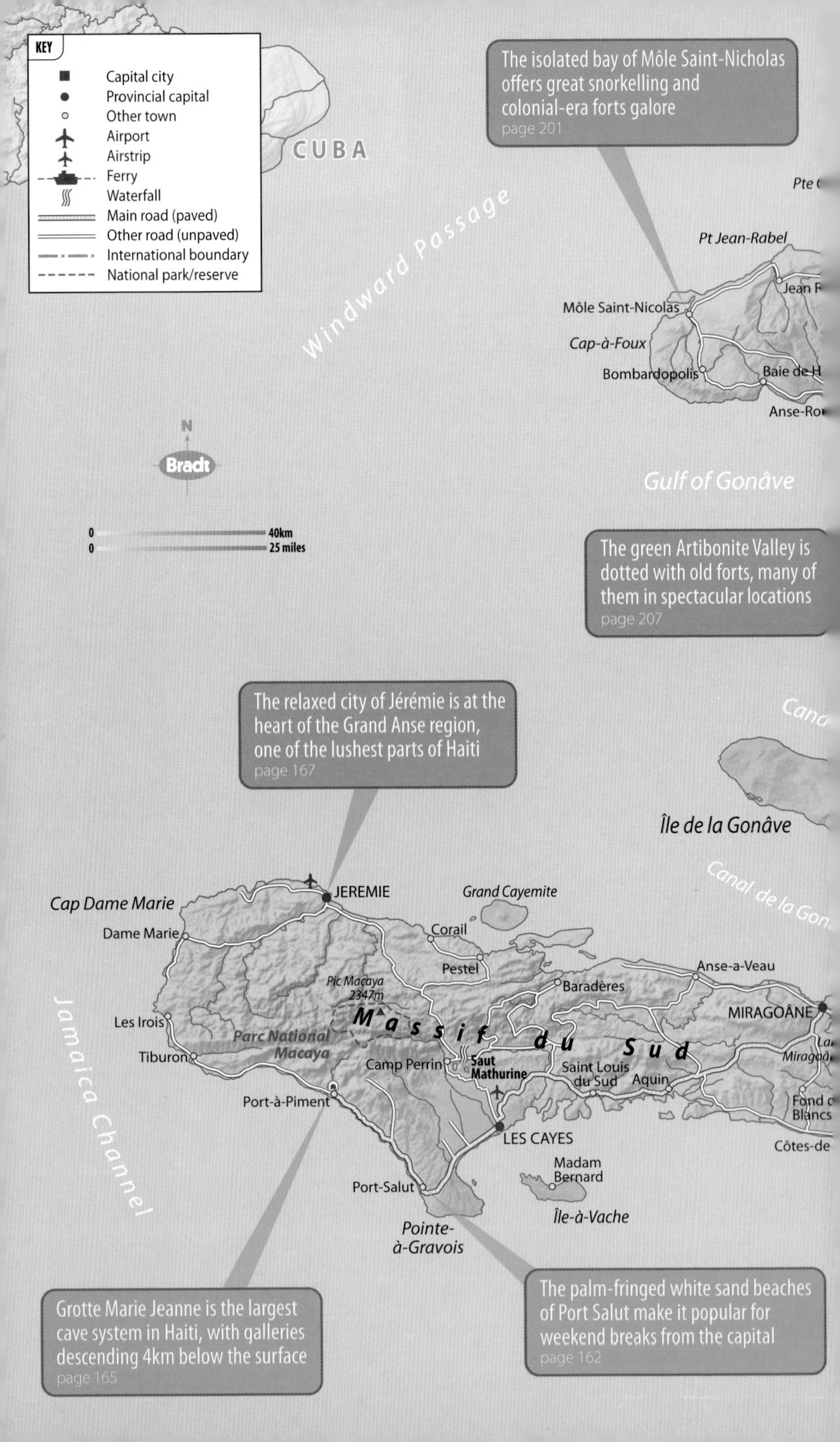

KEY
Capital city
Provincial capital
Other town
Airport
Airstrip
Ferry
Waterfall
Main road (paved)
Other road (unpaved)
International boundary
National park/reserve
CUBA
Windward Passage
The isolated bay of Môle Saint-Nicholas offers great snorkelling and colonial-era forts galore
page 201
Pt Jean-Rabel
Môle Saint-Nicolas
Cap-à-Foux
Bombardopolis
Gulf of Gonâve
0 40km
0 25 miles
The green Artibonite Valley is dotted with old forts, many of them in spectacular locations
page 207
The relaxed city of Jérémie is at the heart of the Grand Anse region, one of the lushest parts of Haiti
page 167
Île de la Gonâve
JEREMIE
Cap Dame Marie
Dame Marie
Grand Cayemite
Corail
Pestel
Baradères
Anse-a-Veau
MIRAGOÂNE
Pic Macaya 2347m
Massif du Sud
Les Irois
Tiburon
Parc National Macaya
Camp Perrin
Saut Mathurine
Saint Louis du Sud
Aquin
Port-à-Piment
LES CAYES
Jamaica Channel
Madam Bernard
Port-Salut
Île-à-Vache
Pointe-à-Gravois
Grotte Marie Jeanne is the largest cave system in Haiti, with galleries descending 4km below the surface
page 165
The palm-fringed white sand beaches of Port Salut make it popular for weekend breaks from the capital
page 162

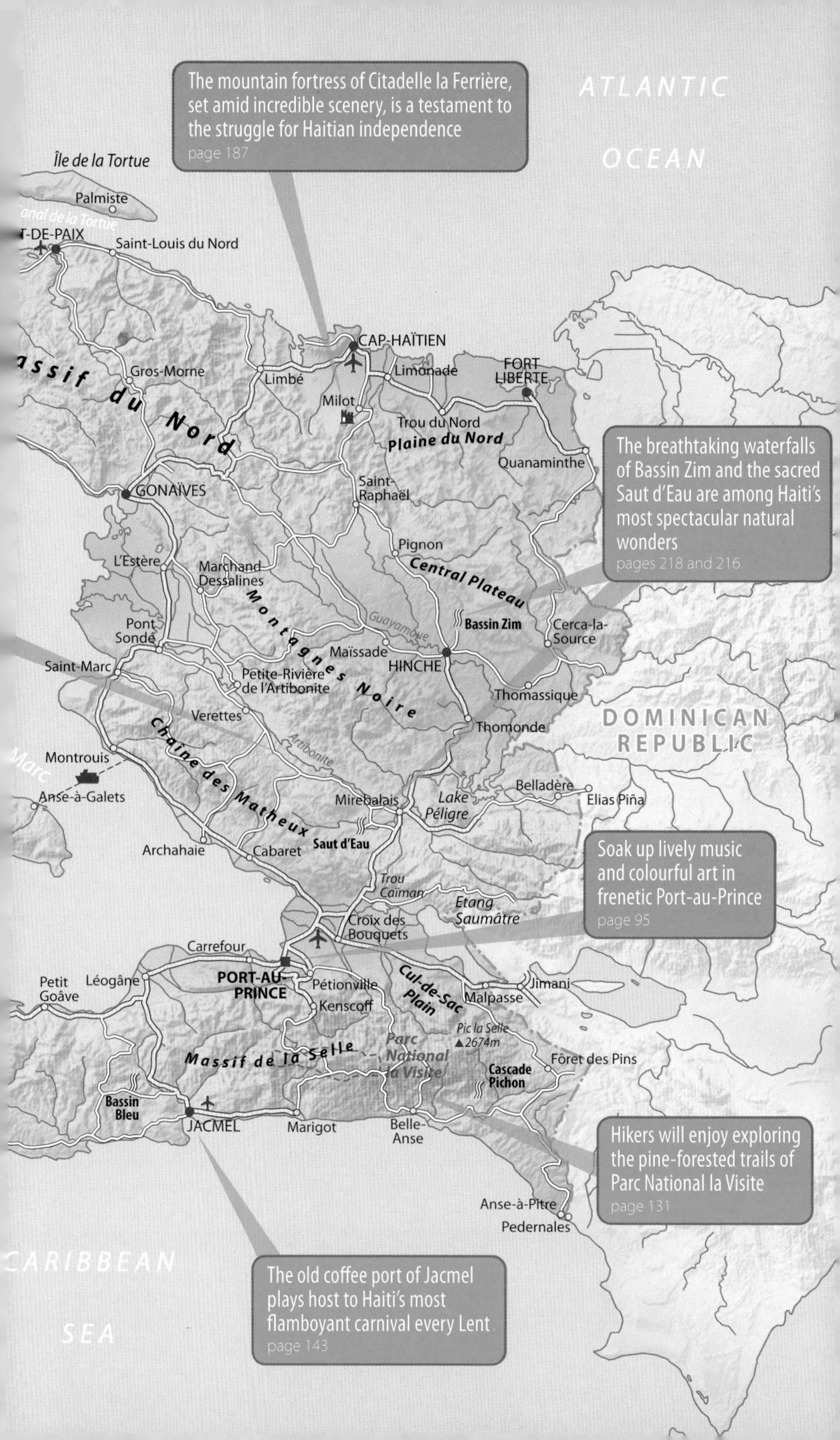

The mountain fortress of Citadelle la Ferrière, set amid incredible scenery, is a testament to the struggle for Haitian independence
page 187
ATLANTIC
OCEAN
Île de la Tortue
Palmiste
Saint-Louis du Nord
Massif du Nord
Gros-Morne
Limbé
CAP-HAÏTIEN
Limonade
FORT LIBERTE
Milot
Trou du Nord
Plaine du Nord
Quanaminthe
The breathtaking waterfalls of Bassin Zim and the sacred Saut d'Eau are among Haiti's most spectacular natural wonders
pages 218 and 216
GONAÏVES
Saint-Raphaël
Pignon
Central Plateau
L'Estère
Marchand Dessalines
Montagnes Noire
Bassin Zim
Cerca-la-Source
Pont Sondé
Maïssade
HINCHE
Saint-Marc
Petite-Rivière de l'Artibonite
Thomassique
Verettes
Thomonde
DOMINICAN REPUBLIC
Chaîne des Matheux
Montrouis
Anse-à-Galets
Belladère
Elias Piña
Mirebalais
Lake Péligre
Archahaie
Cabaret
Saut d'Eau
Soak up lively music and colourful art in frenetic Port-au-Prince
page 95
Trou Caïman
Etang Saumâtre
Croix des Bouquets
Carrefour
PORT-AU-PRINCE
Petit Goâve
Léogâne
Pétionville
Kenscoff
Cul-de-Sac Plain
Jimani
Malpasse
Pic la Selle
2674m
Massif de la Selle
Parc National la Visite
Cascade Pichon
Fôret des Pins
Bassin Bleu
JACMEL
Marigot
Belle-Anse
Hikers will enjoy exploring the pine-forested trails of Parc National la Visite
page 131
Anse-à-Pitre
Pedernales
CARIBBEAN
SEA
The old coffee port of Jacmel plays host to Haiti's most flamboyant carnival every Lent
page 143

Haiti Don't miss...

Beaches
With its ribbon of white sand, Port Salut makes for the perfect lazy holiday getaway
(JS/A) page 162

La Visite National Park
The pine-forested walk between Furcy and Seguin offers some of the country's most exhilarating views (USAID) page 131

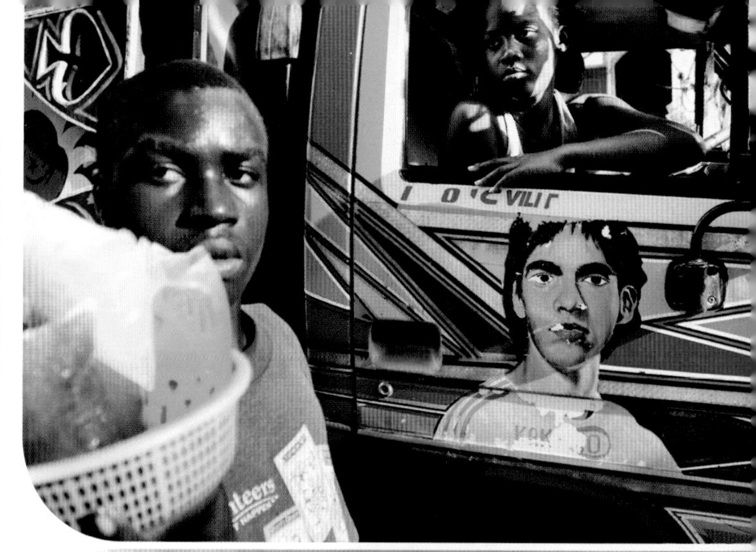

Port-au-Prince
Taptaps with technicolour paint jobs and serious sound systems ply the streets of Haiti's buzzing capital
(JS/A) page 95

Citadelle la Ferrière
The largest fort in the Caribbean, offering sweeping views over the Plaine du Nord, could hold up to 5,000 soldiers
(BCB) page 187

Jacmel
Half of Haiti's population seems to descend on this old southern coffee port every February for Carnival, featuring giant papier-mâché masks, *rara* bands and dancers
(PC) page 143

Haiti in colour

left The venerable Hotel Oloffson is the Haitian gingerbread mansion *par excellence*, dating from 1887 and immortalised in Graham Greene's novel *The Comedians* (H/A) page 104

below The district of Boutilliers, above Port-au-Prince, has a belvedere offering spectacular views over the city (BD) page 128

bottom The capital's main cemetery offers an almost urban vista of colossal sarcophagi and mortuary chapels, testament to the Haitian tradition of honouring ancestors with decorated tombs (MI/A) page 121

above Now fully restored, the Moorish-style pavilion of the Iron Market has become a symbol of rebirth and reconstruction following the 2010 earthquake (SS) page 118

top right The entrance to a temple in Bel Air, Port-au-Prince's oldest residential district and an important centre of Vodou (SS) page 30

right Port-au-Prince has a long and colourful arts and handicrafts tradition, and the walls of streets all over the city are turned into open-air art galleries every day (SS) page 110

below Hundreds of thousands of revellers flock to the Champs de Mars every Lent for the parades, music and free-flowing alcohol that fuel the national carnival (SS) page 108

above The humbling scale of Citadelle la Ferrière is evident on the road up from Choiseul (BCB) page 187

below Allegedly modelled on the palace of Frederick II of Prussia, Sans Souci Palace is testament to the vision of Henri Christophe, self-proclaimed King of Haiti (SS) page 186

AUTHOR

Paul Clammer trained and worked as a molecular biologist before an unexpected encounter in an Iranian teahouse led him into being sucked into the travel industry. He has worked as a tour guide for adventure travel companies in Morocco and Turkey. Since 2003 he was written or contributed to over 25 guidebooks, including Bradt's guide to Sudan, as well as guides to Afghanistan, Pakistan, Morocco and chunks of West Africa. He has been visiting Haiti since 2007, and to research and write this book he based himself in Port-au-Prince for nine months. Follow him online at www.twitter.com/paulclammer and www.facebook.com/HaitiTravelGuide.

AUTHOR'S STORY

It's always been a mystery to me why, when going to the travel section of a bookshop and looking under 'H', you couldn't find a guidebook about Haiti. You always had to move back to 'D', where it was invariably paired with the Dominican Republic, with which it shares the island of Hispaniola. There have been guidebooks before – an early example from 1862 was aimed at African-Americans wanting to emigrate from a country still wracked by slavery – but with this book Bradt has become the first English-language publisher since the 1980s to produce a guide dedicated to this incredible country.

It's a book I've wanted to write since my first visit, a wish that only increased after the 2010 earthquake, when Haiti was flooded with relief workers, often bringing their own preconceptions about the country. To research and write it, I moved to Haiti and rented an apartment in Port-au-Prince. It seemed the only way to try and do the country justice; the resulting manuscript was punctuated by crowing roosters, Carnival theme tunes and delight at the first fresh mangoes and avocados of the season.

These days, most foreigners seem to come to Haiti for some sort of 'project' – from development and volunteer missions to business and consulting. But tourism potentially has a huge part to play in Haiti's reconstruction, and now is also a great time to visit purely for itself. It's a small country, but it's ludicrously full of attractions for the pioneering traveller. So pour yourself a shot of the best Haitian rum, add a squeeze of lime and get stuck in. *Ayibobo*!

PUBLISHER'S FOREWORD

Adrian Phillips, Publishing Director

Paul Clammer's a persuasive chap – he pitched a standalone guide to Haiti several times before we agreed to take it on. We're pleased he persevered because this is not just a useful book but an important one. The damage inflicted by the earthquake of 2010 was immense, and tourism has a key part to play in piecing things back together. Haiti has riches to reward the intrepid visitor – beaches, culture and a fascinating history that includes the world's only successful slave revolution. Paul dived headlong into this project, basing himself in the country for almost a year; whether you want to know where to get the best rum or how to conduct yourself at a Vodou ceremony, he's the man with the answers.

First published November 2012

Bradt Travel Guides Ltd
IDC House, The Vale, Chalfont St Peter, Bucks SL9 9RZ, England www.bradtguides.com
Print edition published in the USA by The Globe Pequot Press Inc,
PO Box 480, Guilford, Connecticut 06437-0480

Project Manager: Maisie Fitzpatrick

ISBN: 978 1 84162 415 0 (print)
e-ISBN: 978 1 84162 742 7 (e-pub)
e-ISBN: 978 1 84162 643 7 (mobi)

British Library Cataloguing in Publication Data
A catalogue record for this book is available from the British Library

Photographs Alamy: JS Callahan/tropicalpix (JS/T/A), Janos Csernoch (JC/A), Hemis (H/A), Jenny Matthews (JM/A), mauritius images GmbH (MI/A), Jan Sochor (JS/A), Universal Images Group/DeAgostini (UIG/A), ZUMA Wire Service (Z/A); Benjamin Cole Brown (BCB); Paul Clammer (PC); Ben Depp (BD); Jacqualine Labrom Voyages Lumière (JL/VL); Lindsay Stark (LS); SuperStock (SS); USAID/Haiti (via Flickr.com) (USAID); Wikimedia Commons (W)
Front cover Île Enchantée, Cap-Haïtien (JS/T/A)
Back cover Dancers at the Jacmel Carnival (BD); gingerbread house, Port-au-Prince (SS)
Title page Taptaps, Port-au-Prince (Z/A); the Marché de Fer, Port-au-Prince (SS); a *rara* band takes a break from performing on Easter Sunday (BD)

Maps David McCutcheon FBCart.S *Colour map* Relief map bases by Nick Rowland FRGS

Typeset from the author's disc by Wakewing
Production managed by Jellyfish Print Solutions; printed in India

Acknowledgements

No guidebook was ever really produced by one person alone, and it's a pleasure to be able to thank those that made producing this book easier than it would otherwise have been. As the Creole saying has it, *men anpil chay pa lou*: many hands make a load lighter.

At Bradt, thanks to Adrian Phillips who gave in to my annual pitch to write a guide to Haiti and commissioned the book, and to Maisie Fitzpatrick for brilliantly managing the project. Rachel Fielding arranged the contracts.

This book has benefited from several fine contributions from others, so thanks to my contributors, Saundra Schimmelpfennig (who wrote on volunteering in Haiti), Diane Wolkstein (Haitian folktales), Kohl Threlkeld (motorbike supremo), and David Eisenbaum (hiking on Pic la Selle). Alexis Erkert also provided a boxed text on women in Haiti, but must also be given special thanks (along with Ben Depp) for fine company and conversations, and revealing the best place to picnic in the mountains above Port-au-Prince.

In Port-au-Prince, *mesi anpil* to the brilliant Jacqui Labrom of Voyages Lumière and to Michael Geilenfeld and everyone at St Joseph's Home for Boys for providing a home from home during the unnecessarily long hunt for an apartment to rent. A big thumbs up to Alain Armand (and Priscilla and Anacaona) and Arikia Millikan. Brian Oakes repeatedly offered insight to some of the more obscure Haitian historical sites, as well as trips in his Polaris. Geffrard was an always reliable and excellent driver. Thanks also to Jean-Cyril Pressoir of Tour Haiti for the Môle trip, along with networking queen Amy King and Philip Kiracofe of Mountain Bike Haiti. Thanks to Monica and Andy Ansaldi for their hospitality. *Merci aussi* to Bertrand Martin of Manman Pemba.

On the road, particular thanks to Maurice Etienne in Milot, Michelle Skaer, Bette Gebrian and Juliette Tardieu in Jérémie, François-Garel Jean-Enard de Vertieres in Cap-Haïtien, David Smyth in Cyvadier, Yanick Martin in Jacmel and Winter Rae in Gonaïves.

During the write-up, thanks to fellow Bradt author Philip Briggs and Melinda Miles (Let Haiti Live). Several journalists also provided interesting conversations and context over varying quantities of Prestige beer and rum sours: Kathie Klarreich, Linda Polman, Trenton Daniels, Jonathan Katz, Susanna Ferreira, and Jacob Kushner. Cheers!

Online, thanks to my followers on Twitter (*@paulclammer*), who were an amazing resource for answering questions and offering feedback during both research and writing. Particularly helpful and friendly were Todd Kaderabek (*@ConsiderHaiti*) and Christine Harms (*@MAFHaiti*). Members of the Corbett List were also excellent at answering specific and frequently obscure questions.

Finally, thanks and love to Robyn, who came along for the entire ride and was truly a sidekick extraordinaire. This book is for her.

Contents

LIST OF MAPS

Introduction

In some ways, the most common question I've been asked about writing a guidebook to Haiti is 'Why?' It's a question that mostly revolves around the earthquake that took place on 12 January 2010 ('Isn't the country just rubble now?') or outdated clichés about the country (for example, 'Is it safe to travel because of the gang violence and the voodoo?').

The short answer, of course, is that Haiti is a fascinating and beautiful place. It has palm-fringed beaches with white sand and turquoise sea. It has a rich cultural heritage that lives through its art, music and literature. Its history – written across its landscape – is astounding, a country born out of the world's only successful slave revolution to become the first independent black republic. When you put it like this, any country trying to build a tourist industry would give their eye-teeth for a portfolio like Haiti's.

And yet, Haiti seems to resolutely remain a 'bad news' country. It gets poked and prodded by the international community, too frequently a laboratory for projects from international development to globalisation and everything in between. Media reports often simply reduce the entire nation to a single line – 'Haiti, the poorest country in the Western hemisphere' – a moniker designed more to obfuscate rather than enlighten. In that sense, this guidebook is firmly about subverting expectations. Yes, Haiti is materially poor with a host of complicated economic, political and developmental problems, but it's hardly unique in that. There's another story out there as well. It's one that you'll find by getting out there and exploring, squeezing into buses or having a cold beer at a street-side bar, learning Creole and listening to locals tell their own stories.

Everyone starts their trip to Haiti in Port-au-Prince. Just 90 minutes by air from Miami, the contrast couldn't be sharper. It's a loud and chaotic place, still bearing the scars of the earthquake, but with an unquenchable spirit, and a lively cultural scene. That said, the country really starts to reveal itself when you leave the capital. In the south, there are beaches galore along the Caribbean coast. The town of Jacmel has a fascinating architectural heritage and is justly famous for its bright handicrafts and even more vivid Carnival celebrations. Port Salut is the perfect lazy holiday getaway, while the province of Grand Anse offers more remote explorations. Heading north, attention focuses on Cap-Haïtien and the simply jaw-dropping Citadelle la Ferrière, a mountaintop fortress built 200 years ago to defend the newly free nation from invasion. Historical sites litter the landscape, from the ramparts of Fort Liberté in the east to Môle Saint Nicholas in the west, where Christopher Columbus made his first landfall in the Americas in 1492. Amid all this, the landscape constantly changes, from dramatic mountains and pine forest to cactus-filled desert and lush green plains. Haiti is a tiny country that packs an awful lot in.

Don't let security preoccupations cloud your mind. Some foreigners working for international organisations are subject to over-zealous restrictions, but Haiti actually ranks near the bottom of the crime table amid Caribbean nations. You need to be prepared for travel in a developing world country, where infrastructure isn't always what you might hope for, and there's poverty among the beauty. But there is also a people who are fiercely proud to be Haitian and keen to show their country off to you, and to challenge the many perceptions held about their home. The travelling can sometimes be a bit rugged but the rewards are immense and frequently unexpected. In the late 1940s, Haiti (along with pre-revolutionary Cuba) practically invented Caribbean tourism. Visitor numbers boomed again in the 1970s and 80s. All the reasons that drew visitors to Haiti then still exist; they've just become obscured in recent years. Maybe now is finally the time to rediscover them.

FEEDBACK REQUEST

At Bradt Travel Guides we're aware that guidebooks start to go out of date on the day they're published – and that you, our readers, are out there in the field doing research of your own. You'll find out before us when a fine new family-run hotel opens or a favourite restaurant changes hands and goes downhill. So why not write to us and tell us about your experiences? We'll include you in the acknowledgements of the next edition of *Haiti* if we use your feedback. Contact us on 01753 893444 or e info@bradtguides.com. Alternatively you can add a review of the book to www.bradtguides.com or Amazon.

If you send an email to info@bradtguides.com about changes to information in this book we will forward it to the author who may include it in a 'one-off update' on the Bradt website at www.bradtguides.com/guidebook-updates. You can also visit this website for updates to information in this guide.

Part One

GENERAL INFORMATION

HAITI AT A GLANCE

Location Caribbean Sea, western third of the island of Hispaniola (bordering the Dominican Republic)
Size 27,750km^2
Climate Tropical
Time Eastern Standard Time (GMT –5 hours)
International telephone code +509
Currency Haitian gourde (HTG). The unofficial term Haitian dollar (H$) is commonly used, where H$1=5HTG.
Electricity 110–125V (60Hz AC), flat two-pin plugs as in the USA
Exchange rate £1=67HTG; US$1=43HTG; €1=53HTG (August 2012)
Population 9.8 million (July 2012)
Capital Port-au-Prince
Languages Creole (Kreyol), French
Religion Roman Catholic (80%), Protestant (various denominations; 20%). Vodou is practised alongside Christianity by up to half the population.
Flag Two horizontal bands of blue and red, centred with a white rectangle bearing a palm tree flanked by flags and cannon and the motto *L'Union Fait La Force* ('Unity Makes Strength')
Economy Agriculture (coffee, mangoes, sugarcane, rice) and garment assembly. The economy is heavily reliant on foreign aid.

1

Background Information

GEOGRAPHY

Haiti occupies the western third of Hispaniola, the island it shares with the Dominican Republic, and covers an area roughly the size of Belgium or the US state of Maryland. Its nearest Caribbean neighbours are Cuba, which sits 85km away across the Windward Passage (visible on a clear day from the tip of Haiti's northwest peninsula), and Jamaica, 180km to the southwest across the Jamaica Channel. Historically, its most important political and economic neighbour is the USA – Miami is less than 1,000km (a 90-minute flight) away from Port-au-Prince.

Geologically, Hispaniola was raised in the Cretaceous period, around 90 million years ago, through a combination of plate tectonics and volcanic activity. The bulk of the country is made of limestone, although the coastal regions are high in rocks made from fossilised coral raised from ancient seas. Both have left a country rich in caves. The region is still seismically active; Haiti sits astride the Enriquillo-Plantain Garden fault in the south and the Septentrional fault in the north. The shallow nature of the faults has left Haiti prone to earthquakes – most famously the

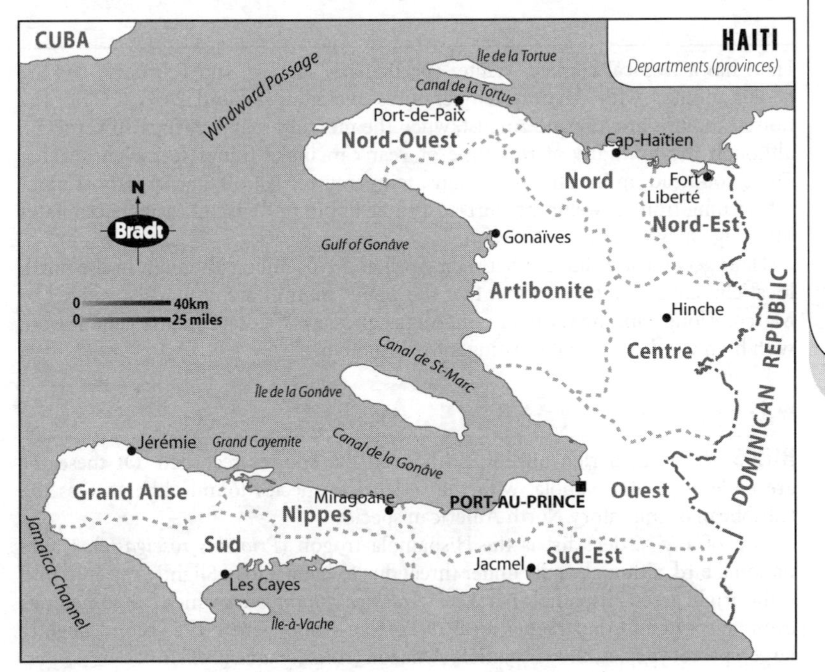

earthquake of 12 January 2010. Tectonic shifts continue to raise the island at a rate of around 2cm per year.

Hispaniola is the most mountainous island in the Caribbean, and a famous Haitian proverb runs *dèyè mon gen mon* – beyond the mountains there are more mountains. There are four main chains squeezed into Haiti's borders. The Massif du Nord runs astride the northern peninsula, while the centre is bisected by the Montagnes Noires and Chaîne des Matheux. In the south the Massif du Sud dominates – called the Massif de la Hotte in the southwest and turning into the Massif de la Selle near the Dominican border. This chain holds Haiti's highest peaks Pic la Selle (2,674m) and Pic Macaya (2,347m). In total, nearly 65% of the land is on slopes of between 20% and 40% – constraining the availability of arable land.

Between the mountains are the agriculturally important lowlands. In the north, around the city of Cap-Haïtien, is Plaine du Nord. In the centre, the Montagnes Noires and Chaîne des Matheux are divided by the Artibonite Valley, named after Haiti's main river. Above the valley is the wide and grassy Plateau Centrale. In the south, the plains around Les Cayes are particularly well watered and fertile.

East of Port-au-Prince is the Plaine du Cul-de-Sac. It contains the slightly salty Lac Azueï (Étang Saumâtre), an ancient hangover from the tectonic shifts which pushed the plates that form Haiti and the Dominican Republic together. It's Haiti's largest lake, followed by the manmade Lac Peligré in the Central Plateau, which sits behind the Peligré Dam, built in the 1950s.

Off the coast, there are four main islands: the largest is La Gonâve, in the central Gulf of Gonâve, followed by the Île de la Tortue, which sits opposite Port-de-Paix on the northern coast. In the south are Île-à-Vache near Les Cayes, and Grand Cayemite near Jérémie.

CLIMATE

Haiti has a tropical climate. Winter (particularly January and February) has the cooler months with daytime temperatures averaging around 24°C (75°F). The hottest months are July and August, when the mercury regularly tops 30°C (87°F), although the humidity at this time of year can make things feel even stickier. Once you head up into the mountains, temperatures fall off, particularly at night – travelling from a sweltering Port-au-Prince uphill to Kenscoff easily necessitates bringing an extra layer to throw on.

Haiti gets most of its rain between April and November, although in the north local climate systems mean that that the wetter months are around November to March. Along with the summer rain, August presages the start of hurricane season, with high winds potentially lasting into November.

NATURAL HISTORY AND CONSERVATION

BIRDS Haiti has a rich birdlife, with over 260 species recorded. Of these, 31 are endemic to Hispaniola, with the rest being species found either across the Caribbean or migratory North American species.

Top of any birder's list is the Hispaniola trogon (*Priotelus roseigaste*), Haiti's national bird, although sadly under threat due to habitat loss. Slightly easier to find is the bright green Hispaniola parakeet (*Aratinga chloroptera*), which can sometimes even be spotted in the greener areas of Port-au-Prince. There is a second, slightly larger, parrot species, the Hispaniola Amazon (*Amazona ventralis*).

HURRICANES

Haiti sits square in the middle of the Caribbean's hurricane corridor and for several months of the year high winds threaten to turn into potentially damaging tropical storms and worse. Technically a form of tropical cyclone, the word 'hurricane' is taken from the Taíno god Huricán, who first created the winds.

Hurricanes are formed every summer over the Atlantic Ocean. When sea temperatures reach at least 26.5°C (80°F) in areas of low pressure, warm moist air rises to form thunderclouds. As the saturated air rises, it releases energy, helping drive the formation of the cyclone and increase wind speeds. Hurricane formation is a complex process, although many climate scientists believe that rising sea surface temperatures will lead to an increased frequency and intensity of hurricanes over the coming century.

Storms are rated in intensity according to their wind speed. A slow-moving system of up to 64km/h (39mph) starts out as a tropical depression, turning into a tropical storm above this speed. As it picks up speed, the weather system officially becomes a hurricane once moving at 120km/h (74mph). Hurricanes have their own classification system, and are rated in increasing severity from one to five. A category-five hurricane can have winds blowing in excess of 250km/h (155mph).

Haiti is peculiarly prone to hurricane damage. Widespread deforestation and mountainous terrain combine in a lethal fashion when storms hit, leaving the land unable to soak up the rain, which pours down the slopes in a muddy torrent to flood the land below. When combined with stormy high tides, low-lying areas can face flooding from both directions. In 2008, Haiti was repeatedly battered, when tropical storms and hurricanes Fay, Gustav, Hanna and Ike caused damage equal to 15% of Haiti's GDP. Gonaïves was completely submerged with a loss of around 450 lives. Hurricane preparedness remains a serious challenge for a cash-strapped Haitian government already beset with severe infrastructural challenges.

The US National Hurricane Center (*www.nhc.noaa.gov*) tracks and provides forecasts for tropical storm systems across the Caribbean.

One of the commonest birds you'll encounter is the white-necked crow (*Corvus leucognaphalus*), which you can find chattering in the tops of trees (particularly palms) across the country. A personal favourite is the bananaquit (*Coereba flaveola*), a tiny grey and yellow bird with a fine curved bill, which can be seen hopping amid flowers to feed on nectar. Haiti also has four species of hummingbird. Eating more substantial meals, there are seven species of hawks and falcons, although the most easily recognisable raptor is the broad-winged and red-faced turkey vulture (*Cathartes aura*), appropriately known in Creole as *mal fini* ('bad end').

On the coast, there are brown pelicans (*Pelecanus occidentalis*), magnificent frigatebirds (*Fregata magnificens*) and a variety of gulls, herons, ibis and many plovers and pipers. Ducks are also plentiful. Hanging on in Trou Caïman east of Port-au-Prince is a small population of the once-widespread Caribbean flamingo (*Phoenicopterus ruber*).

The definitive birding book is *Birds of the Dominican Republic and Haiti* by Stephen Latter and Christopher Rimmer. If you have a smartphone, an app based on the guide is also available, produced by Green Mountain Digital. A locally produced alternative is the child-friendly *A la découverte des oiseaux d'Haïti* ('Discover the Birds of Haiti'), produced by Florence Sergile for the Audubon Society of Haiti.

MAMMALS Hispaniola is not rich in native mammal species – with the exception of various bats, almost everything you see was introduced by humans. There are two possible exceptions, which you should count yourself extremely lucky if you encounter. The solenodon (*Solenodon paradoxus*) is a nocturnal insectivorous mammal that looks like a cross between a mole and an over-sized shrew. The solenodon is almost extinct (the introduction of mongooses to the island was a death sentence), but is thought to persist in Parc National La Visite south of Port-au-Prince and parts of the Massif de la Hotte in the southwest. The second endemic mammal is the Hispaniolan hutia (*Plagiodontia aedium*), an arboreal rodent whose status is made extremely vulnerable by deforestation.

REPTILES AND AMPHIBIANS You'll see lizards everywhere in Haiti. There are plenty of geckos on the walls and a variety of anoles skittering about, of which the males can be identified by their head-bobbing displays and throat sacs, used in territorial displays. You're less likely to see any snakes, although the Haitian boa (*Epicrates striatus*) remains reasonably widespread. Unfortunately, despite the common association with Vodou (notably the snake spirit Damballah, who created the world), the one time you're likely to see a snake is when one has been thrashed to death and displayed by a proud local.

Of the larger species, the most impressive is the rhinoceros iguana (*Cyclura cornuta*), a positively dinosaurian-looking lizard that can grow up to 130cm in length. It's very rare now due to being allegedly quite tasty, as well as predation of its eggs by rats. Populations persist near Etang Saumâtre, as well as around Môle Saint-Nicholas. Found in the waters of Etang Saumâtre is a small and threatened population of caimans, or American crocodiles (*Crocodylus acutus*). Although they can reach lengths of 4m, they eat fish, rather than people.

In the seas around Haiti there are four species of sea-turtle. You'll most commonly encounter the hawksbill (*Eretmochelys imbricata*); its pretty shell means that it's frequently fished for the souvenir market.

Against a backdrop of threatened species loss, a 2010 joint expedition to Parc National Macaya by Conservation International and the International Union for the Conservation of Nature (IUCN) revealed that six species of frog previously thought extinct were still present in the country. Included was the fingernail-sized Macaya breast-spot frog (*Eleutherodactylus thorectes*), one of the smallest species in the world. While hardly a panacea for Haiti's environmental problems, such amphibians are generally known as barometer species, as they are particularly susceptible to environmental changes. As a measure of the health of an ecosystem, they do demonstrate that in the Massif de la Hotte at least there still remain tracts of good original forest.

PLANT LIFE Haiti is geographically diverse for such a small country, and contains several climate zones with a wide variety of plant species. Particularly important trees are the Hispaniola mahogany and the ubiquitous royal palm, the latter featuring on the Haitian coat of arms. Coconut palms, West Indian cedar and wild olive also feature, and many species of low, thorny acacia.

Many of the commonest trees you'll see are the most economically productive. Tall breadfruit and mango trees abound, along with various citrus, avocado and cacao trees. At higher altitudes, coffee bushes grow wild. The mapou have great social significance, as according to the Vodou religion they are frequently home to spirits.

In the southwestern Massif de la Hotte you can find the remainder of Haiti's once-extensive cloudforest. Grand Anse is by some measure the greenest part of the country, in part due to its traditional isolation from the metropolitan areas. It's still possible to trek in the area amid forest trees of considerable size and age. The same goes for the last pine forests in the mountains near Port-au-Prince. By comparison, the Plateau Centrale is an area of mainly open grassland. The northwestern peninsula is arid, and cactus and aloes predominate here.

If Haiti were to have a national flower, it would surely be the hibiscus. Its local name is *choublak*, a corruption taken from the English who used the dried flowers to polish their black boots. It's sometimes made into a refreshing tea.

REEFS AND MANGROVES Hispaniola sits on a high oceanic shelf, giving extensive shallow waters in which coral reefs have thrived. Most are close to the shore, with a few barrier reefs further out in the open sea. Sedimentation, overfishing and climate change all present severe challenges to the reefs. Where reefs remain intact they abound in life: soft plant-like corals swaying in the currents atop the hard limestone-bodied corals that make up the structure of the reef. Crustaceans, urchins, sponges and molluscs live on the reefs, while bright fish swim throughout. There are no dedicated guides to Haitian (or Hispaniolan) reefs, but *Reef Fish Identification: Florida, Caribbean, Bahamas* by Paul Humann and Ned Deloach and its related guide to corals and other creatures make good primers.

The north coast once had extensive mangroves, although these are now reduced severely in area. There are attempts to revive the mangroves to decrease erosion and provide nurseries for fish in the area around Bas Limbé. Unfortunately, some of Haiti's best remaining mangroves are found around the Baie de Caracol – the area currently under development for the Caracol Industrial Park – and are thus at extreme risk.

ENVIRONMENTAL ISSUES Haiti suffers from extreme environmental pressures. It contains half of Hispaniola's population in a third of its space, and the lowest GDP in the Caribbean with which to protect both its citizens and the environment.

NATIONAL PARKS

Haiti has three national parks:

PARC NATIONAL LA VISITE In the Massif de la Selle, southeast of Port-au-Prince. Contains Haiti's remaining high-altitude pine forests, and readily accessible from Port-au-Prince for hiking. Added to UNESCO's World Network in July 2012. See page 131 for more details.

PARC NATIONAL MACAYA In the Massif de la Hotte, in the southwest. Biologically diverse cloudforest, although hard to reach and not for casual travellers. See page 167 for more details.

PARC NATIONAL HISTORIQUE CITADELLE SANS-SOUCI RAMIERS Near Cap-Haïtien. Gazetted for its historical rather than natural significance, it contains the Citadelle fortress and related historic sites. See page 186 for more details.

CHARCOAL

Everywhere you look in Haiti, it seems that you find charcoal – in rural areas you see the smoke from charcoal-making ovens and sacks piled by the road waiting to be sold, in towns the markets are full of vendors selling it by the bag, and food sellers cooking meals on charcoal stoves. Charcoal is big business in Haiti, and together with wood fuel accounts for around 70% of the country's energy consumption.

Charcoal production puts an immense strain on Haiti's natural resources, and although an ostensibly renewable resource, demand far outstrips the ability of the land to supply the wood needed to produce it. The economics are not insignificant – around 200,000 people are financially dependent on the charcoal trade, making it possibly Haiti's single most important employer. Port-au-Prince consumes 80% of Haiti's charcoal, nearly 5,500 tonnes per week, worth somewhere between US$110 and US$150 million per year.

A large sack of charcoal currently costs around 750HTG (just under US$20), although vendors sell it for a few gourdes in small batches called *marmites* for daily use. The relative cheapness of charcoal is its attraction, and although there are continued programmes to promote alternatives, they have frequently foundered against the simple issue of cost. A simple charcoal stove costs around a dollar, more efficient models three to four times that. A propane gas stove can cost anything up to 20,000HTG – a cripplingly high entry point for a more efficient fuel that unit-per-unit costs almost the same as charcoal. Across the border, whilst the slightly wealthier Dominican Republic has had some success with banning charcoal in favour of bottled gas, demand from Haiti has led to a large charcoal-smuggling industry, particularly in the border towns in the central region.

Charcoal alternatives like *briquettes* of recycled paper have had some success in areas where they have been introduced, since their production also generates local employment. *Bagasse*, produced from vegetable waste such as sugarcane is also increasingly used, although neither currently has the capacity to be scaled up sufficiently. Improved coppicing of wood and reforestation projects are also important components. Tackling charcoal production requires action across a number of fields – natural resource management, agriculture, rural economics and education. With so many communities dependent on its production, charcoal is here to stay for Haiti's foreseeable future.

Deforestation has long been Haiti's most important environmental challenge. During the Taíno period, it's estimated that around 75% of the country was forested. Today that number stands at a little under 2%. The French were the first to take the axe to the forests, clearing the Plaine du Nord for sugar plantations. During the 19th century, the logging of valuable trees such as the Hispaniola mahogany was important for customs revenues, a practice that the Americans carried on during their occupation in the early 20th century, driving new roads up into the high-altitude pine forests of the Massif de la Selle. However, it was in the period of 1990–2000, one of the most unstable decades of Haitian history, that the worst damage was wrought, with the country losing 44% of its forest cover in that decade alone. The contrast with the Dominican Republic is stark: in many places the border between the two countries is clearly delineated by a line separating the scruffy brown of Haiti with the green of the DR (the lower population density and series of stern autocratic rulers having slowed that country's rate of tree loss). Today, charcoal production is a major driver of deforestation.

The damage caused by deforestation is manifold. With fewer tree roots to bind the soil together, soil is lost through being washed away by rains or whipped away in a dusty wind. Around 36 million tonnes of topsoil are lost each year. This causes a reduction in the agricultural productivity of the land, reduces rainfall and clogs waterways with silt. Several of Haiti's coral reef systems have become severely degraded through being covered with silt washed into the sea. Haiti has 30 river basins, of which 25 are severely eroded. On top of this is the high monetary value attached to wood – only in rural areas do you still tend to see traditional wooden buildings (which are more earthquake resistant) – in the cities, wood is simply too expensive to build with, and most timber used in construction is actually imported.

Water and sanitation are also major environmental issues. Half of all rural and a third of urban populations lack a potable water source, while just 6% of those in the country and a third of city dwellers have access to improved sanitation facilities. These figures were key in the rapid spread of the cholera epidemic in 2010.

HISTORY

EARLIEST INHABITANTS Haiti's human history begins around 4,500 years ago, when a wave of migrations brought the first people to the island. The earliest arrivals were the so-called Paleo-Indians from the Yucatàn Peninsula, ancestors of the first humans to colonise the Americas from across the Bering Strait. They left few archaeological traces beyond a clutch of stone tools.

Next to follow were the Ciboney, a pre-agrarian Meso-American people who arrived around 1000BC having travelled across the Caribbean chain from South America. They were hunter-gatherers living along the coast, frequently occupying the many caves that riddle the landscape – the name 'Ciboney' means 'cave dwellers' in the language of the Arawak, the people who followed them to Hispaniola and ultimately drove them from the land.

The Arawak were farmers as well as mariners, and they spread quickly throughout the Caribbean. Many early examples of their pottery have survived. Over time, the Arawak in Hispaniola developed into a discrete people known as the Taíno – the 'noble people' – whose culture flourished for around 700 years before Christopher Columbus weighed anchor in 1492.

To the Taíno, their island was Quisqueya ('the cradle of life'), or Ayiti ('the mountainous place'). They had an advanced political structure, with the population divided into six independent chiefdoms called *caciques*. Of these, Marién covered the northern peninsula of modern Haiti, with Xaragua covering the centre and south. Each *cacique* was divided into villages of up to 200 inhabitants, with political power apparently divided equitably between the sexes. Villagers generally went unclothed or with simple garments of cotton or pounded bark, with occasional gold jewellery and tattoos. Like the Arawak, they had sophisticated pottery, which has provided the most tangible evidence of their culture, along with the ritual petroglyphs they carved in caves across the island – many of which can still be visited.

The favoured food crops of the Taíno were cassava, yam and sweet potato, cultivated in raised mounds called *concucos*. Tobacco was also cultivated – another important crop that would spread quickly from Quisqueya to the wider world. Fishing was carried out in dug-out canoes similar to those that had enabled the Arawak to originally colonise the island.

Religious life centred on a pantheon of gods, or *zemis*, associated with different aspects of nature. Rituals were presided over by a shaman, often using natural hallucinogens to commune with the deities. The most important of these were Yúcahu, the spirit of both the sea and cassava, and his mother, Atabey, who represented fresh water and fertility. Lesser gods stood for hurricanes, death and a host of ancestors.

THE SPANISH IN HISPANIOLA The Taíno were 'gentle and without knowledge of what is evil; nor do they murder or steal', according to Christopher Columbus, who landed at Môle Saint-Nicholas on 6 December 1492, on his first great voyage to the Americas. He might have turned the mirror on himself, for the Spanish turned out to be the complete opposite: violent and avaricious. The Taíno population barely survived a century past their first contact.

Columbus named the island La Isla Española ('the Spanish Island'), more typically transcribed as Hispaniola. He marvelled at the natural wealth of its green mountains, and then lusted after the gold with which its native inhabitants decorated themselves. The first Spanish settlement, La Navidad, was founded near Bord de Mer de Limonade, near modern Cap-Haïtien on Christmas Day 1492. Its fort was built with the help of the local chief Guacanacaric, using the salvaged wood from the *Santa María*, the ship Columbus had unfortunately let founder on a nearby reef. He left 39 men there with instructions to trade for gold, and sailed back to Spain. When he returned a year later, all the Spanish were dead, killed by the Taíno in retaliation for the cruelty with which the search for gold had been pursued.

Subsequent Spanish settlements were mostly further east in the modern Dominican Republic, and the newly founded Santo Domingo became the capital of the new colony. Policy for the island was less about settlement than pure wealth extraction. The Taíno were put to work under a system of forced labour called the *encomienda*, digging for gold. It was a harsh system – a forerunner to the sugar slavery later adopted by the French. Coupled with the devastating effects of European diseases to which they had no immunity, the Taíno population crashed. In 1503, the Taíno queen Anacaona (from present-day Léogâne) was arrested and publicly executed, marking the effective end of the rule of indigenous Quisqueya.

PIRATES AND COLONISTS It's a dark irony that barely had the Taíno drawn their last breath, Spain began to lose interest in Hispaniola. The 16th century brought them even greater riches in the forms of the newly conquered Aztec and Inca empires. Even with imported African slave labour, Hispaniola couldn't compete, and quickly became reduced to little more than a trading point for the bullion-rich convoys sailing between the New World and the mother country.

At the same time, Europe became stricken with a series of wars that would burn on and off for the next three centuries. Hispaniola became even more isolated. Tudor England and Spain were deadly rivals, and Admiral Sir Francis Drake sacked Santo Domingo in 1586. Although they sailed for the Royal Navy, England encouraged privateers – pirates under a flag of convenience – to attack Spanish ships across the Caribbean. As a result Hispaniola received fewer and fewer convoys, and the territory it controlled on the actual island shrank to just a few pockets around the major ports. When the colonists that remained tried to trade with foreign powers, Spain sent soldiers to forcibly move them to Santo Domingo. The western part of the island – the future Haiti – was abandoned.

Pirates and foreign colonists filled the vacuum left by the Spanish. Hispaniola became a haven for freebooters of all descriptions, attracted by the security of its hidden harbours and mountainous terrain. The French quickly established themselves as the up-and-coming power. Settlers arrived on the north coast, and traded in meat and hides to passing ships. This quickly turned into full-blown piracy. By the mid 17th century, Tortuga Island (Île de la Tortue) had for all intents and purposes become a full-blown pirate colony, ruled with the lightest of touches by a nominal French governor. Petit Goâve and Île-à-Vache in the south also became important pirate ports.

From time to time the Spanish would send ships to try to expel what they saw as interlopers on their island, but their efforts came to naught. The French were making formal claims on the western third of the island, with settlers arriving in increasing numbers, and beginning to make money from the export of tobacco. They quickly turned to cultivation of sugarcane, newly introduced to the Caribbean. There was potentially even more money to be made through this 'white gold' than through raiding the Spanish, and the pirates were slowly brought into line. Europe too was hit by a rare outbreak of peace. In 1697, the Treaty of Ryswick settled the war between the great powers. As part of the agreement, Spain formally ceded its claim on western Hispaniola. The French colony of Saint-Domingue was born into the world.

FRENCH SAINT-DOMINGUE France did what Spain never could, and turned Saint-Domingue into a going concern. In the 18th century it boomed to the point where it was the richest colony in the world – more valuable to the French than the combined American colonies were to the British. It was the largest producer of sugar and coffee in the world, as well as an important exporter of cocoa, indigo and cotton – all products that were important motors of French economic growth. Cap Français (modern Cap-Haïtien) was 'the Paris of the Antilles', with fine houses and theatres performing the latest plays and operas from the home country.

Great wealth was founded on great violence. Every cup of coffee and bowl of sugar consumed in the finest Parisian salons was indelibly tainted with the blood of slavery. Saint-Domingue had a voracious appetite for slaves imported from Africa. At the height of the colony's prosperity (and the eve of its ultimate destruction), the slave population was nearly half a million strong, outnumbering the free colonists by ten to one. The majority worked on some 700 sugar plantations, clearing fields, cutting and crushing cane and boiling the juice to produce sugar. The plantations were a finely tuned system of 'field and factory', but the grease in the wheels was the sadism meted out to those not deemed to work hard enough. Mortality rates were appallingly high, and the only way that the slave population could be maintained was by importing ever-increasing numbers of captives. In 1790 alone, 40,000 slaves were brought to Saint-Domingue. The colony was a key hub for the so-called 'triangular trade' that crisscrossed the Atlantic: European ships sailed to the west coast of Africa laden with trade goods, which were sold in exchange for captive Africans. This human cargo was then shipped to the Americas, where the ships would load up with sugar and other slave-produced goods, before returning to Europe.

Above the mass of toiling slaves sat the free colonists. They were a divided population. The wealthiest were the *grand blancs*, the rich planters with their mansions. Below them were the *petits blancs*, poorer immigrants who had come west to seek their fortune. Saint-Domingue was also unusual in having a large free coloured population, equal in number to the whites. Often called mulattoes or *affranchis*, they were a surprisingly prosperous class – many owned slaves themselves – and dominated the coffee trade in the south of the colony, where the mountainous terrain made sugar plantations unfeasible.

On the surface Saint-Domingue prospered, but in reality its society was desperately brittle. The planters wanted more autonomy from Paris, while the *petits blancs* resented their wealthy compatriots and the free coloured alike. The latter were deeply discriminated against, and deprived of many legal and political rights. Behind all this was the ever-present threat of slave revolts. Bands of runaway slaves (maroons) tried setting up alternative communities in the mountains far from the plantations, and small-scale revolts were common. In the 1750s the maroon leader Mackandal, who had lost an arm crushed in a sugar mill, led a rebellion across the north that terrified the colonists. Mackandal was eventually captured and burnt at the stake, but the size of the revolt showed that the days of plantation slavery were ultimately numbered.

REVOLUTIONARY FIRES IGNITE In 1791 Saint-Domingue was set alight by flames of revolution that would burn for fully 13 years. The initial spark was provided by the French Revolution. The slogan of *liberté, egalité et fraternité* was as radical to the colonists as to the crowds that stormed the Bastille. Planters and free coloureds alike sent delegations to Paris, but with radically different agendas. The free coloureds demanded equal political rights while the planters sought to entrench their racist agenda by demanding their own political assembly in Saint-Domingue.

Both requests were granted, setting the colony on a collision course. When the planters' assembly refused to acknowledge the free coloureds' political ambitions, the mulatto leader Vincent Ogé raised militias in open revolt against the French. Although Ogé was captured and broken on the wheel, he had opened the door to an even bigger revolt. Both sides had used slave proxies to fight their battles, and those slaves inevitably began to organise for themselves. In August 1791 at Boïs Caiman near Cap Français, a Vodou priest called Boukman led a ceremony where slave leaders pledged themselves to mass insurrection. By the end of the

THE *CODE NOIR*

Regulations governing slavery in Saint-Domingue were covered in the *Code Noir*, a document first drawn up in 1685 by King Louis XIV. It set out rules concerning the baptism of slaves (Catholicism being the only permitted religion), inheritance (since slaves were the property of their owners), types of commerce allowed by slaves (only under express permission of their masters, and never sugarcane), and when a slave could be freed by their master. It also set out suitable punishments that masters were allowed to mete out. Most infractions could be legally settled by whipping or beating. Runaways were branded; repeat offenders were hamstrung or executed.

Despite giving a free hand to planters, the *Code Noir* was still honoured more in the breach. Masters ignored the ban on torture, which was widespread. The brutality with which the French ruled their slaves is reflected in the high death rates on the plantations – the life expectancy of a newly arrived slave was less than five years. Slaves were technically allowed to make complaints about violent masters, but this was understandably rare. In one case in 1788 when slaves did try to complain about a master who had burned off the legs of two female slaves, planters successfully argued that if slaves were allowed to complain, the whole colonial system would collapse. They were right, although not in the way they thought, when those complaints finally broke into irreversible rebellion in 1791.

year, Saint-Domingue was ablaze with burning plantations. The slaves became organised into a potent fighting force under the astute leadership of ex-coachman Toussaint Louverture, who sought and received assistance from the Spanish across the border in Santo Domingo. The planters in turn were so determined to protect their interests they even turned to the hated British for help.

After nearly two years of fighting, Saint-Domingue's slaves had freed themselves. The newly appointed French consul Sonthonax married this simple fact to his own revolutionary principles and formally declared slavery abolished. The effects were felt as far as Paris, and within a year slavery was abolished throughout the French Empire. Louverture immediately switched sides back to France and brought his generals Jean-Jacques Dessalines and Henri Christophe with him. Reconstruction began, and ex-slaves were put back to work on the plantations, albeit this time for a wage. There was still fighting – Louverture campaigned in the south against mulattoes demanding more power, and it took five years to fully kick out an invading British army hoping to grab the colony for themselves. Yet by 1801, the colony was on the road to prosperity again, and Louverture was named governor-general for life.

THE PATH TO INDEPENDENCE In 1799, Napoleon Bonaparte came to power in France. He had no time for the 'gilded African' now ruling Saint-Domingue, especially when Louverture invaded Santo Domingo to liberate the slaves there. In response he sent his brother-in-law, General Leclerc, at the head of a huge army, to restore the old colonial status quo. With him were the mulatto leaders Alexandre Pétion and André Rigaud, representing the old mulatto powerbase in the south. Louverture was instantly suspicious, and retreated to the hills, leaving Cap-François a smouldering wreck behind him. Thus began the war of independence.

The French found the country to be a cemetery. Their forces were ravaged by tropical diseases, as well as the guerrilla war against Louverture's forces. It was a bloody stalemate, but when Louverture was invited to parley with Leclerc, he was clapped in irons and shipped back to France to die a lonely death in 1803, still protesting that his petitions to Napoleon were left unread. As Leclerc himself succumbed to yellow fever, Dessalines, Christophe and Pétion – all now allied against the French war of extermination – began to move the revolution into its endgame. Independence from France was the only remaining option. The violence was terrible on both sides. In the final year of the war, 100,000 people lost their lives, from war, disease and hunger. The conflict had so exhausted the French that Napoleon had to abandon his greater plans for an empire in the New World, and sold France's north American possessions to the USA – the Louisiana Purchase that made the States a true continental power.

At Vertières just outside Cap-François on 18 November 1803, the French army was finally trounced for good. On New Year's Day 1804, Dessalines proclaimed the birth of a new nation, its name taken from the old Taíno word for the country, Ayiti.

DIVIDED AT BIRTH Haiti was born into a tough neighbourhood. A free black nation was an ideological threat to the slave-owning powers of France, Britain and the USA. To rebuild, Dessalines concentrated his powers and pushed the plantation system back onto an unwilling population. At independence, most of the population had been born in Africa, and wanted to stay on their own land and raise crops for themselves, so plantation labour was enforced by the army. The white planters who had remained were massacred, foreign ownership of land forbidden and Santo Domingo invaded again. Less than a year into the young country's life, Dessalines crowned himself emperor. But his subjects deemed his rule too harsh, and in 1806 he was killed in an ambush by his own officers. Pétion was a lead conspirator.

There were two rivals for the succession – Christophe, who controlled the black-dominated north, and Pétion, whose powerbase was with the southern mulattoes. Their differences were irreconcilable, and almost immediately the country split in two by force of arms. Pétion ruled as president from Port-au-Prince, while Christophe sat on the throne in his new kingdom of the north.

Christophe was an absolute monarch like Dessalines. His rule was strict – plantations were still the order of the day – but he also sought to develop his state by inviting European educators and doctors to set up schools and hospitals, as well as building his fabulous palace at Sans Souci and the Citadelle fortress. The British abolitionists William Wilberforce and Thomas Clarkson were recruited to lobby on Haiti's behalf, although recognition from his 'fraternal' monarchs in Europe forever eluded Christophe.

Pétion took another path. His southern state was weak (he immediately faced a rebellion in the Grand Anse), so his choice was to move towards land reform. Parcels of land were divided and distributed among his army and the old mulatto landowners. The peasants were left to their own devices, and taxes on coffee exports became the main state earner. Political power began to become associated with the new mercantile class.

Reunification had to wait until the death of both revolutionary leaders. Christophe shot himself in 1820 when hit by the double-blow of a stroke and rebellion against his autocratic rule; Pétion had died two years earlier, to be replaced as president by his protégé Jean-Pierre Boyer.

GROWING PAINS The foundations for much of Haiti's development over the following century were laid by Boyer, who ruled for an unprecedented 27 years. After sacking Sans Souci, he closed Christophe's schools in the north, and spent much of his rule deeming anyone with an education a threat. The peasant masses were to be kept firmly in their place – learning was to be denied them, Boyer's *Code Rural* explicitly limited their movement and kept them away from cities and the seat of power. Boyer's mulatto elite strengthened their grip on the economy, while foreign merchants arrived in large numbers to prosper in the export trade. Political activity was strictly limited; Boyer was the sort of president who would send troops to threaten parliament rather than hear debates against him.

Boyer's worst legacy was the Faustian deal he struck with France to win recognition of Haitian independence. Pétion had briefly toyed with the idea of paying a small indemnity to France in return for diplomatic recognition. In 1825, King Charles X seized upon the idea, sending and dispatching a squadron of warships to demand a ransom of 150 million francs to compensate French planters for the loss of their property (with the ex-slave very much counting as 'property'). In return, he would 'grant' the Haitians sovereignty over their own country. If Boyer rejected this, the island was to be blockaded. Despite having participated in the war that originally kicked the French out, Boyer blinked. The indemnity was worth US$3 billion in today's terms, and to pay it, the Haitian government were forced to take out loans from French banks at eye-watering rates of interest. By the end of the 19th century, nearly 80% of the national budget was spent on servicing the debt, money that could otherwise have been spent on developing the country.

REBELLIONS AND REVOLVING DOORS The mini revolution of 1843 ultimately did for Boyer. It was an urban revolution led by the small educated class, but when the peasants started to demand their own voices be heard, the commercial and military elites closed ranks. Having power was more important than distributing it equitably. The provinces were cut ever more adrift from the cities, and rebellion became their only method of holding the president to account. There was a seemingly endless changing parade of a dozen or so presidents, with assassination or exile the usual means of exit. In the Haitian maxim, 'constitutions are made of paper, but bayonets are of iron.'

Faustin Soulouque was one notable ruler – a black army officer chosen by the elite to be their puppet, but who turned the tables on his masters by leading an anti-mulatto campaign. Famously crowned emperor in 1849 with a cardboard crown, he eventually came to grief after another ill-advised attempt to conquer Santo Domingo.

The endless instability in Port-au-Prince meant opportunities for foreign powers. Gunboat diplomacy became the standard way of dealing with Haiti; with every rebellion there was invariably damage to foreign businesses, and this damage was invariably recouped by the sending of warships to threaten the capital. The French, Germans, British and Americans were all eager participants. France even ended up owning the national bank. By the turn of the 20th century, Haiti was weak and divided, having burned through nearly 20 heads of state since Boyer's departure.

OCCUPATION Haiti had long had a difficult relationship with the USA. The States was Haiti's biggest trading partner, but Washington refused to recognise Haitian independence until 1861, when Abraham Lincoln was considering emancipating

THE SINKING OF HAITI'S NAVY

For significant parts of its history Haiti has found itself at the sharp end of the worst sort of gunboat diplomacy. The most notorious of these was France's 1825 demand of a 150 million franc indemnity in exchange for recognition of Haiti's independence, exacted through a naval blockade and threat of war. At regular intervals throughout the late 19th century France, Spain, Britain, the USA and Germany all sent warships to threaten Port-au-Prince as a result of real or perceived slights.

Haiti's tiny navy – rarely more than two ships – could do little against such provocations. Its most notorious engagement came in 1902 amid the tumult of the struggle between Pierre Nord Alexis and Anténor Firmin for the Haitian presidency. Admiral Hammerton Killick, an Anglo-Haitian mulatto, declared for Firmin and bombarded Cap-Haïtien, where Alexis was temporarily based. Fleeing the scene, he then reduced the navy to just one vessel by accidentally running the gunboat *Toussaint Louverture* onto a reef. With just the flagship *Crête-à-Pierrot* remaining, Killick attempted a blockade of Port-au-Prince of his own. He seized a German merchant ship that he accused of running arms to Alexis, an act that would doom Firmin's rebellion. Germany reacted with predictable fury and sent a ship of its own to threaten reprisals. The outgunned Killick had other ideas. Having ordered all hands ashore, he dressed himself in the Haitian flag and went to the ship's magazine where he lit a cigar and blew himself and the *Crête-à-Pierrot* out of the water.

The Haitian navy was disbanded following the US occupation in 1916, to be resurrected in the late 1930s as the Haitian coastguard. Its Port-au-Prince base is named for Admiral Killick, whose refusal to surrender has placed him in the pantheon of national heroes.

the USA's slaves. That recognition lasted barely a few decades, when in 1915 the USA sent a military expedition to Haiti and reduced the country to little more than a principality.

The first years of the 20th century were undoubtedly difficult for Haiti. Policies perceived as anti-peasant brought widespread revolts that were in turn co-opted by politicians eager to grab power. Becoming president seemed as short-lived an outcome as a game of musical chairs. The USA looked at the instability in Haiti and began to grow nervous.

The opening of the Panama Canal had increased American desires to lay a controlling hand over the Caribbean, something that only grew when they looked at German penetration into the region (and particularly Haiti) on the eve of World War I. Furthermore, American commercial interests in the country had grown massively, with investments in railroads, sugar and bananas.

The American answer was to seize by force the gold reserves of the Haitian national bank in 1914. A year later, following the killing of President Sam by a mob, they sent in the US marines – with the justification that Haiti had never enjoyed a government competent enough to properly exercise its own sovereignty. The pliable figure of Philippe Dartiguenave was chosen to be president, and the occupation was formalised into a treaty inviting the Americans to stay for 20 years. Having taken control of Haiti's exchequer, the next move was to rewrite the constitution to allow foreigners to own land (the rewriting was done by future US president Franklin Delano Roosevelt). With the marines bringing stability, Haiti was to be the perfect investment destination for American businesses.

Unfortunately for the Americans, the Haitian masses didn't take kindly to foreign occupation. Resistance sprang up almost immediately. Most famous of those to take up arms was Charlemagne Péralte, an officer in the Haitian army. Péralte began his uprising in Hinche, and led a ragtag army of Cacos – a traditional name for those who rose up against the ruling powers. The Cacos only ever had limited success militarily, but they had a galvanising effect on the Americans, who had been fed stories of 'voodoo' rituals and black magic. The Americans did their bit to fuel Haitian resistance by instigating the *corvée*, forced labour gangs put to work on infrastructure projects like road-building. There was much violence associated with the recruitment and running of the *corvée*, which was widely thought of as a return to the slavery days.

Péralte himself was captured in 1919 and executed – an event captured in a widely distributed photograph that seemed to show him as having been crucified and has gone on to provide continuing inspiration to Haitian artists. The States continued to try to remake Haiti in its own image, with anti-Vodou campaigns as part of their civilising mission. Resistance was frequently met with the razing of entire villages by fire.

It wasn't just the countryside that fought the occupation. Unions campaigned against the Americans, and urban culture flourished through the Indigéniste movement led by writers like Jean-Price Mars and Jacques Roumain, who encouraged Haitians to embrace the African roots of their culture.

SECOND INDEPENDENCE Against a backdrop of countrywide strikes, America eventually tired of Haiti, and in 1934 declared that they had stabilised the country enough to withdraw their forces so that Haiti could be independent again. They left behind them several important legacies. Regional ports were closed to concentrate power in Port-au-Prince, and the rural economy began to be shifted away from self-sufficiency towards export-based agriculture. The Americans also reordered the army to fight the Cacos, and left a centralised political force whose only fighting experience was training its guns on its own people.

Haiti's 'second independence' was overseen by President Stenio Vincent. He sought to retain close ties to America, as well as the Dominican Republic. The DR, ruled by the dictator Rafael Trujillo, cared little for Haiti, especially as thousands of migrants had fled to the DR during the American occupation. Trujillo's response was to order the border region cleared through extreme violence – in October 1937 his police and soldiers massacred over 20,000 Haitians. Vincent baulked at even denouncing the murders, although after international condemnation Trujillo sent Haiti half a million dollars in compensation.

Throughout the 1940s, power alternated between establishment presidents and reformers. Dumarsais Estimé saw a progressive future for Haiti and attempted to reform education and labour laws – as well as trying to develop Haiti as a tourist destination. He was hampered by the economy, and a disastrous nationalisation of the banana industry, and was overthrown by army officer Paul Magloire, who as president painted himself as a bulwark against communism to curry favour with the Americans at the advent of the Cold War. His economic medicine proved equally unpalatable and he was run out of office after refusing to call elections in 1956. There were two main candidates for his replacement – the leftist Daniel Fignolé, who enjoyed widespread street support, and a modest country doctor called François Duvalier, who painted himself as an heir to Estimé and bearer of the Indigéniste flame. In a violence-marred election Duvalier prevailed.

THE DARK NIGHT OF DUVALIERISM Duvalier – dubbed 'Papa Doc' – was initially popular, but as his grip on power grew, his extreme ruthlessness became apparent. He identified himself as the personification of the Haitian state itself, and children in school were taught to recite that the early revolutionary heroes, from Toussaint Louverture onwards, were mere precursors to Duvalier.

Frequent purges of the army were carried out to remove potential coup plotters. Force was instead enacted through Duvalier's own private militia, the Tontons Macoutes. They took their name from 'Uncle Knapsack', a figure from Haitian folktales who abducted children. It was an apt name, as disappearances became a regular feature of Haitian life, with organised labour, teachers and even priests targeted for violence. Anyone who could be was co-opted into the regime. Duvalier's paranoia was reflected in the fears of the population. Those who could afford to simply fled the country. By the mid 1960s, 80% of Haiti's qualified professionals, from doctors and engineers to lawyers and administrators, were living outside the country.

In 1964, a referendum declared Duvalier President for Life (the few who dared to vote against were arrested for defacing ballot papers). In the same year, an attempt at an uprising from exiles landing in Jérémie was bloodily squashed. The revolutionaries were publicly executed, while around 300 people in Jérémie – almost the entire mulatto population, from infants to the elderly – were murdered in reprisal. When trusted lieutenant Clement Barbot turned against him, Duvalier ordered all black dogs on the street to be shot on sight, on the basis that Barbot was believed to be a shape-shifter.

For the most part, the USA stood by and offered their support – after Fidel Castro's revolution in Cuba, Duvalier played the anti-communist card with consummate skill. During the Nixon administration, the American ambassador was such a fervent supporter of Duvalier he was dubbed an honorary Tonton Macoute. Development and military aid and international loans flooded in, much of it rapidly expropriated by the predatory state machinery.

Duvalier held sway for 24 years, longer than any president since Boyer. In 1971 he died in office and went to meet Baron Samedi, the Vodou keeper of cemeteries on whom he had partly modelled his image. His last act was to proclaim his 19-year-old playboy son Jean-Claude his successor – 'Baby Doc' taking over from his murderous papa.

Against expectations, the inexperienced Jean-Claude ruled for 14 years. He again sought close relations with Washington, and was rewarded by an influx of US light industrial firms to Haiti, most notably garment assembly factories attracted by tax breaks and cheap labour. A brief window of political liberalisation was allowed in the late 1970s when US president Jimmy Carter pressured Haiti on human rights issues, but it didn't last long before rule by fear was once again the order of the day. Jean-Claude was even more avaricious than his father, and the repression went hand in hand with even greater looting of the state exchequer.

The tide began to turn in the 1980s. The government had carried out a disastrous anti-swine fever campaign that involved the mass extermination of pigs, alienating swathes of the population. Journalists and priests began to speak out more vociferously. There was popular disgust at a lavish party held by First Lady Michèle Duvalier that cost millions and drained the treasury so empty as to cause a fuel shortage when bills for imported gasoline couldn't be met. The final straw was the shooting of several law students at a demonstration in Gonaïves – deaths that tipped the country into popular revolt. In February 1986, Jean-Claude Duvalier finally slipped into French exile.

THE RISE AND FALL OF ARISTIDE The immediate aftermath of Duvalier's ouster saw a great outpouring of optimism, as well as reprisals against the Tontons Macoutes and other symbols of the regime – a *dechoukaj*, or uprooting. A new, more egalitarian, constitution was written, with Creole becoming a recognised national language for the first time. But when the dust settled it became clear that the military who had stepped into the power vacuum weren't very keen on giving it up. Proposed elections in 1987 were drenched in blood, and it was another three years before popular protests forced the junta into holding a more open poll.

One figure stood out above all others during the anti-Duvalier protests of the 1980s – a radical priest called Jean-Bertrand Aristide. He preached social justice for the masses and railed against corrupt elites – sermons that earned him a number of assassination attempts. In 1990 he ran for the presidency, heading a new party called Lavalas ('The Flood'). He won a landslide victory.

Aristide's programme to rebalance Haiti towards the needs of the masses never got off the ground. Less than a year into power the army, supported by members of the business elite, staged a coup and forced him into exile in the USA. It took three years for the USA to broker a deal for the junta, led by Raoul Cédras, to step down and for Aristide to return – an attempt to engineer a transition in 1993 foundered when right-wing militias faced down a US navy ship in Port-au-Prince. In the meantime, Haiti suffered under a trade embargo, and thousands of Haitians fled the country in a wave of 'boat people'. Lavalas supporters who remained were massacred.

In 1994 Aristide finally returned to Port-au-Prince supported by US troops, but the conditions set for his resuming the presidency were strict. He was forced to abandon the most radical parts of his political programme and submit Haiti to strict economic restructuring under guidance from the International Monetary Fund. Constitutionally forbidden from serving two consecutive terms, in 1995 Aristide was succeeded as president by Lavalas prime minister René Préval.

The mid 1990s were difficult for Lavalas. IMF medicine meant privatisation of state assets and resulting lay-offs of workers, as well as tariff-free food imports laying waste to domestic food production. Préval and Aristide split, and Aristide's new party Fanmi Lavalas won enough seats in parliament to reduce the government to deadlock. Préval tried ruling by decree, but the impasse was only broken when presidential elections were finally held in 2000. Despite being marred by violence and allegations of fraud, Aristide again won a broad mandate from the masses.

Aristide's second term was more authoritarian, but scarcely more successful than the first. Opposition parties refused to accept the result, and instability again began to show its face. Violence from right-wing groups operating from across the porous border wreaked havoc. In return, armed gangs of Aristide supporters from the poorest neighbourhoods of Port-au-Prince (often dubbed *chimeres*) often seemed to act with impunity. The USA froze development loans to the government, citing election irregularities, and gave tacit support to the anti-Aristide opposition. Government activity stalled, and security continued to deteriorate. At the start of 2004, when the country was preparing to celebrate its bicentenary, rebels took control of Cap-Haïtien and Gonaïves. Aristide himself was bundled onto a plane to the Central African Republic. The exact circumstances remain highly disputed by all parties: Aristide supporters insist he was kidnapped by US agents – prima-facie evidence of a coup d'état. America, on the other hand, publicly supported his overthrow, but denied active involvement. The end result was the same – more violence and kidnappings, and the return of international forces to attempt to stabilise the country.

FROM MINUSTAH TO MARTELLY Following Aristide's second ouster, the head of the supreme court, Boniface Alexandre, was named interim president. Alexandre invited the UN Security Council to mandate a peacekeeping mission to Haiti, and in June 2004 the Brazil-led force, dubbed Minustah, was dispatched. Minustah had its work cut out from the start. The following two years saw a spike in violent crime, and Port-au-Prince became a hotbed of kidnapping. Attempts by peacekeepers to take control of Cité Soleil, a pro-Aristide slum area of the capital also rife with gangs, seemed as bloody and controversial as the gangs themselves.

By 2006 things began to turn a corner when fresh elections were finally held. Lavalas boycotted the poll, but René Préval was returned for his second term as president. Préval was determined to rule with a much quieter voice, and juggled relations with the USA while also courting Latin American countries – diplomacy which resulted in increased economic aid from Venezuela in an attempt to improve Haiti's energy sector.

At home, Préval was rarely a master of events. In 2008 he faced riots caused by soaring international food prices, for which he lost his prime minister in a parliamentary vote of no confidence. That summer, hurricanes Hanna and Ike wreaked terrible damage on Haiti. The city of Gonaïves was buried under floodwaters and mudslides.

Finally – and most terrible of all – on 12 January 2010, Haiti was hit by a devastating earthquake. The epicentre was only a few miles outside overcrowded Port-au-Prince, producing the worst urban disaster in modern times, with a casualty list comparable to the Asian Tsunami squeezed into an area just over half the size of Wales (or the US state of Connecticut). The international community scrambled to provide aid, but the relief effort struggled with the sheer scope of the task at hand. (For a more detailed account of the earthquake, see box, *35 seconds that shook Haiti*, page 20.)

To compound the issue, in October 2010 there was a cholera outbreak in the Artibonite Valley. The disease, previously unknown in Haiti, is thought to have been introduced by Minustah peacekeepers from Nepal. Given the lack of access to clean water for much of the population, cholera spread rapidly throughout the entire country with cruel effects. By the second anniversary of the earthquake, there had been over half a million cases, with 7,000 deaths.

Against such a difficult backdrop, politics amazingly still continued. Against the protests of some, scheduled presidential elections were held at the end of 2010, with politicians' radio and poster campaigns vying for space with cholera

35 SECONDS THAT SHOOK HAITI

Haiti has been no stranger to devastating earthquakes. In 1751 and 1770, Port-au-Prince was severely damaged by tremors, while in 1842 Cap-Haïtien was completely flattened in a huge quake. But the damage done by these events doesn't begin to match the scale of destruction wrought on 12 January 2010.

The magnitude 7.0 earthquake struck at 16.53. Its epicentre was near the town of Léogâne, dangerously close to the capital. From a depth of 13km (8 miles), a half-minute of shaking flattened that town and tore a destructive swathe through Port-au-Prince, and caused damage as far as Jacmel in the south and Petit Goâve in the west. Anywhere else in the world the earthquake would have been a catastrophe, but the fragile nature of the Haitian state and the vulnerability of its population turned 12 January 2010 into a truly terrible disaster.

When viewed as cold statistics, the numbers are horrific. Over 180,000 buildings were damaged or destroyed outright. That figure includes 90% of schools in Port-au-Prince, 60% of hospitals and clinics and 60% of federal buildings (just one government ministry building survived unscathed; the National Assembly and Supreme Court were levelled). Several iconic buildings were flattened, including the beautiful wedding-cake National Palace and Port-au-Prince's two cathedrals. The headquarters of the UN was reduced to rubble.

The human cost was even harder to fathom. While there are no firm figures, it's estimated that over 200,000 people lost their lives, with 300,000 people injured. With buildings everywhere flattened, more than a third of the population of Port-au-Prince was made instantly homeless. In the immediate aftermath, 600,000 people left the capital, while six months on from the earthquake, there were 1.3 million internally displaced people (IDPs) living in 1,300 camps, with 800 camps in the capital alone.

EMERGENCY RESPONSE It took several days for any serious relief effort to be mounted – both the main airport and dock facilities were put out of action by the earthquake. Haitians were the first responders, rescuing neighbours, sharing food and setting up makeshift clinics. The US military sent 22,000 forces to co-ordinate relief efforts. While this helped to start getting aid flowing, some critics suggested that an over-emphasis on security may have actually hampered some aid getting through (media-led fears of looting and anarchy notably failed to materialise).

Aid and NGOs (non-governmental organisations) flooded in. Governments and private citizens worldwide donated massively to the relief effort. Within three months, billions of dollars had been pledged to help Haiti. In the rush to help there was confusion and duplication, but under the auspices of the UN's Cluster System, where different agencies could share information on their efforts in their health education messages. After a fraught first round marred with accusations and counter-accusations of fraud and manoeuvrings and months of delay, the ex-singer Michel Martelly (also known by his stage name Sweet Micky) was elected president in a run-off ballot in spring 2011. Préval quietly slipped off the scene, having become the first president in Haitian history to serve two full terms of office.

The right-leaning Martelly inherited a full plate. He'd effectively run as an independent candidate, and ran into trouble with a hostile parliament unwilling to lend him their support. It took three attempts for him to find a prime ministerial candidate, leading to months of governmental gridlock when the international

various areas (housing, water and sanitation, protection and so on), some sense of co-ordination was slowly achieved. This wasn't helped by many of the myriad NGOs operating outside the loop and totally unrecognised or registered with the Haitian authorities. Hardly any of the aid was earmarked to go through the Haitian government itself – around 1% of the total monies. Instead, a trans-national body, the Interim Haiti Recovery Commission, was formed, led by former US president Bill Clinton and then Haitian prime minister Jean-Max Bellerive to co-ordinate funds for reconstruction efforts, although this was dissolved in late 2011.

MOVE TO RECOVERY If the initial emergency response phase was complicated enough, any move to recovery and reconstruction has been even harder. The earthquake revealed many of the social, political and economic fault lines already bedevilling Haitian society. For instance, 90% of those living in tent camps had been renting their homes before the earthquake. The question of rehousing, whether in transitional shelters or permanent accommodation has run up against problems of land availability (with much land in the city covered in rubble) or land tenure (where many records were destroyed in the earthquake). Showcase reconstruction camps outside the city have not met with great success, either being too far from economic opportunities for residents or sited inappropriately – the flagship Corail Cesselesse site flooded in its first hurricane season. Meanwhile, many camps received no NGO assistance while in others residents were plagued by insecurity and (especially women) gender-based violence. Nearly two-thirds of camps were on private land, and as time has passed with stalled relocation programmes, forced evictions have become increasingly common.

Recovery in complex disasters usually takes up to five years, even in countries that started from a higher base line than Haiti. Yet less than half the money initially pledged for Haiti by the international community appeared. Further hampering efforts was the cholera epidemic, another symptom of Haiti's chronically inadequate infrastructure. At the time of writing, there was increasing resentment among some about the NGOs and a lack of Haitian participation in reconstruction decisions. Over two-and-a-half years later, nearly 400,000 people were still living in tent camps. With a chronic shortage of new housing being built, it's feared that these camps are becoming institutionalised into permanent shanties.

Haitians have dubbed the earthquake *Goudogoudou*, an onomatopoeia for the sound that the buildings made as they were shaken into rubble. Others simply refer to it as *bagay la* ('the thing'), an event so powerful it can't even be named. Its aftershocks continue to reverberate throughout the country.

HOW MANY DIED IN THE 2010 EARTHQUAKE?

Most media and NGO reports have settled on the number of earthquake dead as being around 250,000, but no-one really knows how many died on 12 January 2010 or its aftermath.

Haitian government figures ranged between 217,000 and 300,000, but unlike the 2004 Asian Tsunami, no-one attempted to count the bodies. The mass graves outside Port-au-Prince at Titanyen were filled largely without supervision in the chaos, others were buried privately and without record, while more dead yet were left in the rubble of destroyed buildings.

Two studies have attempted to put an estimate on the number of casualties through statistical analysis. A report in the journal *Medicine, Conflict & Survival* by Kolbe et al followed up on a 2009 survey of Port-au-Prince households to come up with an estimate of around 158,700 people in the capital having lost their lives in the earthquake and the six-week period following it. More controversially, an unpublished but leaked survey about rebuilding needs commissioned by USAID and written by a long-term critic of aid in Haiti, came up with a figure of around 65,600 deaths. Neither report has been officially accepted.

It's often said that while one death is a tragedy, a million deaths is a statistic, yet Haiti's earthquake has left behind it tragedies that still remain uncounted.

community was waiting to disburse reconstruction funds. In 2011, politics was enlivened even further when, within weeks of each other, Jean-Claude Duvalier and Jean-Bertrand Aristide both controversially returned from exile, stirring up supporters and detractors alike. The cholera epidemic further crystallised popular discontent against the UN mission, matched with dissatisfaction at the seemingly slow pace of post-earthquake rebuilding. That 400,000 people were still living in tent camps in August 2012 when Tropical Storm Isaac blew through the country showed the scale of the task that the country still faces.

GOVERNMENT AND POLITICS

Haiti is a constitutional democracy headed by a president and with two legislative houses – the National Assembly (containing 30 senators) and the Chamber of Deputies (with 99 seats). The government is headed by a prime minister chosen by a president, but subject to confirmation by both parliamentary houses.

Haiti's democracy remains fragile. Jean-Bertrand Aristide, its first democratically elected president, was overthrown twice by coups (in 1991 and 2004). The current president is ex-singer Michel Martelly, elected in spring 2011. The two-round election was toughly contested and required intervention by the Organisation of American States after allegations of vote-rigging. Others boycotted the election following the banning of Aristide's Fanmi Lavalas party from the ballot (by most accounts still the most popular political party in Haiti), while even more could not vote due to incomplete voter registration following the earthquake and cholera epidemic. Martelly ran as a political outsider, and although personally popular, his Repons Peyizan party won few seats in either house. This led to immediate gridlock when his first two nominees for prime minister were repeatedly blocked by opposing senators and deputies, and the successful candidate serving barely four months before resigning after a power tussle with the executive. The largest number of seats in both houses are currently held by Inité, the party of the previous president René Préval.

Presidents may serve two non-consecutive five-year terms: the deliberate break is proscribed in the post-Duvalier constitution, to prevent entrenchment and any possible return to dictatorship. Both the National Assembly and Chamber of Deputies regularly hold elections for a proportion of their seats, leading to endless jostling for power. Turnouts remain stubbornly low however, as many Haitians believe that real political power lies outside the country, with the USA and UN, often in tandem with the tiny Haitian elite class. The Haitian army has also traditionally been an important player and kingmaker in national politics, a fact that led Aristide to abolish the military in 1994. Since his election, President Martelly has repeatedly courted controversy by announcing a desire to reinstate the army, as a matter of national security.

ECONOMY

Domestically, agriculture has traditionally been the mainstay of the Haitian economy. Peasant farmers keep small plots focused primarily on subsistence crops – beans, plantains, sweet potatoes and corn. In places like the Artibonite Valley, rice is an important crop. Fruits are also an important market crop, and at higher altitudes, coffee. Sugarcane is widely grown, but rather than being refined into sugar, tends to go towards local rum production. Despite the relative agricultural richness of the country, Haiti is a net importer of food, particularly from America and the Dominican Republic.

Much of the Haitian economy is informal, particularly in rural areas. Charcoal production is an important revenue generator (see box, *Charcoal*, page 8). Women are often keener traders than men, with female merchants travelling between markets buying and selling on staples. Known colloquially as *Madam Sara*, they stitch much of the retail economy together – in 2011, a temporary shortage of US dollars in Haiti was rumoured to be because of the large amount of cash that Madam Saras were taking out of the country to buy import goods in Panama and other Central American countries.

The Haitian economy has a very small tax base. Since independence, import–export tariffs have been the main source of income for the state. Coupled with the large debts the country accrued since paying the French indemnity of 1825, the government has always had trouble raising adequate revenues. Over the past three decades, Haiti has liberalised its economy to attract foreign investors, offering tax incentives and scrapping tariffs (often with dire side effects – see box, *The high cost of cheap rice*, page 25). Many of the resulting jobs have gone into the low-paying garment or electronic component assembly business. The current government sees attracting increased foreign investment as crucial to kick-starting the economy and tackling the chronic unemployment rate, which languishes somewhere just below 50%. Its flagship programme is the Caracol Industrial Park, a multi-million dollar project just outside Cap-Haïtien, aided by the US HOPE II Act, which gives Haiti duty-free access to the American market. Tourism, a big earner for Haiti until the mid 1980s, is also hoped to become an important pillar of economic reconstruction. Currently around 450,000 tourists visit Haiti each year, although the vast majority of these come by cruise ship to Labadee near Cap-Haïtien, and never leave the exclusive resort complex.

Currently, two of the single largest contributors to Haiti's GDP are external: foreign aid (around 40%) and remittances from the Haitian diaspora, valued by the World Bank at a staggering US$1.5–1.8 billion per year. In 2012 the Haitian government announced to great fanfare that exploratory geological surveys had discovered gold deposits in the northeast of the country potentially worth US$20 billion. With international mining companies set to pile in, Haiti could potentially be due an enormous windfall – provided that promised new legislation provides adequate financial and environmental safeguards for the country.

Nearly 90% of banking activity in Haiti takes place in Port-au-Prince. Access to credit is a perennial issue, but micro-loan social businesses like Fonkoze are increasingly widespread.

PEOPLE

The original inhabitants of Haiti, the Taíno, didn't last long after first contact with the Spanish colonisers. Today, Haiti's population of nine million are almost entirely of African descent, having been brought to the colony as slaves by the French. When the Haitian Revolution broke out, two-thirds of the population were African-born. Although no accurate data was kept by the French, most slaves were imported from west-central Africa, with ethnic groups like the Fon, Yoruba, Ibo and Kongo particularly strongly represented. Traditions and religious practices from these groups all found their way into the culture of newly independent Haiti.

THE SAD TALE OF THE CREOLE PIG

In the late 1970s, Haiti suffered an eruption of African swine fever, following an outbreak in the Dominican Republic. Although it was less lethal than outbreaks elsewhere in the world, there was a fear it could spread rapidly to North America. With this in mind, USAID (the American foreign aid agency) and the Duvalier government came up with what they believed to be a foolproof eradication plan: kill every pig in Haiti.

The authorities went about their task with a rare zeal. Over several months in 1982, nearly two million pigs were slaughtered. In doing so, they did lethal damage to the rural economy.

For the Haitian peasants, their black Creole pigs were quite literally piggy banks. Piglets were a quick source of cash, and whole pigs could be killed and sold for larger sums – to pay for weddings, funerals and school fees. Crucially, over several centuries the pigs had become perfectly adapted to their environment, eating garbage, clearing arable land of roots while adding fertiliser, and requiring little husbandry and no expense to keep. The replacement programme was a disaster – those peasants who managed to claim compensation were given white Iowa hogs, who demanded expensive imported feed and housing in concrete pig pens that (it was darkly joked) were better than the houses the farmers lived in. The Iowa pigs were dubbed 'four-footed princes'. The loss to the rural communities was estimated at US$600 million. Within a year, rural school enrolment had collapsed by 30%, protein intake crashed, and soil productivity decreased.

Since then, the Creole pig has made a comeback, of sorts. Some farmers managed to hide their pigs from the slaughter and breed them with the American pigs, while a French captive-breeding programme crossed similar strains from China, Guadeloupe and the south of France. The pigs will still take several more generations to become truly 'Creole', but their return marks an important pillar of economic activity in rural Haiti – as well as closing the door on one of the most ill-conceived foreign aid programmes in the country's history.

THE HIGH COST OF CHEAP RICE

A plate of food in Haiti is barely considered a meal unless it comes with a serving of rice. Haitian farmers have been cultivating rice since it was brought to the country from west Africa, but it's only in recent decades that it's become a more important source of carbohydrates than more traditional staples like manioc and cassava. Until 20 years ago, Haiti was completely self-sufficient in rice production, but now imports 80% of what it eats, universally known as 'Miami rice' after its main port of origin.

In the 1980s, domestic rice production experienced a slow decline due to rural economic stagnation. Environmental damage has also harmed rice production – harvest time coincided with hurricane season, when the risk of flooding is raised massively due to upstream deforestation degrading Haiti's watersheds. Under the Duvalier regime, farmers were afforded some protection from imports by a hefty 50% rice import tariff. As a result, rice smuggling was big business, and there were regular clashes between smugglers and rice farmers in port towns like Saint-Marc, which sits at the foot of the Artibonite Valley, Haiti's main rice-growing area.

In 1994, when Aristide returned from exile after the first coup against him, he was encouraged by the US government and the IMF to pursue a policy of economic liberalisation. Trade agreements were near the top of his sponsors' list, and the import duty for rice was slashed to 3%. Almost overnight, Haitian markets were full of Miami rice and the price of rice collapsed. While this was good for poor urban Haitians who struggled to feed themselves, it was also a disaster for the rice farmers. Many farmers are share-croppers, giving part of their harvest to their landlords or farming diminishing plots of their own land, and plummeting prices left them unable to make money at market or feed themselves. Many found themselves joining the urban drift to the growing shanties around Port-au-Prince, living in substandard housing that left them severely exposed when the 2010 earthquake struck.

Many campaigners have accused the USA of 'rice dumping' in Haiti, a cheap way of off-loading home-grown rice that receives federal subsidies of over US$430 million a year. In March 2010, Bill Clinton, who championed the tariff cuts when president, admitted that the policy had caused huge damage to Haitian agriculture and primarily benefitted the rice farmers of his home state of Arkansas. Meanwhile, local agriculture continues to stagnate. A lack of rice mills means that Haitian rice often contains grit due to milling by hand. Until there is improved access to capital for farmers, and land and tariff reform, Haiti will struggle to return to its once-vaunted food self-sufficiency.

The French left their genetic mark through having children with their slaves, producing so-called mulattoes. Around 5% of the population, they have historically tended to form a separate urban class, dominating politics and trade. Into this mix can be added a minority Arab population from Syria and Lebanon, who migrated to Haiti in the late 19th century.

Haiti has a predominantly rural population, although over the past three decades the pull of the capital has proved inexorable, and nearly a third of Haitians now live in Port-au-Prince. Despite this, Haiti is a deeply segregated society, and the rural–urban divide remains a strong one. This dates from President Boyer's *Code Rural* of the 1820s, which sought to limit the movements of peasants to the *peyi andeyò*

BANKING ON THE LOTTERY

In Haiti, the lottery is everywhere, and playing it can seem like a national obsession. Whether you're in downtown Port-au-Prince or in the smallest rural town, you're never too far from a brightly painted lottery 'bank'. In a capricious country where people often have little control over their lives, people consciously play for a change to improve their circumstances.

Better known as the *borlette*, the lottery first came to Haiti in the 1950s from Cuba. During the Duvalier period it was state-run, with the numbers often corruptly controlled by the government. These days, the privately run *borlette* draws its numbers from the New York or Chicago lotteries.

A winning draw is called a *tiraj*. Players can pick as little as one number for a gourde or two, with the payout increasing (and the odds decreasing) by picking up to three. But it's how you pick your numbers that's the crucial element. For many people the lottery numbers aren't random at all, but can be predicted through the interpretation of dreams. If you dream of coconuts, you should play 70, or 45 for a dog. Gamblers usually then pair these numbers with their reverse. A book called a *tchala* deciphers the numbers for you, although many people have their own elaborate systems to best interpret their reveries. Although dreamers lose more often than they win, failure is taken to be the fault of bad dream interpretation rather than the system itself. If you have good dreams you should play the lottery, and stop when the dreams turn awry.

The *borlette* is one of Haiti's biggest industries, employing an estimated 100,000 people. The estimated annual spend is a jaw-dropping US$1.5 billion. Incredibly, it all goes untaxed by the state. It's also one of the most efficient industries, paying out twice a day, seven days a week. In Port-au-Prince, the lottery was up and running within a week of the 2010 earthquake.

(outside country) and deny them the right to settle (or often travel to) cities, all the while concentrating power with the elites.

The rural population replied by frequently asking just to be left alone by government. Villages are largely autonomous units based around the *lakou*, houses grouped around a common yard, with a set of essentially egalitarian social conventions such as the communal work team, or *konbit*. Where the rural population has been sucked into the cities, it has taken the social nature of the *lakou* with it, providing a high degree of social cohesion even when rammed up against the harsh nature of life in the *bidonvilles* (slums) of Port-au-Prince.

Power and wealth has filtered upwards in Haiti. The paler-skinned mulattoes formed Haiti's initial mercantile class, and continue to dominate the economy as well as traditionally pulling the levers of political power. French, rather than Creole, is the language of the elite. However, Haitians have always recognised that money as much as colour is the crucial class barrier, codified into the proverb that a rich black is a mulatto, and a poor mulatto a black.

For much of the first hundred years of its existence, Haiti sucked in migrants. In particular it was a magnet for many African-Americans eager to make a new life in the world's only free black republic. But in the 20th century Haiti became a great exporter of people. During the American occupation, large numbers of Haitians left to become migrant workers in the Dominican Republic and Cuba.

The biggest migration took place during the Duvalier period, when a million people – some 15% of the population – fled, including the vast majority of the middle classes and educated professionals. This hollowing out of the state civil society has left a damaging legacy for Haitian civil society, but also created the large diaspora. Around 2.5 million Haitians now live abroad, with the largest numbers concentrated in New York and Florida. The Dominican Republic also has a significant Haitian population, who face severe legal discrimination.

LANGUAGE

Haiti has two official languages: Haitian Creole (Kreyol) and French. There is a distinct linguistic split: Creole is the language of the people, spoken by 90% of the population; French is the language of government, the law and the elite.

Creole is thought to be around 300 years old as a distinct language. It evolved on the slave plantations, and is a fusion of the various tongues brought to Haiti by African captives, with a healthy dose of French vocabulary and a smattering of Spanish, English and even Taíno taken from Haiti's original inhabitants. Despite being the language of the majority, written Creole was only standardised in 1979, and it wasn't until 1987 that it was recognised as an official language.

The officially sanctioned supremacy of French reflects the long-standing trends in Haitian history, with the dominance of the political and economic elites over the masses. The political and legal systems and the majority of the printed media remain in French. Most school education is carried out in French, a fact that handicaps many students from the outset – having to learn by rote in a second language, taught by teachers who frequently aren't fluent in French themselves. Only 10% of those who start high school finish with a pass in their final exams.

RESTAVEKS

Haiti has long had a system of bonded child labour. A *restavek* is a domestic child servant, the name derived from the French 'to stay with'. According to UNICEF, there are around 173,000 restaveks in Haiti, three-quarters of them girls. The restavek system is a condition of poverty. Most restaveks are from rural areas. If a family is incapable of caring for a child, it's not uncommon for that child to be sent (via a broker) to the city to live with either extended family or strangers to work as a domestic servant. The child is never paid, but is meant to go to school as well as being given bed and board, in the hope of eventually improving their life chances.

It doesn't always work like that. The promise of an education is rarely fulfilled (the children are frequently made to work 16-hour days), and restaveks are frequently mistreated, poorly fed and housed and cut off from their families completely. Worse, they are vulnerable to beatings and sexual violence from their host families. Since the earthquake, child trafficking across borders has also become an issue.

It is not illegal to employ a restavek, although many observers have likened it to a form of child slavery – a sensitive charge in a country founded by a successful slave revolution. The Haitian government agency the Institute of Social Welfare and Research and the Ministry of Social Affairs and Labour work with UNICEF and the International Organization for Migration and many smaller NGOs to reunite abused restaveks with their families.

WOMEN'S RIGHTS IN HAITI

Alexis Erkert

The refrain to the popular Haitian feminist song, *Fanm, nou se wozo,* says: 'Women, we are reeds. You can cut off our heads, you can burn our roots, but when it rains, we'll grow again.'

Haitian women articulate their role in society as that of *poto mitan*, or central pillar. Women are the caretakers of children, the sick and the elderly; they head nearly half of Haitian households, carry much of the responsibility for the informal market economy and comprise the majority of the country's subsistence farmers.

HISTORY OF THE WOMEN'S MOVEMENT Haitian women have a history of activism longer than the nation itself. The poisoning of plantation owners by female slaves is among the first recorded acts of insurrection against French colonial authorities, and women battled alongside men in the revolution for independence. Beyond the struggle for their own liberation, women in Haiti have claimed key roles in subsequent movements for sovereignty; for social, economic and political rights; and most recently, for just reconstruction after the earthquake.

Formal advocacy for women's rights began with the formation of the Feminine League for Social Action (Ligue Féminine d'Action Sociale) in the 1930s, partially as a response to sexual violence against women during the US occupation. By 1950, women had won the rights of full citizenship, including suffrage. However, these hard-won freedoms were withdrawn during the Duvalier period, pushing women to become key actors in the social organisations that eventually ousted the regime.

In the months following the end of the dictatorship, more than 30,000 women took to the streets of Port-au-Prince, and thousands more to the dirt roads of Papaye, a village in the Central Plateau, effectively birthing the contemporary women's movement. This movement has been successful in winning access into civil society, allowing women to push more forcefully for their own needs and rights. Over the years, women have made important legal gains, including the rights to own land and to child support.

In 1994, the Ministry on the Status and Rights of Women was created to advocate for gender rights and equality. Haiti is a signatory to the Convention on the Elimination of all Forms of Discrimination against Women (CEDAW) and the Inter-American Convention on Violence Against Women (*Belém Do Pará*), though neither has been fully and effectively implemented.

Although there is an increasing movement to promote Creole, its official use remains stigmatised, and knowledge of French remains important in order to get a decent job.

RELIGION

Haiti is a deeply religious country. Catholicism and Vodou are both recognised as the national religions (the former since independence, the latter only since 1991). A popular adage whimsically reckons it has the balance of practitioners about right, contending that Haiti is 80% Catholic, 20% Protestant and 100% Vodou.

CHRISTIANITY You only have to turn out on a Sunday to see how deeply Christian Haiti is. You're never far from a church, and everywhere you'll see people dressed up for church and carrying their Bibles.

GENDER-BASED VIOLENCE The January 2010 earthquake has intensified the need for women to further advance their rights. In addition to inadequate access to food, water, sanitation and medical and legal services, women and girls living in displacement camps have been subject to alarming rates of rape and gender-based violence.

Haitian women have historically received little legal protection from sexual violence. During the civil unrest that marked Haiti's violent coup years, systematic rape was used as a tool of political oppression. Before 2005, rape was only treated as the equivalent of a misdemeanour. Although it is now classified as a crime against the person, perpetrators are rarely prosecuted: of hundreds of rapes reported post-earthquake, less than 2% have been prosecuted.

In face of these challenges, women's groups are working with the National Consultation Panel against Gender-based Violence (Concertation Nationale contre la Violence Faite aux Femmes) a working group formed in 2003 bringing together grassroots organisations, international agencies and government actors – notably the Women's, Public Health and Justice ministries – to push for legislation that will provide increased legal protection for women, investment into public information campaigns on gender-based violence and provision of government services for victims.

WOMEN TODAY Though today's women's movement as a whole is fractured by politics, the urban–rural divide, and class conflict, women's associations can be found in almost every urban neighbourhood, rural village and university campus, as well as key subsets of Haitian workers' and peasants' movements.

In addition to the fight against gender-based violence, activism by both feminist and grassroots women's groups demands economic rights and full access to social services for women and their families. As they continue to challenge a male-dominated status quo, Haitian women call for decent wages, improved working conditions in factories, universal and free access to education, and quality healthcare.

*Alexis Erkert is a Port-au-Prince-based co-ordinator for Other Worlds (*www.otherworldsarepossible.org*), who support communities working to build just social, economic, environmental and gender-based alternatives.*

Catholicism was brought to Haiti by the Spanish, although they didn't have much of a chance to convert the Taíno before exterminating them through disease and slave labour. Slaves under the French were made to convert, but frequently used their supposed new faith as a cover for their native African religions (see *Vodou*, page 30). Since independence, however, Haiti has very much embraced Christianity. The Church has remained a powerful influence on Haitian life, from the regular anti-Vodou campaigns, to its support for the Duvalier regime – something that famously came out into the open when Pope John Paul II visited Haiti in 1983 and announced 'something must change', giving succour to the anti-Duvalier movements. Those movements themselves were heavily Church-based, not least Aristide's Ti Legliz (Little Church) group, heavily influenced by Latin-American liberation theology.

Protestantism grew rapidly in the 20th century. It arrived in part with the US occupation, but the numbers of missionaries exploded in the 1970s and 80s as part of the great influx of foreign aid groups to Haiti. Evangelical Christianity is very popular and is likely to command increasing congregations over the coming years.

VODOU Haitian Vodou is about as far away from Hollywood ideas of 'voodoo' as it's possible to get. It's a complex belief system, believing in a single God, but one who is so distant from creation that communication has to take place through spirit interlocutors called *lwa*. These lwa form a rich pantheon for believers, and may be summoned in services through a combination of prayer, song, drumming and sacrifice.

Haitian Vodou is unique to the island. It was birthed on the slave plantations and was crucial to the forming of the national identity. Its name and roots come from west and central Africa, the birthplace of the captives who were brought to Saint-Domingue by the French. The name means 'divine spirit' in the language of the Fon, a people from present-day Benin (where, incidentally, Vodun is a national religion). Along with the Yoruba and Kongo, the Fon made up a sizeable proportion of the slave population of the island, and many Haitian lwa share names and characteristics with the spirits of those peoples.

When the slaves were brought to Saint-Domingue, they were forbidden to practise their own religions, and forcibly converted to Catholicism. For many this was a sham, and used the new sacraments to cover their own ceremonies. Many slave owners were wise to this, and instead of being pleased at the conversion of their slaves, were positively afraid of the fervour with which so many slaves apparently embraced Catholicism. This heritage continues in modern Vodou, as each lwa has its counterpart as a Catholic saint – don't be surprised to visit a Vodou temple and find it adorned with images of the Virgin Mary or the Last Supper.

It was a Vodou ceremony at Boïs Caïman in August 1791 that lit the first fires of the Haitian Revolution, but despite (or possibly because of) the fact that it's always been a religion of the people, the authorities have always had a troubled relationship with it. Toussaint Louverture and Dessalines disapproved of it, although the latter has subsequently been claimed as a lwa himself, an aspect of Ogue, the spirit of war. In the 1830s, Boyer's *Code Rural* attempted to outlaw the religion, and since then there have been a variety of official campaigns against practitioners. Foreigners readily went along with this, eager to blame Vodou for the apparently 'backward' nature of Haitian society. Throughout the 19th century, a series of lurid second-hand accounts of cannibalism and human sacrifice made their way into the European and American consciousness, a mini industry that went into overdrive during the US occupation, when memoirs coincided with the dime-store pulp industry to help create the voodoo of popular imagination. In the 1940s, the Haitian government carried out a widespread 'anti-superstition' campaign, backed by the Catholic Church, involving imprisonment, destroying temples and Vodou drums and cutting down sacred *mapou* trees.

The Duvalier period saw the wholesale co-opting of Vodou into the state power structure, with François Duvalier likening himself to Baron Samedi and hiring a US press officer to play up the fact that he kept a Vodou altar in the national palace. Many priests became part of the security apparatus, a fact that led to violent anti-Vodou reprisals in the immediate post-Duvalier period. Duvalier was unusual in playing to the Vodou gallery; a more typical slander is to actually accuse presidents of being involved in Vodou (Aristide's detractors sought comfort in their knowledge that he had apparently taken part in child sacrifice, a story first told about President Simon in 1909). In the 1990s, Vodou was finally recognised as an official religion of Haiti.

HAITI – LAND OF ZOMBIES?

In 1934, Hollywood's *Dracula* actor Bela Lugosi starred in *White Zombie*, a shock-horror movie claiming documentary roots to lift the lid on Haiti's zombie problem, scary jungle drums and all.

Zombies are real, according to many Haitians, although they bear little resemblance to their Hollywood relatives. In Creole, a *zonbi* is someone who has died by poisoning, and is then brought back to life by a *bokor*, or black magician. The poison, thought to be tetradotoxin extracted from puffer fish, is a potent neurotoxin, and brings on a deathlike state. After burial, the antidote is administered, and the person brought back to life, yet under the complete control of the *bokor*. *Zonbis* are then typically put to work in the fields.

Zombification was outlawed in the 1830s, and the statute apparently still sits in the law books. If you ask around, you'll find belief in the existence of *zonbis* almost as common in Haiti as belief in ghosts or guardian angels is in the West. Few people seem to have encountered them though – stories of encounters often revolve around a friend of a friend. The folk origins of *zonbis* are easier to discern however – the fear of returning from the grave to a life of servitude has special meaning in a country that fought so hard to liberate itself from slavery. When the American HASCO sugar mill opened during the US occupation, stories were immediately rife that some of their workers were *zonbis*, a code for previously free peasant farmers being forced to work on the plantations.

The Vodou pantheon Followers of Vodou are known as those who serve the lwa, and for them these spirits are everywhere, tying man to nature in a complex web and providing a link between the visible and invisible worlds. The lwa are independent from God (called Bon Dye or Gran Met in Vodou), but mediate between Him and mankind, as well as connecting practitioners to their ancestors in Africa. The lwa are neither good nor bad – Vodou offers no moral code in the way that other religions do – but are summoned to provide advice, healing or spiritual well-being.

The lwa are divided into a series of families or nations. Of these, the most important are the Rada and Petro. The families have different rituals, music and sacrifices attached to them. The Rada are the most commonly summoned lwa, and include those spirits originally brought over by African slaves – the lwa of Dahomey or Ginen, the Vodou term for ancestral Africa. Of the Rada law, the first to be summoned at any ritual is Legba, the master of the crossroads who can open the gate between the human and supernatural worlds. Next in the hierarchy are Damballah and Ayida Wedo. Damballah, the snake, created the world, and fell in love with the rainbow Ayida Wedo, who he then married. Other important Rada lwa are Ogue Feray the warrior, Zaka the farmer, Ezili Freda who represents motherhood and the husband and wife lwa Agwe and Lasiren (the mermaid), who rule the seas and fresh waters respectively.

The Petro lwa are often referred to as 'hotter' or angrier than the 'sweeter' Rada spirits. These lwa come from Haiti itself. Petro rituals are usually more frenetic, and often associated with the practice of magic. One of the most celebrated of the Petro lwa is Ezili Danto, a mute woman with facial scars who represents motherhood. Ezili originally fought in the Haitian Revolution and had her tongue cut out so she couldn't reveal any of the slaves' secrets.

DECODING THE LWA

Each lwa has a series of recognisable symbols, from the types of offerings made to them and the places they inhabit, to principles they represent and their Catholic counterparts. This table should help you identify some of the major lwa.

Name	Legba
Colour	Red
Family	Rada
Offerings	Cassava, plantains, rice
Attributes	Keeper of the crossroads, protector of the home
Abode	Gates and crossroads
Symbols	Old man in rags
Catholic counterpart	St Peter
Name	Damballah
Colour	White
Family	Rada
Offerings	Anything white – rice, eggs, salt
Attributes	Happiness, order, calmness
Abode	Springs, rivers
Symbols	Snake
Catholic counterpart	St Patrick
Name	Ayida Wedo
Colour	Blue and white
Family	Rada
Offerings	Anything white – rice, eggs, salt
Attributes	Wealth
Abode	Springs, rivers
Symbols	Rainbow
Catholic counterpart	Our Lady of the Immaculate Conception
Name	Baron Samedi
Colour	Black and purple
Family	Gede
Offerings	Black roosters, rum, cigars, black goats
Attributes	Law of the dead, communication with ancestors
Abode	Cemeteries
Symbols	Skeleton, black cross
Catholic counterpart	St Expedit
Name	Ezili Freda
Colour	Blue and pink
Family	Rada
Offerings	Perfume, cakes
Attributes	Love, luxury, promiscuity
Abode	Riverbanks
Symbols	Heart, mirror
Catholic counterpart	Virgin Mary

Name	Ezili Danto
Colour	Navy blue and gold
Family	Petro
Offerings	Black pigs, rum, dolls
Attributes	Motherhood
Abode	Laurel tree
Symbols	Pierced heart, daggers
Catholic counterpart	Black Madonna

Name	Ogue Feray
Colour	Red
Family	Rada
Offerings	Red rooster, bull
Attributes	Fighting, war, leadership
Abode	Bamboo, calabash tree
Symbols	Sword or machete
Catholic counterpart	St James

Name	Zaka
Colour	Blue and red
Family	Rada
Offerings	Corn, bread, tobacco
Attributes	Hardworking, harvests
Abode	Fields
Symbols	Peasant farmer
Catholic counterpart	St Isidore

Name	Agwe
Colour	White and blue
Family	Rada
Offerings	Rams, hens, rum
Attributes	Protector of fishing and husbandry
Abode	The sea
Symbols	Boats, oars
Catholic counterpart	St Ulrich

Name	Marassa
Colour	Yellow
Family	Rada
Offerings	Sweets, dolls (always in double quantities)
Attributes	Twins or triplets, trust, abundance
Abode	Houses
Symbols	Eggs
Catholic counterpart	Sts Cosmas and Damian

After the Rada and Petro, one of the most important lwa families is Gede, the spirits of death and the afterlife. Prime among these is the skeletal and top hat-clad figure of Baron Samedi (or simply Baron) who guards the passage to the next world along with his wife Brigitte. The Gede are the most raucous and lewdly behaved of all the lwa.

Aside from the lwa, there is a widespread belief in magic and magical spirits. The most famous manifestation is the zombie, but another creature that looms large in the popular imagination is the *lougarou*, a shape-changer sometimes said to be akin to a werewolf. Lougarou, who can fly and take any beastly form, come out at night and are particularly feared for their appetite for children and babies.

Vodou in practice A Vodou temple is called an *ounfò*, and is divided into two parts – the inside of the building, which contains one or more altars dedicated to the lwa (covered with offerings and icons), and the outside *peristyle*, where services take place. At the centre of the peristyle is a pillar called a *potò-mitan*, which serves as a bridge connecting the earth to the spirit world and down which the lwa descend during a service. Each ounfò is presided over by a Vodou priest, who can be either male (a *houngan*) or female (a *mambo*). The symbol of their authority in an initiation is an *asson*, or ceremonial rattle, used during rituals.

Singing and drumming is central to any Vodou ceremony, directing the action. The first song to be sung is always the *Priye Ginen*, which symbolises the celebrant's roots to ancestral Africa, and lists ancestors and lwa alike in a mix of Creole, French taken from Catholic hymns and *langaj*, the supposed tongue of mythic Africa. Symbolic pictograms called *vèvè*, each dedicated to a different lwa, are drawn on the floor of the peristyle in flour, cornmeal or charcoal. Many of the symbols are thought to have been inherited by African slaves from the last of the Taíno. After this, the drumming takes over, with different drums, beats and counter-rhythms signifying whether the ritual is dedicated to either the Rada or Petro lwa. Whichever is chosen, the first lwa called upon is always Legba, who opens the gate to the spirit world, allowing the other lwa to descend the potò-mitan to take part.

For the participants, the purpose of the ritual is to be 'mounted' by the lwa – to be literally possessed by the spirits. To the songs of the assembled choir, the devotee is taken over by the lwa, and begins to manifest the characteristics of that lwa. Damballah would show himself through the devotee writhing snake-like on the floor, Ezili Freda might be coquettish, while rude and sexually provocative behaviour is more the domain of the Gede Baron and Brigitte. The lwa dances, talks and sings throughout, possibly offering advice, predicting events or carrying out healings – all behaviours that the mounted initiate won't be able to recall after the event.

As well as music and prayer, sacrificial offerings are essential to bring the lwa to the human realm. An animal is fed with the foods associated with the particular lwa and then ritually washed. The animal is then dispatched, its blood tasted and body presented to the cardinal points. The energy released by the sacrifice is then enough to tempt the lwa to descend and mount a member of the congregation (the animal is later cooked and eaten). Ceremonies can last for some hours, orchestrated by the houngan or mambo until the lwa are satiated.

There are many feasts and festivals associated with Vodou. Fet Gede, at the start of November is the largest, celebrated in cemeteries nationwide. Those with a focus on particular areas are the pilgrimage to Saut d'Eau near Mirebalais in July, and Souvenance near Gonaïves in April. For more information see *Public holidays and festivals*, page 77. If you're interested in tips on attending Vodou ceremonies, see box, *Attending a Vodou ceremony*, page 80.

EDUCATION

Haiti's education system is in a rough shape. According to World Bank figures, less than 1.5% of Haiti's GDP goes on education. Half of all children do not attend primary school and only a fifth of those make it to secondary level. Nationally, the adult illiteracy rate is about 50%.

At independence, the picture was rather brighter. Christophe was a great champion of education, and invested heavily in schools across the north. Sadly, these were all closed during the retrenchment of the Boyer years, when the ruling classes actively chose to keep the masses uneducated and disenfranchised. From the second half of the 19th century, schools were primarily run by the Catholic Church, with lessons in French aimed at the elite (for higher education, children were sent to France). This system persisted largely untouched until the mid 20th century, but even when public schools were opened, the insistence on French as the language of instruction made for poor access for children, especially when many teachers were barely fluent themselves.

Today, education is ostensibly free. In practice, 90% of schools are privately run and insist on some sort of fees – if not for attendance, then for uniforms and materials. Even the smallest fees can keep poor children out of school, or else eat up a huge proportion of family income to maintain their education. The 2010 earthquake disrupted the education system even further by destroying 4,000 schools and several of Haiti's small number of universities. In 2011, the Martelly government introduced a controversial tax on foreign money transfers and international phone calls for its National Education Fund to allow fee-free school attendance.

CULTURE

ART Haiti's visual arts are unmatched in the Caribbean. Much of this can be put down to the influence of Vodou, with its rich visual language of vèvè symbols and painted temples. For first-time visitors to Haiti, even the drive from Port-au-Prince airport is an introduction to Haitian art, with street walls masquerading as impromptu art galleries, hung with a hundred colourful canvases to attract the buyer.

Haitian painting in the 19th century was dominated by European traditions of portraiture, typified by the famous 1822 canvas *The Oath of the Ancestors* by Guillaume Guillon Lethière, representing the union of Dessalines and Pétion under the eyes of God. It wasn't until the 1920s that Haitian painting turned its gaze inward towards its older African roots. The Indigéniste movement actively embraced this heritage, influenced by the writer Jean-Price Mars. Indigéniste art put subjects like peasant life front and centre, and moved away from literal representations towards more expressionist interpretations. Idealised landscapes were also popular, with the whole sometimes dubbed Haitian 'Naive' or 'Primitive' art.

In 1944, an American artist DeWitt Peters 'discovered' the Indigéniste painters, and opened the influential Centre d'Art in Port-au-Prince. Peters collected a stable of artists that went on to form the bedrock of 20th-century Haitian painting, prime among them Hector Hyppolite, Philomé Obin and Préfète Duffaut. Through the Centre, Haitian art was launched into the world – the so-called 'Miracle of '44' celebrating the extraordinary creativity of these previously untutored artists. Among its legacies were the astonishing murals of the Sainte Trinité Episcopalian Cathedral in downtown Port-au-Prince, sadly wrecked in the 2010 earthquake but now undergoing painstaking restoration. Bright colours and magic realism were the order of the day.

By the 1950s, Haitian naive art had been codified into a series of simple themes endlessly copied onto canvases for the tourists arriving by cruise ship. However, there was now a gallery system in place and new artists to take up the challenge. Foremost of these was the Foyer des Arts Plastiques movement, spearheaded by Lucien Price. Indigéniste themes were still embraced, but married to a social awareness of life in Haiti. Peasants weren't to be idealised, but painted with all their hardships.

In the 1970s the wheel turned again. The Saint Soleil movement injected fresh momentum into the commodified primitivism of Haitian art through abstraction and spontaneity. The paintings of the leaders – Leroy Exil, Prosper Pierre Louis and Louisiane Saint Fleurant – strongly interweave lwa, dots and patterns to produce dizzying canvases. Their influence has remained strong to this day within Haitian art, even spreading as far as British artists like Chris Ofili.

Sculpture is another important artistic tradition in Haiti, most notably the metal art of Croix des Bouquets. George Liautaud and Serge Jolimeau are the great masters. Of a more surreal bent are the sculptors of Atis Rezistans, a loose grouping based on

HAITIAN PROVERBS

Creole is rich in proverbs, explaining subtly complex philosophies, and frequently lamenting the toughness of peasant life and the divisions between rich and poor. Here is a sample:

Anpre dans tanbou lou	After the dance the drum is heavy
Bay kou bliye, pote mak sonje	The giver of the blow forgets, the bearer of the scar remembers
Bel anteman pa di paradi	A beautiful funeral doesn't guarantee heaven
Bourik swe pou chwal dekore ak dentel	The donkey sweats so the horse can be decorated with lace
Dèyè mon gen mon	Beyond the mountains are more mountains
Kay koule tronpe solèy, men li pa tronpe lapli	A leaky house can fool the sun, but it can't fool the rain
Konstitisyon se papie, bayonet se fe	The constitution is made of paper, but bayonets are made of steel
Kreyon pep la pa gen gonm	The people's pencil has no eraser
Le yo vle touye chen yo di'l fou	When they want to kill a dog they say it's crazy
Men anpil chay pa lou	Many hands make a load lighter
Pal franse pa di lespri pou sa	Speaking French doesn't make you clever
Piti piti wazo fe nich li	Little by little the bird builds its nest
Pitit se riches malere	Children are the wealth of the poor
Si towo bèf te konn valè l, li pa ta kite you kòd senk kòb touye l	If the bull knew its strength, it wouldn't let a five cent rope kill it
Si travay te bon bagay, moun rich la pran-l lontan	If work was good, the rich would have grabbed it a long time ago
Ti chen gen fos devan kay met li	A little dog is brave in front of its master's house

HECTOR HYPPOLITE

Hector Hyppolite is widely regarded as the great master of Haitian painting. Born near Saint-Marc in 1894, he worked as a sugarcane cutter in Cuba and then a cobbler and housepainter. He was also a *houngan*, dedicated to Lasiren, the lwa of the sea. In 1943 he was discovered by the novelist Philippe Thoby-Marcelin painting doors with bright floral patterns and birds, famously using a brush made of chicken feathers. Through him, Hyppolite was introduced to DeWitt Peters, who had just opened the Centre d'Art in Port-au-Prince.

Hyppolite had been painting for himself for two decades, but in Port-au-Prince he underwent a massive outburst of creativity, producing hundreds of paintings in three years. His style was very much his own – two-dimensional but colourful outsider art, richly seasoned with Vodou imagery. He sometimes claimed the lwa not only dictated the subject matter to him, but had also preordained his success as a painter. When French surrealist André Breton visited Haiti in 1945 he was entranced by Hyppolite's art, and made it a centrepiece of an influential 1947 UNESCO art exhibition in Paris, which introduced Haitian painters to the international art world.

Sadly, Hyppolite didn't have long to enjoy the fruits of his success. He died just a year later at the age of 54, but continues to cast a long shadow over the rest of Haitian painting.

Grand Rue in Port-au-Prince, who recycle anything from human bones and car parts to make wild Vodou-inspired sculptures. In 2011 they represented Haiti at the Venice Biennale, the country's first showing at this art event. In return, they host the Ghetto Biennale, inviting international artists to make pieces in their community.

MUSIC The two most popular blends of Haitian music are *kompa* and *rara*. Rara is the music of the streets (see box, *Rara*, page 39), whereas kompa is the music of dancing and romance – a popular description has it that you must dance so close to your partner as to polish your belt buckle.

Kompa is originally derived from *merengue*, a slow dance music that blended traditional Haitian folk music with the newer sounds of jazz that were introduced by the Americans during their occupation. 'Choucoune' is perhaps the classic merengue song, famous across the country, with the 1950s big bands Super Jazz des Jeunes and Issa el Saleh and his Orchestra its greatest exponents. In the same decade, the influence of the faster Dominican merengue style became more influential, and the renowned band leader Nemours Jean Baptiste twisted the beat to create kompa direct, which has gone on to become Haiti's most popular musical taste. Classic old-style kompa bands like Coupé Cloué and Tabou Combo remain popular to this day, but the music has continued to evolve and suck in other musical influences. The big kompa artists of today are just as likely to be influenced by slick American R&B as any other flavour. One of the biggest stars of kompa in recent years has been Michel Martelly, better known by his stage name Sweet Micky. Once best known for his outrageous stage behaviour (bad language and cross-dressing being favourites), he has since cleaned up his act significantly enough to enter politics: he is currently the President of Haiti. Some of the current big names are Carimi, T-Vice, Top Vice and Djakout Mizik.

Sticking closer to its roots is *twoubadou* music. This is an acoustic style close to Cuban Son, believed to have been brought back to Haiti by migrant workers in the

VODOU FLAGS

Vodou has been the well-spring of Haitian arts, but none are presented with such bling as Vodou flags (*drapo*), creations that have broken free of the Vodou temple to become works of art in and of themselves.

Flags are paraded during Vodou ceremonies, and each *ounfò* will have at least two. The first is dedicated to the warrior Ogue Feray, in a nod to the military origins of the flags and the lwa who inspired many soldiers during the Haitian Revolution. The other is dedicated to the patron lwa of that particular temple. The drapo is usually decorated with the sacred vèvè symbols of the lwa, often complemented with images of their saintly Catholic counterparts.

The flags were once painted or had simple embroidery, but these days they shine and dazzle with thousands of beads and sequins. This is in part a legacy of the 1980s, when garment assembly became big business in Haiti, unwittingly triggering the creativity of artists, including many women who had sewed in the factories. Drapo are now offered for sale by most art galleries in Port-au-Prince as well as internationally, being big hits at events like the influential Santa Fe International Folk Art Market.

Some of the most celebrated traditional flag artists are Yves Telemaque, Georges Valris, and the late Sylva Joseph. Female artists have often moved towards presenting the flags as rich Vodou-inspired tableaux instead of straight religious symbolism – look out in particular for Myrlande Constant and Mireille Délismé. In galleries, the mermaid lwa Lasiren, the hearts of Ezili and the lewd skeletal imagery of the Gede are all popular subjects. A 1m^2 flag can take a month to sew, and prices reflect the amount of detailed work required. If your budget doesn't run to some of the bigger pieces, many enterprising flag makers have also moved into similarly beaded and sequined purses and clutch bags, with more pocket-friendly prices.

early 20th century. In twoubadou, banjos and accordions are as essential, as are gently strummed guitars and lilting vocals.

Mizik rasin (roots music) arrived on the scene with the downfall of the Duvalier regime, a backing track for the big challenges that were facing Haiti. It blends the complex rhythms of Vodou drumming and horns with modern elements from rock, pop and reggae. The two biggest *mizik rasin* bands are still two of its earliest exponents – RAM and Boukman Eksperyans. With lyrics mixing up political commentary and Vodou ceremonial prayers, *mizik rasin* can fulfil the need to protest as well as to party. Songs like 'Ke'm Pa Sote' ('I'm Not Afraid') by Boukman Eksperyans was the Carnival hit of 1990, lampooning the then military dictatorship, while two years later RAM's 'Fèy' ('Leaf') became a popular protest anthem following the first coup against Aristide.

Since the 1990s, there has been a burgeoning local hiphop movement, called *Rap Kreyol*, blending hiphop beats with kompa and rasin rhythms. It was spearheaded by artists like the late Master Dji (credited as the first musician to rap in Creole) and German-Haitian rapper Torch. Perhaps the most celebrated exponents of Rap Kreyol were Barikad Crew, who tragically lost half their group in a car crash in 2008, but are still performing. Ex-Fugees star Wyclef Jean remains a proudly Haitian musician.

Much as the British media love to get in a frenzy about who will grab the Number One spot in the Christmas charts, in Haiti the big annual music tradition is the

Carnival song. Many bands time their biggest releases in the run-up to Carnival, in the hope that their song will dominate the airwaves to become the anthem of the year. Played absolutely everywhere, J Perry's infectious 2012 Carnival smash 'Dekole' ('Take Off') seemed to accompany the writing of this entire guidebook.

Haiti also has a small but strong tradition of classical music, with composers like Ludovic Lamothe ('the Black Chopin'), Occide Jeanty and Férère Laguerre gently blending a Caribbean lilt into the Western classical tradition. The music school of the Sainte Trinité Cathedral in Port-au-Prince (e *saintetrinitemusique@yahoo.com*) holds regular concerts.

LITERATURE French has traditionally been the language of literature in Haiti. The Haitian writers of the 19th century, like essayist Anténor Firmin, often looked outward in their writing, determined to defend Haiti's place as an equal among nations in an often unfriendly world, as well as arguing vociferously for a stake in the country's political development.

The big revolution in Haitian literature took place in the first half of the 20th century, in part as a response to the upheavals of the US occupation. The intellectual life of the light-skinned Haitian elites had hitherto had a strong Francophile bent. The writer and scholar Jean-Price Mars changed all that with his 1928 *Ainsi parla l'Oncle* (*So Spoke the Uncle*), which called on Haitians to reject Europeanised culture and proudly embrace Haiti's history – its African roots, the slave revolution and the rural culture of the peasants. Mars's work was hugely influential, and a key work in the new Indigéniste movement. This movement saw its crowning glory in 1944 with the publication of the novel *Masters of the Dew* by the poet Jacques Roumain, widely considered the greatest work of Haitian literature. The novel tells of a prodigal son returning to his drought-stricken home village from Cuba, and the struggles to find water – an allegory for the founding of a new collective political culture.

RARA

Haiti's most raucous and public music is *rara*. True folk music of the masses, a rara (the term can refer to the music, the band or the entire event) can take place at any time of year, but is most typically associated with the run-up to Carnival and the period between Lent and Easter.

At its core, a rara is a marching band accompanied by a host of revellers, who parade the streets. The instruments are basic – long single-note bamboo trumpets called *vaksins*, smaller metal horns (*kònets*), and a variety of bells, maracas and drums. Each rara has its own society, with their own hierarchies of kings, queens and officers. There's a close association with Vodou, and raras start their parades at their local *ounfò* before sounding out into the streets. The parades then take over the streets, with musicians demanding money from observers caught up in the swell, to a soundtrack described by one observer as 'football fans attempting psychedelic marching tunes on vuvuzelas'.

Raras are also explicitly political, not only in allowing a rare public outing for the rural and urban poor to take over the public sphere, but also in their songs, which frequently poke fun at politics or rally people behind a cause – raras are a standard feature of political demonstrations. Raras are also sometimes used by politicians to drum up supporters, but the best are street music pure and simple, a joyful noisy anarchy that helps bind communities together.

The Indigéniste movement blended with a form of black nationalism to form *Noirisme*, which influenced literature, painting and eventually politics. François Duvalier was elected on a *noiriste* platform, but under his brutal rule literary life was stifled. Novelists like Marie Vieux-Chauvet, whose trilogy *Love, Anger* and *Madness* told of life under a paranoid yet unnamed regime, were forced into exile. Other exiled writers like René Depestre and Pierre Clitandre were even more strident in their criticisms of Duvalier. One literary movement, the surrealism-infused *Spiralisme*, managed to survive throughout the Duvalier period. It did this by moving away from realism and trying to find order in chaos. The poet, playwright and painter Frankétienne (born Franck Etienne) was the leader of the movement. Born in 1936, he was short-listed for the Nobel Prize for Literature in 2009 and is possibly Haiti's greatest living writer. His works include *Dezafi*, the first Haitian novel written in Creole, and the play *Pelin Tet*, about Haitian immigrants in New York. Another work to look for is the strangely magical *Massacre River* by René Philoctète. The terror of François Duvalier's rule also inspired the most famous book about Haiti to be written by a non-Haitian, Graham Greene's darkly satirical 1966 novel *The Comedians*, set in a loosely veiled version of the Hotel Oloffson in Port-au-Prince.

Duvalier's unwitting creation of the Haitian diaspora has helped create a new generation of authors writing primarily in English. Of these, the most widely read and celebrated is Edwidge Danticat. Her clear-eyed realism is perhaps best seen in her novels *Breath, Eyes, Memory* and *The Farming of Bones* about the 1937 massacres of Haitians in the Dominican Republic, her family memoir *Brother, I'm Dying,* and her post-earthquake essay collection *Create Dangerously*. Much current Haitian literature is still only available in French, but the important contemporary writers Dany Laferrière (*How to Make Love to a Negro*) and Lyonel Trouillot (*Street of Lost Footsteps* and *Children of Heroes*) are increasingly also available in English translation.

Amid all this, the great bulk of the Haitian population has largely been illiterate, giving rise to a rich oral culture of storytelling. Stories traditionally start with the question *Krik?*, whereby the teller asks if the audience is ready to hear a tale, to which they cry *Krak!* in return, allowing the story to begin. Like many Haitian proverbs, stories are frequently satirical in nature, poking fun at those in power, or using magical imagery to draw moral conclusions. The most famous Haitian storyteller of the 20th century was Maurice Sixto, a great advocate of Creole whose recordings are still listened to today. Many of his creations have subsequently sprung their binds to enter the wider culture, like Ti Sentaniz the *restavek* (child slave) and Gwo Moso, the feckless. The American storyteller and folklorist Diane Wolkstein collected many traditional stories while living in Haiti in the 1970s, subsequently presented with notes in her collection *The Magic Orange Tree and Other Haitian Folktales.*

CINEMA Haiti had its first public cinema screening in 1899, and silent newsreels were regularly made during the American occupation. Today there is a thriving local film scene (sometimes dubbed 'Bellywood'), although films tend to be shot on digital and released locally on DVD. Haiti doesn't currently have any active cinemas; the famous Rex Theatre on Champs de Mars in Port-au-Prince is now a sadly empty shell.

Internationally, Haiti's best-known director is Raoul Peck, whose work includes *Lumumba* (2000) about the 1960s Congolese leader Patrice Lumumba, and the recent *Moloch Tropical* (2009). This tells of the final paranoid days of a fictional Haitian

PAPA GOD AND GENERAL DEATH

One evening, two men were walking on a hillside, Papa God and General Death. As they walked along, General Death pointed to a large yellow stone house overlooking the valley and said, 'Last week I took one from there.' Then he pointed to a smaller house down the path: 'Tomorrow I shall take one from there.'

'You are always taking from people,' said Papa God, 'and I am always giving to them. That is why people prefer me.'

'Oh, I wouldn't be so sure of that,' said General Death.

'Well, let's see,' said Papa God. 'Let's ask the man you will be visiting tomorrow for some water and see whether he gives more water to you or to me.'

So Papa God walked up the path to the small house and General Death stood waiting by the road.

'Good evening,' Papa God called from outside the gate. 'Have you some water for a thirsty man?'

'I haven't a drop,' the man answered.

'I beg of you,' said Papa God. 'I am very thirsty. And I am sure Papa God would be pleased if you would give me some water.'

'My good fellow, don't talk to me of Papa God. Do you know how far I have to go out for water? Ten miles! Five miles to the spring and five miles back! And Papa God makes places where there is so much water people are swimming in it. No, don't talk to me of Papa God.'

'My good man,' Papa God said patiently, 'if you knew with whom you are speaking, I am certain you would give me some water.'

'Who are you?' asked the man.

'I am Papa God.'

'Papa God,' said the man, 'I still do not have any water. But I will tell you this: if General Death should pass this way, then I would have water.'

'How is that?' asked Papa God.

'Because death has no favourites. Rich, poor, young, old – they are all the same to him. Last week, he took the owner of the large house on the hill, the week before he took my neighbour's wife, the week before a young baby, and the week before that an old man. Death takes from all the houses. But you, you give all the water to some people and leave me here with ten miles to go on my donkey for just one drop.'

Papa God saw Death motioning to him. It was Death's turn. Shaking his head sadly, Papa God walked away.

Several minutes later, General Death walked up the path.

'Good evening,' he said. 'Can you give me some water?'

'What is your name?' asked the man.

'I am General Death.'

The man excused himself and went into his house. He returned with a calabash full of cool water.

'Drink!' he said to General Death. 'Drink as much as you wish.'

And General Death drank. He drank long and he drank fully. And he must have been pleased, for the next day he did not stop at the small house but continued on his route down the hill.

president holed up in his palace as the country rebels against him. Although it is a loose reworking of the end of Henri Christophe's reign (it's partly set in the Citadelle), the film is easily read as a satire on Jean-Bertrand Aristide.

A highly regarded documentary film-maker is Arnold Antonin, who made his name in 1973 with *Duvalier Accused*, a film for which he had to go into exile, immediately following up with *Haiti – The Road To Freedom*. He now makes short documentaries on social issues.

Modern Haitian film-makers often divide their productions between Haiti and the diaspora centres of Miami, New York and Montréal. Two of the most popular Haitian films of recent years have been Wilkenson Bruna's *Le Vent du Désir* (*Wind of Desire*) and *I Love You Anne* by Richard Senecal, a romance starring popular comedian Tonton Bicha. Other notable films include Jean-Gardy Bien-Aimé's *Le Cap a la Une* (*Cap Has the One*), from 1997, with actor Smoye Noisy, *La Rebelle* by actor-director Reginald Lubin and *La Peur d'Aimer* (*Fear of Love*), another Tonton Bicha vehicle. Every year, gongs are handed out to the best films of the year at the Motion Picture Association of Haiti awards ceremony in Boston.

Haiti has also served as a canvas for many foreign films, although these are rarely actually filmed in the country. A rare exception is Jonathan Demme's unmissable 2003 documentary *The Agronomist* about the life and death of campaigning Haitian radio journalist (and sometime film-maker himself) Jean Dominique, assassinated in 2000. Rather more lurid is the quasi-documentary *Ghosts of Cité Soleil* (2006) by Asgar Leth, about the street gangs of Cité Soleil in the run-up to Aristide's second ouster.

In fictional form, Haiti's cinematic representations are a decidedly mixed bag. Haiti as a dangerous other has been a frequent theme, kicking off the Bela Lugosi flick *White Zombie*, made in the final years of the US occupation, and 1943's *I Walked With A Zombie*. Both focus on innocent white heroines facing possession at the hands of evil witch-doctors bearing voodoo dolls, and set the tone for subsequent Hollywood treatments, from 1987's shock-horror *The Serpent and the Rainbow* (ironically adapted from a more serious-minded ethno-botanical investigation into Vodou and zombification) to the Blaxploitation-inspired James Bond outing *Live and Let Die*, where the fictional island of San Monique stands in for Haiti, with a Papa Doc-esque dictator Mr Big and a scary 'voodoo' henchman called Baron Samedi (as well as Roger Moore's ever-arching eyebrows). Bond's grittier incarnation, Daniel Craig has also made a brief visit to Haiti in *Quantum of Solace* in 2008, even adding a bit of spicy commentary about foreign involvement in overthrowing Aristide.

Haiti is the focus of the 2005 Charlotte Rampling film *Heading South*, about sex tourism during the Jean-Claude Duvalier era, adapted from a short story by novelist Dany Laferrière. Also well-worth checking out is the lush 2011 French two-part film *Toussaint L'Ouverture* about the Haitian Revolution, with Haitian-American Hollywood star Jimmy Jean-Louis as the eponymous hero. For a more sympathetic (and fascinating) look at traditional Vodou, watch anthropologist Maya Deren's posthumous *Divine Horsemen: The Living Gods of Haiti*, made from film shot by her in the 1940s and 50s.

ARCHITECTURE Haiti's most important contribution to world architecture is the gingerbread house. Found mostly in Port-au-Prince, but with important examples in Jacmel and Cap-Haïtien, they are paragons of elegant tropical living, designed for the merchant and political classes of the late 19th and early 20th centuries. Gingerbreads are primarily wooden houses, with wide verandas and elegant high balconies, steeply pitched roofs and plenty of detailed latticework. The biggest concentration can be found in the downtown districts of Pacot and Bois Verna in the capital. Many gingerbreads suffer from neglect – to the point of being put *en masse* on the World Monument Fund watch-list of endangered buildings. However, there has been renewed interest in them of late when it was realised the flexibility of these wood-framed buildings allowed them to mostly sail through the 2010 earthquake, when more modern buildings (as well as contemporary buildings made of reinforced concrete, such as the National Palace and Notre Dame Cathedral) quickly collapsed.

Much vernacular urban architecture also fared badly in the earthquake. Typical houses are made of concrete cinderblocks with steel rebar frames, but there is scant attention to building codes. Cinderblocks are often made privately rather than industrially, with poorly graded river sand, making them prone to collapse. In rural areas, houses are often made of thick lath and plaster, with palm thatch or tin roofs, with the move to concrete buildings seen as a step up the housing ladder. Split palm logs may also be used – look out for the tiny houses on stilts, used as grain stores. Whatever the material, all houses have an open veranda at the front, a feature of the communal *lakou* system of living in the country.

Little of Haiti's French colonial architecture remains, although it's still possible to find the remains of old *habitations* (plantations) and the chimneys of sugar mills, particularly in the north of the country. Best preserved are the remains around Fort Drouet, north of Port-au-Prince, which still has intact slave quarters.

CEMETERIES

One of the most elaborate forms of architecture you'll see in Haiti is its tombs. Bodies are buried in graves above ground rather than in it, with colourful crypts as grand and baroque as a family's budget will allow.

In the country, people are buried on family land wherever possible; formal cemeteries are the domain of towns and cities. Where a crypt serves as a repository for the family bones, it is usually kept firmly locked against the possible depredations of tomb robbers. Given the importance in Vodou of the ties between the living, their ancestors and the lwa, it's often held that bones can possess magical properties. After the flight of dictator Jean-Claude Duvalier in 1986, one of the first actions of the celebrating crowds was to ransack his family crypt in Port-au-Prince, although the remains of Papa Doc had reportedly been spirited away to prevent their destruction. Cemeteries often have a grave dedicated to Baron Samedi, marked by a ceremonial cross (in one of his aspects, Baron is depicted as Christ on the cross).

Funerals are very much public affairs, with funeral processions possibly even including a New Orleans-style marching band to commemorate the deceased. Vodou followers are buried with a mix of Vodou and Catholic ritual. On dying, the body is immediately treated with a rite called *dessounen* to disengage the person's protective spirit, and make them ready for burial. The body is washed, and conversations may be held with the departed to give them messages to carry to the next world. A wake for the dead is held nine nights after their death, but for some time after, the family may continue to offer food for the dead (*manje lèmò*) while the spirit continues its journey 'across the water' back to the invisible world and ancestral Africa.

Tombs are often repainted every year in the run-up to Fet Gede, the Vodou festival of the dead at the start of November.

French forts also bear witness to the colonial era, with the most accessible being Fort Picolet near Cap-Haïtien, the ring of bastions around Fort Liberté and, in the south, the two forts outside Saint-Louis du Sud. Fort building was also a major feature of the early years of independence, a flurry of construction that produced the Citadelle, the Caribbean's most imposing fortress, as well as the quasi-Versailles palace of Sans Souci.

SPORT Haiti is **football** (soccer) mad. You'll regularly see painted Brazilian and Argentine flags painted on walls, and one gets the feeling that if the Barcelona and Argentina star Lionel Messi were to run for Haitian president, he'd be elected with a landslide. Bars regularly show matches from the Spanish Liga and English Premier League.

Domestically, Haitians follow the Division 1 Ligue Haïtienne. Key clubs are Racing Club Haïtien (Port-au-Prince) and Baltimore Sportif Club (Saint-Marc), the most recent league champions. The headquarters of the Fédération Haïtienne de Football, who have run the league since its inauguration in 1937, were destroyed in the 2010 earthquake, and the national stadium, Stade Sylvio Cator, in Port-au-Prince operated as a camp for displaced people for nearly 18 months after the earthquake.

HAITI'S WORLD CUP HERO

The national hero of Haitian football is the striker Emmaneul 'Manno' Sanon, who led Haiti in their only World Cup appearance, at the 1974 World Cup in West Germany. Haiti's amateur team had narrowly missed out on qualifying for the 1970 tournament, but Jean-Claude Duvalier bankrolled the squad as well as refurbishing the Sylvio Cator Stadium in Port-au-Prince. Home crowds for the qualifying matches reportedly even contained government-paid Vodou *houngans*, to tempt the spirits to aid the players.

Haiti's opening match in West Germany was against Italy, a tournament favourite. In a dozen matches, no side had put a goal past the Italian keeper Dino Zoff, then rated as the best in the world. Haiti held the Italians to a goalless draw in the first half, but at the start of the second half, Manno Sanon astounded the Italians – and the footballing world – by beating the Italian defence and slotting the ball past Zoff. Watching the goal on YouTube, the Haitian delight and Italian shock is clear to see. The celebrations were sadly short-lived, and the Haitians eventually lost the match 2-1. The defeat was compounded the following day when centre half Ernst Jean-Joseph became the first player to be ejected from a World Cup following a positive drugs test. Haiti went on to lose their two remaining matches against Poland and then Argentina (with Sanon scoring the consolation goal in that match too).

Sanon went on to play professionally in Holland and the USA, and scored 47 goals in 106 appearances for Haiti before a knee injury ended his career. He died in 2008 of pancreatic cancer. At his funeral in Port-au-Prince, his 1974 teammates acted as pallbearers to his coffin, and the capital ground to a halt as people paid their respects.

Speaking years after the World Cup, Sanon called that goal his greatest moment in football. 'Zoff's face – he was absolutely furious with his defence, and I was joyful too because I knew that back home, everyone would be going wild.' For that reason alone, Sanon's goal lives on in the collective memory.

Haiti's national side, dubbed the Grenadiers, have a middling international record, but have only qualified once for the FIFA World Cup, back in 1974. Many Haitian footballers have found international success playing under foreign colours, including Joe Gaetjens, who played for the USA at the 1950 World Cup and scored the winning goal against England that caused one of the most famous upsets in football history. Gaetjens's family later became outspoken opponents of 'Papa Doc' Duvalier, and Gaetjens himself was abducted by the Tontons Macoutes in 1964, and was never heard of since.

Cockfighting is popular as both a pastime and spectator sport, and every town has its *gagè*, or cockfighting ring. The birds do not fight to the death or wear spurs as in some other countries, but animal lovers may still prefer to stay away. There's usually a fee of a few gourdes to attend, with the real money changing hands as the (entirely male) crowd bet on the outcome – often over in a quick flurry of feathers. Owners take great care over their fighting cocks (*kok bataye*), often resting them a month between bouts. The unluckiest birds end up in the cooking pot.

Much less common is traditional **Haitian bullfighting**. This doesn't involve matadors or a choreographed fight between man and animal, but is more a test of strength: two bulls in a field, wrestling with their horns until one concedes the field. It's another opportunity to gamble, but there's no space between you and the animals – spectators get as close as they dare. You can see it at weekends in Port Salut and sometimes Léogâne.

One pastime that you'll see a lot of is groups of men on the street playing **dominoes**. It can be fiercely competitive, but unlike the gambling that takes place around cockfighting or the lottery, domino players play for forfeits. Those on a losing streak can be picked out easily by the clothes pegs clipped to their faces and arms. It's a simple but painful way of marking out the winners and losers – if you're looking for an incentive to improve your dominoes game, this is it.

2

Practical Information

WHEN TO VISIT

Tropical Haiti is a year-round destination, with a strong Caribbean sun and temperatures fluctuating from warm to hot. April to November is the hottest time of year, when average temperatures fluctuate just above 30°C (86°F). December to March are the coolest months, with the temperatures averaging around 22°C (72°F). Whatever time of year, you'll rarely be out of short sleeves, although nights can be cool in the mountains. There are roughly two rainy 'seasons' – May–July for the centre and south of the country, while from November to January, northern Haiti gets most of its rain. August to November is the time of tropical storms and hurricanes across the Caribbean. Travel during wet periods can be potentially tricky, as rough roads can be affected and thus increase travel time.

HIGHLIGHTS

Haiti packs a lot in for such a small-sized country. Even if you're based mostly in Port-au-Prince, it's still possible to reach most places over a weekend, especially if you're prepared to travel earlier or grab a short flight.

The **Citadelle**, the mountain fortress that all but symbolises the great victory of the Haitian Revolution, is the country's stand-out tourist sight. It's an hour from Cap-Haïtien, set in fabulous scenery. If at all possible, it's the one thing you mustn't miss from a trip to Haiti.

Quicker to reach from Port-au-Prince (a morning's drive away) is the old southern coffee port of **Jacmel**, equally rich in historic architecture and bright art and handicrafts. Its annual Carnival is the most visually spectacular day out in the national calendar. Nearby are the waterfalls and swimming holes of **Bassin Bleu**. There are good beaches near Jacmel too, but sand-and-sun lovers usually make first for the long picture-postcard beach at **Port Salut**. Hikers should enjoy **Parc National la Visite**, with its pine-forested walk from Furcy to Seguin. It's pretty easy to get off the beaten track – Fôret des Pins has simple mountain cabins amid the trees and trails, but there's great potential for hiking in the **Central Plateau** as well. All these areas are also good for birdwatching. Haiti's geology also means that it's blessed with many caves – the **Grotte Marie Jeanne** near Port-à-Piment is the most accessible, while more remote examples are often covered with petroglyphs from the island's original Taíno inhabitants. There are **waterfalls** aplenty too – not just Bassin Bleu, but the sacred falls at Saut d'Eau, at Bassin Zim near Hinche and the tough to reach but astounding Cascade Pichon in the southeast.

While the Citadelle is the most obvious historical site, Haiti's history means that it is simply littered with **old forts**, many in quite spectacular locations. At Saint-Louis du Sud the overgrown Fort Anglais guards a lonely tropical island, while the green

Artibonite Valley is dotted with them. Fort Drouet, only recently rediscovered, is just a couple of hours away from Port-au-Prince. At Môle Saint-Nicholas in the far northeast, half-a-dozen forts guard a beautiful coast, little visited by foreigners.

Art lovers may find themselves with groaning luggage at the end of their trip. Some of the picks include Jacmel's papier-mâché art, the intricate Vodou-inspired metal of Croix des Bouquets, as well as the painted canvases that hang across Port-au-Prince, from the open-air galleries to the high-end boutiques of Pétionville.

Haiti is a relatively small country, and it's possible to reach almost any corner from Port-au-Prince by road in a day – distances that shrink even further when you consider that internal flights to even the farthest cities take no longer than 40 minutes. With that in mind, Jacmel, Port Salut and even Cap-Haïtien become easy weekend destinations. If you have more time, a slow meandering along the south coast could easily fill a week – the same can be done for the north, building an even longer trip to loop through the centre. Your speed of travel depends on your mode of transport – there's plentiful public transport on the main roads, but your own vehicle lets you stop and enjoy the road wherever it takes you.

SUGGESTED ITINERARIES

Haiti is a small country, and, despite a few bad roads, most corners can be visited relatively easily – even more so if you include internal flights in the equation.

Almost all visitors arrive in Port-au-Prince, and its location makes a good base for further exploration. In two or three days you can cover both the sights in the capital as well as throwing in a couple of trips to nearby locations like Furcy in the mountains above the city or the artisan village at Croix des Bouquets.

The most popular overnight trip is to Jacmel on the south coast, but there's enough here to divert you for several nights if you have time. The same goes for Cap-Haïtien – a day's drive from Port-au-Prince, but a little over 30 minutes if you fly, making a short trip to the Citadelle and Sans Souci palace an easy option.

Cap-Haïtien is a good central point to further explore the north, from the beaches around Labadie to the coastal forts around Fort Liberté. If you have your own vehicle, driving either there or back through the Central Plateau is a great trip.

The area around Les Cayes and Port Salut, half a day's drive from Port-au-Prince, is a good base for trips in the south. The beaches around here are some of the most beautiful in the country, while there are caves and waterfalls to be explored in nearby Port-à-Piment and Camp Perrin. Head to Jérémie for the greenest and wildest part of the country.

It is easy enough to cover the Haitian essentials in a week, but with more time you can get a little more off the beaten track. A perfect way to make a circuit between Port-au-Prince and Jacmel is to hike over the mountains through Parc National La Visite via Seguin. If you have your own vehicle, there's great pleasure to be had in covering some of the backroads with a drive through the Artibonite Valley, the long but fascinating trip to Môle Saint-Nicholas on the north-eastern tip of the island, or the bumpy roads of the Grand Anse in the southwest.

TOUR OPERATORS

HAITI

Na Sonje ☎3702 9234; e nasonje@gmail.com; http://nasonje.blogspot.com. Offers immersive visits & tours to its 'memory village' outside Port-au-Prince, living with locals & learning about Haitian culture & history.

Pegasus Diving ☎3555 9633/3624 9486; e haitidivingpegasus@yahoo.com. Trustworthy scuba diving & boat tours including PADI certification. Based on the Côte des Arcadins north of Port-au-Prince.

Tour Haiti ☎ 2813 2223/3711 1650; e info@tourhaiti.net; www.tourhaiti.net. Package & tailor-made tours across Haiti as well as group logistics. Strong on adventure/activity trips.

Voyages Lumière ☎ 3607 1321/3557 0753; e voyageslumierehaiti@gmail.com, lojistik.haiti@gmail.com; www.voyageslumiere.com. Tailor-made individual & group tours, including vehicle hire, flights, guiding & logistics for visiting volunteer groups. Excellent personal service.

USA

Global Exchange Reality Tours ☎ +1 415 255 7296; e web@globalexchange.org; www.globalexchange.org. Political & educational solidarity tours of Haiti with a positive slant.

Mountain Bike Ayiti www.mtbayiti.org. Sustainable adventure travel start-up, planning a network of trails & mountain bike depots in Haiti. Organisers of the Haiti Ascent Race in Feb, an annual mountain bike challenge running from Port-au-Prince across Parc National La Visite, descending to Jacmel in time for Carnival.

Destination North Haiti ☎ +1 800 545 3381; e info@destinationnorthhaiti.com; www.destinationnorthhaiti.com. Historical, cultural & eco tours across northern Haiti.

Spring Break Haiti e springbreakinhaiti@yahoo.com; www.springbreakinhaiti.com 'Alternative' college spring break company, aimed at introducing students to Haitian culture, including volunteering opportunities.

Village Experience ☎ +1 917 862 9236; e info@experiencethevillage.com; www.experiencethevillage.com. Socially conscious cultural exchange tours of Haiti, visiting grassroots organisations, development projects & local artists.

TOURIST INFORMATION

Haiti doesn't maintain any tourist offices outside the country. In Haiti there are no tourist bureaux as such, but you can pick up the occasionally useful pamphlet at the **Ministry of Tourism** (*8 Rue Légitime, Champs de Mars, Port-au-Prince;* ☎ *2223 2143/2223 5631*). There are sub-offices in Jacmel, Cap-Haïtien and Les Cayes (see relevant listings for details), which are often more enthusiastic than offering concrete help. Given the prominence that the Martelly administration has given to promoting tourism as an economic developer in Haiti, it's hoped that this situation will improve.

As if to mark the new pro-tourism outlook, in mid 2011 the national **Association Touristique d'Haïti** (*www.haiticherie.ht*) launched a new glossy magazine ***Magic Haiti*** (*www.magichaiti.com*) aimed squarely at promoting local tourism among foreign nationals residing in Haiti. You'll frequently find copies being handed out on arrival at the airport, otherwise the website has PDFs of each issue to download. Each issue has a useful listings section, and news on places to visit, stay and eat.

RED TAPE

VISAS All visitors to Haiti require a passport, the expiry date of which must be valid for six months beyond the length of your stay. If you are arriving by air, a return flight ticket is also required, but entry itself is visa-free, except for nationals of the Dominican Republic, Colombia and Panama. A stay of up to three months is permitted on arrival. When being stamped in, the green immigration landing card you must complete has a tear-off slip at the bottom marked 'Départ/Departure' which you'll be given back – keep this safe, as you need to hand it in when leaving Haiti.

If you are intending to stay in Haiti longer than three months, there are two options. The first is to leave the country and re-enter, thus giving you a fresh three-

HAITI'S GOLDEN AGE OF TOURISM

The current government has heavily promoted tourism as a pillar of economic development. At a major investment conference in Port-au-Prince in November 2011, international hotel chains seemed to be queuing up to announce plans to build in the country. Haiti has been here before however, and the atmosphere harks back to the golden age, or *bel epek*, of Haitian tourism, in the decade from the end of World War II.

1949 was the year of Port-au-Prince's bicentenary, marked by President Estimé's International Exposition, which gave a facelift to the city and helped introduce Haitian art to the wider world. Tourism numbers jumped by a quarter in that year alone and continued to grow. A year later, Estimé was dumped out of power by the army and replaced by the anti-communist Colonel Paul Magloire. Dutifully elected president several months later with 99% of the popular vote, Magloire surfed a boom based on high coffee prices and international loans. To a soundtrack of newly fashionable Haitian *merengue* albums, tourists flooded in. Downtown Port-au-Prince was the place to be, with shopping on Grand Rue (the orientalist Marché de Fer was claimed to be a bigger draw than even the Citadelle), and beachfront clubs and casinos stretching all the way to Carrefour. Port-au-Prince was as fashionable as pre-revolutionary Havana, with the likes of Noel Coward and Truman Capote taking rooms at the Hotel Oloffson.

The high watermark came in 1954 with *le Tricinquantenaire* – Haiti's 150th anniversary – commemorated with a re-enactment of the Battle of Vertières and the unveiling of Gonaïves's modernist cathedral. But Magloire's days were numbered. The same year, Haiti was battered by Hurricane Hazel, the economy was in hock to international debtors and popular discontent towards the regime was being twisted into violence and-coming François Duvalier. By the time American vice-president Richard by supporters of the up-Nixon visited in 1956, the shine had already rubbed off. There's still a photo of his visit hanging in the Ibo Lele Hotel in Pétionville – he looks somewhat like a comic on the verge of losing his audience, but for Haiti the laughs really were ebbing away, as the long night of Duvalierism was about to descend.

month entry stamp. This is most easily and economically done by making a side trip to the Dominican Republic – there are direct road transport links from Port-au-Prince to Santo Domingo through the border at Malpasse/Jimaní, and from Cap-Haïtien to Santiago through the border at Ouanaminthe/Dajabón. With your own vehicle this can be a day trip or less, and is relatively hassle-free. For more information, see *Getting there and away*, *By land*, page 54.

If you want to put your long-term stay in Haiti on a sounder footing – if you're working, for example – a *permis de séjour* gives you the right to residency in Haiti. The process is straightforward, although slightly bureaucratic. Applications are made at the Ministry of Interior (Service du Contentieux), 29 Rue Duncombe, Bois Verna, in downtown Port-au-Prince. The following paperwork is required: passport photocopy, a doctor's certificate, recent bank statement, a letter of employment stating the reason for your stay, your immigration landing card, a police record (*casier judiciaire*) from your country of residence, and a copy of your birth certificate. You'll also need two ID photos and 150HTG for the application itself. The *permis de séjour* itself is 5,000HTG (around US$125). Assuming your paperwork is in order, it takes up to a month to issue, and is valid in the first instance for a year (renewable).

If you've found yourself overstaying, you need to get a *visa de sortie* to leave the country. Most travel agents can arrange this for 500–1,000HTG, which takes around a week to process, with your passport being sent to the Ministry of Interior. The resulting stamp in your passport legalises your position, but you must then leave the country within a month of issue.

CUSTOMS Along with their personal effects, visitors to Haiti are allowed to bring in up to 200 cigarettes, a litre of spirits and up to 200,000HTG in local or foreign currency (around US$5,000). Given the large number of people entering Haiti for humanitarian or mission purposes, it's not uncommon for individuals to bring small amounts of supplies packed in their checked luggage.While customs at Port-au-Prince airport is generally laid-back for passengers with a usual amount of luggage, those seeking to bring in large quantities of supplies should seek to formalise their arrangements – see box, *Importing aid to Haiti*, below.

IMPORTING AID TO HAITI

In the immediate aftermath of the 2010 earthquake, stories about the byzantine nature of Haitian Customs and aid sitting for months awaiting customs clearance seemed legion. However, if you're bringing large amounts of supplies (aid or otherwise) into Haiti, there are bureaucratic hoops you'll need to jump through to import to Haiti to clear your goods. While not exhaustive, the following guidelines should help you get started, but be aware that regulations can change at the drop of a hat.

Non-governmental organisations (NGOs) registered with the Haitian government qualify for duty/tax exemption on imported goods. Many NGOs and missions effectively act as private organisations under the radar of the authorities, so your first port of call might be ensuring your papers are cleared with the Ministère de la Planification et de la Coopération Externe (MPCE; *www.mpce.gouv.ht*). Registered organisations must then get a *Quitus Fiscale* from the Direction Générale de Impôts (DGI; *www.mefhaiti.gouv.ht/dgi.htm*) and then a *Demande de Franchise* from the Ministry of Finance (*www.mefhaiti.gouv.ht*). For the goods themselves, you'll then need to provide various papers, including a declaration form, packing list, bill of lading and freight certificate.

If your organisation is not registered with the government, you should go first through the Direction de la Protection Civile (DPC; *www.protectioncivilehaiti.net/DPC.htm*), but you'll still need the *Quitus Fiscale* and *Demande de Franchise*.

By far the simplest method to navigate the system is to use a customs broker – you can find them listed on the online business directory of Peace Dividend Marketplace Haiti (*http://haiti.buildingmarkets.org*). Note that if your goods are held up at customs, you will be charged a storage fee before they're released, so it's essential to plan as far in advance as possible. Getting copies of your papers to a customs broker before the goods arrive means that the clearance process can be started early, although you'll still need the original documents to finally collect your goods.

EMBASSIES AND CONSULATES

E Argentina Av Figueroa Alcorta 3297, Buenos Aires; +54 11 4807 0211; e embahaiti@interar.com.ar
E Bahamas Sears Hse, Shurley St, Nassau; +242 326 0325; e lhjosepH43@earthlink.net
E Belgium 139 Chaussée de Charleroi, Brussels; +32 2 649 7381; e amb.haiti@brutele.be
E Brazil SHIS QL 10, Conjunto 6 Casa 16, Lago Sul, Brasilia; +55 61 3248 6860; e embhaiti@zaz.com.br
E Canada (Embassy) 85 Albert St, Suite 1110, Ottawa; +1 613 238 162; e bohio@sympatico.ca; (Consulate) 1100 Bd René Lévesque Ouest, Montréal; +1 514 499 1919; e consulgeneral@haiti-montreal.org; www.haiti-montreal.org
E Chile Zurich 255, Las Condes, Santiago; +56 2 231 0967; e embhai@terra.cl
E Cuba 5ta Av 6804 e, Miramar, Havana; +53 7 204 5421; www.embhaiti.cu
E Dominican Republic 33 Av Juan Sanchez Ramirez, Santo Domingo; +1 809 686 5778; e amb.haiti@codetel.net.do
E France 10 Rue Théodule Ribot, Paris; +33 1 47 63 47 78; e haiti01@francophonie.org
E Germany Meinekestrasse 5, Berlin; +49 30 8855 4134; e haitbot@aol.com
E Italy 7-7A Via di Villa Patrizi, Rome; +39 6 4425 4106; e amb.haiti@tiscali.it
E Jamaica 2 Munroe Rd, Kingston; +876 927 7595
E Japan 38 Kowa Bildg, 4-12-24, Nishi-Azabu, Minato-Ku, Tokyo; +81 3 3486 7096
E Mexico Presa Don Martín 53, Delegación Miguel Hidalgo, Mexico City; +52 55 5557 2065; e ambadh@mail.internet.com.mx
E Panama Edificio Dora Luz 2, Calle 1, El Cangrejo, Panama City; +507 269 3443; e ambhaiti@panama.c-com.net
E South Africa 808 George St, Arcadia, Pretoria; +27 12 430 7560
E Spain Marqués del Duero, 3 1 Izq, Madrid; +34 91 575 2624; e embhaiti@ctv.es
E USA (Embassy) 2311 Massachusetts Av NW, Washington, DC; +1 202 332 4090; e embassy@haiti.org; www.haiti.org; (Consulates) 259 SW 13th St, Miami, FL; +1 305 859 2003; 271 Madison Av, 17th Floor, New York, NY; +1 212 697 9767; e contact@haitianconsulate-nyc.org; www.haitianconsulate-nyc.org; 11 E Adams, Suite 1400, Chicago, IL; +1 312 922 4004; e chicago@haitianconsulate.org; www.haitianconsulate.org; 545 Boylston St, Suite 201, Boston, MA; +1 617 266 3660; e conbos@msn.com
E Venezuela 59 Av Rosas-Urban, San Rafael de Florida, Caracas; +58 2120 730 7220

For foreign missions in Haiti, see the listings in the Port-au-Prince chapter. Note that there is no Haitian embassy in the UK – the nearest embassy is in Paris.

GETTING THERE AND AWAY

Most people enter Haiti by air through Port-au-Prince, although it's also possible to fly directly into Cap-Haïtien. Hispaniola is the only island in the Caribbean divided between two countries, making it possible to enter Haiti overland from the Dominican Republic.

BY AIR Haiti's main entry point is **Aéroport International Toussaint Louverture** (code PAP; *2250 1120/1123*) in Port-au-Prince. The busiest route to Haiti by far is through Miami, allowing plentiful connections from international and domestic American flights. The secondary airport is **Aéroport International Cap-Haïtien** (code CAP; *2262 0313/8539*). At the time of writing this had strictly limited international connections. The airport is currently undergoing a major overhaul and runway extension to be completed by early 2013, with the expectation of being able to receive more direct flights from the USA.

Of the major international carriers, **American Airlines** offers the most flights to Port-au-Prince – twice daily from Miami and once a day from New York JFK and Fort Lauderdale, Florida. **Delta Airlines** fly daily from JFK. **United Airlines** fly three times a week from New York/Newark (EWR). **Air Canada** connects to Port-au-Prince with four flights a week from Montréal. **Air France** fly four times weekly from Miami and from Paris (via Pointe à Pitre in Guadeloupe). You can also fly from Paris to Port-au-Prince with Air Caraïbes.

Smaller airlines also abound. Haiti's **Tortug'Air** connects Port-au-Prince to Santo Domingo (Dominican Republic) and Providenciales (Turks and Caicos Islands). **Spirit Air** fly to Fort Lauderdale, Florida. **Insel Air** fly to Miami, as well as Curaçao and St Maarten in the Dutch Antilles. **Aerocaribbean** fly from Havana, Cuba. **Air Turks and Caicos** fly to Providenciales. The Christian airline **Missionary Flights International** fly from Fort Pierce, Florida to both Port-au-Prince and Cap-Haïtien, but takes bookings from affiliated missionary groups. **IBC Airways** fly from Cap-Haïtien to Miami and Fort Lauderdale, plus Marsh Harbour in the Bahamas.

The airport at Port-au-Prince was damaged in the 2010 earthquake. The departure terminal has been fully renovated, but at the time of writing the arrivals terminal was still an over-sized shed, although this should be replaced during the lifetime of this guidebook. Baggage reclaim can sometimes be chaotic – porters can swiftly remove luggage from the carousel, and stack it alongside, so you need to keep your eye out. As soon as you reach for your bags, you'll undoubtedly be approached by a porter keen to carry it for you – a couple of US dollar bills is asked for in return – so be clear if you don't need any assistance. On clearing the arrivals hall, there's a short walk to the outside. If you're being met, make sure your pickup has your name clearly marked on a sign, as well as his mobile phone number. Otherwise you'll be approached by official taxi drivers (with a badge from the Association des Chauffeurs Guide d'Haiti) keen for your fare, and outside the gate, even more people offering you a vehicle. Depending on your final destination in Port-au-Prince, you can expect to pay around US$20–40 for your ride.

Flying out of Port-au-Prince is a straightforward affair – the only potential hassle being porters who want to speed you to the front of the security queue in exchange for a small fee. Security screening for flights to the USA can be strict but efficient – queues at the duty-free stand for Barbancourt rum invariably seem to be longer.

Airline contact details Airline offices in Port-au-Prince are listed below. Unless stated otherwise, all international airlines maintain their main offices at the airport.

✈ **Aerocaribbean** www.cubajet.com

✈ **Air Canada** Aéroport International Toussaint Louverture; ☎ 2250 1115/1116; www.aircanada.com

✈ **Air Caraïbes** Belvédère, corner of rues Clerveaux & Chavanne, Pétionville; ☎ 2813 1037/1829; e reservation.haiti@aircaraibes.com; www.aircaraibes.com

✈ **Air France** Aéroport International Toussaint Louverture; ☎ 3115 5000; www.airfrance.ht

✈ **Air Turks and Caicos** Aéroport International Toussaint Louverture; ☎ 2942 6711; e res@flyairtc.com; www.airturksandcaicos.com

✈ **American Airlines** Choucoune Plaza, Rue Lamarre, Pétionville; ☎ 2999 6000/2229 6000; www.aa.com. Another office in Delimart Plaza, Delmas 32.

✈ **Delta Airlines** Complexe Promenade, Rue Grégoire, Pétionville; ☎ 2943 3582; e delta@sorahaiti.com; www.delta.com

✈ **Insel Air** Belvédère, corner of rues Clerveaux & Chavanne, Pétionville; ☎ 2813 0403/0401; e info@hatenterprises.com; www.fly-inselair.com. Another office at 69 Rue Pavée in Port-au-Prince.

✈ **Missionary Flights International** ☎ +1 772 462 2395 (USA); e mfi@missionaryflights.org; www.missionaryflights.org

✈ **Spirit Air** 30 Av Marie Jeanne, Bicentenaire; ☎ 2940 4421/4422; e customersupport@spirit.com; www.spirit.com

Tortug'Air Aérogare Guy Malary; 2812 8000; e reservation@tortugair.com; www.tortugair.com

United Airlines 30 Av Marie Jeanne, Bicentenaire; 2946 4682; www.united.com. Formerly Continental Airlines.

BY LAND There are four official border points between Haiti and the Dominican Republic. The busiest is at Malpasse (to Jimaní) between Port-au-Prince and Santo Domingo, followed by Ouanaminthe/Dajabón, between Cap-Haïtien and Santiago in the north. In both cases, there are direct public transport links between the cities on either side of the border, taking the hassle out of the crossings. The two less frequently used border points are from Anse-à-Pitre to Pedernales in the far south, and Belladère to Elías Piña (Comendador) in the centre.

Immigration is open from 08.00 to 18.00 (from 09.00 in the Dominican Republic, but note that the country is one hour ahead of Haiti). There are various charges levied on both sides of the border, all payable in US dollars: US$10 each way to enter/leave the DR, and US$10 to leave Haiti. Technically, US$10 must also be paid to enter Haiti by land too, but for some reason I've only ever been charged a token US$1.

From Port-au-Prince, three coach companies have daily services to Santo Domingo: **Terra Bus** (*Av Pan Americaine, Pétionville; 2257 2153*), **Caribe Tours** (*corner of rues Clerveaux & Gabart, Pétionville; 2257 9379/3785 1946*), and **Capital Coach Line** (*8 Rue Borno, Pétionville; 2512 5989; www.capitalcoachline.com*). Capital also has departures from a depot on Route de Tabarre, near the US embassy. The coaches are air conditioned and a sandwich and drink is provided en route. One-way tickets cost around 1,600HTG (US$40), but you can also opt to have the border fees bundled into the cost of the ticket. Travel time is eight hours.

From Cap-Haïtien, Caribe Tours (*Rue 24B; 2260 1258/3614 0264*) have a similar coach service to Santiago, taking six hours and costing 1,000HTG (US$25) one-way, plus border fees. The coach continues to Santo Domingo, an 11-hour trip costing 1,200HTG (US$30).

Both of these borders are busy marketplaces, particularly on Mondays and Fridays when traders from both sides – especially Haiti – descend for an orgy of cross-border trade. The scene can be a little overwhelming, and if you're on your own or on foot you may have to fight to get through the crush at immigration. Or perhaps not – commenting on the Dominican side about the steep passport fees, the immigration officer suggested half-jokingly that if I was just there for a day trip, then next time I should simply walk across the border without even showing my passport!

A quieter time is guaranteed if you cross between Anse-à-Pitre to Pedernales. Immigration officers will be surprised to see you, but there's no hassle. Bear in mind however that the road from Anse-à-Pitre through Belle Anse towards Jacmel is pretty broken up, leading to some uncomfortable bumping in the back of a pick-up.

Belladère to Elías Piña (the colloquial name for the Dominican town of Comendador) is remoter still. There's a walk of nearly 1km between immigration offices, with everyone between hassling for money, moto-taxi rental, and money changing. Although Belladère is relatively run-down, it's noteworthy as a planned community built in 1948 under President Estimé, and has some interesting modernist architecture. From here, you'll need to take onward transport to Mirebalais.

HEALTH *with Dr Felicity Nicholson*

Travelling somewhere like Haiti presents different potential health issues compared with Europe or North America. By taking sensible precautions you can greatly reduce your risk of catching any serious diseases, and visitors are unlikely to encounter any medical problems more acute than a possible attack of travellers' diarrhoea (see page 58).

It's recommended to visit your doctor or travel clinic at least six weeks before travelling to allow plenty of time for any potential course of vaccinations. Last-minute injections can give only partial cover for some diseases. It's strongly advised to have immunisations against diphtheria, tetanus and polio which come as the all-in-one vaccine Revaxis which lasts for ten years. Vaccination against hepatitis A and typhoid, both diseases transmitted through infected food and water, are also strongly recommended, as is vaccination against cholera. The oral cholera vaccine, Dukoral, is available for those aged six and over as a two-dose schedule. The two doses should be given one–six weeks apart and at least one week before arriving in Haiti. For those aged two–five years then a three-dose schedule is used. Other vaccines

LONG-HAUL FLIGHTS, CLOTS AND DVT

Dr Felicity Nicholson

Any prolonged immobility, including travel by land or air, can result in deep-vein thrombosis (DVT) with the risk of embolus to the lungs. Certain factors can increase the risk and these include:

- Having a previous clot or a close relative with a history
- People over 40, with increased risk in the over-80s
- Recent major operation or varicose-veins surgery
- Cancer
- Stroke
- Heart disease
- Obesity
- Pregnancy
- Hormone therapy
- Heavy smokers
- Severe varicose veins
- People who are tall (over 6ft/1.8m) or short (under 5ft/1.5m)

A deep-vein thrombosis causes painful swelling and redness of the calf or sometimes the thigh. It is only dangerous if a clot travels to the lungs (pulmonary embolus). Symptoms of a pulmonary embolus (PE) – which commonly start three to ten days after a long flight – include chest pain, shortness of breath, and sometimes coughing up small amounts of blood. Anyone who thinks that they might have a DVT needs to see a doctor immediately.

PREVENTION OF DVT

- Keep mobile before and during the flight; try to move around every couple of hours
- Drink plenty of fluids during the flight
- Avoid taking sleeping pills and excessive tea, coffee and alcohol
- Consider wearing flight socks or support stockings (see *www.legshealth.com*)

If you think you may be at increased risk of a clot, ask your doctor if it is safe to travel.

that should be considered are hepatitis B, especially if you are working in hospitals or with children, meningitis (ACWY) and rabies. Hepatitis B and rabies schedules are a series of three vaccines over three–four weeks so allow plenty of time for vaccination.

You should also get the most up-to-date advice on anti-malaria prophylaxis.

If you're planning to be in Haiti a long time a dental check-up before flying out is a good idea. If you wear glasses, take a spare pair and a copy of your prescription. It's also very important to take out comprehensive medical travel insurance before travelling to Haiti. Make sure the policy covers medical evacuation.

MEDICAL FACILITIES IN HAITI Medical care is of reasonable quality in Haiti – the best naturally being in Port-au-Prince, although many hospitals are very under-resourced. Most hospitals and clinics are private, but even at public facilities patients have to pay for treatment. It's a harsh irony that in the immediate aftermath of the earthquake, many local doctors and hospitals found themselves out of a job: instead of being the backbone of medical recovery, they were out-competed by international organisations offering free medical care. You'll often find private laboratories near hospitals offering tests and supporting services. Most embassies maintain lists of recommended hospitals and doctors. Many physicians speak English, because after completing their basic medical education in Haiti they tend to study abroad to specialise in their chosen field, often in the USA. By contrast, you'll have to speak French in most pharmacies, which are usually well stocked, at least in the larger towns. Pharmacists tend to be well versed in most of the common ailments you might pick up. If you follow any particular treatment regime, it's a sensible idea to bring your prescription, although many drugs are available over the counter.

PERSONAL FIRST-AID KIT

A minimal kit contains:

- A good drying antiseptic, eg: iodine or potassium permanganate (don't take antiseptic cream)
- A few small dressings (Band-Aids)
- Suncream
- Insect repellent; anti-malarial tablets; impregnated bed-net or permethrin spray
- Aspirin or paracetamol
- Antifungal cream (eg: Canesten)
- Ciprofloxacin or norfloxacin, for severe diarrhoea
- Tinidazole for giardia or amoebic dysentery (see below for regime)
- Antibiotic eye drops, for sore, 'gritty', stuck-together eyes (conjunctivitis)
- A pair of fine pointed tweezers (to remove hairy caterpillar hairs, thorns, splinters, coral, etc)
- Alcohol-based hand rub or bar of soap in plastic box
- Condoms or femidoms

TRAVEL CLINICS AND HEALTH INFORMATION A full list of current travel clinic websites worldwide is available on www.istm.org/. For other journey preparation information, consult www.nathnac.org/ds/map_world.aspx. Information about various medications may be found on www.netdoctor.co.uk/travel.

UK

+ Berkeley Travel Clinic 32 Berkeley St, London W1J 8EL; ☎ 020 7629 6233; ⌚ 10.00–18.00 Mon–Fri, 10.00–15.00 Sat

+ CityDoc 42 Wimpole St, London W1G 8YF; ☎ 0207 935 6260; 16 City Rd, London EC1Y 2AA; ☎ 0207 256 8668; www.moorgatemd.co.uk; both clinics ⌚ 09.00–18.00 Mon–Fri, 10.00–15.00 Sat.

Also check the website for clinics throughout the UK (0845 0260 830). Walk in or same day travel clinic appointments. Vaccinations, anti-malarials & travel advice.

The Travel Clinic Ltd, Cambridge 41 Hills Rd, Cambridge CB2 1NT; 01223 367362; e enquiries@travelclinic.ltd.uk; www.travelcliniccambridge.co.uk; 10.00–16.30 Mon & Fri, 10.00–16.00 Tue & Sat, 12.00–18.30 Wed & Thu

The Travel Clinic Ltd, Ipswich Gilmour Piper, 10 Fonnereau Rd, Ipswich IP1 3JP; 01223 367362; 09.00–16.30 Mon, 09.00–17.30 Wed, 10.00–17.30 Fri

Edinburgh Travel Health Clinic 14 East Preston St, Newington, Edinburgh EH8 9QA; 0131 667 1030; www.edinburghtravelhealthclinic.co.uk; Extended hours including some evenings. Travel vaccinations & advice on all aspects of malaria prevention. All current UK prescribed anti-malaria tablets in stock.

Fleet Street Travel Clinic 29 Fleet St, London EC4Y 1AA; 020 7353 5678; e info@fleetstreetclinic.com; www.fleetstreetclinic.com; 08.45–20.00 Mon–Thu, 08.45–17.30 Fri. Vaccinations, malaria advice & travel products.

Hospital for Tropical Diseases Travel Clinic Mortimer Market, Capper St (off Tottenham Ct Rd), London WC1E 6JB; 020 7387 4411; www.thehtd.org; 13.00–17.00 Wed & 09.00–13.00 Fri. Consultations are by appointment only & are only offered to those with more complex problems. Check the website for inclusions. Runs a Travellers' Healthline Advisory Service (020 7950 7799) for country-specific information & health hazards. Also stocks nets, water purification equipment & personal protection measures. Travellers who have returned from the tropics & are unwell, with fever or bloody diarrhoea, can attend the walk-in emergency clinic at the hospital without an appointment.

InterHealth Travel Clinic 111 Westminster Bridge Rd, London SE1 7HR; 020 7902 9000; e info@interhealth.org.uk; www.interhealth.org.uk; 08.30–17.30 Mon–Fri. Competitively priced, one-stop travel health service by appointment only.

MASTA pre-travel clinics 01276 685040; www.masta-travel-health.com/travel-clinic.aspx. Call or check the website for the nearest clinic; there are currently 50 in Britain. They also sell malaria prophylaxis, memory cards, treatment kits, bednets, net treatment kits, etc.

NHS travel websites www.fitfortravel.nhs.uk or www.fitfortravel.scot.nhs.uk. Provide country-by-country advice on immunisation & malaria prevention, plus details of recent developments, & a list of relevant health organisations.

Nomad Travel Clinics Flagship store: 3–4 Wellington Terrace, Turnpike Lane, London N8 0PX; 020 8889 7014; e turnpike@nomadtravel.co.uk; www.nomadtravel.co.uk; walk in or appointments 09.15–18.00 Mon, Tue, Wed & Fri, 11.45–19.30 Thu, 09.15–18.00 Sat. See website for clinics in southwest & central London, Bishops Stortford, Bristol, Loughton, Manchester & Southampton. As well as dispensing health advice, Nomad stocks mosquito nets & other anti-bug devices, & an excellent range of adventure travel gear.

Trailfinders Immunisation Centre 194 Kensington High St, London W8 7RG; 020 7938 3999; www.trailfinders.com/travelessentials/travelclinic.htm; 09.00–17.00 Mon, Tue, Wed & Fri, 10.00–18.00 Thu, 10.00–17.15 Sat. No appointment necessary.

Travelpharm www.travelpharm.com. The Travelpharm website offers up-to-date guidance on travel-related health & has a range of medication & equipment available through their online store. Online consultation for malaria prevention.

Irish Republic

Tropical Medical Bureau 54 Grafton St, Dublin 2; 01 2715272; e graftonstreet@tmb.ie; www.tmb.ie; until 20.00 Mon–Fri & Sat mornings. For other clinic locations & useful information specific to tropical destinations, check their website.

USA

Centers for Disease Control 1600 Clifton Rd, Atlanta, GA 30333; 800 232 4636 or (800) 232 6348; e cdcinfo@cdc.gov; www.cdc.gov/travel; 08.00–20.00 Mon–Fri. The central source of travel information in the USA. Each summer they publish the invaluable *Health Information for International Travel*.

IAMAT (International Association for Medical Assistance to Travelers) 1623 Military Rd #279, Niagara Falls, NY 14304-1745; 716 754 4883; e info@iamat.org; www.iamat.org. A non-profit organisation with free membership that provides lists of English-speaking doctors abroad.

Canada

✚ IAMAT 67 Mowat Ave, Suite 036, Toronto, Ontario M6K 3E3; ☎ 416 652 0137; www.iamat.org

✚ TMVC Suite 106, 4180 Lougheed Hwy, Burnaby BC, V5C 6A7; ☎ 604 681 5656; e vancouver@tmvc.com; www.tmvc.com. One-stop medical clinic for all your international travel health & vaccination needs.

Australia and New Zealand

✚ TMVC (Travel Doctors Group) ☎ 1300 65 88 44; www.tmvc.com.au. 30 clinics in Australia & New Zealand, including: *Auckland* Canterbury Arcade, 174 Queen St, Auckland 1010, New Zealand; ☎ (64) 9 373 3531; e auckland@traveldoctor.co.nz; *Brisbane* 75a Astor Terrace, Spring Hill, Brisbane, QLD 4000, Australia; ☎ 07 3815 6900; e brisbane@traveldoctor.com.au; *Melbourne* 393 Little Bourke St, Melbourne, Vic 3000, Australia; ☎ (03) 9935 8100; e melbourne@traveldoctor.com.au; *Sydney* 428 George St, Sydney, NSW 2000, Australia; ☎ (2) 9221 7133; e sydney@traveldoctor.com.au

✚ IAMAT 206 Papanui Rd, Christchurch 5, New Zealand; www.iamat.org

South Africa

✚ Netcare Travel Clinics ☎ 011 802 0059; e travelinfo@netcare.co.za; www.travelclinic.co.za. 11 clinics throughout South Africa.

✚ TMVC NHC Health Centre, cnr Beyers Naude Dr & Waugh Ave, Northcliff 2195; ☎ 0861 300 911; e info@traveldoctor.co.za; www.traveldoctor.co.za. Consult the website for clinic locations.

TRAVELLERS' DIARRHOEA Travelling in Haiti carries a reasonable risk of getting a dose of travellers' diarrhoea; the newer you are to exotic travel, the more likely you will be to suffer. By taking precautions against travellers' diarrhoea you will also avoid cholera, typhoid, paratyphoid, hepatitis, dysentery, worms, etc. Travellers' diarrhoea and the other faecal-oral diseases come from getting other peoples' faeces in your mouth. This most often happens from cooks not washing their hands after a trip to the toilet, but even if the restaurant cook does not understand basic hygiene you will be safe if your food has been properly cooked and arrives piping hot. The most important prevention strategy is to wash your hands before eating anything, or use an antibacterial hand gel: since the introduction of cholera to Haiti, this is widely available, and many restaurants keep a supply handy. You can pick up salmonella and shigella from toilet door handles and possibly bank notes. The maxim to remind you what you can safely eat is:

PEEL IT, BOIL IT, COOK IT OR FORGET IT.

This means that fruit you have washed and peeled yourself, and hot foods, should be safe but raw foods, cold cooked foods, salads, fruit salads which have been prepared by others, and foods kept lukewarm in hotel buffets are potentially dangerous. Many visitors also avoid ice in their drinks, but most commercially-sold ice is made with treated water. That said, plenty of travellers and expatriates enjoy fruit and vegetables, so do keep a sense of perspective, as it would be shame to miss out on Haiti's great fruit and street food completely. If you are struck, see box opposite for treatment.

MALARIA The island of Hispaniola is the only part of the Caribbean where malaria remains endemic. Spread by the malarial parasite-transmitting Anopheles mosquito, malaria is found in regions lower than 300m in altitude. Prevalence is partly tied to the rainy seasons, with transmission peaking in November–January and May–July, but it should be considered to be a risk all year round and in all areas. Localised outbreaks often make media headlines – a recent slight to national pride took place in February 2011 when Haiti's Under-17 football team were forced to withdraw from a CONCACAF cup match in Jamaica due to malarial infection.

TREATING TRAVELLERS' DIARRHOEA

Dr Jane Wilson-Howarth

It is dehydration that makes you feel awful during a bout of diarrhoea and the most important part of treatment is drinking lots of clear fluids. Sachets of oral rehydration salts give the perfect biochemical mix to replace all that is pouring out of your bottom but other recipes taste nicer. Any dilute mixture of sugar and salt in water will do you good: try Coke or orange squash with a three-finger pinch of salt added to each glass (if you are salt-depleted you won't taste the salt). Otherwise make a solution of a four-finger scoop of sugar with a three-finger pinch of salt in a 500 ml glass. Or add eight level teaspoons of sugar (18g) and one level teaspoon of salt (3g) to one litre (five cups) of safe water. A squeeze of lemon or orange juice improves the taste and adds potassium, which is also lost in diarrhoea. Drink two large glasses after every bowel action, and more if you are thirsty. These solutions are still absorbed well if you are vomiting, but you will need to take sips at a time. If you are not eating you need to drink three litres a day plus whatever is pouring into the toilet. If you feel like eating, take a bland, high carbohydrate diet. Heavy greasy foods will probably give you cramps.

If the diarrhoea is bad, or you are passing blood or slime, or you have a fever, you will probably need antibiotics in addition to fluid replacement. A dose of norfloxacin or ciprofloxacin repeated twice a day until better may be appropriate (if you are planning to take an antibiotic with you, note that both norfloxacin and ciprofloxacin are available only on prescription in the UK). Ciprofloxacin is considered to be less effective in Haiti. If the diarrhoea is greasy and bulky and is accompanied by sulphurous (eggy) burps, one likely cause is giardia. This is best treated with tinidazole (four x 500mg in one dose, repeated seven days later if symptoms persist).

It's unwise to travel in malarial areas whilst pregnant or with children: the risk of malaria in many parts is considerable and these travellers are likely to succumb rapidly to the disease.

Malaria prevention There is no vaccine against malaria that gives enough protection to be useful for travellers, but there are other ways to avoid it; travellers must plan their malaria protection properly. Seek current advice on the best antimalarials to take: chloroquine (Nivaquine or Avloclor) is considered effective and easy to take being a weekly dosage. Two tablets should be taken together with food and washed down with a soft drink. They should be started one week before reaching Haiti, taken through the trip and for four weeks after. They may not be suitable for people with bad psoriasis, epilepsy, if you are on medication for cardiac arrhythmias, on zyban to stop smoking, or if you have poor renal function. An alternative to use if it is not suitable is paludrine. Both of these drugs have been around for decades and can be used in pregnancy if necessary. However, it is wise to avoid malarial areas wherever possible when pregnant, as pregnant women are more prone to acquiring malaria.

No anti-malaria tablet should be considered 100% effective and other precautions should be taken such as wearing cover-up clothing and using insect repellents that contain DEET.

Malaria: diagnosis and treatment Even those who take their malaria tablets meticulously and do everything possible to avoid mosquito bites may

CHOLERA

In October 2010, Haiti suffered a devastating cholera epidemic. From its initial epicentre in the Artibonite Valley, it spread rapidly to every corner of the country, its passage aided by poor sanitation. At the time of going to press it had caused more than 7,200 deaths, with over half a million people infected.

Cholera is not endemic to Haiti. The outbreak was traced to Nepali soldiers at a Minustah base outside Mirebalais that was dumping raw sewage in the Artibonite river – although the UN have not formally accepted responsibility, genetic fingerprinting showed the cholera strain to be identical to one from Nepal, which was having a cholera outbreak at the time.

As well as medical support, a large-scale public health education campaign was needed to inform people about this previously unknown disease that can kill in hours. Hand-sanitiser gel is now widely available, along with street signs and banners advising people *lave men ak savon pou pwotoje sante* ('wash hands with soap to protect your health'). When I visited a health clinic in Grand Anse in 2011, five hours walk from the nearest road, attendees demonstrated the songs with actions used to spread simple hygiene information. Unfortunately, cholera is now likely to remain endemic in the country, with reservoirs in rural areas where the population has little access to potable water and good sanitation. A two-dose oral vaccine does exist for cholera, but public health advocates strenuously debated whether or not to bring it to Haiti or to concentrate on improving access to clean water. After much wrangling, a pilot cholera vaccination project was finally rolled out in spring 2012 jointly run by Partners in Health and Gheskio, aiming to vaccinate up to 1% of the population, including the most vulnerable communities in Port-au-Prince and the Artibonite Valley.

In late 2011 cholera victims, supported by the Institute for Justice and Democracy in Haiti, launched a landmark legal action against the UN for damages caused by the introduction of the disease. The case is still ongoing.

contract a strain of malaria that is resistant to prophylactic drugs. Untreated malaria is likely to be fatal, but even strains resistant to prophylaxis respond well to prompt treatment. Because of this, your immediate priority upon displaying possible malaria symptoms – including a rapid rise in temperature (over 38°C), and any combination of a headache, flu-like aches and pains, a general sense of disorientation, and possibly even nausea and diarrhoea – is to establish whether you have malaria, ideally by visiting a clinic.

Diagnosing malaria is not easy, which is why consulting a doctor is sensible: there are other dangerous causes of fever in Haiti, which require different treatments. Even if you test negative, it would be wise to stay within reach of a laboratory until the symptoms clear up, and to test again after a day or two if they don't. It's worth noting that if you have a fever and the malaria test is negative, you may have typhoid or paratyphoid, which should also receive immediate treatment.

With malaria, it is normal enough to go from feeling healthy to having a high fever in the space of a few hours (and it is possible to die from falciparum malaria within 24 hours of the first symptoms). In such circumstances, assume that you have malaria and act accordingly – whatever risks are attached to taking an unnecessary cure are outweighed by the dangers of untreated malaria. Experts differ on the costs and benefits of self-treatment, but agree that it leads to over-treatment and to many people taking drugs they do not need; yet treatment may save your life. There is some division about the best treatment for malaria, so discuss your trip with a specialist either at home or in Haiti.

DENGUE FEVER Malaria is by no means the only insect-borne disease to which the traveller may succumb. Dengue fever is endemic in Haiti, and the mosquitoes that carry the virus bite during the daytime, so it is worth applying repellent during the daytime as well as in the evening. Symptoms include strong headaches, rashes, excruciating joint and muscle pains and high fever. Viral fevers usually last about a week or so and are not usually fatal. Complete rest and paracetamol are the usual treatment; plenty of fluids also help. Some patients are given an intravenous drip to keep them from dehydrating. It is especially important to protect yourself if you have had dengue fever before, since a second infection with a different strain can result in the potentially fatal dengue haemorrhagic fever.

EYE PROBLEMS Bacterial conjunctivitis (pink eye, locally called *pish-pish*) is a common infection in Haiti; people who wear contact lenses are most open to this irritating problem. The eyes feel sore and gritty and they will often be stuck together in the mornings. They will need treatment with antibiotic drops or ointment – pharmacists are used to diagnosing the complaint. Bathing your eyes with cold tea can also be an effective treatment. Lesser eye irritation should settle with bathing in salt water and keeping the eyes shaded.

SKIN INFECTIONS Any mosquito bite or small nick in the skin gives an opportunity for bacteria to foil the body's usually excellent defences; it will surprise many travellers how quickly skin infections start in warm humid climates and it is essential to clean and cover even the slightest wound. Creams are not as effective as a good drying antiseptic such as dilute iodine, potassium permanganate (a few crystals in half a cup of water), or crystal (or gentian) violet. One of these should be available in most towns. If the wound starts to throb, or becomes red and the redness starts to spread, or the wound oozes, and especially if you develop a fever, antibiotics will probably be needed: flucloxacillin (250mg four times a day) or cloxacillin (500mg four times a day). For those allergic to penicillin, erythromycin

AVOIDING INSECT BITES

As the sun is going down, don long clothes and apply repellent on any exposed flesh. Pack a DEET-based insect repellent (roll-ons or stick are the least messy preparations for travelling). Few hotels have bed nets, so bringing your own impregnated with permethrin is sensible. Permethrin treatment makes even very tatty nets protective and prevents mosquitoes from biting through the net when you roll against it. Otherwise retire to an air-conditioned room or burn mosquito coils (which are widely available and cheap) or sleep under a fan. Coils and fans reduce rather than eliminate bites. Note that plug-in repellents are only as good as your accommodation's electricity supply. Travel clinics usually sell a good range of nets, treatment kits and repellents.

Mosquitoes and many other insects are attracted to light. In hotel rooms, be aware that the longer your light is on, the greater the number of insects that will be sharing your accommodation.

(500mg twice a day) for five days should help. See a doctor if the symptoms do not start to improve within 48 hours.

Fungal infections also get a hold easily in hot, moist climates so wear 100%-cotton socks and underwear and shower frequently. An itchy rash in the groin or flaking between the toes is likely to be a fungal infection. This needs treatment with an antifungal cream such as Canesten (clotrimazole); if this is not available try Whitfield's ointment (compound benzoic acid ointment) or crystal violet (although this will turn you purple!).

HIV/AIDS Haiti has an adult HIV infection rate of 2.2%, with around 120,000 people in total carrying the virus – around half the total number of carriers in the Caribbean region. While the virus puts a heavy burden on health services (along with the social stigma associated with infection), Haiti has made impressive gains in reducing HIV levels through both improved treatment and public education, bringing the infection rate down from an early-90s high of around 9%.

The risks of sexually transmitted infection are high in Haiti whether you sleep with fellow travellers or locals. About 80% of HIV infections in British heterosexuals are acquired abroad. If you must indulge, use condoms or femidoms, which help reduce the risk of transmission. If you notice any genital ulcers or discharge, get treatment promptly since these increase the risk of acquiring HIV. If you do have unprotected sex, visit a clinic as soon as possible; this should be within 24 hours, or no later than 72 hours, for post-exposure prophylaxis.

MENINGITIS This is a particularly nasty disease as it can kill within hours of the first symptoms appearing. The tell-tale symptoms are a combination of a blinding headache (light sensitivity), a blotchy rash and a high fever. Immunisation protects against the most serious bacterial form of meningitis and the tetravalent vaccine ACWY has been recommended for Haiti by British travel clinics, in the aftermath of the earthquake in 2010 Although other forms of meningitis exist (usually viral), there are no vaccines for these. Local papers normally report localised outbreaks. A severe headache and fever should make you run to a doctor immediately. There are also other causes of headache and fever; one of which is typhoid, which occurs in travellers to Haiti. Seek medical help if you are ill for more than a few days.

RABIES Haiti is considered to be a high risk country for rabies. The disease can exist in theory in any warm-blooded mammal although dogs and related species and bats are the most common. The disease can be transmitted by a bite, scratch or saliva getting into broken skin or into eyes, nose or mouth. Wash any skin wound immediately with soap and running water for a good 15 minutes, then, if you have some antiseptic, use that. If the exposure is through the eyes, nose or mouth then rinse with the cleanest water you can find.

The treatment for non-vaccinated people involves a blood product called Rabies Immunoglobulin (RIG), which ideally should be human (HRIG) but horse (ERIG) will do. This ahould be administered as soon after the exposure as possible together with the first of four or five vaccines given over a month. RIG can be very hard to come by and is very expensive. If you have had three pre-exposure vaccines over a minimum of 21 days then RIG is no longer needed and treatment involves two doses of vaccine given three days apart. The scarcity and expense of RIG is a good reason for pre-exposure rabies vaccine to be offered wherever possible, Remember rabies is almost 100% fatal and is one of the worst ways to go.

SUN EXPOSURE Try to keep out of the sun during the middle of the day and, if you must expose yourself to the sun, build up gradually from 20 minutes per day. Be especially careful of exposure in the middle of the day and of sun reflected off water, and wear a T-shirt and lots of waterproof suncream (at least SPF20) when swimming. Sun exposure ages the skin, makes people prematurely wrinkly and increases the risk of skin cancer. Cover up with long, loose clothes and wear a hat when you can. The glare and the dust can be hard on the eyes, too, so bring UV-protecting sunglasses and, perhaps, a soothing eyebath.

SAFETY

People who have never been to Haiti tend to ask two things when you tell them you're going there: Is anything still standing after the earthquake? And, is it safe? Haiti, it's safe to say, has had a troubled image abroad ever since it freed itself in the world's only successful slave revolution. The US State Department (*www.travel.state.gov*) has – for many Haitians – traditionally been monolithic in its travel warnings for the country, frequently advising against any travel irrespective of the situation on the ground. Even during the research of this book, that situation seems to have changed, and along with the British Foreign Office (*www.fco.gov.uk/travel*) now offers better and more nuanced advice. (If your government *does* advise against travel, this can invalidate regular travel insurance, so while government advisories are only part of planning for a trip, they're still important to take note of.)

INSECURITY AND CRIME While perceptions of crime and insecurity predominate media perceptions of Haiti, the actual situation on the ground is rather better than one might expect. While the UN peacekeeping mission Minustah has hardly been without controversy, its presence has fostered a political situation stable enough to hold presidential elections in 2006 and 2010 largely without incident, while also helping to tackle the epidemic of kidnappings that swept the country in 2005–06.

While you'll frequently see Minustah troops in vehicles, day-to-day law enforcement is carried out by the 11,000-strong Haitian National Police (PNH). While their numbers are still inadequate, Haiti actually has a much lower violent crime rate than most other Caribbean countries. There are around seven murders a year per 100,000 people, compared with the tourist magnets of neighbouring Dominican Republic (24) and Jamaica (52). To put that figure into an even wider context, the USA has five murders a year per 100,000 people.

This is not to say that crime and insecurity don't exist. Kidnappings do still sometimes take place, although they are almost exclusively specifically targeted against the middle classes and wealthy Haitians. That said, there have been a small number of incidents against foreigners working long-term in Port-au-Prince, so it's worth taking simple precautions to reduce your exposure to risk. Kidnappings are almost always preceded by reconnaissance and planning rather than being opportunistic so mitigate against this by not setting patterns of movement and timings. This is particularly important for those working in Haiti, going to the office and returning home at set hours in a vehicle emblazoned with your organisation's logo. Vary your movements if possible, remain aware while driving and keep doors locked.

Street crime is a small but serious risk. By comparison to the vast majority of the local population, any foreigner in Haiti is extremely affluent and is a potential target of, at the very least, petty crime. Don't walk around at night on your own, as muggings can occur. If you are out on foot, it can be a good idea to leave your wallet at home and only carry what money you need on you at the time.

THE HAITIAN RUMOUR MILL

Keeping your ear to the ground is important, but it's equally vital to understand that Haiti can sometimes seem to be a country that runs entirely on rumours and word of mouth. The pertinent Creole word here is *teledyòl*, meaning 'grapevine'. A good example is the opposition-fuelled debate about whether President Martelly actually holds a US passport (dual nationality would rule him ineligible for office). In March 2012 things came to a head when Martelly announced a press conference to clear things up once and for all. For a brief afternoon, Port-au-Prince seemed to go crazy. The press conference was repeatedly delayed, while SMS and BlackBerry messages spread rumours of imminent curfews, crisis and threats of violence. Politicians on the radio fanned the panic by talking of imminent disturbances. The Haitian Twittersphere went into frenzy, while parents were told to take their children out of school early. As the press conference finally took place, the streets were empty as people wondered what was going to ensue. As it happened, nothing. When Martelly's nationality was confirmed, you could hear the sort of cheers that Haitians normally reserve for the winning goal of a Barcelona–Real Madrid match, and everyone carried on as before. But in just a couple of hours, an atmosphere so febrile had been worked up as to give the impression that a full-blown crisis was erupting. Such is the power of *teledyòl*.

Political demonstrations (*manifestasyon*) are a regular fact of life in Haiti, and crowds of under-employed people are easy to gather. It's usually best to avoid them – while most are peaceful, a mix of an emotive issue, over-zealous policing and frustrated demonstrators can produce unpredictable results. If you hear of roads being blockaded, avoid the area altogether, and if you see people running, get off the streets as quickly as you can.

HASSLES While it pays to be sensible, going the other direction to paranoia is unwarranted. Most of the safety concerns related to Haiti are exactly the same as in any other developing nation. One of the more annoying issues is the frequent lack of working street lights. This isn't just an issue about the risks of being mugged, but broken pavements, open sewers and the occasional need to walk in the road all contrive to make after-dark strolls off-putting. Public transport is often poorly maintained or simply badly driven, increasing the risk of accidents. This particularly applies to the moto-taxis that weave through congested traffic with reckless abandon.

I'm unsure as to how much of a hassle it is, but one thing you should be prepared for is to be called a *blan* a lot. This is the Creole word for foreigner, and isn't colour-specific (I once talked to a Nigerian working in Port-au-Prince who was bemoaning being called 'blan', despite having darker skin than most Haitians). People may call out *blan* to address you or simply get your attention. Some days you might not notice, on other days it can be slightly wearing.

WOMEN TRAVELLERS

Haiti lacks the macho Hispanic culture of neighbouring Dominican Republic, although most foreign women will receive some amount of unwarranted romantic attention during their stay. Most of this is simply annoying, from whistling or making kissing sounds to get attention, although it can still make an individual feel uncomfortable. It's best to be prepared and, if possible, develop a sense of humour (or at least public indifference) to it.

Women should take the standard safety precautions, such as not walking alone at night (good advice for men too) or hitchhiking alone. In terms of dress, it's fine to wear shorts or singlets around town – dress codes are suited to the Caribbean.

GAY/LESBIAN TRAVELLERS

Homosexuality is not criminalised in Haiti, but relatively few people openly self-identify as either gay or lesbian (in Creole, *masisi*, often used as a pejorative) due to fear of stigmatisation or persecution. In 2008, when Michele Pierre-Louis became prime minister, rumours about her sexuality forced her to make a radio broadcast denying that she was a lesbian, before her nomination was confirmed. Interestingly, some gay men and women find Vodou to be a more sympathetic religion than Christianity; the lwa often helping to find an explanation and expression for their sexuality. Anyone interested in homosexuality in Haiti should look out for the 2002 documentary *Of Men and Gods*, directed by Anne Lescot and Laurence Magloire.

For visitors, there shouldn't be any problems visiting Haiti, although discretion is advisable. There is no openly gay/lesbian scene; in 2011, **Kouraj** (*www.kouraj.org*), Haiti's first lesbian/gay/bisexual/transgender support group was founded in Port-au-Prince, with plans to open a centre in the capital.

DISABLED TRAVELLERS

Haiti is not somewhere that puts much comfort in the way of disabled travellers – the country's overstretched and under-maintained infrastructures can at times put plenty of challenges in front of even the most able-bodied. The number of lifts in the country can be counted on one hand, while steps, stairs and broken streets abound. An adventuring spirit and equal doses of stamina and pragmatism are required, and you are likely to need your own vehicle and driver/guide.

There have long been social stigmas attached to those born with physical disabilities in Haiti, although the number of those maimed in the earthquake have made such conditions increasingly visible, particularly in Port-au-Prince. Wheelchairs, and to a lesser extent amputees, aren't such an uncommon sight as they once were. Haitians are generally very considerate to those who have particular needs and one could certainly expect help from strangers if it is required.

WHAT TO TAKE

The type of luggage you bring will depend on the sort of travel you'll be doing: if you plan on using public transport a lot, a rucksack or suitcase/kitbag that converts to a backpack will be most practical, especially for manhandling on buses and *taptaps* (minibus or covered pick-up truck). Lockable bags will deter casual, opportunistic theft. There's little call for camping gear in Haiti, but a sheet sleeping bag or liner can be handy. Mosquito nets are only rarely provided in hotels, so consider one of those too, especially if you're travelling in the rainier times of the year.

When packing for clothes, remember that Haiti is a tropical country. Pack light, natural fabrics if possible. A couple of pairs of trousers (or skirts for women), three light-fitting shirts or T-shirts, and a week's supply of underwear should be adequate, although the longer your stay the more options you may wish to have. If you're going to be working in Haiti, smart wear for the office may also be appropriate. Nights in the mountains (even above Port-au-Prince) can be cool, so an extra layer may be required, although nothing as drastic as a heavy sweater. A light, breathable waterproof or umbrella may prove useful during the rains. As for footwear, light shoes are most convenient, plus a pair of sandals or flip-flops.

A long-term resident of Port-au-Prince adds these thoughts on packing clothes: 'One mistake a lot of first-time travellers make when they come to Haiti is to dress for safari, packing cargo pants, combat boots, bucket hat, etc. This is a Caribbean country, and whether rich or poor, people generally take pride in their appearance. They have style! If travellers don't want to stick out any more than they already do, I'd recommend they pack at least one nice or stylish outfit, including sandals for the ladies. There are ample options to shop for lovely, locally made jewellery and accessories here as well. You might go to a nicer restaurant, or concert, or be invited to a baptism or marriage reception, and you'll want to look your best, if not out of pride then out of respect. I've heard female aid workers complain frequently how frumpy they feel as compared to their Haitian colleagues, and how much they wished they had brought some nicer clothes.'

Suggestions for a personal medical kit are listed in the *Health* section on page 56. A torch is pretty much essential for power cuts, while a Swiss army knife or similar multi-purpose tool is a personal favourite. Electricity in Haiti is 110V AC at 60Hz cycles, with American-style flat two-pin plugs in use. Most (but not all) sockets take the American-style third round grounding pin. An unlocked mobile phone will allow you to buy a cheap local SIM card. A money belt that can be hidden under clothing is useful, for keeping your cash, cards and passport safe.

For toiletries, bring what you can't do without, although shops in Port-au-Prince are well stocked with American and French brands. Decent English-language reading material can be hard to find though, so stock up before travelling.

MONEY

Haiti's currency is the gourde (rhyming with 'food'; HTG). It's a reasonably stable currency, with exchange rates floating at around 40 to the US dollar at the time

CURRENCY READY RECKONER

Where US$1 = 40HTG approximate (based on rates in August 2012)

Gourde	Haitian dollar	US dollar
1,000HTG	H$200	US$25
500HTG	H$100	US$12.50
250HTG	H$50	US$6.25
100HTG	H$20	US$2.50
50HTG	H$10	US$1.25

US dollar	Gourde	Haitian dollar
US$5	200HTG	H$40
US$10	400HTG	H$80
US$20	800HTG	H$160
US$50	2,000HTG	H$400
US$100	4,000HTG	H$800

of writing. Bank notes come in denominations of 10, 25, 50, 100, 250, 500 and 1,000HTG, and 1HTG and 5HTG coins. The smallest denominations can be very grubby indeed, but you're well advised to hoard them whenever possible, as getting change from street vendors and motorbike-taxis is frequently a challenge: no Haitian seemingly likes to give up their small change if at all possible.

While prices are generally listed in gourdes, you'll as often as not be quoted prices in US dollars. This is where money in Haiti becomes interesting (or a headache, depending on your viewpoint). From the US occupation in 1915 until just after the end of the Jean-Claude Duvalier regime in the late 1980s, the gourde was pegged to the US currency at a rate of five gourdes to the dollar. As such, it became common practice to refer to a unit of five gourdes as a Haitian dollar (H$), a term that has remained firmly embedded in day-to-day usage. Thus a bag of oranges that costs 50HTG may be quoted to you as costing H$10. You'll get used to multiplying or dividing by five as necessary, but it's a system that's guaranteed to cause at least short-term confusion (particularly if you're simultaneously trying to convert the sum in your head into a base currency like US dollars). It can be handy to picture the bank notes as denominations of Haitian dollars themselves – thus the 100HTG bill is actually H$20, 250HTG is H$50, and so on.

The Haitian dollar merely gives the impression that Haiti has a dual-currency economy, but the power of the American greenback actually makes this supposition a reality. Big-ticket items like hotel rooms, car hire, plane tickets and many services are quoted and payable in US dollars. The greenback really is king in Haiti, and you should bring plenty of them – in both high and low denominations. In major towns you can usually also change euros, Canadian dollars and Dominican pesos, but forget about bringing any other currency.

Cash is the most practical way to go in Haiti. **Changing money** is straightforward enough, provided that you avoid the horrendously long queues at any bank. Money-changing shops are widespread, but you can also change money at almost any minimarket or supermarket – there's often a separate counter by the cashier. You'll often also see men with rolls of notes in the street, who'll approach you to change cash. I've invariably found them to be straightforward and honest, but the obvious security caveats about whipping your wallet out on the street to fumble through your stash of US$100 bills apply – such transactions work best if you need a quick 20 bucks changed and have the note ready to go in your pocket.

ATMs are mostly a practical concern in Port-au-Prince, which is hardly a surprise when you learn that nearly 90% of the banking activity in the country takes place in the capital. The biggest concentration of **ATMs** (mostly Sogebank, and, to a lesser extent, Unibank) are found away from downtown Port-au-Prince in Pétionville, but you can also find machines in some of the larger supermarkets, as well as the fast-food chain Epi d'Or. I've only been able to find a handful outside the metropolitan Port-au-Prince area, in Jacmel, Cap-Haïtien, Jérémie and Saint-Marc, but hopefully this will improve over the lifetime of this guide. This may well change in the future, but for now you're advised to carry plenty of funds when travelling beyond the capital.

Credit cards are increasingly accepted at hotels – if you're paying over about US$80 for a room you'll almost certainly be able to put it on your plastic, although it's sensible to check in advance. Upscale shops, travel agents and even the bigger supermarkets also take credit cards, although invariably being outside Port-au-Prince makes it more likely that you may have to resort to cash. Before arriving in Haiti, make sure that your bank knows you'll be using your card in the country.

HOW MUCH IS ... ?

1.5 litre bottle of water	20–30HTG
Bottle of beer	50HTG
Street snack (*fritay*)	20HTG
Gallon of petrol	240HTG
Moto-taxi ride (short hop)	25–50HTG
Minibus from Port-au-Prince to Jacmel	100HTG

Finally, if you need funds sent from home, you can either get an international transfer made to a local bank (more long queues again), or get it wired to a money transfer agency. You can find these in even the smallest town in Haiti – the importance of remittances from the diaspora make them a crucial pillar of the Haitian economy. Branches of **Western Union** (*www.westernunion.com*) and **C.A.M.** (*www.camtransfert.com*) are the most common. Agency fees are paid by the sender, while the recipient pays around US$1.50 – a levy introduced in 2011 to help fund the Martelly administration's free primary education programme.

BUDGETING

Visitors are often surprised that in a country like Haiti, where so many people survive on a dollar a day, travel can be relatively expensive. Once largely self-sufficient, the Haitian economy is now heavily dependent on imports and US dollars. This makes for a strangely paradoxical situation where some things can be very cheap (public transport, street food), and others quite expensive (private transport, hotels).

Accommodation will be the biggest proportion of your budget. Finding a room under US$50 is difficult, and it's more realistic to assume that you'll be paying US$80 or more. Local buses and the like are very inexpensive (a matter of a few dollars for trips of a couple of hours), but once you get into private car hire, your daily spend can easily hit US$200. Eating out at restaurants, you can get by on as little as US$15 a day (less if you stick to street food and stay off the booze), while at a restaurant in Pétionville it's easy to spend that alone on a main course.

GETTING AROUND

Haiti is not a large country to travel around, and has a road network of variable (although improving) quality, and a decent selection of internal flights from Port-au-Prince.

Port-au-Prince sits squarely in the centre of the national highway system, and the fact that all roads lead to the capital makes it either a convenient base to travel from, or an unavoidable annoyance if you'd prefer to avoid getting sucked into its traffic gridlock. From Port-au-Prince, Route National 1 heads north to Gonaïves and then over the mountains to Cap-Haïtien. At Gonaïves, the road also splits to lead to Port-de-Paix along RN5. East of the capital, RN3 passes through Mirebalais and Hinche, and continues on to Cap. In the south, RN2 passes through Léogâne and Miragoâne on the way to Les Cayes and Port Salut. Side branches split off towards Jacmel (RN4) and Jérémie (RN6). For the most part, these roads are well paved. Notable exceptions include the terribly pot-holed roads from Gonaïves to Cap-Haïtien and Port-de-Paix, and the unsealed stretches from Hinche to Cap-Haïtien and from Les Cayes to Jérémie, although at the time of writing all were either under active improvement or were scheduled for work. Away from the national highways, road quality can be highly variable. The rainy climate means that unmaintained tarmac roads quickly attract pot-holes, while unsealed roads of packed earth or gravel can become equally slow and treacherous in heavy rains.

For trip planning, by far the best map commercially available is the *Haïti Carte Touristique*, produced by the Ministry of Tourism. You can find it in larger supermarkets and some bookshops in Port-au-Prince and Pétionville. It's a little outdated in places and carries a few errors (all corrected in this book), but has a useful street map of Port-au-Prince on the reverse side.

BY AIR Three airlines operate flights within Haiti, with Cap-Haïtien (nine hours by road from Port-au-Prince) being the best-served destination. Flight times are short – no flight lasts more than 40 minutes, while at ten minutes, the hop from Port-au-Prince to Jacmel feels barely long enough for the plane to reach altitude before you realise you are descending to land. All domestic flights from Port-au-Prince depart from **Aérogare Guy Malary** (*2250 1127*), next door to the international terminal.

The busiest operator is **Tortug'Air** (*2812 8000/3771 8550;* e *info@tortugair.com; www.tortugair.com*), who run four flights a day to Cap-Haïtien, as well as daily flights to Jérémie and Port-de-Paix. Ignore their own advertising claiming to run a service to Les Cayes – this hasn't operated in several years, and is unlikely to return. However, rumours regularly abound that its once-popular weekend flight to Jacmel will return to the flight schedule.

A newer operator is **Salsa** (*2813 1222/1223;* e *reservations@flysalsa.com; www.flysalsa.com*), who have up to five flights a day to Cap-Haïtien. In September 2011, Salsa suffered an air crash when one of its planes came down near Cap-Haïtien during heavy rain. Both the pilots and the only passenger were killed.

One-way prices are around US$110 to Cap-Haïtien and US$130 to Jérémie and Port-de-Paix. Online booking is available – reliable if you're departing from the more organised airports at Port-au-Prince or Cap-Haïtien, but regular travellers advise that you're as well to also call to confirm your seat if you're flying out of Jérémie or Port-de-Paix.

The aircraft used are small – typically 16-seater Beechcraft – which means that strict baggage limits apply, usually 23kg (50lb). Tortug'Air in particular has a poor reputation with bags: you can happily purchase excess baggage but the finite amount of space on the plane means that if the flight is fully booked, other bags may get left on the ground to follow on later. This is frustrating enough if you're flying to Cap-Haïtien and the bags can be put on a flight later in the day, but potentially disastrous if your bags go astray to Jérémie. Needless to say, it's best to try to keep an eye on your bags at all times if possible (I've sometimes been on flights where I could carry my bags on to the tarmac and put them on the plane myself), but you should always carry anything valuable – money, laptop, medicines – in your carry-on bag.

American-run **Mission Aviation Fellowship** (MAF; *+1 208 498 0800 (USA);* e *flyhaiti@maf.org; www.mafhaiti.org*) has the most extensive domestic network in Haiti, flying to some of the country's most remote airstrips. It has two scheduled daily flights, to Pignon (near Hinche) and Jacmel. It also offers charters to Les Cayes, Fond des Blancs, Jérémie, Dame-Marie, Anse Rouge, Môle Saint-Nicolas, Port-de-Paix, Cap-Haïtien, Ouanaminthe, La Gonâve, Gonaïves and Hinche. MAF do not operate on Sundays. There are three price brackets for the flights, in order of increasing cost: mission groups, NGOs, and the general public. One-way tickets to Pignon cost around US$45, while charters start at US$240 for the smallest plane. In all cases, you should email your flight request as far in advance as possible.

MAF operate three single-propeller Cessna planes in Haiti – two five-seaters and a nine-seater. Luggage is limited to 11kg (25lb), and according to how full the flight is, excess baggage may or may not be allowed.

If you need to charter a helicopter, your best option is **Helico** (*40 Rue Lamarre, Pétionville;* ☎ *2512 8888/3683 8200;* **e** *info@helicohaiti.com; www.helicohaiti.com*).

BY CAR Having your own vehicle gives you the maximum amount of freedom to get around in Haiti. You'll need either your driving licence from your home country or an international driving permit to get behind the wheel. Wearing seatbelts is compulsory, although more honoured in the breach than in the observance.

If you're working with an organisation, it's possible you might have access to one of their vehicles, otherwise there are plenty of car-rental companies in Haiti, including most of the international companies (who are mostly based near the airport in Port-au-Prince. The default vehicle of choice is some sort of 4x4 – few people drive regular cars if they have a choice, as Haitian roads are demanding on vehicle maintenance. Be warned that rental prices are high – starting at around US$150 per day or US$200 if you also want a driver. At the time of writing, fuel costs floated around 240HTG (US$6) for a gallon of petrol, 160HTG (US$4) for diesel.

Traffic drives on the right, and wherever there's a clear road there's a tendency for drivers to put their foot down. Too many Haitians drive offensively rather than defensively, and this can take some getting used to. In heavy traffic, no space seems small enough to squeeze a vehicle into, and no corner blind enough to try to overtake on. Get used to using your horn. If at all possible, avoid driving at night – a frightening proportion of drivers seem to eschew the use of headlights, and pedestrians walking in the dark can be hard to see. When parking, it's not uncommon to pay a guardian a few gourdes to watch your vehicle (you'll usually be approached beforehand).

BY BUS Haiti's towns and cities are stitched together by a wide variety of transport of varying shapes and sizes. I'm using the terminology 'bus' here in its loosest sense – you can be lucky enough to get an air-conditioned mini coach, travel with the chickens on a bone-rattling bus, or (most likely) squeeze into a minibus or covered pick-up truck known as a *taptap*.

For most destinations you'll get a choice of different transport types, but most will leave from a standard departure point, called an *estasyon*. The words 'bus station' are far too formal to apply here – in most cases they're more like a car park surrounded by a moderate swirl of anarchy. Touts shout out for passengers, while even more people offer food and drinks for the journey and mobile-phone top-ups.

The longest distances are covered by the biggest vehicles. Imported American school buses are what most people use to travel between Port-au-Prince and, say, Cap-Haïtien or Jérémie. The more organised bus companies brightly repaint them (often involving a love of God, Jesus or the Psalms), but don't be too surprised if you get on a bus whose apparent destination appears to be a school somewhere in the midwest of the USA. Inside, basic seats take three passengers on each side of the aisle, with a seventh quite often squeezed onto a stool in the aisle itself. Do not expect comfort (buying two seats to garner a little more space can be a good idea). Your luggage will hopefully squeeze into the above-seat racks or below, otherwise you'll be expected to tip the guys who put your bag on the roof. For long distances, tickets are sold a day in advance, and buses roughly adhere to a set departure time. If the journey is more than about four hours, expect at least one meal stop.

More common for journeys of up to a few hours are *taptaps*. These are fill-and-go vehicles – either minibuses or pick-up trucks with a roof added and bench seating along the back. Seats next to the driver are more comfortable, and attract a slightly higher fare. A pick-up taptap should take six passengers on each bench, but invariably squeezes in a few more in the middle (often sat on the sacks and pots of

MOTORBIKES IN HAITI

Kohl Threlkeld

When I first arrived in Port-au-Prince in the middle of August I immediately noticed two things: the staggering heat, and all the motorcycles. It was the latter that made me particularly pleased – I knew before I came that I wanted to buy one, but I wasn't sure how 'motorcycle friendly' Haiti would be. Haiti basically runs on motorcycle transportation thanks to the cheap Chinese bikes that are for sale just about everywhere. They cost between US$800 and US$1,200, and maintenance is cheap too; even in remote villages, I've easily found spare parts.

Navigating the paperwork process to buy the motorcycle is the hardest part. To buy a motorbike you need a National Identification Number, which requires you to have a *permis de séjour* (residency visa) – people who come to Haiti for a short time may want to look at either borrowing a motorcycle or buying one and putting it in the name of a local friend. Either way, you need a driver's licence with a motorcycle endorsement on it, be it Haitian or international. I used a larger and more reputable motorcycle dealer who offered the services of obtaining all necessary documents for me for an extra US$100. When driving always keep a copy of your insurance and registration papers along with your driver's licence and passport/*permis de séjour*. Police checkpoints are common and not having the paperwork proving you own the motorcycle could result in it being seized.

Watching helmetless Haitians wearing flip-flops dart in and out of traffic, I'll admit that the thought of driving a motorbike in Port-au-Prince initially seemed like a suicide mission. But there's a system to the chaos and, after zipping by cars that were stuck in the endless traffic jams that plague Port-au-Prince, I realised it's really the only way to get around in the city. However, I learned the hard way not to expect cars to give me the right of way. Also, it's best to ride at night only if you are familiar with the road you are on to avoid any open sewers or large holes; heavy rains can also make flash flooding a real hazard.

The Chinese bikes aren't without their quirks, so a careful and knowledgeable mechanic is crucial. After watching the first mechanic I went to put my front shocks on backwards, and the next one put my brake caliper on upside down, I decided to invest in finding a good one. Most motorbike-owning expats shared similar stories to mine, so ask around for some recommendations.

On the other hand, if I have a flat tyre I am never far from a *kawochouman* (tyre-repair guy) who will pull out my inner tube and, using an impressive homemade contraption involving petrol, burning rubber, and a piston from a car engine, have me back on the road in no time. Experiences like these define owning a motorcycle in Haiti. For me this has not only been a traffic-beating convenience, but it has also been a gateway to learning the language, culture, and seeing incredible sights I would otherwise not have discovered.

fellow passengers), and maybe a couple more on the roof rack. As well as transport between towns, taptaps also ply set routes within cities. In Port-au-Prince, taptaps have even been elevated to the realms of travelling art, with radically converted chassis and bright paint jobs that verge on the psychedelic, covered in paintings of anything from Bible scenes to hiphop and football stars. Just stand at the side of the road and flag them down as they approach – take the same approach in rural areas where transport is scanty.

The next level down is the truck (*camion*). These can be monster vehicles, heavily overloaded with both inanimate and human cargo – the latter either perched on top of the freight or hanging onto strapping on the inside. They're deservedly the cheapest transport option available.

Finally, a few inventive companies are taking advantage of the improved road network to lay on proper air-conditioned coaches. For now, these are restricted to the route between Port-au-Prince and Les Cayes, but have proved so popular that they put the matching domestic air route out of business. You get a seat to yourself, and frequently a cup of coffee and slice of cake while you wait for departure. Prices are at a premium compared to other options, but the comfort makes it more than worthwhile. It can only be hoped that the services roll out to other cities before too long.

BY TAXI AND MOTO-TAXI Taxis aren't much of a feature of the Haitian transport scene. It's only really in Port-au-Prince and Cap-Haïtien that you'll find regular taxis plying the streets. They're referred to as *publiques*, as unless they pick up a private fare, they tend to run set routes, picking up passengers along the way. You

THE ART OF THE *TAPTAP*

A bus in Haiti doesn't have to be a bus – it can also be a canvas for great art. Brightly painted *taptaps* are as Haitian as rum and Vodou. Most forms of public transportation undergo some form of personalisation by their driver, even if it's just the addition of bullbars on the front of the vehicle and a stencilled slogan (frequently religious) across the windscreen. Intercity buses tend to get a bright new livery, but it's the taptaps of downtown Port-au-Prince where artistic sensibilities are given their most free rein. Chassis are stripped down and rebuilt, with new windows carved from wood into stylish shapes. Fenders are extended, multiple mirrors added, and frequently a loud sound system patched in for some extra loud tunes on the go. When completed, the painters set to work, covering the whole with a bright confection of colour. Anything and everything can be painted on the body of a bus – from nature scenes to jetplanes, hiphop and football stars to bikini girls and the Virgin Mary. Spaces not large enough for a full painting are covered in bright geometric patterns.

Taptap conversion isn't cheap – a ride might only cost a few gourdes, but a decent paint job starts at over US$1,000, with minimum artistic standards regulated by the National Union of Taptap Artisans. So why bother? Drivers see them as peacock displays in a Darwinian competition – the prettiest bus fills up first at the taptap station, leaving dowdier vehicles behind it. Passengers might also surmise that anyone spending big on a paintjob is hopefully also taking care of vehicle maintenance and will drive with at least a modicum of care. Either way, once you've seen them you won't want to drive in a plain minibus ever again.

need to get your eye in to spot them though – rather than going for a distinctive livery, they're marked out by the red ribbon hanging from their rear-view mirror, and licence plates marked 'TP' for transport. Neither leaps out at a great distance, but as drivers will hopefully be looking as actively for a fare as you are for a pickup, you'll hopefully find each other. The set routes have set fares usually around 30HTG (US$0.75), otherwise it's up to you to bargain for the fare (assuming you want a private hire). A few cities such as Les Cayes have private radio taxis that can be booked in advance.

In practical terms, the quickest and easiest way to get around town (and frequently between towns) is to grab a motorbike taxi (moto-taxi, or just plain moto). Fares vary – a ten-minute ride in Port-au-Prince will cost two or three times the equivalent distance in somewhere like Jacmel. Drivers occasionally wear crash helmets themselves, but I've never come across one offering a helmet to a passenger. Two adults can ride pillion, but it's not uncommon to see motos picking up four kids at the school gate to take them home. Bikes are usually sturdy Chinese imports, although places like Jacmel and Gonaïves seem to specialise in weedy little scooters. Either way, moto drivers are often reckless with both their bikes and passengers: hitting the gas whenever the road is clear, or trying to narrowly squeeze between trucks when traffic is tight. Feel free to tell your driver to slow down or otherwise take care as you see fit (I once had to reprimand a driver for sending text messages while driving at high speed). The corollary to this is that if you find a particularly good and trustworthy driver, take his number and use him again.

While taking motos is almost unavoidable in Haiti if you don't have your own vehicle, not all travel insurance policies cover riding pillion on a motorbike, so check your fine print. Accidents are certainly not rare – one resident of Cap-Haïtien joked to me that the emergency unit of the local hospital was dubbed 'Haojin' by medical staff, after the most popular brand of motorbike ridden by accident victims.

BY BOAT Given that nine of Haiti's ten departmental capitals are ports (Hinche being the exception), it's unusual that boat transportation isn't more of a feature in the country. Boats are almost entirely for local travel only – the most notable exception is the weekly overnight ferry between Jérémie and Port-au-Prince. You're more likely to need to use boats if you're travelling to any of the islands such as La Gonâve or Île de la Tortue – in both cases there are a mix of traditional wooden sailing boats and motor boats. There are also short hops aplenty, such as to Île-à-Vache (boat transport is generally provided to your hotel) and around Labadie, where you need to get a boat-taxi (*bateau-taxi*) to the village.

ACCOMMODATION

Haiti offers a reasonable selection of accommodation, yet for the most part finding somewhere to sleep is going to bite into a sizeable proportion of your budget. There's a dearth of good, cheap hotels, and you have to hunt around to find value for money. Paying US$80 for an adequate room isn't uncommon, and paying a lot more for something really decent even more so. As such, even the budget listings included in this guide are higher than would be expected. As you range from moderate to upmarket, there are some excellent hotels. Although rates listed are for double rooms, some places list rates for the room, and either don't distinguish between single and double occupancy, or more rarely, assume that a double means two double beds in the room. Where possible, prices include the 15% tax added on to most bills. Breakfast of some sort is normally included.

ACCOMMODATION PRICE CODES FOR A DOUBLE ROOM

Upmarket	**$$$$**	>US$150
Mid range	**$$$**	US$100–150
Budget	**$$**	US$50–100
Shoestring	**$**	<US$50

As a rule, rooms come with bathrooms. Most places offer air conditioning unless they're in the shoestring category, although even at that price you're likely to get a fan of some sort. The efficacy of any sort of air cooling is dependent on Haiti's less-than-reliable electricity supply. At the bottom end of the spectrum, this may well mean frequent power cuts, while the more you spend, the better your electricity. Some hotels add on a fuel surcharge (typically US$10 per day) to cover generator costs; others may only run their generators at set hours. No matter the level of your accommodation, however, having a torch or candle to hand is never a bad idea.

Wi-Fi is becoming increasingly standard in hotels, except at the cheapest end of the spectrum. Bed-nets to ward off biting insects are the exception rather than the norm.

Shoestring and many budget hotels operate on an hourly as well as a nightly rate. This doesn't automatically mean that they are brothels; many couples take rooms on a short basis because privacy is otherwise hard to find, and such hotels can be as clean and well run as any other. You'll know if you're in a hotel like this if the receptionist asks you if you want a room for a night or just *un moment*. Mirrors on the ceiling can also be a giveaway.

A notable shoestring option in Port-au-Prince are the small number of private guesthouses, often catering to Church mission groups and volunteers. A good, if basic, alternative to hotels, they can be highly sociable as meals are taken together (half-board is the standard). Many operate under a strong Christian ethic (which can include a night curfew) although others are more relaxed about their guests, making these a good way of easing the pain that hotels can inflict on your wallet.

There's no real seasonal difference to prices, except at holiday times. The most notable instances are at Jacmel during Carnival and any beach hotel during Fet Gede at the start of November, which is often wrapped around a long weekend. In both cases, booking as far in advance as possible is advised, and some hotels may insist on a minimum number of nights to confirm the room.

EATING AND DRINKING

Haitian cuisine is an interesting blend of African and French influences, with an occasional taste of hot peppers thrown in for a Caribbean twist. Eating out is typically an unceremonious affair, at a 'bar-resto' or quite possibly served up in a

RESTAURANT PRICE CODES FOR A MAIN COURSE

Expensive	$$$$$	>US$20
Above average	$$$$	US$10–20
Mid range	$$$	US$5–10
Cheap and cheerful	$$	US$2–5
Rock bottom	$	<US$2

polystyrene food box on the street by a woman cooking several pots over a charcoal brazier. Port-au-Prince (specifically Pétionville) has the fanciest restaurants with a wide variety of cuisines, although elsewhere there's not much international food besides burgers, pizza and spaghetti. All the more reason then to stick to Haitian cuisine – *manje kreyòl.*

FOOD If Haiti has a national dish, it has to be rice slowly cooked with beans and served with stock or sauce. *Diri ak sos pwa*, as it's locally known, is everywhere, and you'll eat a lot of it. The sauce, called *bouyon* or *ragu*, is almost always a stew with some potato, onion and tomatoes, spices and preferably meat of some description. This can be beef (*bèf*), goat (*kabrit*) or chicken (*poule*). *Legim* is a stew containing just vegetables, although vegetarians should note that wherever possible, meat is used as a flavouring in the stock. Plantain (*bannann*) is a common accompaniment, either sliced and fried, or stewed. Other starch vegetables to look out for are yam (*yanm*) and *militon* (a type of squash). A variant on rice and beans is *diri djon djon* – tiny dried mushrooms are cooked with the rice, turning it black but imparting a great flavour. Avocadoes (*zaboka*) make a good accompaniment to almost any meal. Their size and creamy yellow-green flesh put modern supermarket varieties to shame.

Soups are popular. Most famous is *soup jomou* (sometimes also called *soup giramoun*) made with pumpkins and eaten every 1 January (Independence Day). Also common is *mayi moulen*, a thick cassava porridge, served as an accompaniment to a main meal, or a countryside staple.

An unexpected addition to Haitian cuisine is the influence of Arab dishes brought in by Syrian and Lebanese immigrants in the early 20th century. Most notable is *kibbeh* – ground beef and bulgur wheat made into balls and fried. Haitian tastes have added a little more spicy hotness to the traditional recipe. Spaghetti is widely available, although it has been adopted almost exclusively as a breakfast dish, often with herring and ideally served liberally covered in tomato sauce. Most hotels will offer eggs and bread as well. Local guava (*gwayav*) jam is excellent, as is the peanut butter, served straight (*mamba*) or with a hint of chili (*mamba piman*).

For a country with such an extensive coastline, it's no surprise that seafood is plentiful. Anywhere near the sea you can find plenty of fish (*pwason*), lobster (*woma*) and especially conch (*lambi*), which is harvested in great numbers. Possibly the numbers are in fact too great: since 2003 the export of queen conch – the mollusc that provides the lambi meat – has been banned by the Convention on International Trade in Endangered Species (CITES), due to collapsing populations across the Caribbean. Anecdotal evidence suggest that lambi is best avoided – while it's common to see conch shells 30cm in length used as house decorations, one lambi fisherman unloading his catch couldn't produce a specimen more than a third fully grown, out of nearly a dozen sacks of conch.

There are plenty of good and cheap street food options for quick eating, mostly falling under the umbrella of *fritay*, or fried food. Pieces of chicken, beef (*tasso*, rather than *bèf* in this case), fish or goat are fried up, but tastiest of all is *griyo*, or fried pork. Vegetarian options include *marinad* (fried dough balls), *accra* (fritters of *malanga*, a starchy root vegetable), and the ubiquitous *bannann pese* (fried plantain). Fritay is best accompanied with a spoon of *pikliz* – cabbage and carrot slaw made with chili-spiced vinegar. Plantain is also thinly sliced to make a local equivalent of potato chips, called *papite*, sold in small bags, often with similarly prepared breadfruit (*lanm veritab*). Another good snack to eat on the go is *pate*, small savoury pastries with meat, fish or chicken.

MUD COOKIES AND PEANUT PASTE

One menu item that can't be recommended is *bonbon té*, better known in the English media as mud cookies. Looking like flat discs, the cookies are made from an edible clay found near Hinche, mixed with salt and vegetable shortening or fat. Once a traditional food supplement for pregnant women (the clay is rich with minerals), they're more often now associated with poverty – a cheap way to fill bellies when rising rice prices hit the poorest hard. Unfortunately, the clay can also be rich in parasites, and cause further health problems.

Chronic undernourishment is sadly not uncommon in Haiti. The World Food Programme estimates that about a third of the population is estimated to be food insecure – living in fear of hunger. Ironically, Haiti itself produces its own food supplements that can be used in emergency situations, a ready-to-use therapeutic food (RUTF) akin to that used by NGOs addressing famine in other countries. A blend of ground peanuts, powdered milk, cooking oil and sugar, fortified with vitamins and minerals, it's used to treat malnourished children. Two NGOs make the paste – **Meds & Food for Kids** (*www.mfkhaiti.org*), based in Cap-Haïtien, and **Partners in Health** (*www.pih.org*), through their Zanmi Agrikol programme in Cange in the Central Plateau. The RUTFs are locally dubbed *Medika mamba* ('peanut butter medicine') and *Nourimanba* respectively, and form an ingenious local solution to a perennial problem.

Haitians don't have a massive sweet tooth, although there's plentiful fruit to be had. Mangoes are deservedly celebrated here. Bananas are also plentiful, but take care to ask for *fig* rather than *bannann*, as the latter will get you plantain. A notable dessert is *pen patate*, sweet potato bread made with milk, nutmeg and cinnamon. *Komparet* is a speciality of Jérémie, a halfway-house between a bread and a cake, sweetly flavoured with ginger, nutmeg and coconut. If you're after straight-up sweets, *dous* is a sort of milky toffee sold in slabs, while *tablet* is a brittle, made with peanuts or cashews.

DRINKS Fruit juices are very popular. Best of all is *shadek*, made from the Haitian grapefruit, and sweeter than regular grapefruit. In season look out for *grenadya* (passion fruit), *seriz* (cherry), as well as *zoranj* (orange). A colder option than a straight juice is a *fresco* made with juice syrup poured over shaved ice. Sold in the street, a fresco cart is invariably surrounded by a small swarm of bees.

Treated water is widely available, and is provided free in most restaurants. You can buy small bottles everywhere (local brands include Crystal and Aquafine), while the Culligan brand has become synonymous with treated water, and is frequently used as shorthand for the five-gallon containers that most treated water comes in. On the street, you'll also see vendors selling small sachets of treated water, for a few gourdes each. Do not drink the tap water.

Coffee is grown throughout Haiti, and is almost uniformly excellent – rich in flavour and lacking in bitterness. Of the locally available brands, Café Rebo and Café Selecto both offer good blends. In the country (and a few guesthouses, if you're lucky), people grow and roast their own. It's not uncommon for home-grown coffee to be sweetened during the processing, with the beans ground with a sugar paste called *rapadou*, giving the final blend a singular taste compared to adding sugar after brewing.

As befits any Caribbean country, Haitians are proud of their rum (*rhum*). The most celebrated brand is Barbancourt, a double-distilled dark rum made from local sugarcane (not molasses, like many rums), and a noted Haitian export. Barbancourt produce a very drinkable three-star rum (aged four years), an even smoother five star (aged eight years) and an eye-wateringly expensive 15-year reserve. Also available is the slightly cheaper rum produced by Bakara.

Very much for the domestic market is *klerin*, a cheaply produced white rum made from molasses. Although available commercially, it's as often produced in local distilleries – Léogâne has several in the centre of town, unmissable open-sided sheds containing wooden vats half the size of a house. Buy directly by taking your own bottle to be filled, noting that since klerin isn't often filtered it can range in appearance from clear to milky-white. It's truly fiery and strong, and not a taste everyone can acquire. Klerin can be infused with fruit or herbs to make traditional medicines – presumably operating on 'the hair of the dog that bit you' principle of curative drinking.

Haiti has one national beer, Prestige. A light lager, it won a gold medal at the 2000 and 2012 World Beer Cups. The Dominican brand, Presidente, is also widely available.

WHERE TO EAT AND DRINK The standard eating establishment in Haiti is the bar-resto, slightly informal places which serve up a handful of dishes along with cold beers and rum. Breakfasts can be big, but lunch tends to be the main meal of the day (as a result, some places in smaller towns will open in the morning but close for food by early evening). Menus are frequently open to loose interpretation, and you may find it easier simply to ask what's on offer. Bar-restos are big on beans and rice with plantains and one or two meat options.

Street food is widespread, and you don't have to go far to find women with simple stalls and a couple of big pots of food serving up meals into polystyrene containers, which must all surely be Haiti's most popular and ugliest street trash item. Food is cooked over coals and then usually covered to slowly cool until it's all been served up, a potential breeding ground for food poisoning (for similar reasons I'd exercise a similar degree of caution over *fresco* sellers. The other popular street food sellers are those frying up batches of fritay to eat on the go.

At the other end of the spectrum are more formal restaurants. Port-au-Prince has the widest selection of restaurants on offer, more specifically in Pétionville, where you can eat anything from Chinese and Thai food or dine in fine French restaurants or hip salad bars. Outside the capital the choice becomes more restricted, with Creole fare the order of the day, but you can usually also find pasta, pizza and burgers, as well as great seafood along the coast.

PUBLIC HOLIDAYS AND FESTIVALS

The following are fixed public holidays in Haiti, when you can expect government offices and many businesses to shut. In addition, the moveable Easter feast day of Good Friday (usually falling in April) is also a public holiday.

1 January	Independence Day
2 January	Ancestors' Day
12 January	Anniversary of the 2010 earthquake
1 May	Agriculture and Labour Day
18 May	Flag Day

17 October	Anniversary of Jean-Jacques Dessalines's death
1 November	All Saints' Day (Day of the dead)
2 November	All Souls' Day
18 November	Anniversary of the Battle of Vertières
25 December	Christmas Day

Taken together, 1–2 November are more popularly celebrated as Fet Gede, the Vodou festival of the dead. This is the biggest holiday of the year, and many people take the opportunity to wrap it around a long weekend – if you're travelling to the beach at this time, book accommodation well in advance.

The weekends flanking Shrove Tuesday, immediately before Lent (falling in February or March) are the time to celebrate Haitian Carnival (*Kanaval*). The exact dates are usually only fixed a few months in advance. The two biggest Carnival celebrations are in Jacmel and Port-au-Prince, and are held on subsequent weekends so as not to clash. The three days after Carnival are a national holiday. As with Fet Gede, it's a popular time to travel, so beach accommodation books up some time in advance. This is also the case for Carnival in Jacmel, where hotel rooms fill up months in advance for the party.

CARNIVAL Carnival is Haiti's biggest party. It is held annually after Shrove Tuesday, to mark the start of Lent. Every town has its own celebrations, with the national

FETES PATRONALES

The following towns and cities celebrate their patron saints' days (*fêtes patronales* or *fêtes champetres*) on the following days:

Port-au-Prince	19 March (St Joseph), 26 July (St Anne), 15 August (Our Lady of the Assumption)
Camp Perrin	26 July (St Anne)
Cap-Haïtien	25 July (St James), 15 August (Our Lady of the Assumption)
Croix des Bouquets	1st Sunday of October (Our Lady of the Rosary)
Fermathe	25 July (St James)
Fort Liberté	19 March (St Joseph)
Gonaïves	1 November (St Charles)
Hinche	8 December (Our Lady of the Immaculate Conception)
Jacmel	1 May (St James and St Philip)
Jérémie	25 August (St Louis)
Labadie	16 July (Our Lady of Mount Carmel)
Léogâne	23 August (St Rose of Lima)
Les Cayes	15 August (Virgin Mary)
Milot	8 December (Our Lady of the Immaculate Conception)
Miragoâne	24 June (St John the Baptist)
Mirebalais	25 August (St Louis)
Môle Saint-Nicholas	6 December (St Nicholas)
Ouanaminthe	15 August (Virgin Mary)
Pétionville	29 June (St Peter)
Petit Goâve	15 August (Our Lady of the Assumption)
Port-de-Paix	28 April (St Louis Marie de Monfort)

ATTENDING A VODOU CEREMONY

Many *houngans* and *mambos* will be happy for foreigners to attend a Vodou ceremony, although it's essential that you check in advance. This isn't just a matter of politeness; ceremonies are often not pre-announced, so you'll need to visit the *ounfò* or *peristyle* to see if anything is planned. Here are some tips to help you get the most out of your attendance:

- Vodou temples are often brightly painted on the outside with images of the *lwa*, but can otherwise be hard to find – ask around to find the nearest *peristyle*.
- Bring an offering to the ceremony for the houngan or mambo. Rum is used widely in Vodou ceremonies, so a good bottle of Barbancourt makes an excellent gift.
- Always ask for permission before getting your camera out, and note that there may be some religiously sensitive parts of the ritual that you may not be allowed to witness.
- Cash donations (for the lwa or upkeep of the temple) aren't uncommon, so be prepared.
- Go with a local who can translate if necessary and point out many of the hidden symbols of the ceremony.
- With dancing a big part of ceremonies, be ready to join in if asked, although it's also fine just to sit on the sidelines (taking part in the dancing does not mean you'll be mounted by a lwa).
- Not all Vodou ceremonies necessarily involve animal sacrifice, but many do. Be prepared for this.
- Many ceremonies can go late into the night – have transport back to your residence lined up in advance.

Carnival held in downtown Port-au-Prince. There are long parades with decorated floats and monstrous speakers, and long before the event bands release special songs they hope will become adopted as the official Carnival anthem – the weeks running up to the party are dubbed 'pre-Carnival', with plenty of sound systems building up the excitement and rara bands parading in the streets. Thousands of people hit the streets in a blurry revel of music, dancing and drinking.

Jacmel holds its Carnival a week before the national event. For visual spectacle, it manages to out-do the Port-au-Prince party by dint of its seemingly endless parade of bright papier-mâché sculptures and surreal street theatre. For more information, see box, *Jacmel Carnival*, page 148.

VODOU FESTIVALS There are many small local Vodou festivals, usually tied to a particular lwa and location, but several have slipped their bounds to become big events on the national calendar – either celebrated across the country, or as a focus for pilgrimage to a particular spot.

By far the most widely celebrated festival is **Fet Gede**, strung across 1–2 November (All Saints' and All Souls' days). This is the Vodou festival of the dead, marked across the country in honour of the Gede, the intertwined lwa of death and sexuality. Fet Gede celebrations often start with a traditional Catholic church Mass, but then proceed to the cemeteries. Black and purple costumes are the colours of the Gede, with celebrants also whitening their faces to make themselves corpse-like. One-eyed sunglasses and top hats are also *de rigueur*, in honour of Baron Samedi, master of the dead. The Gede are tricksters and enemies of hypocrisy, and regarded as being particularly close to the masses, which may account for the festival's popularity. Those possessed by them exhibit the most lewd and raucous behaviour. Sacrifices are made, ancestors are communed with and much rum is drunk. Gede celebrations usually take place in the evening, and continue late into the night.

Souvenance is a huge festival every Easter, held at a site of the same name near Gonaïves. The lwa Ogue (or Ogue Feray) is venerated here, and people bathe in sacred pools. It is a time of spiritual revitalisation, and many of the rituals here can be traced back to west Africa. Souvenance's importance relates to that ancient nature, as well as the role that Ogue is said to have played in inspiring the freed slaves of the Haitian Revolution. For more information, see box, *Souvenance*, page 212.

Every July, Vodou and Catholic pilgrims alike make their way to **Saut d'Eau** near Mirebalais. A beautiful waterfall streams from the hills, a spot beloved by Ezili Danto, and also the site of a 19th-century apparition of the Virgin Mary (frequently used as a counterpart to Ezili). A statue of the Virgin is paraded through town, while Vodou celebrants bathe in the waterfalls, offering prayers to the lwa. For more information, see *Saut d'Eau*, page 216.

Also taking place every July is the pilgrimage to **Plaine du Nord**, just outside Cap-Haïtien. A sacred muddy pool here is dedicated to Ogue Feray, and hosts a week-long celebration of rituals, baptisms and purifications. For more information, see *The Plaine du Nord*, page 192.

OTHER FESTIVALS In addition to these bigger festivals, every town and city also celebrates their patron saints' days, with music parades and other events. Particularly away from the cities, these are big days out and are worth diverting for to get an unvarnished taste of Haitians traditionally celebrating their own culture. See box, *Fêtes patronales*, page 78, for a list of dates for the main towns (smaller towns have their dates listed where relevant in the guide).

SHOPPING

When it comes to bringing home souvenirs, the problem is what *not* to buy: the richness of Haiti's arts and crafts scene means that you can be overwhelmed by choice.

There are plenty of shops run by artisan co-operatives in Port-au-Prince and elsewhere; in the handicrafts capital Jacmel you'll frequently be able to buy direct from the artists themselves. Particularly good places to find arts and crafts include the Marché de Fer in downtown Port-au-Prince, Croix de Bouquets for its elaborate metal art, and Jacmel for papier-mâché masks and painted wood. Haiti's most celebrated artists are sold in the more rarefied galleries of Pétionville; if you're just looking for something cheap and cheerful there are plenty of vendors turning the streets into open-air galleries by hanging canvases on public walls. Pétionville also has several good shops selling beautiful clothes, bags and shoes by local designers.

For more everyday items, Port-au-Prince seems to abound in supermarkets stocked with both local and imported goods. If you're hankering after your favourite breakfast cereal, there's a good chance you'll be able to find it somewhere.

When it comes to shopping in the markets for fresh produce and the like, it inevitably takes some time to discover the 'true' price of goods. Fruit and vegetables tend to be sold in piles or measured out in volume rather than by weight, and some vendors seem to be happy to charge what they think a *blan* will pay rather than what they would normally sell for. It's worth asking at a few places to see how prices are set (always remembering how easily people slip between gourdes and Haitian dollars). One tip is to ask for a certain price – say, 100HTG of mangoes – rather than a set amount, to get a feel of the cost of things. If you do end up haggling, it's best to keep things leavened with humour rather than outrage at the prices on offer. Try to retain a sense of proportion too; if it comes down to arguing over just a few gourdes, remember that you're undoubtedly a lot better off than the person you're dealing with.

ENTERTAINMENT

Music often seems to be everywhere in Haiti, and makes up a good proportion of the entertainment scene.

Seeing RAM play their regular Thursday night concert at the Hotel Oloffson is a particularly great Haitian experience. There are plenty of nightclubs that go on until the small hours, often with live music. In Pétionville you can take dance classes to learn how to dance properly to kompa music. If you're after something a little different, Port-au-Prince hosts its own **International Jazz Festival** (*www.papjazz.org*) every January. There are also regular concerts by the Sainte Trinité Chamber Orchestra, which is attached to the music school of the Episcopalian cathedral of the same name in downtown Port-au-Prince. The orchestra celebrated its 50th anniversary in 2012, and seeing them is a rare introduction to Haitian-composed classical music.

The best way to get an idea of upcoming concerts is to look for the big temporary billboards that spring up at busy road junctions. The review and listings website **Manman Pemba** (*www.manmanpemba.com*) is also a good place to start, although its main focus is on Port-au-Prince. There aren't many large music venues, so bigger concerts tend to be restricted to places like the Parc Historique de la Canne à Sucre on the outskirts of Port-au-Prince, or some of the beach hotels on the Côte des Arcadins. Cover charges can be high – US$50 or more isn't unknown for big events. In the country, many musical events are tied to a town's *fête patronale* (see page 79).

Football (soccer) is the main spectator sport, and going to a Ligue Haïtienne match is a great way to take the pulse of the country. If you can't make this, it's just as much fun to go to a bar and down a few Prestiges with the locals while watching Manchester United or Barcelona play on satellite.

PHOTOGRAPHY

Haiti is an amazingly photogenic country, and photography is an integral part of travelling, but taking photos with sensitivity is essential. Haitians can be acutely aware of how their country is represented in foreign media as being poverty- and disaster-stricken, and such attitudes can come into play the moment you get out your camera. This sensitivity is long-standing, and was captured in the satirical poem *Tourist* by the poet Félix Morisseau-Leroy back in 1951, when Haiti was experiencing its first tourist boom:

Tourist, don't take my picture/Tourist, don't put me in/I'm too ugly/Too dirty/I'm much, much too thin … Tourist, don't take my picture/You don't understand my pose/You don't understand a thing/It's none of your business, I say/Gimme five cents, tourist/And then – be on your way!

Scenic views are one thing, but be extremely circumspect about photographing scenes of clearly visible poverty. Post-earthquake tent camps and rubble are sadly likely to persist for the foreseeable future, and it's easy to cause offence by blithely taking out your camera. Even taking street scenes, you may find people turning away or hiding behind their hands. If taking pictures of individuals, always ask permission, and if you promise to send someone a copy, do make sure you follow up on it.

MEDIA AND COMMUNICATIONS

TELEVISION AND RADIO Haiti has two main television stations, Télé Haiti and the state-run Télévision Nationale d'Haïti, as well as several smaller stations that purely broadcast locally. Broadcasts are in a mix of Creole and French. Neither is a thrilling watch, but as with television all over the world, watching the adverts gives an interesting insight into local culture. Satellite television (French and American channels) is pretty widespread, and you can bet that whenever there's a big English or Spanish football match on, it'll be showing somewhere near you.

Radio is by far the most important media. Every town has its own selection of FM stations, but some of the most popular include Metropole (100.1FM), Radio Kiskeya (88.5FM), Radio Caraïbes (94.5FM) and Signal FM (90.5FM). The first station to broadcast in Creole rather than French was the now-defunct Radio Haïti Inter, founded by the journalist Jean Dominique in the 1960s. Regularly calling Haiti's leaders to account, Dominique was assassinated in 2000. His perpetrators have never been called to justice.

NEWSPAPERS Haiti's press is primarily in French. The two biggest daily newspapers are **Le Nouvelliste** (*www.lenouvelliste.com*) and **Le Matin** (*www.lematinhaiti.com*), in print since 1898 and 1907 respectively. Also available are the weekly **Haiti Progrès** (*www.haitiprogres.com*) and **Haiti Liberté** (*www.haiti-liberte.com*), published in French, Creole and English.

French newspapers and magazines are relatively easy to find, especially in Port-au-Prince. English-language press is harder to track down, and expensive – there's not much choice between *Newsweek*, *Time*, the occasional copy of *The Economist* and a smattering of American lifestyle and gossip magazines. Haiti has its own glossy fashion and lifestyle magazine, **Rebelle** (*www.rebellehaiti.com*), aimed squarely at the moneyed elite.

TELEPHONE There are three main providers: Natcom, Digicel and Voila. Natcom is the old national Telelco, privatised in 2010 and now owned by the Vietnamese company Viettel. Natcom primarily provides land lines, and is currently undergoing a massive investment in fibre-optic cabling across the country. In late 2011 it also launched into the highly competitive mobile-phone market, dominated by **Digicel** (*www.digicelhaiti.com*) and **Voila** (*www.voila.ht*). Digicel is the largest

MISSED CONNECTIONS

Haiti's telephone system often appears to be in a state of permanent revolution. Land lines are often out of service, and the national provider, Natcom, is only very slowly recabling the country, upgrading to fibre-optic lines as it goes. Many businesses keep several numbers, each belonging to the different operators, and changing with frustrating regularity. While every effort has been made to keep contact details current, it's more than likely that many telephone numbers will change during the life of this guidebook.

telecoms provider in Haiti, and its red-and-white branding can be seen absolutely everywhere, with Voila's lime-green livery in second place.

Roaming charges quickly add up, so if you're in Haiti for any length of time you're best buying a local phone or SIM card (Haiti uses the GSM network). SIMs cost about 200HTG (US$5), although you'll need to take some form of ID to buy one. You can top up your credit by buying scratchcards from street vendors – easily identifiable as they tend to wear phone company tabards. They can also top your phone up by sending credit direct to your number. In both cases, note that if you buy, say, 100HTG of credit, you actually receive 90HTG – the remainder is the vendor's fee.

There are no local phone codes in Haiti.

INTERNET Getting online is straightforward in Haiti. Wi-Fi access is increasingly common in hotels, and cybercafés are plentiful, typically charging around 30HTG (US$0.75) per hour.

For more portable internet, USB modems are available from **Natcom**. These cost around 1,600HTG (US$40) for the modem plus SIM card, and then unlimited internet access for about 1,500HTG (US$38) a month. An alternative is to get a fixed modem from **Access Haiti** (*www.accesshaiti.com*) or **Multilink** (*www.multilink.ht*), although initial set-up costs are slightly higher than the USB option.

POST Haiti's postal service is faltering at best. Anything more valuable than a postcard is best sent through an international courier – DHL, FedEx (through local contractor Anndex), TNT and UPS all maintain offices in Port-au-Prince. If you're here longer-term, courier firm **Aeropost** (☎ *3779 0700/3776 0700; www.aeropost.com*) offers a mail and package service, providing customers with an address in Miami and then shipping direct to Port-au-Prince – a service explicitly touted to allow residents the joys of internet shopping.

BUSINESS

A key plank of Michel Martelly's presidency has been the message that Haiti is 'open for business'. Investment conferences seem to take place on an almost monthly basis in Port-au-Prince, while organisations like Brand Haiti seek to encourage a newer, more positive, image of the country as a place for business. The four main investment sectors being pursued by the government are garment assembly, tourism, agribusiness and telecommunications. There are undoubtedly great investment opportunities for the patient investor, but despite official enthusiasm Haiti ranks poorly in the World Bank's annual *Doing Business Report*. According to the 2012 survey, Haiti sits 176th out of 183 countries for ease of doing business (for more details see *www.doingbusiness.org*). It's likely that the pro foreign-investment government will attempt to tear up regulations in the next few years to make Haiti more attractive to incoming businesses.

There are half-a-dozen separate procedures involved in registering a business, and the process takes about a week. A limited-liability corporation takes about three months and a dozen processes to register – half of what it was five years ago. Registration is done at the Direction Générale des Impôts (DGI), which is part of the Economic and Finance Ministry. Those setting up a business must have a residence permit (*permis de séjour* – see *Red tape*, page 50), as well as be registered for tax in Haiti.

Foreigners are permitted to own property in Haiti (a key part of the USA's rewriting of the Haitian constitution during the 1915–34 occupation). There are no restrictions on opening bank accounts or on bank transfers of capital. Access to credit was improved by legal reform in 2010, but importing or exporting materials is slow, taking a month on average to move a container through customs. Getting construction permits is painfully slow, and in 2012 the government increased permit fees at the Ministry of Public Works – a possibly unhelpful move given the need to improve regulation of building standards in an earthquake zone.

Haiti has a 30% corporate tax rate, 15% capital gains tax, and social security tax of 6% on gross salaries. Larger-scale businesses are being encouraged to Haiti by the establishment of duty-free industrial zones in Port-au-Prince (near the airport), as well as the flagship Caracol industrial zone near Cap-Haïtien. Garment-assembly businesses continue to be particularly encouraged by the US Hope II Act, which allows duty-free access to the American market.

Corruption isn't always out in the open, but is present behind the scenes. In 2011 Transparency International rated Haiti 175th out of 183 countries for levels of public corruption – a declining rating since the 2010 earthquake, as it's widely believed that the vast influx of aid money has increased opportunities for both petty and institutional graft. It's not uncommon to make a payment to speed up a bureaucratic process although international businesses can and should try to operate without resorting to such measures.

OTHER USEFUL DETAILS

American Chamber of Commerce in Haiti 8 Rue Moïse, Pétionville; ☎ 2511 3024/2940 3024; http://amchamhaiti.com

Brand Haiti http://brand-haiti.org

Centre de Facilitation des Investissements 27 Rue Armand Holly, Debussy; ☎ 2514 5793/2813 0369; www.cfihaiti.net. Government-run investment agency.

Chambre de Commerce et d'Industrie d'Haïti Bd Harry Truman, Port-au-Prince; ☎ 2512 5141/3556 7116; www.ccih.org.ht

Chambre Franco-Haïtienne de Commerce et d'Industrie 5 Rue Goulard, Pétionville; ☎ 2510 8965/2257 1874; www.chambrefrancohaitienne.com

Direction Générale des Impôts 62 Chemin de Dalles, Port-au-Prince; ☎ 2513 0386/0387; www.mefhaiti.gouv.ht/dgi.htm

Ministère du Commerce et de l'Industrie 8 Rue Legitimé, Port-au-Prince; ☎ 2942 1088; http://mci.gouv.ht

LIVING IN HAITI

Large numbers of foreigners travel to Haiti every year to live, whether as aid workers, volunteers or missionaries. The exact number of foreign residents in Haiti is unknown. It's estimated that there are around 50,000 US citizens in Haiti at any one time (although this includes Haitians with dual nationality), while the Minustah contingent alone was around 12,000 strong at the beginning of 2012. Port-au-Prince inevitably attracts the highest proportion of expats.

If you're moving to Haiti with an organisation, it's likely that they'll arrange somewhere to live for you. Most people are shocked at how expensive accommodation in Port-au-Prince can be. Rents were driven through the roof following the earthquake, by a combined influx of free-spending international organisations and a decimation of available housing stock. At the start of 2012 it wasn't uncommon to find a two-bed apartment in Pétionville (where many NGOs are based) renting at US$1,500 a month. Prices depend on two things: location and amenities. Naturally, prices drop the further you are away from the popular areas, but this has to be balanced by potentially long commutes in the city's horrendous traffic jams.

In terms of facilities, you need to be explicitly clear when signing a lease as to exactly what's on offer –how dependent you'll be on city power (the less the better) or what electricity you'll be getting from inverters or generators. Water is another important consideration, as most places have their own reservoirs that need to be filled with deliveries from water trucks (rooftop reservoirs also require power for pumping). Building security is also something to be aware of in terms of locked gates, whether there is a building guardian and so on. The larger international organisations including the UN agencies also demand accommodation meets stringent Minimum Operating Residential Security Standards, which may include an armed guard on the gate.

Needless to say, residential prices drop dramatically outside the capital – an apartment in Jacmel will probably cost half of an equivalent place in Port-au-Prince. You can find plenty of rental real estate agents for Haiti online, although somewhat inevitably the best deals are those you hear about once you're in the country.

Many organisations in Haiti ban their employees from taking certain forms of local transport. Taptaps and moto-taxis are usually top of the list. Check in advance what your transport options are, if you'll be provided with a vehicle to drive yourself, or even have a car and driver. Particularly in Port-au-Prince, many organisations have strict security policies that limit travel. This can be frustrating for work but also limits social opportunities such as going out to eat or seeing friends. Be prepared if this will be the case, as several people have described to me the feeling of being trapped by their restrictions.

INVERTERS

Mains electricity in Haiti is provided by the national generating company EDH, but demand far outstrips supply and long power cuts are common in the cities. Large swathes of rural Haiti are simply off the grid altogether. Alternative sources of power are noisy generators or battery inverters, which are more common in domestic use. Solar power is also starting to make inroads into Haiti.

An inverter is essentially a box that converts DC electricity (from batteries) to AC (for use with regular electrical appliances), allowing you to draw power when there's no other electricity. The usual system is to have the inverter also rigged up to the regular power grid so that it can then keep the batteries charged up when there's mains electricity. Many inverters also have a built-in uninterruptible power supply (UPS) to provide protection from power surges. If not, it's worth investing in a UPS to protect your appliances. Several batteries can be rigged up to an inverter to provide increasing amounts of power, although using electrical goods with high wattage (electric cookers) will drain your power very quickly or blow the power completely.

A decent inverter should pretty much run itself, although they do need regular maintenance to keep them in good working order. If the batteries are unsealed, they need to be regularly topped up with distilled water (never tap water, which contains potentially damaging electrolytes). The terminals also need to be kept clean to prevent potential corrosion. Batteries should always be kept off the floor (most typically in locked cages). When you move into a property, always check the system you have, and whether you will be responsible for maintenance or if there's a building guardian who takes cares of things.

Assuming you're free to move around, you may be pleasantly surprised at what's available to you. Port-au-Prince has plenty of large supermarkets stocking imported foods and goods, and most things you want will be available (if you have certain dietary requirements, you can even buy otherwise unexpected items like gluten-free foods, soy milk and so on). Although the choice drops off outside the capital, you can usually find a reasonable range of products, and in most towns there are reasonable pharmacies carrying items like women's sanitary products.

A particularly good resource is the book *How to Work in Someone Else's Country* by Ruth Stark, as well as *The Expert Expat* by Melissa Brayer Hess and Patricia Linderman.

CULTURAL ETIQUETTE

Cultural sensitivity mostly boils down to common sense and having some respect for the people and places you're visiting, and being able to adapt to local customs. Trying to learn some Creole, rather than relying on French, will have an immediate positive impact. Greetings are important, and it's rude to start asking questions of someone you've just met – even if just asking for directions – without exchanging greetings. Older members of society are treated with extra respect. Always ask permission before taking photos but don't be offended if the answer is no, as it often is in Haiti (take note that for some reason, Haiti can seem to have a higher-than-average number of self-appointed busybodies who may approach you to object to your merely taking photos of a street scene in 'their' neighbourhood).

From sex to politics, there are few taboos in Haitian conversation, but be aware that the 2010 earthquake remains an incredibly sensitive subject. Everyone in the affected areas has their own story, but that doesn't mean that they necessarily want to share it, so be very circumspect about bringing the topic up. That said, those interested in politics and aid will frequently be engaged (and occasionally lambasted) over the thorny topic of the pace of post-earthquake recovery.

Haiti is a resource-poor country, so be careful to use energy resources such as water and electricity efficiently, and not to wash in lakes or rivers (regardless of local practices, because of pollution). Try to buy souvenirs from the craftspeople who made them rather than via middlemen (artisan co-operatives are listed in this guide) and patronise small street vendors rather than big supermarkets where possible. Don't bargain unreasonably; although some prices can become inflated due to the 'blan tax', the difference may be the cost of a drink to you but a whole family meal to the vendor – haggling is best done with a sense of humour rather than naked competition.

Here's one particularly egregious example of being a 'bad' visitor to Haiti, which I witnessed a couple of years ago. I was visiting with friends in a town when we came across a group of foreigners standing outside a school that had just finished lessons for the day. They were literally throwing sweets into the throng of children that had gathered around them, who were churning up the surrounding mud in a sugar-filled melee. The street vendors you find outside every school in the country looked on glumly, having lost all chance of custom for the day. We talked with the group when they had finished their 'distribution', and they were pleased to have done something good for the kids they'd turned into a crowd of begging hands. While most of the group were one-week volunteers, their leader had been visiting Haiti for a decade but proudly told us that he'd never seen the need to learn any Creole. When we asked if they'd met the local mayor, who apparently had never heard of their project in his town, they said they'd never had the time but might consider it next time. You may draw your own conclusions.

Ultimately, one of the best ways to travel to Haiti may ultimately be to return home and tell people about your experience. Haitians are acutely aware that most of the world does not see them as a country proud to have found their freedom through the world's only successful slave revolution and gone on to build a country with an immensely rich cultural heritage. Instead, media stereotypes continue to dominate – from 'voodoo' and boat people to dictators and disaster. Haitians love their country and know there is another narrative, so going home with an honest picture of Haiti and being able to tell even as simple an anecdote about having a cold beer on the beach with new friends can be an important counter to those stereotypes. In this instance, the responsible traveller may even be he or she who goes out to *enjoy* Haiti the most, as well as trying to understand its complications.

TRAVELLING POSITIVELY

A trip to Haiti is about being a guest in someone else's home. Haitians welcome guests, but can frequently be sensitive about the motivations of foreigners coming to Haiti, an understandable reaction given the country's history. Reading up on that history, as well as Haiti's culture and many achievements (as well as its troubles) before you travel will help you settle in once on the ground, as well as helping to break the ice with locals once you're there.

You can find good advice on being a responsible tourist from the UK-based Tourism Concern (☎ *020 7753 3330; www.tourismconcern.org.uk*). If you'd like to offset the carbon footprint of your flight, try www.carbonneutral.com, a website which has an easy-to-use emissions calculator and a range of offset programmes.

ORGANISATIONS IN HAITI It's not for nothing that Haiti is jokingly referred to as the 'Republic of NGOs'. The country has the highest density of NGOs per capita in the world. These range from the big players such as Oxfam and the Red Cross through tiny 'mom and pop' set-ups and Church groups to the many Haitian grassroots organisations. The figure of 10,000 organisations is often wheeled out by the media, and while this is almost certainly an exaggeration, no-one really knows the exact number, as the majority of them are not centrally registered with the Haitian government.

Before donating, take time to listen and learn about operations on the ground. Are they building long-term capacity or offering short-term aid? (Note that development is harder than emergency work.) Are they Haitian-led? Are they trying to do themselves out of a job through lasting and self-sustaining programmes? It can be hard to find easy answers, but asking the questions is an important first step.

If you're travelling to Haiti as part of a church volunteer group, a thought-provoking read is *When Helping Hurts* by Steve Corbett and Brian Fikkert, which tackles many of the complicated issues (and unintended consequences) arising from short-term mission trips.

The following is a small selection of primarily local NGOs operating in Haiti:

EarthSpark International www.earthsparkinternational.org. Promoting energy-efficient eco-stoves in Port-au-Prince & Les Anglais to reduce charcoal consumption.

Fonkoze www.fonkoze.org. Haiti's largest micro-finance institution offering financial services to the rural-based poor in Haiti.

Gheskio www.gheskio.org. Pioneering HIV/AIDS organisation founded in 1982. Offers free screening & medical treatment for both HIV & tuberculosis.

Haiti Communitere www.haiti.communitere.org. Runs the Sustainability Resource Center, a hub for international groups to manage on-the-ground projects & network with local organisations.

Haiti Partners www.haitipartners.org. Helping Haitians change Haiti through alternative education, open space & leadership training.
Haitian Sustainable Development Foundation www.sustainablehaiti.org. Supporting community development solutions in Jacmel.
HELP http://uhelp.net. Scholarship programme developing young professionals in Haiti.
Institute for Justice and Democracy in Haiti www.ijdh.org. Working on a local level in Haiti with the Bureau des Avocats Internationaux, human rights lawyers working on post-earthquake displacement issues, women's rights & general advocacy & legal support for the consolidation of constitutional democracy & human rights.

VOLUNTEERING IN HAITI

Saundra Schimmelpfennig

Haiti has always been a popular destination for volunteering, and the number of opportunities has only increased since the 2010 earthquake. Volunteers often come with the belief that any and all assistance is both helpful and desperately needed. Unfortunately, some projects are developed more to meet the needs of the volunteers rather than the people they're trying to help, and some assistance can do more harm than good. Before planning a trip, take the time to choose your volunteer programme carefully.

Three of the commonest projects are construction, education and childcare, but all carry complicating issues.

Construction projects are popular because they feel very concrete and seem to meet an obvious need. This has led to the construction of numerous buildings that are not needed or are quickly abandoned. There's no shortage of local people who are desperate for work and just as good if not better than you at construction, so why is the organisation bringing in volunteers instead of hiring locally?

Teaching English is a common volunteer activity. Unfortunately, unless it is part of a clear and regular curriculum, bringing in volunteers to teach random songs and games can be a distraction that takes time away from teaching core subjects and turns the teacher into the volunteer's assistant. Think carefully, what qualifies you to teach English? How effective a teacher can you be if you don't speak Creole?

While it's an unpleasant thought, there are cases in **childcare** volunteering where unscrupulous people have used non-profits and orphanages to gain access to vulnerable children. Did the organisation conduct a background check on every single volunteer? Children who repeatedly bond with and then are abandoned by volunteers can develop attachment issues and other emotional problems. Why is the organisation bringing in foreign volunteers for childcare when this is something plenty of Haitians are able to do?

Before volunteering for any project here are two things to think about:

First, what is it that you are bringing to the project that local people could not be hired to do – especially if the project had all the money you will spend on plane tickets, immunisations, hotels, and transportation? Often you can provide more help by donating money to a local charity than by going there yourself.

Second, it's worth analysing your own personal goals and incentives for the trip. People often volunteer because they want adventure, personal fulfilment, or a life-changing experience. However, good volunteering is about meeting the needs of beneficiaries, not your own. What are your core motivations?

So how do you make the best volunteer choice? Consider the following:

CREATE JOBS – DON'T COMPETE FOR THEM The unemployment rate in Haiti is extremely high. More than handouts or houses, people want jobs. Jobs let them

KOFAVIV (Commission of Women Victims for Victims) www.kofaviv.org. Provides emergency medical services, peer counselling & safe houses for women who have been raped. Operates an advice hotline, neighbourhood watches, training for men & work with at-risk children in tent camps. Partnered with MADRE (www.madre.org), a global network of community-based women's groups.

Lambi Fund of Haiti www.lambifund.org. Well-regarded organisation strengthening local communities through sustainable agriculture, environmental protection, improved animal husbandry & similar projects.

Let Haiti Live www.lethaitilive.org. Has 2 partner projects: Rebwaze Ayiti (Reforest Haiti), working with JADPE (Youth in Action for Development &

buy food, clothing, or household goods. Weekly wages means they can send their children to school or build their own homes. Without jobs they are reduced to waiting for help and handouts from non-profits.

Well-intentioned volunteers can out-compete disaster survivors for jobs. Volunteers not only work for free, but they also often pay money to be allowed to work. Make sure whatever job you do is not something a local person could be paid to do.

DON'T BRING HANDOUTS WITH YOU Volunteer groups often arrive with boxes of goods to hand out. By bringing in free stuff, you are out-competing local people trying desperately to make a living selling similar goods. To take one example, a colleague of mine saw several people selling shoes in Port-au-Prince within two weeks after the earthquake. At the same time volunteers and celebrities were taking up collections of thousands of shoes to hand out. Handing out donated shoes could destroy their livelihoods, while purchasing shoes from them helps them feed their families.

SPEND MONEY LOCALLY One of the biggest ways you can help is to spend money in the local economy. Stay in local guesthouses, eat at locally run restaurants and buy from street vendors and local stores.

OFFER SPECIALISED SKILLS Small, local non-profits can often benefit from specialised assistance. They don't need help in the villages because their local staff can work with villagers far better if they don't have to translate for and supervise volunteers who don't understand the local language, culture or politics. Although this is not what most volunteers envision, the best support you can give is in the office.

Assistance that local organisations may need might include creating promotional material and presentations, translating websites and promotional materials, applying for grants, giving presentations to English-speaking audiences, computer training for staff or setting up networks, teaching English to staff or tracking down technical resources.

CONSIDER JUST BEING A TOURIST RATHER THAN A VOLUNTEER You can do a lot of good just being a tourist and spending money locally. It's much more helpful to be a good tourist than to work for a bad volunteer programme.

Saundra Schimmelpfennig runs the aid donor advice website Good Intentions Are Not Enough (www.goodintents.org).

ADOPTION AND ORPHANAGES IN HAITI

Several hundred children are internationally adopted in Haiti each year, mostly by Americans. There are around 600 orphanages in Haiti, although most children living in them are not actually orphans, but have been placed there by parents too impoverished to care for them. While many of these orphanages are well run, a number are run as for-profit enterprises with poor standards of care for their children, and look either to maximise income through charitable donations, or generate income through international adoption. The Ministry of Social Affairs, through its over-stretched Institute for Social Well Being & Research (IBESR) is charged with regulating orphanages. Haiti is not a signatory to the Hague Convention on inter-country adoption.

A typical adoption process takes around two years. Permission must be granted from the child's legal custodians (almost always their parents), then prospective adoptive parents are investigated by the IBESR, who give authorisation for the adoption. Finally, a court order grants legal custody, at which point a Haitian passport must be obtained for the child, and an immigration visa for the country of their adoptive parents. During this whole process, the child remains in the orphanage, and may only see those planning to adopt them a couple of times a year.

The earthquake brought several adoption scandals to the fore in Haiti. The US temporarily waived visa restrictions for children who were brought to the States without their adoptive parents having been completely screened, including children from orphanages in areas unaffected by the earthquake. A Baptist missionary was jailed in 2011 for illegally transporting 33 children from orphanages across the Dominican border in the immediate post-earthquake chaos. While enquiries from prospective adoptive parents spiked after 12 January 2010, organisations like UNICEF and Save the Children argue that children's needs are best served by their remaining in their home country and supporting them there – especially in a case like Haiti where their parents are still living and have only placed them in the care of others due to poverty.

Many orphanages rely on foreign charity for support. Do some research if you plan on donating. Are they IBESR registered, with trained staff and well supervised? Is the orphanage located in the child's community, and do they provide information on how the child's contact with its family is maintained? Is the orphanage set up as a family-like setting, with siblings kept together? A good place to start is with the UN's 2009 *Guidelines for the Alternative Care of Children* (available online at *www.iss-ssi.org*) and the 2010 report *Misguided Kindness: Making the right decisions for children in emergencies* (available from *www.savethechildren.org.uk*).

Protection of the Environment) in Cyvadier, Jacmel, through tree nurseries & community compost, & training for local farmers. Also Bri Kouri Nouvèl Gaye (Noise Travels, News Spreads), an alternative media & community mobilisation team working in tent camps, urban neighbourhoods & some rural areas.

Li, Li, Li! www.lililiread.org. Tackling post-earthquake trauma & psycho-social damage in children, by reading aloud in Creole in tent camps.

Meds & Food for Kids www.mfkhaiti.org. Based near Cap-Haïtien, producing the Ready To Use Therapeutic Food *medika mamba*, using locally sourced foods. Also runs emergency feeding programmes.

Mennonite Central Committee in Haiti www.mcc.org. Orgabnisation that has been working in Haiti since 1958, currently running programmes in the Artibonite Valley. Focusing on reforestation &

environmental education, human rights & advocacy for food security.

Partners In Health www.pih.org. Pioneering health NGO co-founded by Paul Farmer, & a major healthcare provider in central Haiti, with community-based treatment & socio-economic support. Operates the impressive new teaching hospital in Mirebalais.

Quixote Center www.quixote.org. Supporting the Jean Marie Vincent Center for Reforestation in Gros Morne, with projects including a model forest, community garden & composting programme & a large network of satellite tree nurseries, as well as horticultural training.

Restavek Freedom www.restavekfreedom.org. NGO working with restaveks (child slaves) in Haiti, including advocacy, direct support for children & families, & community education.

SAKALA, Pax Christi Haiti and Bochika http://paxchristiusa.org/programs/sakala. Multi-dimensional programme in Cité Soleil in Port-au-Prince. Includes a community garden (*Jaden TapTap*), football & education programme, & ecological sanitation.

Sonje Ayiti www.sonjeayiti.com. Working in northern Haiti, mainly around Limonade, on community development through education, micro-credit & promotion/support of social business programmes.

Sustainable Organic Integrated Livelihoods SOIL; www.oursoil.org. Working mostly in Port-au-Prince on ecological sanitation, with integrated approaches to public health, agricultural productivity & environmental destruction.

The Peasant Movement of Papaye www.mpphaiti.org. One of Haiti's largest & most active peasant networks based in the Central Plateau. Working in agricultural development, soil protection, community education & peasant co-operatives.

Ti Kay www.tikayhaiti.org. Based at Port-au-Prince's General Hospital, providing free, high-quality medical care to tuberculosis & HIV patients.

Zafèn www.zafen.org. Offers funding to local businesses & social enterprise projects through credit loans, business advice & education.

Zanmi Lakay www.zanmilakay.org. Providing outreach services, educational grants & medical support for street children in Port-au-Prince.

Bradt Travel Guides

www.bradtguides.com

Africa

Access Africa: Safaris for People with Limited Mobility £16.99
Africa Overland £16.99
Algeria £15.99
Angola £17.99
Botswana £16.99
Burkina Faso £17.99
Cameroon £15.99
Cape Verde £15.99
Congo £16.99
Eritrea £15.99
Ethiopia £17.99
Ethiopia Highlights £15.99
Ghana £15.99
Kenya Highlights £15.99
Madagascar £16.99
Madagascar Highlights £15.99
Malawi £15.99
Mali £14.99
Mauritius, Rodrigues & Réunion £15.99
Mozambique £15.99
Namibia £15.99
Niger £14.99
Nigeria £17.99
North Africa: Roman Coast £15.99
Rwanda £15.99
São Tomé & Príncipe £14.99
Seychelles £16.99
Sierra Leone £16.99
Somaliland £15.99
South Africa Highlights £15.99
Sudan £15.99
Tanzania, Northern £14.99
Tanzania £17.99
Uganda £16.99
Zambia £18.99
Zanzibar £14.99
Zimbabwe £15.99

The Americas and the Caribbean

Alaska £15.99
Amazon Highlights £15.99
Argentina £16.99
Bahia £14.99
Cayman Islands £14.99
Chile Highlights £15.99
Colombia £17.99
Dominica £15.99
Grenada, Carriacou & Petite Martinique £15.99
Guyana £15.99
Nova Scotia £14.99
Panama £14.99
Paraguay £15.99
Turks & Caicos Islands £14.99
Uruguay £15.99
USA by Rail £15.99
Venezuela £16.99
Yukon £14.99

British Isles

Britain from the Rails £14.99
Bus-Pass Britain £15.99
Eccentric Britain £15.99
Eccentric Cambridge £9.99
Eccentric London £14.99
Eccentric Oxford £9.99
Sacred Britain £16.99
Slow: Cornwall £14.99
Slow: Cotswolds £14.99
Slow: Devon & Exmoor £14.99
Slow: Dorset £14.99
Slow: Norfolk & Suffolk £14.99
Slow: Northumberland £14.99
Slow: North Yorkshire £14.99
Slow: Sussex & South Downs National Park £14.99

Europe

Abruzzo £14.99
Albania £16.99
Armenia £16.99
Azores £14.99
Baltic Cities £14.99
Belarus £15.99
Bosnia & Herzegovina £14.99
Bratislava £9.99
Budapest £9.99
Croatia £13.99
Cross-Channel France: Nord-Pas de Calais £13.99
Cyprus see *North Cyprus*
Dresden £7.99
Estonia £14.99
Faroe Islands £15.99
Flanders £15.99
Georgia £15.99
Greece: The Peloponnese £14.99
Helsinki £7.99
Hungary £15.99
Iceland £15.99
Kosovo £15.99
Lapland £15.99
Lille £9.99
Lithuania £14.99
Luxembourg £14.99
Macedonia £16.99
Malta & Gozo £12.99
Montenegro £14.99
North Cyprus £13.99
Serbia £15.99
Slovakia £14.99
Slovenia £13.99
Spitsbergen £16.99
Switzerland Without a Car £14.99
Transylvania £14.99
Ukraine £15.99

Middle East, Asia and Australasia

Bangladesh £17.99
Borneo £17.99
Eastern Turkey £16.99
Iran £15.99
Iraq: Then & Now £15.99
Israel £15.99
Jordan £16.99
Kazakhstan £16.99
Kyrgyzstan £16.99
Lake Baikal £15.99
Lebanon £15.99
Maldives £15.99
Mongolia £16.99
North Korea £14.99
Oman £15.99
Palestine £15.99
Shangri-La: A Travel Guide to the Himalayan Dream £14.99
Sri Lanka £15.99
Syria £15.99
Taiwan £16.99
Tibet £17.99
Yemen £14.99

Wildlife

Antarctica: A Guide to the Wildlife £15.99
Arctic: A Guide to Coastal Wildlife £16.99
Australian Wildlife £14.99
Central & Eastern European Wildlife £15.99
Chinese Wildlife £16.99
East African Wildlife £19.99
Galápagos Wildlife £16.99
Madagascar Wildlife £16.99
New Zealand Wildlife £14.99
North Atlantic Wildlife £16.99
Pantanal Wildlife £16.99
Peruvian Wildlife £15.99
Southern African Wildlife £19.99
Sri Lankan Wildlife £15.99

Pictorials and other guides

100 Alien Invaders £16.99
100 Animals to See Before They Die £16.99
100 Bizarre Animals £16.99
Eccentric Australia £12.99
Northern Lights £6.99
Swimming with Dolphins, Tracking Gorillas £15.99
Through the Northwest Passage £17.99
Tips on Tipping £6.99
Total Solar Eclipse 2012 & 2013 £6.99
Wildlife and Conservation Volunteering: The Complete Guide £13.99
Your Child Abroad £10.95

Travel literature

Fakirs, Feluccas and Femmes Fatales £9.99
The Marsh Lions £9.99
Two Year Mountain £9.99
Up the Creek £9.99

Part Two

THE GUIDE

3

Port-au-Prince

Haiti's buzzing capital is uncompromising and irrepressible. As the economic, political and cultural hub of the country, it's seemingly irresistible to Haitians too, ceaselessly sucking in migrants from across the country – when people say that the 'Republic of Port-au-Prince' is a completely separate country to the rest of Haiti, they're only half-joking.

Around two million people live in the greater metropolitan area, squeezed in between the coastal plains and the high slopes of the mountains that rise above them. Designed for a population a quarter of its size, Port-au-Prince's infrastructure creaks and groans under the pressure, a state of affairs that has only grown since swathes of the city crumbled in the 2010 earthquake. Rebuilding has been slow, and the scars are still plain to see, but contrary to the expectations of many first-time visitors, the city is not just one giant rubble pile.

Far from it. Port-au-Prince's spirit is very much alive. It's a sweaty and noisy place, its streets clogged with street vendors and traffic jams, but it's also a place of lively music, vibrant art and great restaurants, of impromptu soccer games watched with a cold beer from a street vendor, church singing, and impeccably uniformed school children streaming to class every morning. The concrete-block houses of the developing world sit cheek by jowl with fancy 'gingerbread' houses, while the city remains surprisingly green given its uncontrolled development – don't be surprised if you catch sight of a flock of parrots winging their way between mango trees. In all this, perhaps the jokers are right after all – Port-au-Prince *is* Haiti, in all its glory and contradictions, and a mile away from the dangerous and chaotic reputation that swirls around it.

A note on this chapter: most visitors to Port-au-Prince tend to divide their time between either downtown ('la Ville') or up the hill in Pétionville. The majority of sights are found downtown, while Pétionville has a better variety of eating options and shops. Choices for accommodation are split fairly evenly between them, but for the sake of the guide I've divided the listings in two for ease of use.

HISTORY

In the mid 18th century, the French colonial authorities were looking for a site for a purpose-built capital, somewhere between the economic powerhouse of Cap-Français (modern Cap-Haïtien) and the increasingly wealthy southern plantations of the Cul-de-Sac and Léogâne plains. They settled on the wide horseshoe-shaped bay at the foot of the Massif de la Selle, named for the French ship *Prince* that had first weighed anchor there in 1706. In 1749, Port-au-Prince was formally chartered by the King of France as the capital of Saint-Domingue.

Port-au-Prince prospered, and was a key battleground in the Haitian Revolution, during which it was briefly renamed Port-Républicain. The British army held it against Toussaint Louverture, while Dessalines eventually recaptured it for the revolutionaries. Port-au-Prince was a mulatto stronghold supporting Dessalines's eventual rival, Pétion, and two years after independence was finally declared, Dessalines was assassinated at Pont Rouge on the city outskirts. The murder split the country in two, a fact formalised when Pétion successfully repelled a siege of the city against his northern rival Christophe.

The original layout of the city corresponded to the area around the modern districts of Champs de Mars and Bel Air, but in 1831 a new town, Pétionville, was founded on the mountain slopes above the port, with the intention of becoming a new capital. The move never stuck, and Port-au-Prince continued to boom. It was no stranger to trouble. An earthquake in 1770 had devastated the city, leading to an ordinance to enforce building in wood only but leaving it prone to a series of ferocious fires. After the last city-wide blaze in 1925, wooden buildings were finally banned, putting an end to the tropical gingerbread architectural style for which Port-au-Prince was becoming known. On top of this the city was regularly occupied with locally raised armies, which had become the traditional tool of settling disputes in 19th-century Haitian politics.

Port-au-Prince saw its next great facelift during the US occupation, with large-scale infrastructure projects to improve roads and sanitation, as well as the expansion of the city's nascent tram network, extending light rail out to Léogâne and the Cul-de-Sac. At the same time, the closure of regional ports saw Port-au-Prince's economic and political power begin to grow inexorably. Under President Estimé, the city hosted a World Fair to celebrate its bicentennial. The waterfront area around Boulevard Harry Truman (but popularly known as Bicentenaire) was redeveloped as a model city, with parks and fountains.

Such model growth was left to stagnate during the Duvalier years. The rural poor were sucked in from the countryside with the biggest growth taking place in areas like La Saline, north of the port and the regularly flooded slum district of Cité Soleil – conveniently located next door to the new industrial parks specialising in low-wage garment and electrical component assembly. Port-au-Prince's population quickly outgrew the city's capacity, with uncontrolled growth putting increasing strains on its infrastructure, a trend that only accelerated throughout the 1990s. The once separate town of Delmas, between Pétionville and Port-au-Prince, was quickly subsumed into the city limits, while Pétionville itself is now seen by many as just another suburb. Downtown, the city of Carrefour now finds itself within the metropolitan sprawl, and it can only be a matter of time before Croix des Bouquets meets the same fate.

While the poor have packed themselves ever more densely into the city, the wealthy have retreated uphill, into villas in the suburbs above even Pétionville. But unmonitored construction across Port-au-Prince left it horribly exposed to the earthquake of 12 January 2010, when the city found itself the epicentre of the world's largest urban disaster.

GETTING THERE AND AWAY

Aéroport International Toussaint Louverture [99 F1] and Aérogare Guy Malary (domestic departures) are located off Route National 3 on the northern edge of Port-au-Prince. For detailed information on these entry points, see *Chapter 2*, pages 52–3. Taxis from the airport cost around US$20–40 according to where you're headed in Port-au-Prince proper.

There is no central bus station in Port-au-Prince, rather a series of general areas where road transport congregates. They can seem anything but organised

– series of buses, minibuses and pick-ups parked up along the street and disrupting traffic, while ticket touts bark out directions and street vendors wind between vehicles selling refreshment in the fumes. A first visit is usually a bracing experience.

The two major transport terminals are Portail Léogâne (for transport to the south), and Carrefour Aviation (for northbound transport). Transport doesn't run to a set timetable – instead you wait for your vehicle to fill and depart. Portail Léogâne is the more sprawling, and covers a couple of blocks between the Sylvio Cator stadium and Grand Rue (Boulevard Jean-Jacques Dessalines) – you'll need to ask for the particular *estasyon* for your destination. From here, transport leaves to Jacmel (2½ hours), Léogâne (1 hour), Les Cayes (4 hours), and all points along Route National 2. To Les Cayes, there are air-conditioned minibuses leaving at set hours, from next to the stadium (see *Les Cayes*, page 157).

To get to Jérémie (9 hours), buses leave from a cluster of transport offices on Grand Rue. For Cap-Haïtien (8 hours), Gonaïves (4 hours), Port-de-Paix (8 hours), Hinche (3 hours) and points north on Routes National 1 and 3, Carrefour Aviation in the old industrial area near Cité Soleil is the main departure point. To head south up the mountains to Fermathe (30 minutes) and Kenscoff (50 minutes), transport leaves throughout the day from Rue Geffrard in Pétionville. Road transport starts rolling slightly before dawn.

For a list of airline offices in Port-au-Prince, see *Airline contact details*, page 53.

ORIENTATION

Port-au-Prince can be a rather tricky city to get your head around initially – it stretches up from the coast over several hills, and there are few obvious vantage points or landmarks to help you get your bearings. It's best thought of as a city of discrete districts, held together by a number of major road arteries. The main distinction is between Port-au-Prince 'proper' and Pétionville, which are technically different cities, but which have become blended together through years of uncontrolled growth.

ALTERNATIVE STREET NAMES

Many important streets in Port-au-Prince have an official name and a more commonly used colloquial name – it's useful to learn these as quickly as possible.

Official name	Colloquial name
Avenue Jean Paul II	Turgeau
Avenue John Brown	Lalue (turning into Rue Panaméricaine in Pétionville)
Avenue Lamartinière	Bois Verna
Avenue Martin Luther King	Nazon
Boulevard Harry Truman	Bicentenaire
Boulevard Jean-Jacques Dessalines	Grand Rue
Boulevard Toussaint Louverture	Route de l'Aéroport
Delmas 60	Musseau
Delmas 105	Frères
Rue Paul VI	Cassernes

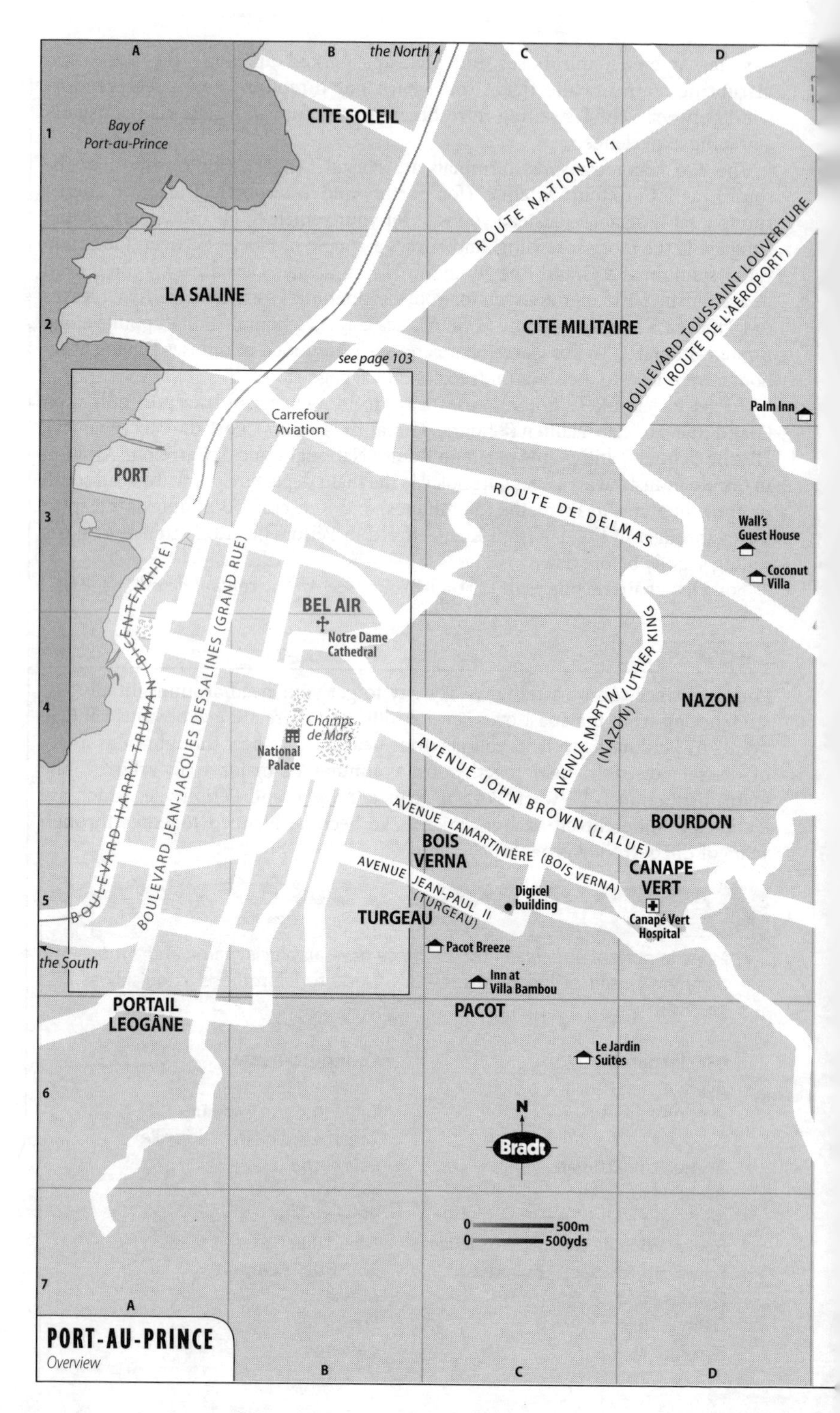
PORT-AU-PRINCE
Overview
Bay of Port-au-Prince
CITE SOLEIL
LA SALINE
PORT
CITE MILITAIRE
the North
the South
ROUTE NATIONAL 1
BOULEVARD TOUSSAINT LOUVERTURE (ROUTE DE L'AÉROPORT)
see page 103
Carrefour Aviation
ROUTE DE DELMAS
Palm Inn
Wall's Guest House
Coconut Villa
BEL AIR
Notre Dame Cathedral
Champs de Mars
National Palace
BOULEVARD HARRY TRUMAN (BICENTENAIRE)
BOULEVARD JEAN-JACQUES DESSALINES (GRAND RUE)
AVENUE MARTIN LUTHER KING (NAZON)
NAZON
AVENUE JOHN BROWN (LALUE)
BOURDON
AVENUE LAMARTINIÈRE (BOIS VERNA)
BOIS VERNA
AVENUE JEAN-PAUL II (TURGEAU)
TURGEAU
CANAPE VERT
Digicel building
Canapé Vert Hospital
Pacot Breeze
Inn at Villa Bambou
PACOT
PORTAIL LEOGÂNE
Le Jardin Suites
N
Bradt
0 500m
0 500yds
A
B
C
D
1
2
3
4
5
6
7

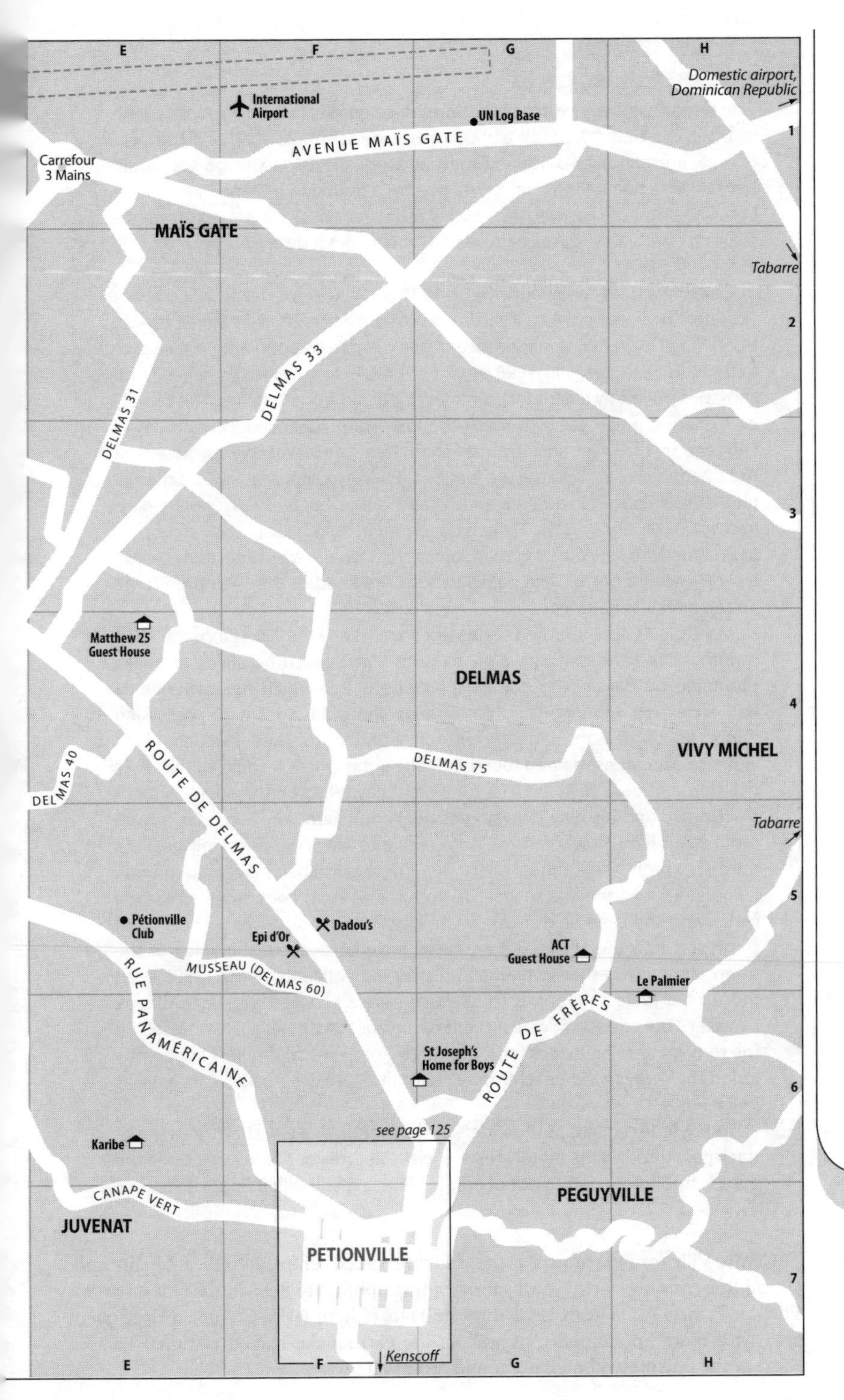
E
F
G
H
Domestic airport, Dominican Republic
International Airport
UN Log Base
1
AVENUE MAÏS GATE
Carrefour 3 Mains
MAÏS GATE
Tabarre
2
DELMAS 33
DELMAS 31
3
Matthew 25 Guest House
DELMAS
4
VIVY MICHEL
ROUTE DE DELMAS
DELMAS 75
DELMAS 40
Tabarre
5
Pétionville Club
Dadou's
Epi d'Or
ACT Guest House
MUSSEAU (DELMAS 60)
RUE PANAMÉRICAINE
Le Palmier
ROUTE DE FRÈRES
St Joseph's Home for Boys
6
see page 125
Karibe
PEGUYVILLE
CANAPE VERT
JUVENAT
PETIONVILLE
7
Kenscoff
E
F
G
H

HAITI'S LOST RAILWAY

One thing that every visitor to Port-au-Prince quickly becomes intimate with is its terrible traffic. *Taptaps*, trucks, SUVs and moto-taxis snarl and compete for space on an over-burdened road network. Yet 80 years ago you could have taken a tram along Champs de Mars or a train down Grand Rue as far as Léogâne. After the earthquake, several urban regeneration projects touted a return to light rail to ease congestion, but why did it disappear from the city in the first place?

Haiti's first trams were launched in 1878 and linked the district of Croix des Bossales (near the port) to Champs de Mars. The trams were horse-drawn, but difficulties in maintenance meant that despite its popularity, the service folded after ten years. In 1896 a light rail replacement was launched, with carriages pulled by steam locomotives imported from Belgium. This rapidly expanded in a few years to reach the important sugar-producing areas of Léogâne to the west and towards Thomazeau in the east. This growth of the Chemin de Fer d'Haïti – the National Railway Company – was aimed at ultimately linking Port-au-Prince with Cap-Haïtien, but by 1910 funding loans had again run dry, and the Haitian government sold it lock, stock and barrel to an American speculator named James MacDonald, who reportedly swung the deal with a gift of fake pearls to turn the head of the then president's Vodou priestess daughter.

MacDonald was granted extensive concessions to develop the land running along the railway's path to Saint-Marc, which he aimed to make profitable by developing banana plantations (for which he conveniently had an export monopoly). Unfortunately the plans meant dispossessing hundreds of peasant farmers, who responded to their evictions with violence. The unrest helped fuel the heady atmosphere leading to the USA's decision to invade Haiti in 1915, for which they relied on the advice of both MacDonald and his new railway president John Farnham. Eager for private profits, Farnham slowly ran the company into the sidings, taking nearly a third of its profit as his annual salary. By 1932, the urban trains ceased running completely, and the tracks were torn out. The rural lines survived largely by serving the cane fields outside the city, running a passenger service of some sort into the 1950s. But repeated presidencies saw the value of the trains more as a cash cow than a transport network and by the 1960s, even those lines were moribund. The service barely survived into Jean-Claude Duvalier's presidency, at which point his wife let loose her cronies to sell off the remaining rolling stock for scrap metal. Many metal sleepers apparently found their way to the beachfront villas of the Côte des Arcadins, to serve as fence posts.

Today, little remains as reminders of Haiti's trains – a few short stretches of track pass through the metal artists' enclave at Croix des Bouquets, while the bypass through Carrefour out of Port-au-Prince is still called Route de Rail.

Centre Ville (or Downtown) is the old commercial centre, with Bicentenaire and Grand Rue running north–south, and heading uphill into Bel Air, the oldest part of Port-au-Prince. At its heart is Champs de Mars (Chanmas in Creole), a large open area with many monuments, as well as the earthquake-ruined National Palace. Most of the downtown hotels are found around here.

Grand Rue is the main downtown road, turning into Route National 1 to head north out of the city, and at the other end Route National 2 to the south of Haiti, after traversing Carrefour (once a separate town, now a suburb).

Heading uphill, two main roads lead to Pétionville: Lalue (which turns into Panaméricaine on entering Pétionville), Delmas and Canapé Vert. Roads coming off Delmas are numbered sequentially – odd to the left going uphill, even to the right. Important junctions are Delmas 15 (where Nazon links Delmas to Lalue), Delmas 33 (to the airport) and Delmas 60 (Musseau, linking Delmas to Panaméricaine). A fourth potential option from Pétionville is Frères, which will lead you down a back route to Route de Tabarre for the airport. Pétionville itself is easy to navigate, as it is laid out in a grid system, with roads leading up to Place Saint-Pierre and out to Route de Kenscoff.

GETTING AROUND

Not only does Port-au-Prince sprawl, it's also heavily congested. Big traffic jams (*blokis*) are common, pedestrians and markets extend onto the roads and accidents are common. Always allow more time than you anticipate to get to your destination.

Taptaps are the stitches that thread Port-au-Prince's transport network together. They're mostly beaten-up covered pick-ups, although there's a tradition of downtown taptaps being brightly decorated trucks, with heavily converted bodywork, serious sound-systems and technicolour paint jobs. Taptaps run set routes, which are painted on the cab doors. Fares are around 10HTG. If you don't get on at a terminus, just flag one down on the street, and shout 'Merci chauffeur!' when you want to get off. Some of the most useful cross-city taptap routes are Delmas–Pétionville, Lalue–Pétionville and Canapé Vert (or Bourdon)–Pétionville. Aéroport–Nazon conveniently bisects Delmas and Lalue, as does Delmas 65–Portail Léogâne, while Saline–Martissant runs the length of Grand Rue.

Downtown Port-au-Prince has shared taxis called *publiques*, tatty cars with a red ribbon hanging from the rear-view mirror, operating roughly set routes between neighbourhoods. Fares are around 30HTG, sharing the cab with other passengers. Any *publique* can also be hired privately for a negotiable fee. The red ribbons can sometimes be hard to spot, so also look out for cars with 'TP' on their number plates, denoting that they're registered for public transport.

From Pétionville, **Nick's Taxis** (*30 Rue Panaméricaine; ☎ 2948 7777*) operate a reliable 24-hour radio-taxi service. Fares start at 100HTG plus 15HTG per minute – a better deal for evenings than traffic-clogged daytime roads.

The fastest way of getting around is by moto-taxi, which are everywhere. Drivers will squeeze and dodge through the busiest jams, although they're not always particularly safe. Short fares will be around 50HTG, ramping up considerably for anything longer distance.

TOUR OPERATOR

Voyages Lumière ☎ 3607 1321/3557 0753; **e** voyageslumierehaiti@gmail.com; www.voyageslumiere.com. Organises city, historical & artisanal tours. Prices depend on the number of passengers & if you provide your own vehicle.

WHERE TO STAY

One of the biggest decisions you'll make is where in Port-au-Prince to stay – downtown or in Pétionville. While most of the recent growth has taken place up

GRAFFITI ART IN PORT-AU-PRINCE

The walls of Port-au-Prince are rich in graffiti. On every other wall you can see a litany of slogans supporting or condemning political figures. From *Aba Minustah* (Down with Minustah) to Jen Koré Jen (The youth support the youth), policies are criticised or people are exhorted to stand together. Throw in a multitude of fading electoral posters and it creates a messy but fascinating palimpsest of recent political history.

One graffiti artist has managed to transcend the sloganeering. Jerry Rosembert, better known simply as Jerry, has been tagging walls in Port-au-Prince since 2002, but first came to be more widely known in 2009 with a series of cartoon portraits memorialising the singer Michael Jackson. Aiming at an often illiterate audience, Jerry also used his art to make sharper political points: a corner in Pétionville popular with sex workers was sprayed with a confused prostitute torn between a leering customer and her hungry child, elsewhere broken pipes were idealised by spraying them gushing with life-giving water. Jerry's most famous creation came the day after the 2010 earthquake, when he depicted the map of Haiti with a crying eye at its centre and a pair of praying hands with a simple slogan in English: 'We need help.'

Jerry's artwork seems to be ubiquitous, and somewhat inevitably he's been dubbed 'the Haitian Banksy'. But unlike that more sardonic prankster, since the earthquake Jerry has moved into art that aims to inspire more than just criticise. Coming up with motto *Haiti pap peri* (Haiti won't die), he's depicted the independence heroine Catherine Flon re-stitching the Haitian flag amid the rubble, children and flowers climbing out of the wreckage, as well as being employed to brightly paint water storage tanks in tent camps with cartoon characters and hand-washing messages.

Any wall is temptation to the sloganeers, so some of Jerry's pieces are already being covered up with more graffiti. But keep your eyes out and your camera ready – once you've seen one you'll probably want to photograph them all.

the hill in Pétionville, there are developments in downtown too with some good new guesthouses opening since the earthquake, while Digicel is moving into the hospitality business in partnership with the Marriott chain to build a 173-room hotel in Turgeau, due to open in 2014. Added to the Royal Oasis and Best Western hotels due to finish shortly after this guide went to press, Port-au-Prince's hotel scene is undergoing its biggest boom since the 1950s.

PORT-AU-PRINCE

Upmarket

The Inn at Villa Bambou [98 C5] 1 Rue Marfranc, Pacot; 3702 1151/2813 1724; e info@villabambouhaiti.com; www.villabambouhaiti.com. A charming & exclusive top-end boutique hotel in a restored 1920s villa, with lovely garden & views across the city. Hard-to-beat service & Michelin-quality dining on request. Pool, Wi-Fi. **$$$$**

Le Jardin Suites [98 C6] Mont Joli #24, Turgeau; 3170 8500/3701 9919; e info@lejardinsuites.com; www.lejardinhaiti.com. Somewhere between a small hotel & a series of apartments, high quality & well-presented accommodation in green surroundings with views over Port-au-Prince. **$$$$**

Le Plaza Hotel 10 Rue Capois, Champs de Mars; 3701 9303/2940 9800; e info@plazahaiti.

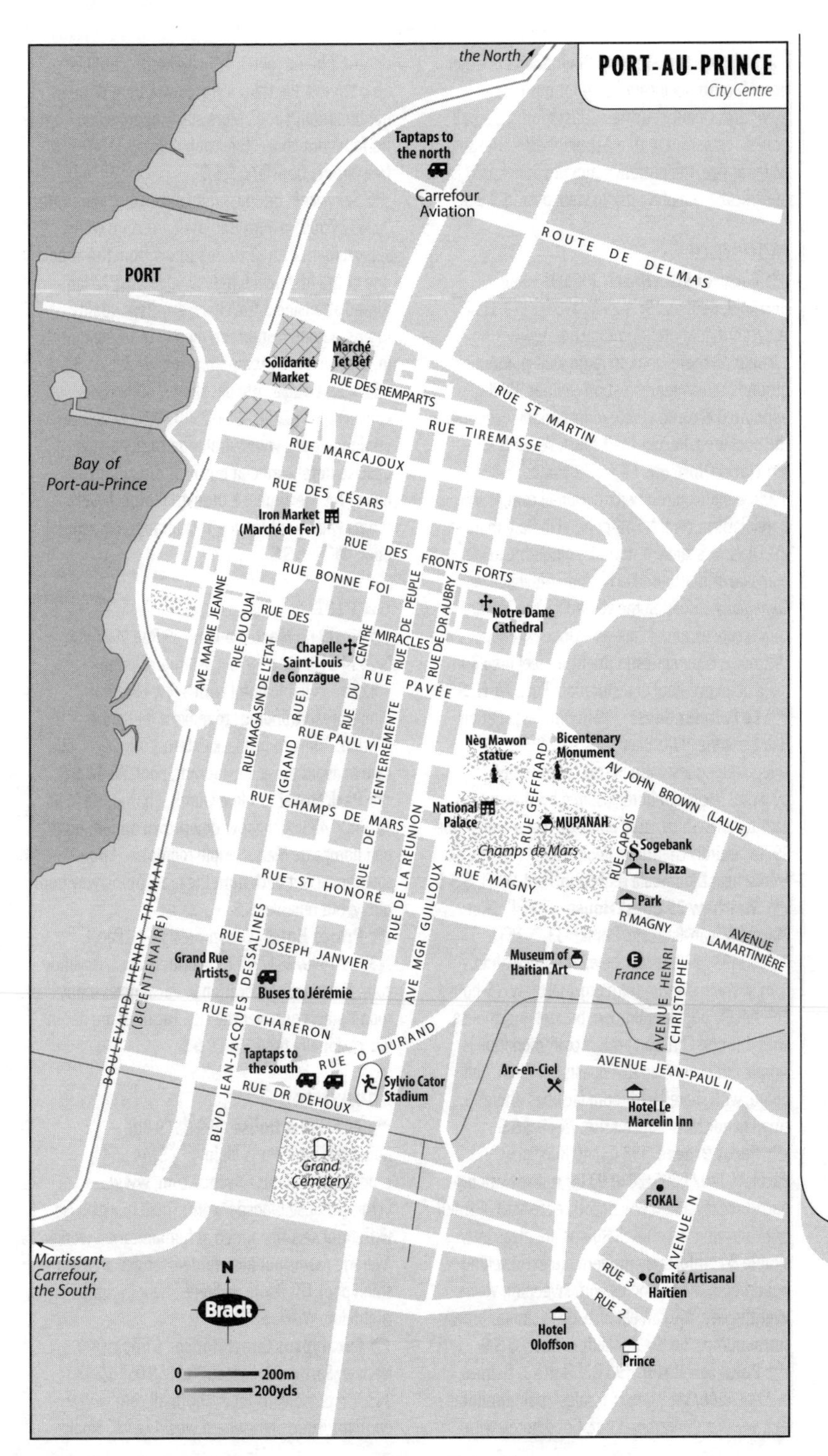
PORT-AU-PRINCE
City Centre
the North
Taptaps to the north
Carrefour Aviation
ROUTE DE DELMAS
PORT
Marché Tet Bêf
Solidarité Market
RUE DES REMPARTS
RUE ST MARTIN
RUE TIREMASSE
RUE MARCAJOUX
Bay of Port-au-Prince
RUE DES CÉSARS
Iron Market (Marché de Fer)
RUE DES FRONTS FORTS
RUE BONNE FOI
RUE DES MIRACLES
Notre Dame Cathedral
Chapelle Saint-Louis de Gonzague
AVE MARIE JEANNE
RUE DU QUAI
RUE MAGASIN DE L'ETAT
RUE DU CENTRE
RUE DE PEUPLE
RUE DE DR AUBRY
RUE PAVÉE
(GRAND RUE)
RUE PAUL VI
RUE DE L'ENTERREMENTE
Nèg Mawon statue
Bicentenary Monument
RUE GEFFRARD
AV JOHN BROWN (LALUE)
RUE CHAMPS DE MARS
National Palace
MUPANAH
Champs de Mars
RUE CAPOIS
Sogebank
Le Plaza
RUE DE LA RÉUNION
RUE MAGNY
RUE ST HONORÉ
Park
R MAGNY
AVENUE LAMARTINIÈRE
BOULEVARD HENRY TRUMAN (BICENTENAIRE)
RUE JOSEPH JANVIER
AVE MGR GUILLOUX
Museum of Haitian Art
France
AVENUE HENRI CHRISTOPHE
Grand Rue Artists
Buses to Jérémie
BLVD JEAN-JACQUES DESSALINES
RUE CHARERON
RUE O DURAND
Taptaps to the south
Sylvio Cator Stadium
RUE DR DEHOUX
Arc-en-Ciel
AVENUE JEAN-PAUL II
Hotel Le Marcelin Inn
Grand Cemetery
FOKAL
AVENUE N
Martissant, Carrefour, the South
N
Bradt
RUE 3
Comité Artisanal Haïtien
RUE 2
Hotel Oloffson
Prince
0 200m
0 200yds

com; www.plazahaiti.com. Downtown's premier hotel & centrally located spot for business meetings. Quality business-class rooms, a small pool & restaurant with a popular buffet. Despite its large size, the entrance (next to Sogebank) is inexplicably small & easy to walk past. **$$$$**

Moderate

Coconut Villa Hotel [98 D3] 3 Rue Berthold, Delmas 19; 2510 4901/3179 3752; e coconutvillahotel@prodigy.net; www.coconutvillahotel.com; In large well-planted grounds conveniently just off Delmas. Well-appointed & comfortable rooms, many overlooking the pool area. Racquetball court, Wi-Fi. **$$$**

Hotel Oloffson 60 Av Christophe; 3810 4000; e oloffson.reservation@gmail.com; www.hoteloloffson.com. No other hotel in Haiti matches the Oloffson's fame, a stunning gingerbread mansion immortalised in Graham Greene's *The Comedians*. Drinks on the veranda & the Thu RAM concert are essential Port-au-Prince experiences, but the rooms & service can sometimes feel tired & in need of an overhaul or restoration. Pool, Wi-Fi. **$$$**

Le Palmier Guest [99 H6] Impasse Pétion, Rue Lamothe, Puits Blain 4; 3702 9648; e lepalmier.guest@gmail.com. Surrounded by palms, a circular hotel inspired by Mayan architecture which could only have been built in the 1970s. Weirdly charming. Pool, Wi-Fi. Off Route de Frères, near Djoumbala Nightclub. Pool, Wi-Fi. **$$$**

Matthew 25 Guest House [99 E4] 6 Rue Martial & Jean-Baptiste, Delmas 33; 2511 7273/3493 1900; e Matthew25house@yahoo.com; www.parishprogram.org/matthew-25-house. Perennially popular midtown budget guesthouse with a strong Christian ethic. Accommodation is simple but cheery; up to 4 guests per room, half board, with shared bathroom facilities. There's a small handicrafts store on site. Wi-Fi. **$$$**

Pacot Breeze [98 C5] 40 Rue Pacot, Pacot; 3402 0895/2810 0316; e reservation@pacotbreeze.com; www.pacotbreeze.com. A small but charming new hotel. Rooms are pleasantly simple & comfortably modern, an extra selling point being the balconies with sweeping views over the city. You can eat outside in similar breezy surroundings, on the poolside terrace. **$$$**

Palm Inn Hotel [98 D2] Hatte 3, Delmas 31; 2947 4266/3889 0162; e sales@palminnhotel.net; www.palminnhotel.net. Good hotel, with decent if bland rooms & several self-contained apartments. Pleasant terrace restaurant & green garden around pool. More easily approached from Bd Toussaint Louverture than Delmas 31. Wi-Fi & free airport transfers. **$$$**

Servotel Bd Toussaint Louverture, Maïs Gate; 2812 7500; e info@servotelhaiti.com; www.servotelhaiti.com. A stone's throw from the airport, one of the first new hotels to open post 12 Jan. Aimed at business travellers, excellent quality rooms, a good restaurant, gym to burn the day off in, & poolside courtyard for evening drinks. **$$$**

Visa Lodge Rte des Nîmes, off Bd Toussaint Louverture; 2250 1561/2510 3424; e services@visalodge.com; www.visalodge.com. Popular upscale hotel aimed at business consultants, & handy for the airport & industrial zone. Lovely rooms with good service, restaurants & bar plus pool. Wi-Fi. **$$$**

Budget

Hotel Le Marcelin Inn 29 Rue Marcelin; 2514 3172/3409 0104; e lemarcelininn@aol.com. Reliable hotel with a few external gingerbread trappings to make it feel more Haitian. A few rooms lack external windows; take care to avoid these. Restaurant, pool, Wi-Fi. **$$**

Park Hotel 23 Rue Capois, Champs de Mars; 2940 1453. A cheaper downtown option, right on Champs de Mars. Simple rooms in a large townhouse set back from the road. Some way from glitzy, but reliable. **$$**

Prince Hotel Corner rues 3 & N, Pacot; 3791 1549/2517 0597; e princehotelha@yahoo.com. A convenient location in Pacot gives many rooms views out over the city. Facilities are decent, if occasionally tired. Wi-Fi. **$$**

Shoestring

ACT Guest House [99 G5] 9 Rue Boisrond Canal, Puits Blain 4; 2944 5544; e actallianceghouse@yahoo.com; www.actguesthouse.blogspot.com. Small guesthouse with tight security aimed at humanitarian workers. Average rooms but nice garden/terrace area & a small pool. Off Route de Frères, near Djoumbala Nightclub. Wi-Fi. **$**

Eucalyptus Guest House 6 Impasse Nezivar, Sarthe 59, Cazeau; 3558 0576/3480 3833; e ernsojean_louis@hotmail.com; www.eucalyptusguesthousehaiti.weebly.com. Small

& friendly guesthouse near the airport (opposite the Cazeau police station). Decorated with art, with a pleasant garden & even a tennis court. Some rooms are shared, all are half board. Weekly/monthly rates available. Wi-Fi. **$**

St Joseph's Home For Boys [99 G6] 21, Delmas 91; 2257 4237/3449 9942; e sjfamilyhaiti@hotmail.com; www.heartswithhaiti.org. An art-filled refuge for ex-street boys turned welcoming home-from-home for foreign visitors. Completely destroyed in the earthquake, but beautifully rebuilt from the rubble, even brighter & better than before. Some rooms, which are half board, may be shared. Wi-Fi. **$**

Wall's Guest House [98 D3] 8 Rue Mackandal, Delmas 19; 3703 4788/3622 0684; e walls@haitianmail.com; www.fida-pch.org/walls-international-guest-house. Small & friendly, popular with volunteers & mission groups. Some rooms shared, all half board. Pool, Wi-Fi. **$**

PÉTIONVILLE

Upmarket

Hotel Ibo Lele Route Ibo Lele, Montaigne Noir; 2257 5668/8500; e info@ibolelehaiti.com; www.ibolelehaiti.com. Built in the 1950s tourist boom, perching over the top of Pétionville. A big pool & bar with great views (the setting is all), although some rooms can feel a little ordinary for the price. **$$$$**

Karibe Hotel [99 E6] Juvenat 7; 2812 7000/2256 8903; e info@karibehotel.com; www.karibehotel.com. Currently Port-au-Prince's top hotel & conference centre, popular with the movers & shakers in business & political circles alike. Business-standard rooms with excellent service. Well-priced restaurant, pool with swim-up bar, gym, spa & related services. **$$$$**

Royal Oasis Hotel 115 Rue Panaméricaine; 2940 6472; e info@oasishaiti.com; www.oasishaiti.com. A huge V-shaped complex painted in bright colours to dominate the top of Rue Panaméricaine. Due to open as this guide went to press, with nearly 130 rooms, restaurant, shops & a host of international-standard hotel facilities. **$$$$**

Villa Creole Impasse des Hôtels, Rue Panaméricaine; 2941 1570/1571; e info@villacreole.com; www.villacreole.com. Really good service at this hotel, with its low-slung area around the pool & separate accommodation block. Comfortable & spacious rooms. It's business class, but has been around long enough to remember what tourists are. Wi-Fi. **$$$$**

Moderate

Best Western Corner rues Louverture & Geffrard; 2945 7777; www.bestwestern.com. Still under construction as this guide went to press, due to open in the heart of Pétionville early in 2013. Expect the high standards befitting this international chain. **$$$**

Kinam Hotel Pl St Pierre; 2944 6000/2945 6000; e reservation@hotelkinam.com; www.hotelkinam.com. A modern hotel masquerading as a gingerbread house to pleasing effect. Effective rooms & a nice restaurant bar area above the pool. Lethal rum punches. Wi-Fi. **$$$**

Budget

Doux Sejour Guest House 32 Rue Magny; 2257 1553/2514 4528; e douxsejourhaiti@yahoo.fr; www.douxsejourhaiti.com. Small but slightly rambling hotel. Some rooms a little rough around the edges in places, but good value & centrally located. Restaurant, Wi-Fi. **$$**

Kay Blanch Guest House 16 Rue Pipo, Juvenat 7; 3824 6446; e info@kayblanch.com; www.kayblanch.com. Secluded & slightly grand guesthouse in a quiet area near the Karibe Hotel. Some rooms are shared (& cheaper). **$$**

Splendid Guest House 13 Route de Kenscoff; 3820 1110/3838 5096; e info@splendidhaiti.com; www.facebook.com/splendidhaiti. Compact & cosy hotel right on the main road, near turning for Morne Calvaire. Modern, well-appointed rooms, & terrace bar & restaurant. Close to Pl St Pierre, but the busy road makes walking difficult. Wi-Fi. **$$**

WHERE TO EAT

You don't have to go far to get a bite to eat, either shelling out a handful of gourdes or doing some serious damage to your stash of US dollars. The simplest form of street food comes from the *ti machann*, or women market vendors. At its most basic this can be a woman selling bread rolls, hardboiled eggs and bananas – a cheap lunch for many people – also look out for men carrying plastic boxes on their heads with *pate* (small savoury pastries with meat, fish or chicken) for a few gourdes. Next up are the *ti machann* with their own pitches, allowing them to serve up rice with sauce, *fritay* (fried snacks) or cuts of barbecued chicken.

Simple bar-restos are widespread, serving Creole food, along with fast-food places serving up American fare. By far the biggest selection of restaurants is in Pétionville. Traditionally the haunt of the moneyed class, the growth of the aid and reconstruction economy since 2010 saw something of a boom in new restaurants and bars in the area (with an equally big turnover of new places) – the listings below are only a taste. See the review and listings website Manman Pemba (*www.manmanpemba.com*) for the newest and trendiest options.

PORT-AU-PRINCE

Mid range

Arc-en-Ciel 24 Rue Capois; 10.00–23.00 daily. A bar-resto that stands slightly above the competition. Handsome portions of Creole standards, a few fast-food dishes, & lively music in the evenings. **$$$**

Hotel Oloffson 60 Av Christophe; 3810 4000; 10.00–22.00 daily. Veranda restaurant of the iconic hotel (or eat inside the equally atmospheric bar). The menu leans somewhere between American & Creole – the food is decent enough, but the ambience is all. Great (& potent) rum punches are also served up here. **$$$**

La Table de Caïus 16 Rue Légitime, Champs de Mars; 2940 7227; 11.00–16.00 Mon–Sat. Tucked in the gardens of the Musée d'Art Haïtien, this is an unexpected treat. Charming surroundings & a menu featuring good seafood & meat dishes, salads & pasta. Popular with business diners. **$$$**

Le Plaza Hotel 10 Rue Capois, Champs de Mars; 3701 9303/2940 9800; 06.30–23.00 daily. There aren't many upscale dining options downtown, but Le Terrasse Restaurant inside the Plaza is one. The international à la carte menu is available throughout the day, but it's worth making a detour for the Creole buffet every Wed lunchtime, or Sun evenings for their barbecue buffet (accompanied by a *twoubadou* band). **$$$**

Cheap and cheerful

5 Coins 210 Rue Nicholas (corner of Rue Magloire Ambroise); 2511 1044; 11.00–21.00 daily. Fritay is very much thought of as a street food, but 5 Coins elevates it to gourmet standards. It's all here – buy your marinated meat & fish by weight for it to be fried up for you, then load up with *pikliz*, rice & other sides. Haitian soups & bean salads are also great. Wash down with a cold beer, or a freshly squeezed juice. **$$**

Assiette Creole 12 Route de l'Aéroport; 2940 0041; 11.00–18.00 Mon–Sat, 07.00–16.00 Sun. A new branch of the popular Pétionville outfit, dishing up canteen-plates piled high with great-value, tasty Creole food. **$$**

Dadou's [99 F5] 349, Delmas 81; 3873 4747; 11.00–21.00 Mon–Sat, 10.00–17.00 Sun. Home cooking, Haitian-style: great servings of Creole standards in cheery surroundings, plus a few unexpected items like goat or chicken curry. Sandwiches, burgers & fries are also on the menu, & traditional soups at the weekend. **$$**

Epi d'Or [99 F5] 4, Delmas 56; 3893 2182; 06.00–21.00 daily. This popular local chain started doing burgers, pizzas & Subway-style sandwiches, but has now grown to offer a full range of Creole dishes & really rather good crêpes. Sit in the large & busy fast-food dining hall, which has a rapid turnover. Smaller branches can be found at Delmas 33 & 51 Rue Rigaud (in Pétionville). **$$**

PÉTIONVILLE

Expensive

La Plantation Impasse Fouchard, Rue Borno; 3555 2935/3458 2699; 12.00–22.00 daily. Pétionville's oldest restaurant, tucked away & popular with the society movers & shakers. Intimate atmosphere, a menu leaning heavily on classic French (with a hint of Caribbean) & a good wine list. $$$$$

Papaye 48 Rue Metellus; 3558 2707/3701 2707; 12.00–23.00 Mon–Sat. Stylish & expensively fashionable restaurant, blending international cuisines from French to pan-Asian with occasional Creole twists. The garden pavilion at the rear hosts the slightly less-expensive Papaye Café, offering wood-fired pizzas & the like. $$$$$

Above average

Chicken Fiesta 124 Rue Panaméricaine; 2813 9866; 12.00–22.00 daily. Chicken wings in as many flavours as you could want – anyone for passion fruit & chilli? Tasty Chinese dishes too, & many servings are big enough for 2. Summon your waiter with a squawking rubber chicken, or dial out for home delivery. $$$$

Lunchbox L'Esplanade, Rue Darguin; 2942 3138/4412 3138; 11.00–23.00 Mon–Sat. Café-cum-bistro in airy surroundings in a small shopping arcade. Generous & delicious salads, a good selection of sandwiches & pasta, but the unexpectedly excellent sushi is the main draw. Top service. $$$$

Quartier Latin 10 Pl Boyer; 3460 3326/3445 3325; www.brasseriequartierlatin.com; 12.00–23.00 Mon–Sat, 10.30–22.00 Sun. Perennially popular brasserie with a pleasant garden front & back. Good French & Italian-influenced dishes, with regular Indonesian & Thai buffet nights & a busy Sun brunch session. There's frequent live music, & Wi-Fi for working lunches. $$$$

Mid range

Fior di Latte Choucoune Plaza (corner of rues Lamarre & Chavannes); 2256 8474/2813 0445; 11.00–22.00 Mon–Sat. The tables laid out under a pleasantly vine-clad gazebo always attract a steady stream of customers. Italian is the order of the day, with good pasta & pizzas, & sizeable salads. Those with a sweet tooth will find they keep coming back for the gelato. $$$

La Coquille 10 Rue Rebecca; 2942 5225/3466 3908; 11.00–18.00 Mon–Sat, 08.00–12.00 Sun. Friendly & folksy restaurant serving traditional Creole food in cheerily painted surroundings. Food is buffet-style, so pile your plates high, & get ready for queues on Sun mornings when the place packs out for their famous *soup joumo* – definitely worth rising early for. $$$

Muncheez Corner rues Panaméricaine & Rebecca; 2813 1524/1530; 11.00–23.00 daily. Fast food – good pizzas, half-decent burgers, steak sandwiches & chicken wings. Something of an establishment, & a popular meeting place for people-watching on the street below. $$$

O Brasileiro 103 Rue Louverture; 3716 5511/2813 1050; 12.00–23.00 daily. Fashionably laid-back bar & restaurant, with cosy indoor seating & relaxed outdoor garden area, frequently with live music at the weekends. Good international dining & great ambience. $$$

Presse Café 28 Rue Rigaud; 2944 3131; 07.00–23.00 Mon–Sat. Small bistro that changes its nature throughout the day – open early for breakfasts, busy at lunchtime for its Creole buffet at 12.30, & then chilling at the bar for tapas or à la carte dining in the evening (with live music on Thu & Fri). Wi-Fi. $$$

Cheap and cheerful

5 Coins 20 Rue Panaméricaine; 2511 1044; 11.00–21.00 daily. The Pétionville branch of the celebrated fritay outfit. Marinated meat & fish, traditional soups & side dishes, fresh juices & a lively dining atmosphere. $$

Assiette Creole 6 Rue Ogé; 2940 0041; 11.00–18.00 Mon–Sat, 07.00–16.00 Sun. Canteen-plates with generous servings of Creole food, from *ragu* & *griot* to fish, chicken & *tassot*, all accompanied by plenty of rice, *pikliz* & *bannan peze*. Popular with local office workers. $$

Marie Belliard Corner rues Faubert & Lambert; 2813 1515/2943 1515; 06.30–17.00 daily. Patisserie & boulangerie selling delicious pastries, *pate*, sandwiches & paninis – take-away or eat in with a coffee. Also the place for expensive special-occasion cakes. $$

Rebo Expresso 25 Rue Metellus; 2945 0505; 07.00–18.00 Mon–Sat. Somewhat inevitably dubbed 'the Starbucks of Pétionville', this small but cosy outfit brings a bit of coffee-shop zing to the scene. Sandwiches, paninis, cakes, lots of good coffee & big windows mean you can sit & watch the outside world go by – something of a local rarity. Wi-Fi. $$

ENTERTAINMENT AND ACTIVITIES

LIVE MUSIC Concerts tend to be announced via big roadside billboards, often at busy junctions. They're meant to be temporary, but often linger for several months after an event, which can lead to some confusion and disappointment. You can find a more up-to-date guide to coming events on the listings website **Manman Pemba** (*www.manmanpemba.com*).

The biggest concerts tend to be held at the open-air **Parc Historique de la Canne à Sucre** (*48 Bd 15 Octobre, Tabarre; ☎ 2256 8051*) or at weekends outside the city at the beach hotels on the Côte des Arcadins, particularly **Club Indigo** (*Km 77, Route National 1; ☎ 3650 1000/3651 1000; www.clubindigo.net*) and **Kaliko Beach** (*Km 681, Route National 1; ☎ 2940 4609/3427 7615; www.kalikobeachclub.com*). Cover charges for these events can be high, easily topping out at US$50.

The mother of all regular live music nights in Port-au-Prince is **RAM at the Hotel Oloffson** (*60 Av Christophe; ☎ 3810 4000; www.hoteloloffson.com*) every Thursday night. The band tends to come on around 22.30–23.00 – if you get there late there's a cover charge of 500HTG, but those arriving early to take dinner at the hotel restaurant don't pay. The band play at the back of the hotel – there isn't a stage as such so the dozen or so band members and their dancers squeeze up against the crowd, presided over by bandleader (and hotel owner) Richard Morse and the bewitching vocals of his wife Lunise. It's hard to keep still, and as the Prestige and

CARNIVAL IN PORT-AU-PRINCE

The national carnival in Port-au-Prince is quite simply the biggest party in the country. On the first Sunday after Shrove Tuesday (typically in February), several hundred thousand people descend on Champs de Mars and the surrounding area downtown for the parade, the music and the free-flowing and alcohol-fuelled celebration. It's such a big event that the three days after Carnival are a national holiday, to allow a gentle come-down after the party.

The parade marks the culmination of a month of pre-Carnival festivities. Every Sunday for a month in the run-up to the big day, rara bands are active in the streets, and clubs and bars hold big parties. Bands release special Carnival songs, each vying with the other to become that year's anthem.

The parade typically starts around Stade Sylvio Cator in Portail Léogâne in the early afternoon, and heads up Boulevard Jean-Jacques Dessalines (Grand Rue). It then cuts towards Champs de Mars, which is the heart of the Carnival experience. Large viewing stands are erected here. After processing around Champs de Mars, it cuts down Rue Oswald Durand to eventually finish back near the stadium. With all the floats, dancers and Carnival queens, rara bands and crush of people, the parade can take as much as ten hours to complete.

Carnival in 2010 fell a month after the earthquake and was famously cancelled for the first time in living memory. When it returned a year later, it was a scene of great emotional release, although hoardings had to be erected in Champs de Mars to put the tent camps out of sight. In an attempt by the government to spread the party's economic benefits, the 2012 Carnival was held in Les Cayes, much to the indignation of Port-au-Prince. As a part reply, the traditional of the Carnival des Fleurs (Flower Carnival), not held since the Duvalier period, was revived the same year, in the last weekend of July, with more of the same music and costumed parades

FESTIVAL TIME

Port-au-Prince's biggest day out by far is the annual Carnival, held every February, but there are several other cultural festivals worth looking out for.

The **Artisanat en Fête**, a grand annual celebration of Haitian handicrafts hosted by the Institut de Recherche pour la Promotion de l'Art Haïtien (IRPAH; *www.irpah.com*) is held every October at the Parc Historique de la Canne à Sucre. Artisans from all corners of the country descend on the site to display their creativity. Concerts are also held (often with big-name Haitian bands), and the festival has also started hosting local food producers offering regional specialities to taste along with the art.

Also held at Canne à Sucre is **Livres en Folie** (*www.livreenfolie.com*), Haiti's largest and longest-running literature festival, founded in 1993 and held every June. There are readings, signings and talks, as well as plenty of Haitian books on sale. The festival attracts the most prominent writers from Haiti and the diaspora; in 2011 Edwidge Danticat and Lyonel Trouillot were guests of honour. Note that events are mostly in French or Creole.

Every January, Port-au-Prince holds its **Festival International de Jazz** (*www.papjazzhaiti.org*), which attracts jazz musicians from across the globe as well as highlighting local talents. The main concerts tend to split between Quartier Latin (which hosts weekly jazz throughout the year) in Pétionville and Fokal downtown. The festival seems to get bigger and better each year, and for the first time in 2012, it spread its wings beyond Port-au-Prince to hold concerts in Les Cayes, a successful programme that looks likely to be repeated. Many of the concerts are free.

Dubbed a 'Salon des Refusés for the 21st Century', the **Ghetto Biennale** (*www.ghettobiennale.com*) is held on alternate years (the next will be in 2013) in downtown Port-au-Prince, focused on the Atis Rezistans art collective of the Grand Rue. Visiting artists collaborate on art projects with the local community, and there are usually accompanying concerts, Vodou ceremonies and film screenings.

Along similar lines, the **Transcultural Forum of Contemporary Art** (*http://www.africamerica.org*) is held every September to celebrate Haitian art, with visiting international artists, exhibitions, lectures and presentations.

Barbancourt flows, it's an experience that everyone should experience at least once during their time in Port-au-Prince.

Quartier Latin (*Pl Boyer, Pétionville;* ☎ *3460 3326/3445 3325*) is well known for live jazz every Wednesday night, following up on Thursdays with Latin music. You can also hear live jazz every Thursday evening at **Café Place Saint-Pierre** (*corner of rues Chavannes & Lamarre, Pétionville;* ☎ *2940 3131*), or go along on Tuesday nights for an evening on slam poetry in Creole and French. On other nights, there's a piano bar. **Presse Café** (*28 Rue Rigaud, Pétionville;* ☎ *2944 3131*) has live music on Thursday and Friday evenings, mixing up traditional *kompa* and jazz.

There's a variety of live music options at **Garden Studio** (*101 Rue Grégoire, Pétionville;* ☎ *2226 5371; www.gardenstudiopv.com*) – great *twoubadou* every Wednesday, open mic and acoustic on Thursdays, and even karaoke on Tuesdays if you get bitten by the performing bug yourself. The venue is big enough to host larger concerts with named bands (attracting a cover charge), as well as salsa nights and a variety of good DJs.

The popular bar and nightclub **Mangos Lounge** (*104 Rue Louverture, Pétionville; ☎ 2943 0571*) has live music every Thursday night, ranging from *kompa* and *rap kreyol* to reggae, as well as weekend club nights. A cover charge of around 250HTG usually applies.

Two long-established nightclubs with regular live music from *kompa* to *rap kreyol* are **Djoumbala** (*corner of Route de Frères & Rue Boisrond Canal; ☎ 2257 0525*) and **X-Treme** (*64 Rue Grégoire, Pétionville; ☎ 3556 0026*). Things tend to get going here around 22.00.

Although the Saint Trinité Cathedral collapsed in the earthquake, its school of music survives and plays regular **classical music concerts**. They are well worth seeing – contact e saintetrinitemusique@yahoo.com for details of upcoming concerts.

CULTURAL CENTRES **Fokal** (*143 Av Christophe; ☎ 2813 1694/2510 9814*) is a wide-ranging cultural institution with a broad remit to promote Haitian culture and the arts. It is involved in projects ranging from the preservation of gingerbread houses, environmental restoration (including the memorial park in Martissant – see *What to see*, page 122) as well as providing youth access to the arts through educational grants. It holds regular concerts, film showings, plays, book readings, art exhibitions.

The **Institut Français** (*99 Rue Lamartinière, Bois Verna; ☎ 2244 0016; www.institutfrancaishaiti.org*) has a very active cultural programme. As well as film screenings and music concerts, it hosts excellent lectures and discussions (in French) covering a wide spread of Haitian culture. Along with Fokal, it's one of the best places in Port-au-Prince to see Haitian theatre and dance, which feature strongly in their programme. The institute also runs French- and Creole-language classes.

The **Institut Haitiano-Américain** (*corner of rues Capois & Saint Cyr; ☎ 2222 3715/2947; e haipaph@gmail.com; www.haitian-americaninstitute.org*) also hold regular music concerts and other events, as well as running good Creole-language classes for long-term residents.

SPORT The **Stade Sylvio Cator** (Rue Oswald Durand) is home to the football clubs Racing Club Haïtien and Violette Athletic – you'll need to check the local press for fixtures. The stadium is also the ground for international matches. Tickets to see the Grenadiers, the national team, run from 150HTG to 1,000HTG according to seating. The stadium has been recently refurbished with new floodlights and astroturf pitch.

On the edge of Cité Soleil, **L'Athlétique d'Haïti** (*www.athletiquedhaiti.org*) is a local NGO focused on youth development, run by ex-footballer and Duvalier-era political prisoner Bobby Duval. They run frequent tournaments and other events, including matches for the Haitian Association of Amputee Football (since the earthquake, Port-au-Prince has four amputee football teams). In 2012 plans were announced to build a new 'Phoenix' stadium at the site, designed to eventually have a capacity of 20,000 – developments can be followed at www.phoenixstadium.org.

SHOPPING

ART AND HANDICRAFTS Some of the preferred shops are listed below, but there is plenty of art and handicrafts on sale on the streets. Noted areas are Place St Pierre in Pétionville around the Kinam Hotel, whose walls are turned into an open-air gallery every day. Downtown, Route de l'Aèroport also has many vendors, clustering around the huge **UN Logbase**. Rue Panaméricaine is strong on metal art – you'll find sellers around Musseau (the turning for the cut-through to Delmas 60). At Christmastime look out here for *fanal*, festive model gingerbread houses made of card (and sometimes wood), to be lit up with candles during Advent. You can find more *fanal* for sale on Route de Bourdon.

The original Haitian handicraft co-operative is **Comité Artisanal Haitïen** (*29 Rue 3, Pacot;* ☎ *2510 3575/3558 1498; www.cahaiti.com*) – in 2012 it celebrated 40 years of supporting artisans through fair trade deals. It has lots of metal art from Croix des Bouquets and papier-mâché from Jacmel, as well as some beautiful basketry.

Better known as the Iron Market, the **Marché de Fer** (*Bd Jean-Jacques Dessalines*) has an enormous range of art and handicrafts under its ornate metal roofs. You can probably find anything you're after here (it's strong on Vodou art), and the shopping experience is certainly a world away from the rarefied galleries of Pétionville.

A good selection of handicrafts can be found at **IRPAH** (*6 Rue Ogé, Pétionville;* ☎ *2256 2282; www.irpah.com*) from painted wood to stone carvings and Vodou flags. Run by the Institut de Recherche pour la Promotion de l'Artisanat Haïtien (IRPAH), who host the annual Artisanat en Fête at Canne à Sucre. It's in the same compound as the Assiette Creole Restaurant.

At the gingerbread-styled **Galata** (*153 Rue Faubert, Pétionville*), you can find the traditional mix of crafts, plus a few larger items like brightly painted rocking chairs from the south. If you ever yearned for a mouse-mat shaped like a *taptap*, come here.

Creole food is added to the mix at **Kay Atizan** (*43 Rue Magny, Pétionville;* ☎ *3456 6989; www.kayatizan.net*); you can come here to eat lunch while shopping for a good variety of folk art.

You can get beautiful wooden bowls from **Einstein Originals** (*16 Impasse Citoyenne, Rue Paloma, Carrefour;* ☎ *3458 4978/3403 5184; www.einsteinoriginals.com*), made from the fast-growing *obeche* tree by a workforce that's 85% female. Princess Diana was a fan – the Diana bowl is named for her and remains the most popular design. Call ahead for an appointment.

Cheap-and-cheerful canvases have been mass-produced for foreign visitors since the 1950s, often stealing themes and images from the big names in Haitian painting. Open-air street galleries will sell you paintings for a few dollars, but if you want to do your wallet serious damage and invest in something more substantial, try the following galleries in Pétionville:

Expressions (*55 Rue Metellus;* ☎ *2256 3471/3558 7584; www.expressionsgaleriedart.com*) A large gallery with canvases crammed in with barely an inch of free wall space. A wide selection of artists, both young and established.

Galerie Marassa (*17 Rue Lamarre;* ☎ *3558 8484/4739 3923; www.galeriemarassa.com*) A small gallery with a strong focus on contemporary naive and avant-garde artists, plus metal sculpture and Vodou beadwork.

Galerie Monnin (*23 Rue Lamarre;* ☎ *2257 4430; www.galeriemonnin.com*) The oldest art gallery in the city, exhibiting and selling a wide variety of schools of Haitian art by renowned artists, including some good Vodou pieces. A rarity in that the family have also produced their own internationally regarded artist, Pascale Monnin.

Galerie Nader (*50 Rue Grégoire;* ☎ *2257 5603/3510 0036; www.galeriedartnader.com*) A gallery also housing the largest private collection of Haitian art in the world, previously displayed in the Nader Museum which was flattened in the earthquake.

A huge gallery with a wide selection of paintings from contemporary artists and Haitian masters alike.

BOOKS AND MUSIC Bookshops often mean stationery shops in Port-au-Prince, and the city isn't great for English-language bookshops. **The Bookstore** (*Esperanza Bldg, 87 Rue Grégoire, Pétionville*) has a reasonable selection, albeit nothing on Haiti, although it makes up somewhat by serving coffee, cake and sandwiches. You can find a few English titles at **Librairie La Pleiade** (*Complexe Promenade, corner of rues Grégoire & Moise, Pétionville*) and **Asterix** (*Rue Ogé, Pl St Pierre, Pétionville*) – both have extensive Haiti sections (in French), along with some English-language international press. Asterix also has a good selection of postcards. **J'Imagine** (*Complexe Louverture, 49 Rue Chavannes, Pétionville*) is better for fiction, and also has a good coffee bar and sandwiches.

If you're after CDs of Haitian music, your best bets are **Melodisque** (*30 Rue Rigaud, Pétionville*), **CD Selection** (*340 Route de Delmas, near Delmas 40*), and **La Boite à Musique** (*11 Rue Pavée*), close to the intersection with Rue Montalais downtown.

FASHION

Artisans du Soleil (*21 Rue Rigaud, Pétionville; 3467 4801; www.artisansdusoleilhaiti.com*) Intricate Haitian-flavoured jewellery in glass, shell and stone, as well as sequin-encrusted bags from Port-au-Prince-born designer Giovanna Menard.

Vèvè Collections (*17 Rue Gabart, Pétionville; 2942 6344; www.vevecollections.com*) Amazing Vodou flag-inspired handbags by local designer Phelicia Dell, along with a small range of *prêt-à-porter* fashion.

SUPERMARKETS AND HOMEWARES Port-au-Prince seems to recently have had an explosion in the number of supermarkets and minimarkets, and wherever you are in the city you'll be able to stock up on most things you need. Pétionville has the two biggest and most extensively stocked: **Giant Supermarket** (*corner of rues Ogé and Géffrard*) and **Caribbean Supermarket** (*51 Rue Metellus*).

If you're going to be based in Port-au-Prince long-term, good-value shops for homeware include **Valerio Canez** (*branches on Delmas 65 & Bd 15 Octobre, Tabarre*), **Acra** (*corner of rues Louverture & Grégoire, Pétionville*) and **Handal** (*Pl Boyer, Pétionville*).

OTHER PRACTICALITIES

CLUBS Long-term residents with a sporting bent may wish to join the **Pétionville Club** (*1 Rue Metraux, off Rue Panaméricaine, Pétionville; 2940 5449/3430 0584; e thepetionvillecluboffice@yahoo.com*), which has tennis courts, a pool, restaurant/bar and other sports facilities. Annual membership costs US$800. The club became famous after the earthquake when its golf course became home to a large tent camp, managed by actor Sean Penn's NGO J/P HRO.

The **Colony Club of Haiti** (*e colonyclubofhaiti@yahoo.com; 16.00–18.30 Fri*) is an English-language library also based at the Pétionville Club – the slightly anachronistic name dates from its founding by the wives of US officers in 1924 during the American occupation. It has around 3,000 titles including an excellent Haiti section, and has a 'tea-wine' social on alternate weeks, as well as regular outings. Annual fees are US$35, or US$45 for a couple.

COMMUNICATIONS Wi-Fi is increasingly widespread in Port-au-Prince (hotels and restaurants are listed in the relevant sections earlier in the chapter) as well as 3G and, increasingly, 4G internet phone services. You can pick up SIM cards in branches of Digicel, Voila and Natcom across the city. For internet services, head to **Haiti Access** (*60 Rue Geffrard, Pétionville; 2812 6000; www.accesshaiti.com*) or **Multilink** (*Delmas 18; 2511 3411; www.multilink.ht*).

There are post offices on Rue Bonne Foi (*Bicentenaire*), Delmas 45 and Place St Pierre (*corner of rues Grégoire and Pinchinat*) in Pétionville. They'll undoubtedly be surprised to see you clutching a postcard. All the major international courier firms have offices in the city:

AnnDex 33 Av Marie Jeanne; 2813 1277/3702 2348; www.anndex.com. Haitian franchise of FedEx.
DHL 17 Bd Toussaint Louverture, corner of Rue Jean Gilles; 2812 9400; www.dhl.com. Also a branch at 19 Rue Clerveaux, Pétionville.
UPS 195, Delmas 29; 2511 8181/2246 2592; www.ups.com. Also a branch on the corner of rues Geffrard & Chavannes, Pétionville.

FOREIGN EMBASSIES IN PORT-AU-PRINCE

Brazil Hexagon Bldg (3rd Floor) (corner of rues Clerveaux & Darguin), Pétionville; 2256 7556/2256 7574; e ppinto@mr.gov.br
Canada Between Delmas 71 & 75; 2249 9000/8000; e prnce@dfait-maeci.gc.ca; www.port-au-prince.gc.ca
Cuba 3 Rue Marion (cnr Rue Chevalier), Peguyville; 2256 3811/3812; e ecuhaiti@hainet.net
Dominican Republic 121 Rue Panaméricaine, Pétionville; 2257 9215/0383; e embrepdomhai@yahoo.com; (Consulate) 85 Rue Rigaud, Pétionville; 2257 1968/1208
France 51 Rue Capois; 2999 9000/9001; e contact@ambafrance.ht.org; www.ambafrance.ht.org
Germany 2 Impasse Claudinette, Bois Moquette, Pétionville; 2257 6131/2949 0202; e info@port-au-prince.diplo.de; www.port-au-prince.diplo.de
Holland (Consulate) 66 Pl Boyer, Pétionville; 2940 9642; e rpadberg@bndhaiti.org
Italy (Consulate) 26 Bis, Bd Toussaint Louverture (opposite DHL), Delmas; 2257 1113/3449 9894; e joanny.matteis@agacorp.com
Japan Hexagon Bldg (corner of rues Clerveaux & Darguin), Pétionville; 2256 3333/5885; www.ht.emb-japan.go.jp
Switzerland 12 Rue Ogé 12 (3rd Floor), Pl St Pierre, Pétionville; 2257 9862/0503; e ppc.vertretung@eda.admin.ch; www.eda.admin.ch/portauprince
UK (Honorary consulate) 337 Route de Delmas (by Delmas 73, opposite ERF); 3744 6371; e florence.boucard-hon@fconet.fco.gov.uk. As the guide was going to press, it was announced that the UK would open a full embassy in Port-au-Prince in 2013.
USA 41 Route de Tabarre, Tabarre; 2229 8000; http://haiti.usembassy.gov
Venezuela 2 Bd Harry Truman; 2222 0971/3949; e embavenzhaiti@hainet

Please note that Ireland, Australia and New Zealand do not have diplomatic representation in Haiti.

HEALTH There are plenty of hospitals in Port-au-Prince, of varying quality. Pharmacies can be found on any main road, and are well versed in diagnosing the most common complaints.

For non-emergencies, many embassies maintain lists of medical practitioners; the list from the US embassy (*http://haiti.usembassy.gov*) can be downloaded as a PDF. A 24-hour ambulance service is run by **OFATMA** (*2943 2907; www.oftama.gouv.ht*).

✚ **Clinique Lambert (Margaret Degand)** 75 Rue Lambert, Pétionville; ☎ 3702 3646/3470 3646

✚ **Hôpital Bernard Mevs (Medishare)** Route de l'Aèroport; ☎ 3604 7572/3999 2099

✚ **Hôpital de la Communauté Haïtienne** Rue Audant, Route de Frères; ☎ 2816 1313/2816 1212 (emergency); www.haitihosp.org

✚ **Hôpital du Canapé Vert** 83 Route de Canapé Vert; ☎ 2245 0984/0985

✚ **Hôpital Français** 378 Rue du Centre; ☎ 2511 9873/2223 2110

LANGUAGE COURSES Regular Creole-language beginner, intermediate and advanced courses are offered at the **International Haitian Creole Institute** (e *creoleinstitute@gmail.com*). Classes are taught at the Quisqueya Christian School on Delmas 75; a course of 30 two-hour lessons costs US$750 (including teaching materials).

The **Institut Haitiano-Américain** (*corner of rues Capois & Saint Cyr;* ☎ *2222 3715/2947;* e *haipaph@gmail.com; www.haitian-americaninstitute.org*) offers an 11-week Creole-language course, costing US$150.

The **Institut Français** (*99 Rue Lamartinière, Bois Verna;* ☎ *2244 0016; www.institutfrancaishaiti.org*) has French- and Creole-language classes, costing US$150 for each 20-hour course.

MONEY AND BANKING Port-au-Prince has an increasing number of **ATMs**, mostly operated by Sogebank. Useful ATMs include: branches on Delmas 30 and Delmas 48, on Impasse Père Huc, on Route de Frères, Rue Capois downtown, on Route National 2 in Martissant and Carrefour, and inside Eagle Market on Delmas 83. In Pétionville ATMs include the Sogebank branches at the corner of rues Louverture and Géffrard, inside Giant Supermarket at the corner of rues Ogé and Géffrard, and at the Hotel Karibe in Juvenat. The fast-food chain Epi d'Or also has ATMs in its branches on Delmas 56 and Rue Faubert in Pétionville. Unibank has ATMs at its branches on Rue Capois, Canapé-Vert, Frères and the corner of rues Clerveaux and Lambert in Pétionville.

To change money, avoid the banks and go to a supermarket – they all have a counter where you can change US dollars, and usually a sign up giving the day's exchange rate. You'll sometimes see people in the street clutching wads of bills offering to change money, but these come with the usual caveat about flashing large amounts of money in public.

POLICE The emergency telephone number for the police is 122 or 3842 1111. The main police stations are on Rue Légitime downtown, and Place St Pierre in Pétionville, but all districts have their own smaller stations (*commissariat*).

TRAVEL AGENTS

Agence Citadelle Complexe Promenade, cnr of rues Grégoire & Moise, Pétionville; ☎ 2940 5900/2257-3868; e info@agencecitadelle; www.agencecitadelle.com. Long-established & reliable travel agent.

Uniglobe 149 Rue Faubert, Pétionville; ☎ 2941 0741/2941 0742; e uniglobe@hainet.net. Efficient service.

WHAT TO SEE AND DO

MUSEUMS

National Pantheon Museum (Musée du Panthéon National, MUPANAH)

(*Rue de la Republique, Champs de Mars;* ☎ *3610 3457/2222 8337;* ⌚ *08.00–16.00*

Mon–Sat, 10.00–16.00 Sun; admission 125HTG) Haiti's national museum is a compact affair, sat across the road from the Palais National. Part of its charm comes from the building itself, sunk into the ground with blue mosaic chimneys (said to echo the houses of the Taíno) rising from a roof-top pool, like some peculiar tropical bunker.

You enter into a round atrium with a glittering gold sculpture of the cannons, flags and palmiste tree that make up Haiti's coat of arms. The surrounding walls are an honour list of national heroes – from Caonabo and other Taíno who fought the Spanish to the leading figures of the Haitian Revolution. Busts of Toussaint Louverture, Dessalines, Pétion and Christophe look on approvingly – their last mortal remains are interred beneath the sculpture.

A long gallery curls behind the atrium, with key artefacts from Haitian history. First up is a large Taíno dug-out canoe and some splendid examples of their intricate pottery, including a large ritual bowl found in a cave at Gros Morne. Polished stone axes and amulets and tiny masks with gargoyle faces further hint at Taíno cultural life, but there's little explanation from the captions as to their wider meaning.

The Spanish period is represented in the swords and armour of a conquistador, and a huge ship's anchor thought to be from the *Santa María*, Columbus's ship that ran aground near Bord de Limonade in 1492. Some frankly terrifying iron slave shackles herald the arrival of French Saint-Domingue; a sugar loaf resembling a giant mortar shell rams home the bloody story behind the European sweet tooth.

Moving into the revolutionary period, there's a splendid *tambou* drum once owned by Pétion, painted with the Haitian coat of arms, and letters from Christophe announcing the arrival of the French invasion to Toussaint. There are various weapons, but one of the most striking inclusions is a painting commissioned for Haiti's centenary celebrations of the independence heroes raising their swords while overlooked by angels, while Haiti, represented as a red-and-blue-clad woman, walks proudly forward with a sword and banner proclaiming liberty or death.

A personally signed copy of Christophe's *Code Rural* and coins with Pétion's head skirt around their dividing of Haiti, while the display of Boyer's treaty of friendship with France neglects to mention the imposition of the crippling indemnity he'd been forced to pay. Then it's swiftly along to the bling of Emperor Faustin's crown and ceremonial swords, a burnt fragment of Admiral Killick's doomed flagship, then a rush through to the US occupation (the famous photograph of the 'crucified' Charlemagne Péralte is on display) and beyond – finishing with some fragments of moon rock and a tiny Haitian flag presented by Richard Nixon, having been sent to the moon and back by the Apollo 11 mission.

There's a second gallery behind the exhibits, with an exhibition of Haitian painting. There are some great canvases, including works by masters like Castera Bazile and Rigaud Benoît, but like the rest of the museum, they're let down by poor labelling and lack of any accompanying context. It's certainly fascinating to see Papa Doc's cane, homburg hat and carbine rifle, but only if you've already been primed with the historical background. Guides are available for further explanations, but don't always speak English.

Museum of Haitian Art (Musée d'Art Haïtien) (*16 Rue Légitime, Champs de Mars; 2222 2510; 10.00–17.00 Mon–Sat, 10.00–16.00 Sun; admission 50HTG*) Established in 1972 on the edge of Champs de Mars to give an introduction to Haitian art, this small museum holds a great and important collection of paintings by Haitian masters. Frustratingly, it consistently punches below its weight, and keeps a lot of its permanent collection in storage, instead devoting much of its space to temporary exhibitions and retrospectives that are often poorly displayed. It's quite frustrating, especially since the museum passed through the earthquake largely unscathed, while the famous Centre d'Art, the murals of the Sainte Trinité Episcopalian Cathedral and the Musée d'Art Nader all fell victim. Passing art fans might find it of interest, but casual visitors won't feel like they're missing out by not looking for it (although its restaurant – La Table de Caïus – is well worth checking out; see *Where to eat*, page 106).

CHAMPS DE MARS The biggest open space in downtown Port-au-Prince is Champs de Mars (Chanmas in Creole). It's home to the National Palace, the National Museum and a series of monuments marking key moments in Haitian history, set in a number of parks intersected by wide tree-lined avenues. Given the busy press of people, traffic and buildings in most of the city, the sudden sense of space comes as a mild, but pleasant, surprise. That said, Champ de Mars was heavily affected by the earthquake and its scars are still clear for anyone to see – not least in the crumpled ruins of the destroyed Palais National (National Palace).

Champs de Mars was parkland used for army parades for much of Port-au-Prince's history until it was turned into a racetrack in 1912, with grand wrought-iron viewing stands facing the Palais National. In 1945 it was officially renamed the Place des Héros de l'Indépendence. Its current layout is from 1999, when the area was remodelled to celebrate Port-au-Prince's 250th anniversary.

GINGERBREAD HOUSES

Gingerbreads are Port-au-Prince's most emblematic houses. They're instantly identifiable, usually tall buildings with steep metal roofs, and wide porches and balconies decorated with fine latticework. In short, they look like something from a Caribbean fairy tale. There are about 200 in Port-au-Prince, concentrated in the areas of Bois Verna, Pacot and Turgeau.

The first gingerbreads were built following the construction of the National Palace by George Baussan in 1881, who introduced new themes into Haitian architecture: wood frames lined with brick, carved wooden façades and high ceilings and windows with large galleries. Although this version of the National Palace was destroyed in 1912 (by an accidental gunpowder explosion – the palace also served as a military magazine), the style was instantly copied. Of the gingerbreads of this period, the most famous (and readily accessible to modern visitors) is the Hotel Oloffson, built in 1887 as a private residence, turned into a military hospital during the US occupation and finally converted to a hotel in 1935.

The majority of Port-au-Prince's gingerbreads were built by just three men: Baussan, Léon Mathon and Joseph Eugene Maximilian, architects who returned to their native Haiti in 1895 after training in Paris. They refined and modified the gingerbreads to create some truly Baroque buildings perfectly suited to their environment, decorating them with turret roofs resembling witches' hats or lacy filigree ironwork, with designs inspired by Haitian folk-art and *vèvè* symbols from Vodou. As well as beautiful, the houses were practical, with shady porches, high ceilings directing hot air above the living spaces, and plenty of side-windows to catch the breeze.

The gingerbread boom came to an end in 1925, when the Mayor of Port-au-Prince banned wooden construction due to the risk of fire. Although once the province of the rich, many descendants of the original owners can no longer

At the heart of Champs de Mars is the **Palais National**, the site of the French governor's residence during the colonial period, and home to every Haitian president since Pétion. There have been several palaces since independence, their fate a seeming reflection on the turbulence of Haitian history. The first, built in the late 18th century, was destroyed under bombardment by a warship in the 1869 civil war. Its replacement wasn't built until 1881, but when completed its elegant new style kick-started the fashion for gingerbread houses. Unfortunately, a section of it was used as a gunpowder store and the whole thing blew sky-high in 1912, killing the incumbent President Lecanto. The present building dates from 1915, a gleaming white triple-domed building, blending French renaissance style and the White House in Washington, DC.

The palace collapsed in the 2010 earthquake, the image of its cracked façade and slumping domes becoming instant media shorthand for the earthquake. As of summer 2012, only part of the structure has been cleared. When rebuilding will finally take place is anyone's guess – another metaphor perhaps, this time for the halting pace of Haiti's reconstruction.

On a square in front of the palace is a proud statue of **Toussaint Louverture** – elsewhere in the parks around Champs de Mars are equally prominent statues of a mounted Jean-Jacques Dessalines, Pétion and Henri Christophe (also on horseback). The statues were erected to celebrate Haiti's 150th anniversary in 1954.

afford to maintain the properties, with the result that some are falling into severe neglect (the wood is particularly termite-prone). Despite this, the gingerbreads weathered the 2010 earthquake surprisingly well – around 5% of them were damaged or collapsed compared with 40% of concrete buildings in Port-au-Prince (of those that were seriously damaged, most had undergone bad restorations that compromised the flexibility of their wooden frames).

In 2010, the World Monument Fund carried out the first comprehensive review of the gingerbreads, in partnership with the cultural foundation FOKAL (*www.fokal.org*) and ISPAN, Haiti's national heritage body. Fokal ultimately hopes to have the square mile that contains most of the houses turned into a heritage area, a project that could cost US$10 million, although there are many hurdles to overcome before that can come to pass – from the legal status of the private buildings (Haiti has no equivalent to the UK's system of listed buildings or the US's National Register of Historic Places) to the hard economics of protecting the buildings (which often sit in large grounds) from the covetous wallets of developers.

Modern constructions like high security walls have masked some gingerbreads from view, but it's still possible to make a worthwhile tour. One of the highest concentrations is found along Avenue Lamartinière in Bois Verna, including the twin-steepled #15, #32 built by president Tancrede Auguste in 1914, the slim-fit #52, and the grandly roofed #84. Le Manoir at 126 Avenue John Brown is another fine example, along with the Peabody House in Pacot. And of course, you can always take a drink on the veranda at the Hotel Oloffson.

For more information, see the 2010 report *Preserving Haiti's Gingerbread Houses* by the World Monument Fund (*www.wmf.org*), as well as Anghelen Arrington Phillips's beautiful sketchbook *Gingerbread Houses: Haiti's Endangered Species*, available in Port-au-Prince bookshops.

The statue of Toussaint Louverture stands between the palace and the iconic statue of the **Nèg Mawon** (Marron Inconnu, or Unknown Slave). Sculpted by Albert Mangonès, it's the most famous statue in Haiti. The slave has broken his shackles, and with a machete in one hand puts a conch shell to his lips with the other, blowing a call to revolution. Rather less inspiring, next to the Nèg Mawon is a scroll-like monument that used to contain an Eternal Flame, commissioned by Jean-Claude Duvalier. It went out in 1986 when he fled the country, but was relit in May 2012 on the first anniversary of President Martelly's inauguration.

Across the street from the Unknown Slave is **Place des Martyrs**, a tiny park centred on a bronze statue of a man releasing a dove, held up by a mass of people. It was erected in 1994 following the return of Aristide to power and has frequently been a focus for political demonstrations (note the trampled soldier at the rear of the base – the army was abolished the same year the statue went up).

One monument in Champs de Mars stands above all others – a huge squat pyramid in raw concrete. This is the **Monument Bicentenaire**, ordered by Aristide to celebrate 200 years of Haitian independence, but the 2004 coup meant that it was never finished. Finally, on Rue Capois opposite the Plaza Hotel is a black marble monolith dedicated to the Haitian constitution.

In the days after the 12 January 2010 earthquake, the whole of Champs de Mars quickly became a giant tent city. The statues of the founding fathers were barely visible, poking above a sea of tarpaulins. It took around 18 months for it to be cleared, but the surrounding area remains fringed with damaged and fractured buildings. The destruction stretches back towards the sea, with the area behind Champs de Mars to Grand Rue and Bicentenaire being one of the hardest hit.

IRON MARKET (MARCHÉ DE FER) (*Bd Jean-Jacques Dessalines*) If the destroyed Palais National on Champs de Mars stands as one of the most potent symbols of the destruction of 12 January 2010, Port-au-Prince's other truly iconic building, the Marché de Fer, is a real symbol of rebirth and reconstruction. Largely ruined in the earthquake and its aftermath but now completely restored, a busy centre of commerce on Boulevard Jean-Jacques Dessalines (Grand Rue) as it has been for 120 years.

The Marché de Fer (also known as the Marché Hyppolite, or just the Iron Market) sits on the site of the original market that sprang up near the waterfront on Port-au-Prince's founding in 1749. Today, it consists of two large halls, joined together by a central pavilion with four clock towers, all painted in a striking scarlet and deep green. It was erected in 1891 under the auspices of President Hector Hyppolite, who expended a great deal of energy on public works to improve the city (the 1889 date inscribed on the pavilion relates to the start of his presidency rather than the market's construction). The structure is almost entirely made of cast iron. The parts were imported from France to be erected like a giant model kit, but the source of the building's design is shrouded in mystery – the Moorish-styled pavilion, with its minaret-like towers, has given rise to the story that it was originally intended to be the main hall of Cairo's train station, but when the sale fell through it was snapped up by Hyppolite.

The market was wrecked by the earthquake, but its rapid restoration was personally underwritten by Digicel founder Denis O'Brien to the tune of US$12 million, working with British architects and the Haitian heritage organisation ISPAN. Many of the market holders were employed in the reconstruction, and their pitches held for them until the market's reopening – just 11 months after the earthquake. The rebuild included earthquake strengthening and solar panels for electricity.

The two halls are given over to different types of goods. The southern hall (on the left as you enter) is for food, with stalls piled high with sacks of rice, fruit, meat on the block and kitchenware. The air is thick with ginger, tamarind and the earthy aroma of dried *djondjon* mushrooms. The north hall is full of arts and handicrafts. While tourists might be thin on the ground today, in the 1960s when cruise ships docked nearby, this market claimed to be the most popular tourist destination in Haiti, a bigger draw even than the Citadelle. While many of the goods – woodcarvings and paintings – seem instantly familiar, the most fascinating part is the third of the hall section given over to Vodou. Here you'll find not just sequined Vodou flags, but stalls selling nothing but tiny bottles of perfume or powder (each to be used in rituals for a specific *lwa*) icons, rattles, crucibles and more.

There's undoubtedly a little bit of hustle at the Marché de Fer, but it's not too pushy. Many stall holders speak pretty good English, so even if you don't want to buy, you might want to tip one to take you around to explain some of the Vodou paraphernalia.

A five-minute walk from the Marché de Fer is another striking example of the late-19th-century vogue for metallic architecture. The **Chapelle Saint-Louis de Gonzague** (*180 Rue de Centre*) is another cast-iron kit building, erected in 1896. Its pretty blue-grey façade with silver detailing and mosaics over the porch and rose window is worth a detour.

GRAND RUE ARTISTS (*622 Bd Jean-Jacques Dessalines; www.atis-rezistans.com*) It's easy to think of Haitian art in clichés – so many bright canvases of rural life enlivening the street walls of Port-au-Prince, or their more elegant cousins hung in the galleries of Pétionville. The sculptors of Grand Rue, also known as by their collective name Atis-Rezistans, take that notion and turn it thoroughly on its head to produce art of the most incredible visual potency.

The artists live and work in a part of Port-au-Prince surrounded by auto workshops, hemmed in by the backwash of uncontrolled urbanisation. Their response has been to turn their surroundings into art, scavenging car parts, old wood, TV sets – anything – to reinterpret Haitian culture for the 21st century. Vibrant Vodou spirits of life, death and sex all figure prominently, often topped off with real human skulls (or doll's heads). There's a sense of dystopia – a disregard for the cycle of Haitian politics and the reality of material poverty, yet the art is transformative too, with self-reliance and recycling of found materials enabling the artists to recreate their own identities and community.

The two lead artists are André Eugene and Jean Hérard Celeur, but the purpose of Atis-Rezistans is to engage all around them. Their youth offshoot, Ti Moun Resiztans involves children as young as six in the creation of art. As well as making art a focus for their own community, Atis-Rezistans have worked hard to attract foreign artists to Port-au-Prince, acting as hosts for their very own Ghetto Biennale (*www.ghettobiennale.com*) every other December (the next is due to be held in 2013). The focus is very much on collaboration – in 2011 over 50 international artists visited to work with the community and produced their own and shared pieces of art, which were presented along with concerts, screenings, talks and Vodou ceremonies. In a happy parallel, André Eugene, Jean Hérard Celeur and Jean Claude Saintilus were chosen to represent Haiti for its first presentation at the Venice Biennale.

To find the artists, look for the sculpture of the Vodou lwa Papa Legba on Grand Rue – he's a hard-to-miss 8m-high figure made from an old truck chassis, sporting an impressive giant red phallus. Immediately behind this there is a small exhibition space for Ti Moun Rezistans – their art is also displayed on the surrounding walls – followed by the gallery-home of André Eugene. There is an open area here displaying art by all the members of the collective. As with any gallery, the art is for

BICENTENAIRE AND GRAND RUE

For a city founded as a port, the sea in Port-au-Prince can often seem a distant thing, seen from a hillside. Little-visited now, the seafront area used to be a major draw for foreign visitors. In 1949, the city hosted a World Fair to celebrate its bicentennial. The area near the docks was developed into the model Cité de l'Exposition, with wide boulevards and waterside parks. At its heart were a ceremonial tower and a fountain with its own *son et lumière*. The dock received cruise tourists, who would spend their dollars at the souvenir stores along Grand Rue, and their nights at the many clubs and casinos.

Since the Duvalier period, the area has fallen into slow disrepair. The imperious statue of Christopher Columbus was toppled into the bay in 1986 after the ouster of Jean-Claude Duvalier. The old Cité, at the top of Bicentenaire, feels deserted, something only exacerbated by damage from the earthquake, which levelled the Legislative Palace at its centre. The musical statue still stands (albeit silently), along with a grand statue of Simón Bolívar. The area has been surveyed by Haiti's historical preservation organisation ISPAN with a view to further regeneration; recently rebuilt bank buildings behind the Marché de Fer and the bright Chapelle Sixtine on Avenue Marie-Jeanne (once the Vatican's World Fair Pavilion) may hopefully point to a brighter future for this prime real estate.

Boulevard Jean-Jacques Dessalines – Grand Rue – fared similarly on 12 January 2010, and even today the material damage is there to see. However, where buildings have been wrecked, business continues in the street. At the junction with Delmas is Croix Bossales, one of the biggest market areas. Above this, the street turns into Route National 1 at Carrefour Aviation – the old Pont Rouge where Dessalines was assassinated (a cenotaph marks the spot). Commerce continues unabated as you head south past the Marché de Fer towards Portail Léogâne, with its cheap hotels, bars and auto-shops. It isn't always pretty – the streets can be clogged with rubbish, standing water and traffic fumes aplenty – and yet, this oldest of Port-au-Prince's thoroughfares remains one of the most vital and alive parts of the city.

sale, although some pieces are absolutely huge (others might shock your granny if you displayed them on your mantelpiece). There is usually someone around to show you the place, and you'll need to be taken further back through the close-packed cinderblock houses to the workshops of the other artists.

NOTRE DAME CATHEDRAL (*Rue Dr Aubrey, Bel Air*) The spiritual heart of Bel Air – indeed, of Port-au-Prince – has always been the Cathédrale Notre Dame de l'Assomption. It was built between 1889 and 1914 and for a long time stood alongside an older 18th-century cathedral, which was sadly razed by arsonists during political unrest in 1991 (its old bell is on display at MUPANAH).

The cathedral was one of the most high-profile casualties of the 2010 earthquake, when its roof collapsed, bringing down its upper walls and turrets. The cathedral was the oldest public building in Haiti to be made of reinforced concrete, and its age apparently made it particularly susceptible to tremors (the second oldest, the Palais National, was an equal victim).

The site was left largely uncleared for over a year while the diocese, together with ISPAN explored preservation options for the ruins. In spring 2012 an international design competition was launched for a new cathedral to cost US$40 million, and hopefully be consecrated by the tenth anniversary of the earthquake. Plans and progress can be seen on the website www.ndapap.org.

PORT-AU-PRINCE CEMETERY (GRAND CIMETIÈRE) Port-au-Prince's main cemetery is almost a city in itself, spread out behind the Sylvio Cator stadium at Portail Léogâne. It's a strange place of monolithic sarcophagi, mortuary chapels and family shrines, all testament to the Haitian tradition of raising decorated tombs to the honour of ancestors.

It's a jumbled-up place, with grand tombs mixed up with others ruined in the earthquake, overgrown weeds and even the occasional scattered human bones, either taken from one of the tombs designed for short-term occupancy, or left over from broken-open and abandoned coffins. You'll undoubtedly be approached by someone offering to show you around. You'll almost certainly be taken to see the wrecked tomb of François Duvalier, who was buried here with great ceremony in 1971. Following the collapse of his son's rule 15 years later, crowds made their way here to show their displeasure by tearing his mausoleum open with their bare hands. However, when the tomb was opened, his coffin had vanished, presumably smuggled out of the country on Jean-Claude Duvalier's flight into exile.

The image of Duvalier *père* seems particularly appropriate in the cemetery, given how he so often publicly associated himself with the Vodou lwa Baron Samedi. The Baron is the guardian of the crossroads between life and death, and he is

THE SAINTE TRINITE MURALS

One of Haiti's artistic icons was the Sainte Trinité Episcopalian Cathedral. Built on the site of an older church founded by 19th-century African-Americans fleeing slavery, from 1947 to 1950 the cathedral commissioned painters from the Centre d'Art to decorate its interior with murals. The results were a bright and giddy textbook of the Haitian masters, with scenes from the Bible reinterpreted as having taken place in a Haitian context – something that scandalised polite society at the time. Préfète Duffaut showed the procession to Calvary taking place in the streets of his native Jacmel, while Wilson Bigaud had Jesus turning water to wine to a backing of *rara* bands at the Wedding at Cana. Behind the apse, three huge panels depicted the Nativity (by Rigaud Benoît), Crucifixion (Philomé Obin) and Ascension (Castera Bazile) in glorious magic realist style.

The cathedral came down on 12 January 2010. Of the 15 murals, only three survived in cracked but recognisable form – Castera Bazile's *Baptism* (with Christ and John the Baptist in a very Haitian scene surrounded by women washing clothes at the river), Préfète Duffaut's Jacmel-meets-Calvary *Native Procession*, and Philomé Obin's three-walled *Last Supper*. The rest were reduced to dust. The Haiti Cultural Recovery Project (*http://haiti.si.edu*), run by the Smithsonian Institution with the Ministry of Culture has worked to conserve what remains, with international conservation experts training Haitian counterparts. The murals spent the first six months after the earthquake exposed to the elements, before being properly covered. All were then painstakingly removed from their walls, and taken away for conservation and storage. The plan is to eventually install them when the cathedral's replacement is built, perhaps even to be augmented with murals from the current generation of Haitian masters.

BEL AIR

The district of Bel Air is the oldest residential part of Port-au-Prince. It was designed as the administrative centre, in the clean air away from the docks and market. Bel Air begins uphill of Grand Rue and takes in the whole of the Champs de Mars area up towards Delmas 2, but is more generally referred to as the area above the cathedral. Once a sought-after locale, overcrowding in the late 19th century saw the moneyed classes move out in favour of greener Pacot and Bois Verna; Bel Air is now one of the poorer parts of the city.

Bel Air carries something of a reputation before it. It has always been an important centre of Lavalas support, and has subsequently suffered in the periods following the two coups against Aristide. In 2005 in particular, the district was considered particularly dangerous due to gang violence and heavy-handed policing that led to the deaths of many residents. Despite the reputation, Bel Air is no longer considered a no-go area and contains many important ateliers for local craftsmen, in particular Vodou flag-makers. They have organised themselves into the **Coordination des Artistes et Artisans du Bel-Air** (CAABEL; *Mario Calixte 3663 1436; www.belair.net*), and now welcome visitors.

At the junction of Rue Macajoux and Rue du Peuple is the statue of Madan Kolo, a French female colonist who has become one of Bel Air's symbols. The streets around the statue are full of market traders.

everywhere in the cemetery, from the skeletal murals of him with his wife Maman Brigitte and the other Gede (spirits of the dead), to the black crosses that are his signifiers. The stubs of candles, empty bottles of rum and smudged *vévé* symbols are all signs that, for followers of Vodou, the cemetery is a place of everyday worship and communion with past generations.

The cemetery is at its busiest every 1 and 2 November, for Fet Gede, the Vodou festival of the dead. Celebrations and rituals last all day and through the night, with adherents dressed in white and purple, and a lot of music, rum and lewd behaviour.

MARTISSANT PARK (PARC DE MARTISSANT) (*Martissant 23; 2813 1695; www.parcdemartissant.org; Tue–Sun; admission free*) The crush of traffic, fumes and people along Route de Carrefour as it grinds through Martissant seems the unlikeliest place in Port-au-Prince to seek the green restorative power of the natural world. And yet as you climb the hill, here it is – 15 acres of beautiful wooded parkland.

The park is the brainchild of the cultural organisation **FOKAL** (*www.fokal.org*), and is part of an ongoing community regeneration project in Martissant. The park is divided over three linked properties – the Habitation Leclerc, Residence Katherine Dunham and Residence Albert Mangonés. Restoration has been ongoing since 2008, and at the time of research, only the last named (at the top of the hill) had been opened to the public.

Albert Mangonés was a celebrated architect and sculptor who oversaw the 1980s restoration of the Citadelle and designed the famous Nèg Mawon statue in front of the Palais National on Champs de Mars. The grounds of his house have been landscaped to form the **Mémorial du Parc de Martissant**, commemorating those lost to the 2010 earthquake. The gardens are lovely to walk around and a place for quiet contemplation. While there is no central monument, in places the paths are paved with the ghostly outlines of figures, and there is a central platform looking out over Port-au-Prince bay. A banner spreads across the scene with a quote from St Therese of Lisieux, 'I understood that Love is everything, that it embraces all times and places, that it was eternal.'

The largest section of the park will be the **Habitation Leclerc** – the first property you reach uphill from the main road. The *habitation* was owned by the French general Leclerc, sent to crush the rebellious slaves in 1802, but ending up dying of yellow fever. His wife Pauline was Napoleon's sister, and reputedly lived here. In the 1940s it was bought by the dancer Katherine Dunham, and then turned into a luxury hotel in the 1970s. Mick Jagger and Jackie Onassis were famous guests. It was badly damaged by the earthquake and is undergoing restoration. The grounds are thickly planted

CITÉ SOLEIL

Home to around 300,000 people, Cité Soleil is Port-au-Prince's most famous – that is to say, notorious – slum area. Its name is frequently invoked as a byword for gang violence although as with many things in Haiti the reality is rather different and less alarming than the hype. Far from being a pit of anarchy, Cité Soleil has one of the strongest senses of community identity in Port-au-Prince.

Cité Soleil was always intended to be for the poorest of the poor – it was founded in 1958 by François Duvalier to be a source of cheap labour for the nearby industrial zone on the northern outskirts of Port-au-Prince, originally naming it Cité Simone after his wife. Unfortunately the location chosen, a low-lying marshy area, was less than ideal for residential purposes, and the municipality floods regularly during the rainy season.

Cité Soleil came to national prominence during the Aristide era, and formed a strong backbone of support for the Lavalas movement. In turn, the area suffered in the period following the two coups against him, with widespread reprisals by the security forces. At the same time, Cité Soleil became a centre for gang activity (pro-Lavalas gangs were often dubbed *chimères*, or monsters). The worst years were 2004–05, with kidnappings at their height, as well as being the period of Operation Baghdad, Minustah's armed (and much-contested) anti-gang response. Today, the gang situation has greatly subsided, and Cité Soleil's crime rate is on a par with any other part of Port-au-Prince. Preconceptions remain, however, and perceived security concerns meant that it took longer than almost any area in the city to receive aid after the earthquake.

There are around 34 quarters to Cité Soleil, each with names such as Brooklyn, Norway or Philadelphia. In January 2012, a new quarter called Paris was demarcated, an event celebrated by the community raising their very own Eiffel Tower, a 1:100-scale replica of the original. Although its popular image is of tightly packed cinderblock houses, around half of Cité Soleil is actually rural, and includes the Barbancourt factory and several co-operatively run organic banana plantations.

Although a large number of NGOs are active in Cité Soleil, there are many community organisations working on finding solutions to their own problems, such as **La Différence**, a local committee working since 2003 to clean up neighbourhoods through communal work groups (*konbits*) clearing rubbish, street cleaning and house-painting. **Soley Leve** (*www.soley-leve.org*) is a coalition of similar *konbits*, all working through self-reliance to rehabilitate their neighbourhoods – and Cité Soleil's image in the process.

with mature trees and are rich in birdlife – when finally opened to the public it should become a major draw for people craving some nature in the city.

Slightly uphill on the right is the **Residence Katherine Dunham**, latterly the dancer's private home. Redevelopment plans here include a cultural centre and library, with the gardens being turned over to plants used in traditional Haitian medicine.

PETIONVILLE Pétionville has traditionally been Port-au-Prince's mirror image. Where the capital sweated with congestion and overcrowding, Pétionville was cooler and spacious, a residential suburb in the mountains. However, over the years Pétionville has itself grown and become crowded, a commercial hub sucking business away from downtown. This process has only accelerated since the earthquake. Today, Pétionville is where you find the best restaurants, hotels and boutique shops, as well as the headquarters for many of the larger NGOs.

The town was founded in 1831 as a potential alternative capital, at a place called La Coupe Charbonnière which was a large charcoal-producing area. It was popularised as a destination in the 1850s by Emperor Faustin Soulouque, who frequently holidayed here. Although urban sprawl has now well and truly wrapped the town into Port-au-Prince, as late as the 1950s tourist guidebooks could tout its attractions as a green mountain resort high above the city (if you want to note where Port-au-Prince ends and Pétionville begins, look for the municipal signs just above Delmas 91, or near Musseau on Rue Panaméricaine).

The centre of Pétionville is laid out in a grid, with Place St Pierre at the top, framed on one side by St Pierre Church (which contains some lovely stained-glass windows), and on the other by the gingerbread-style Kinam Hotel, at the corner where Route de Kenscoff leads up into the mountains. At the bottom of the square

KATHERINE DUNHAM IN HAITI

The African-American dancer Katherine Dunham was a widely influential figure in 20th-century dance. As much anthropologist as choreographer, in the 1930s she travelled widely in the Caribbean to study local dances and, if possible, trace their roots back to African forms. In 1936 she visited Haiti for the first time and began an association with the island that lasted her entire life. Haitian dance shaped her own, with Vodou rituals and drumming being a particularly strong influence – Dunham went on to study Vodou and became a *mambo* in her own right. Back in the USA, she incorporated the dances and rhythms into her own work, and met great success when her company toured internationally. She was a glamorous figure, but also a social activist, and fought against racial segregation in the States.

Whenever time allowed, Dunham made Haiti her retreat, purchasing the Habitation Leclerc in the 1940s, to which she added a pavilion for dance performances and her own personal Vodou *peristyle*. A memoir of her time in Haiti, *Island Possessed*, published in 1969 makes for a fascinating read, bringing the spirits and folk stories attached to the property alive, as well as painting a lively portrait of Haiti and its political scene of the 1940s and 50s.

Dunham's last great act of solidarity with Haiti came in 1992 when she went on hunger strike at the age of 82 to protest against the American treatment of Haitian boat people following the first coup against Aristide. She starved herself for 47 days until Aristide personally asked her to stop – he later called her the 'spiritual mother' of Haiti. She died in 2006, aged 96.

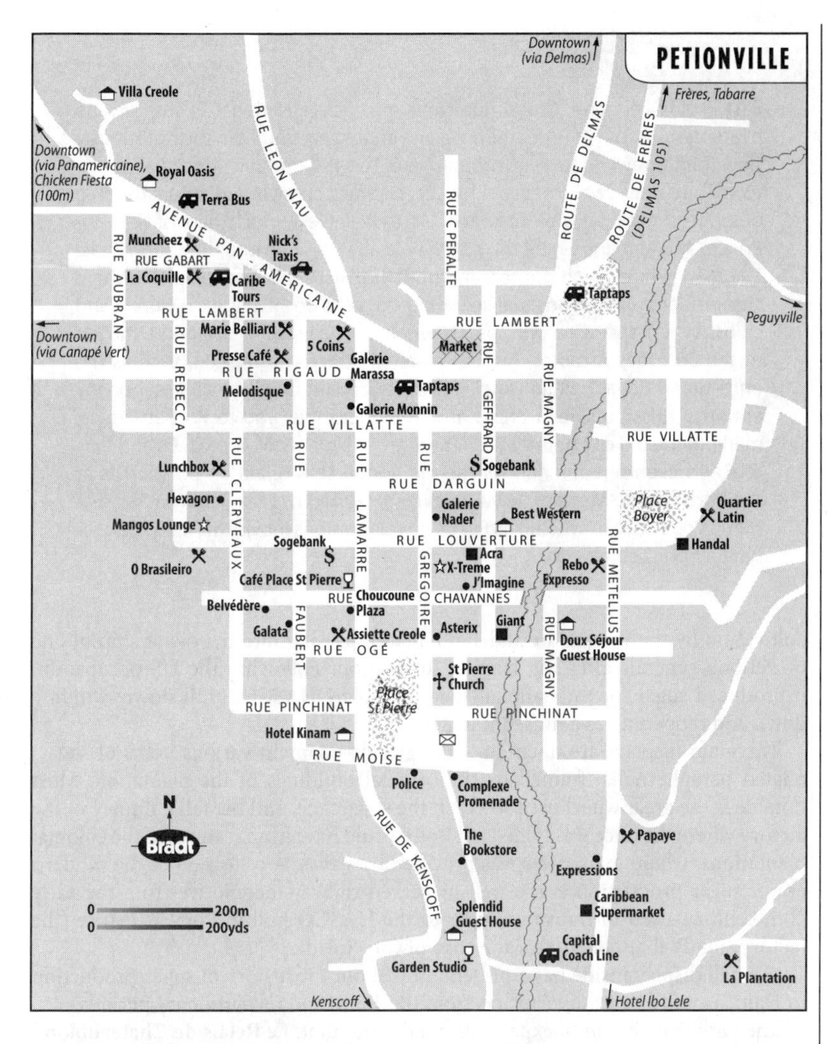

there's a permanent flower market. At the centre of the square is a statue of Pétion with an allegorical figure representing Haiti, erected in 1904 to celebrate the centenary of independence. The square holds occasional open-air art shows and artisanal fairs; it has recently undergone restoration, having served as a tent camp for nearly two years after the earthquake (nearby Place Boyer, Pétionville's other public space, was similarly occupied).

At the bottom of Pétionville, where Rue Panaméricaine, Route de Delmas and Route de Frères all roughly converge, there's a busy and moderately chaotic street market. The traffic clogs terribly here – the nearby cemetery was controversially razed in 2011 to make way for a new bus and *taptap* station – but at the time of writing the area had been fenced off for at least a year with little sign of any building work.

PARC HISTORIQUE DE LA CANNE À SUCRE (*48 Bd 15 Octobre, Tabarre; ☎ 2256 8051; www.parchistorique.ht*) On the outskirts of Port-au-Prince, this museum-park stands on the site of an old sugar plantation. The site was first used for sugar

CARREFOUR

Past Portail Léogâne, Grand Rue turns into Route National 2, and anyone heading south out of Port-au-Prince inevitably gets caught in the notoriously slow traffic crawling its way through here. This is Carrefour – once a separate town but now swallowed up by the capital's sprawl, and often used to describe the whole area between Martissant (very much part of Port-au-Prince) and Mariani, where the highway finally runs free into the countryside. The road runs close to the sea, and until the 1980s this was the place where city residents and tourists alike would come to relax at beach hotels and clubs. When the area was overtaken by urbanisation, attention moved to the Côte des Arcadins, but there are still traces to be seen, such as the once-grand Royal Haitian Hotel with its sweeping driveway and mahogany entrance (just outside, a brand-new sign welcomes you to Port-au-Prince, marking the old city boundaries). There are still plenty of nightclubs and bars too, and even one remnant of the old Vodou shows laid on for tourists at the **Peristyle de Mariani** (*www.vodou.org*) owned by Max Beauvoir, head of Haiti's Vodouisants, who hosts Fet Gede celebrations for visitors in a purpose-built amphitheatre.

cultivation by the French around 1700, before passing into the ownership of one of Pétion's generals after the Haitian Revolution. Following the US occupation, it produced sugar for the national sugar company HASCO, until slowly winding down and reopening as a museum in 2004.

The main displays are open-air – the grounds contain various items of sugar-related paraphernalia, framed by the original buildings of the plantation. Most notable is the great wheel used to crush the sugarcane, and the tall chimney of the factory where the juice was boiled off. Both would have been features of the colonial plantations, where manpower was provided by slaves. A reflection of the modern era of sugar production is the well-preserved railway locomotive from the early 20th century, used to transport sugar to the HASCO mill in Port-au-Prince (the factory stands abandoned near the edge of Cité Soleil).

A small display inside has a presentation about the history of sugar production in Haiti, as well as various artefacts from the Taíno and revolutionary periods.

The park contains an unexpectedly good restaurant, **Le Relais de Chateaublond** (*2940 1101/3449 7407*), named after the original family owners of the plantation, serving decent sandwiches, steaks and salads and the like, and a lunchtime buffet. It's also a venue for regular live music concerts, advertised on billboards around the city.

4

Around Port-au-Prince

The gravitational pull of Port-au-Prince can sometimes seem irresistible. The city has plenty of diversions, but the constant buzz of traffic and press of people can easily leave you tired. This chapter has plenty of options for quick escapes from the city, either for the day or simple overnight trips.

The chapter is divided into four sections, each corresponding to the four cardinal points. To the south, the Route de Kenscoff leads into the cool mountain air of the Massif de la Selle. There are day walks to be had in pine forests here around Kenscoff and Furcy, and a great trek through Parc National la Visite to Seguin, which leads you in a day and a half down towards the Caribbean Sea near Jacmel. West of Port-au-Prince, Route National 2 leads through Léogâne towards Petit Goâve, an area with a number of good beach hotels and restaurants. They're relatively little visited in comparison to the Côte des Arcadins, the long stretch of coast that extends north from the capital, a popular weekend beach destination for well-heeled city-dwellers. Finally, heading east towards the Dominican border through the Plaine du Cul-de-Sac, there are the metal artists of Croix des Bouquets, the lakes of Trou Caïman and Étang Saumâtre, and the Forêt des Pins, where the most adventurous can hike Pic la Selle, Haiti's highest mountain.

In reality, Haiti is a small enough country that most places could be visited as overnight trips from Port-au-Prince/Jacmel and Port Salut (see *Chapter 5, Southern Haiti*, pages 142 and 162) are perennially popular for weekend getaways, while if you time the flights carefully enough it's possible to visit the Citadelle near Cap-Haïtien (see *Chapter 6, Northern Haiti*, page 184) as a day trip. A third option is the waterfalls of Saut d'Eau and Bassin Zim (see *Chapter 7, The Artibonite Valley and Central Plateau*, pages 216 and 218 respectively).

SOUTH OF PORT-AU-PRINCE

Route de Kenscoff is the main road south of the capital, starting at the top end of Place St Pierre in Pétionville by the Kinam Hotel, and winding slowly up into the mountains. It's a steep road, and as you climb the surroundings become noticeably greener and the air cleaner and fresher. Pack an extra layer to put on, and if it's anywhere near the rainy season, a waterproof. Compared with many parts of the country it's a relatively prosperous area – not only has it been a traditional retreat for the moneyed elite to build their villas, it's also agriculturally very productive. The slopes of the mountains are endlessly terraced into fields, and the market towns of Fermathe and Kenscoff in particular provide huge amounts of fresh produce for the hungry city below.

If you don't have your own transport, *taptaps* to Fermathe and Kenscoff leave from the bottom of Rue Grégoire (near the market) in Pétionville. Change at Kenscoff for onward transport to Furcy.

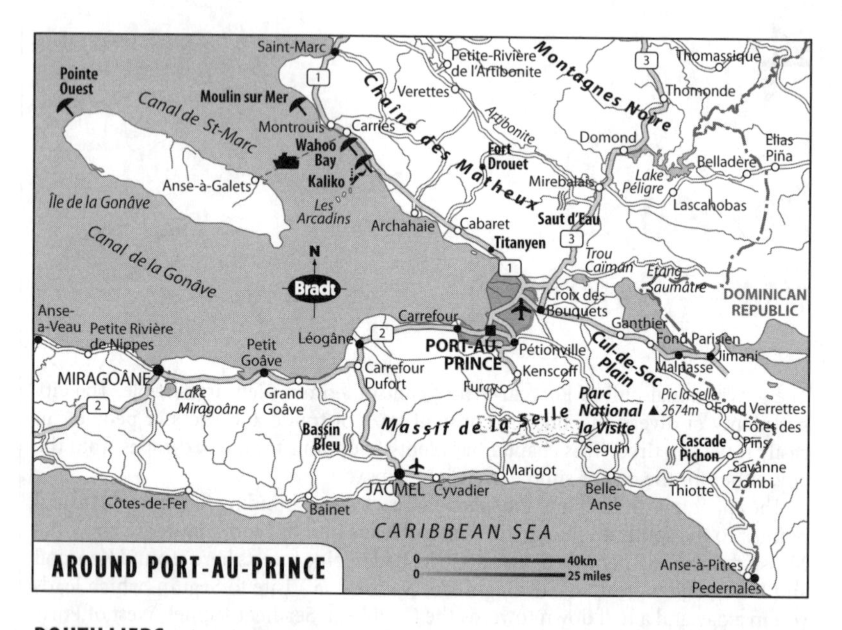

BOUTILLIERS The districts above the centre of Pétionville stretch and blur as you climb Route de Kenscoff. Passing through Pelerin, the first place of any size is Boutilliers, about 20 minutes from Place St Pierre. There is a famous belvedere with an **observatory** here, which is well worth a diversion. To reach it, turn right at Laboule 12 – the junction is just opposite a series of shops on the main road (including a Delimart supermarket with a useful Sogebank ATM), and a giant concrete head in a similar style to Haitian woodcarving. The viewpoint (*vue panoramique*) has quite stunning views over the whole of Port-au-Prince, along the coast in both directions and in towards the Plaine du Cul-de-Sac. Near the viewpoint is the old **Château Jane Barbancourt**, built in a quasi-medieval style. Owned by the rum company, it used to be a popular lunch and dinner spot for tourists, who could also test out a few special rum cocktails. Now closed, the weirdly kitsch building remains. As this guide went to press, the Ministry of Tourism announced plans to restore the viewpoint, install telescopes and develop craft stalls and possibly a new restaurant.

Paris St Tropez (*88 Laboule 12;* ☎ *3410 7219/3873 2285; mains* **$$$**) opposite Delimart, does good pizzas and other similar dishes, although the tropical island-style décor seems a little incongruous for the mountain setting.

FERMATHE After passing Boutilliers, the mountain views really start to open up, affording some really spectacular vistas by the time you reach Fermathe, the first of the market towns on Route de Kenscoff. It's notable for **Fort Jacques**, one of the chain of forts constructed by Pétion on the orders of Dessalines following independence (the fort is named after him). It's the closest fort to Port-au-Prince, and is commemorated on the back of the 500HTG note. To reach it from the main road, take a sharp left opposite the covered market fronted by stands piled high with *fritay*. From here it's a short walk or drive through the many market stalls selling fresh produce from the surrounding area.

Fort Jacques certainly has a commanding position, looking out from a height of 1,300m over Port-au-Prince and its bay. It has thick double walls forming an embankment, three sharply pointed bastions and on its fourth corner, a wide rotunda. Inside the courtyard are a series of rooms and munitions stores with vaulted ceilings, and a rainwater cistern. At least one of the cannons still remaining on the site is British, captured in battle by Toussaint Louverture. Outside the walls, near the parking area, are the ruins of a powder magazine. A second, more ruined bastion, Fort Alexandre (named for Pétion) sits on a nearby hill, protecting Fort Jacques's only exposed flank. It was never completed and is now quite ruined, but there is some talk of converting it into an amphitheatre to host cultural events.

The forts were abandoned when Haitian independence was recognised by the French, and fell into disrepair. Fort Jacques was restored in the 1980s, but suffered some damage to its thick curtain walls in the 2010 earthquake. Visitors will be approached by would-be guides and a few souvenir sellers, but will need to tip the guardian to get him to unlock the gate to the main fort.

Fermathe's other notable landmark is the **Mountain Maid Baptist Mission** (*www.bhm.org; ⌚ Mon–Sat*). Established in 1948 (two years before the sealed road from Pétionville was completed), this is one of Haiti's longest standing foreign aid programmes. Evangelical in nature, it also focuses strongly on agriculture, health and education projects. Most people visit it for their shop, which sells a good variety of locally produced handicrafts and foodstuffs including jam and really good bread and cookies. If you're here at Christmas, their plant nurseries also sell festive poinsettia in great numbers. Attached to the shop is a small restaurant, **The Mountain Maid Tea Terrace**, which shows its American roots by serving up plenty of burgers, hot dogs, doughnuts and ice cream. Next door is a small but interesting museum full of historical artefacts collected by the founders of the mission. The mission is on the right as you enter Fermathe.

Fermathe has one of the best restaurants on Route de Kenscoff, **Les 3 Decks** (*3 Bis, Fermathe 54; 📞 3462 6201/3418 8511; mains* **$$$$**). It does excellent French-influenced cuisine served in a relaxed dining atmosphere, decked out in wood with views over the mountains. There's a good wine list, but you may choose to finish your meal with a local lemongrass tea. It's not particularly well signed – the turning is a little way after the main centre of Fermathe, on the right just before the red Total petrol station.

KENSCOFF Kenscoff is the main market town in the mountains. En route you'll pass plenty of trucks coming to and from here laden down with produce – onions, carrots, cabbages and potatoes aplenty. The altitude means that coffee has also been an important crop, but is less so now than in the past. The biggest markets are held on Tuesday, Thursday and Friday, when farmers from across the region descend on the town to sell their crops.

The whole area from Kenscoff uphill to Furcy seems tailor-made for hiking – you could put on a pair of boots and start walking almost anywhere. Everywhere you turn it seems there is a new vista – prettily terraced fields, dotted with wild flowers against the oxide red earth. It's changed a little since Pétion visited in 1797, but his sentiments still apply: 'Amidst so much beauty, grandiose and impressive panoramas are a feast for the eyes and fill the heart with admiration … Eternal spring reigns here, and summer is felt at the oddest times.' As you climb, there is plenty of the original pine forest, although it's under increasing pressure from local farmers, who either cut the trees for wood or graze their cattle beneath them, preventing new saplings from taking root. Where the trees do persist, they're frequently clad in moss and other epiphytes, taking moisture from the air. A warning about the local weather – clouds can rush in at any time, cutting visibility and sending the temperature plummeting. I've experienced a hailstorm here during the rainy season, probably the only time in

Haiti I've been left shivering from the damp cold. If you're hiking, bring suitable attire. Some of the best walks with views can be had by heading for **Belot** (turn off the main road at Kenscoff 74), or from Morne Tranchan.

Kenscoff is also home to the **Wynne Farm Ecological Reserve** (*Kenscoff 97;* e *info@wynnefarm.org; www.wynnefarm.org*). It was founded in 1953 as an experimental farm by an American, Victor Wynne, who first came to Haiti as a road builder during the US occupation, but later returned to marry a Haitian woman and develop an interest in more sustainable forms of agriculture. Today it is run by his daughter Jane Wynne. The farm has 32 acres, much of it given over to permaculture, reforestation and reintroduced native species, as well as working with local farmers to improve crop productivity through the USAID Winner programme. It is sometimes possible to arrange visits, but arrange well in advance (contributions to the farm's work are welcomed).

Where to stay and eat

Le Florville Route de Kenscoff; 3551 3535/3449 6161. On the left-hand side of the main road just below Kenscoff proper, a small bed & breakfast with a clutch of decent rooms, although better known as a restaurant. Dishes are Creole & international, with good service. There's frequent live music on Sun (the busiest day), & concerts & other events throughout the year. **$$$**

Le Montcel Km 14, Belot, Kenscoff; 3701 4777/1755; e montcel@aol.com. Quite some way from the main road (but signed), this large ranch is only open to guests at the weekend. Rooms are in charming Swiss chalet-style. The property seems to encompass a whole ridge of mountain, & it's usually possible to hire horses & guides to explore the area. **$$$**

Bois d'Avril Guest House Carrefour Maraka, Kenscoff; 2942 1460/3443 0137; e deb.currelly@gmail.com. A small new guesthouse with a cosy atmosphere, vegetarian food (half board) & a warm welcome. The hosts can advise on local hiking routes. Somewhat out of the way (the guesthouse had to build its own rough road to the property), so call ahead to be met or be picked up (US$5 transfer). **$$**

Ti Kay Kreyòl Obléon, Morne Tranchan, Kenscoff; 3614 9404/3504 1520; www.titakaykreyol.com. This small hotel painted in bright cheery colours was sadly closed on a recent visit, but will hopefully reopen again before too long. As well as good, simple rooms, it had a popular & inexpensive Sun buffet. Hikes up to the mountain ridge from the road give particularly good views. **$$**

FURCY Furcy is a half hour's drive from Kenscoff – when you get here you've reached the heights of the Massif de la Selle, and you're surrounded in every direction by ridges and ravines in dusty reds and rich greens, like so many folds in a uncrumpled ball of paper. If you're looking for a literal representation of the Haitian proverb *Dèyè mon gen mon* ('Beyond the mountains there are more mountains'), this is surely the place. The road, which has been deteriorating in quality since leaving Kenscoff, gives out soon after this point. To get any further you have to do as the locals do and walk. Of course, that's partly the point of coming here, as Furcy is the trailhead for the hike through Parc National la Visite to Seguin, and then on to Jacmel.

You hit the start of the trail *before* Furcy. The road splits at a spot called Carrefour Badyo – you either carry straight on towards Seguin, or turn right and follow the road for another ten minutes as it winds into Furcy. The turning is impossible to miss: a building on the junction has a large red tin roof with 'Rustik/Furcy' painted in giant letters.

Furcy proper sits amid the pine trees – the administrative centre must be one of the prettiest in the country; a cluster of candy-coloured chalets amid the pines, more Hansel and Gretel than Caribbean. Even if you're not doing the long trek, hikes from Furcy start pretty much anywhere. A popular one is to the waterfalls, which takes one to two hours depending on your fitness. Ask for *le cascade*. It's also locally known as Bassin Bleu, but this is not to be confused with the more famous waterfalls of the same name near Jacmel. Since it gets plenty of foreign visitors, this is a rare place in Haiti that has a little bit of tourist hassle, with plenty of would-be guides offering their services, and groups of children wanting to tag along with you.

Getting there and away There's very little public transport to and from Furcy – it's easiest to go to Carrefour Badyo and catch a bus or truck heading to Kenscoff. Furcy guide Syffal St Vertus (*3434 0401; www.facebook.com/FurcyPony*) offers pony-trekking in the area, along with tree planting to educate locals and foreigners about deforestation. Tours cost around US$20–30 according to duration and the number of people.

Where to stay and eat There are two sleeping options in Furcy, both past the administrative centre. Be reminded that nights can be surprisingly chilly here, so pack some warm layers.

The Lodge Furcy; 3458 5968/1052; e info@thelodgeinhaiti.com; www.thelodgeinhaiti.com. A stone & wood hotel looking very much part of its natural surroundings. A popular weekend restaurant (**$$$$**), the accommodation is something of a mixed bag – distinctly average rooms with inexplicably small windows refusing to make the most of potentially grand views. **$$$**

Rustik Furcy; 3880 5170/3858 3898. Rustic by name & nature – a guesthouse & restaurant amid the trees built with scavenged & recycled wood, with cable drums as tables & beer-bottle windows. Feels a bit like an overgrown teenager's den. Rooms have bunk beds & outdoor showers. Rents out mountain bikes. **$**

Near the entrance to Furcy, **Resto Kris Kapab** does good breakfast omelettes, and chicken with rice and the like for lunch and dinner – a cheap, filling option.

LA VISITE NATIONAL PARK Hiking across Parc National la Visite has to be one of the most exhilarating forms of exercise that Haiti can offer, and if your time in the country has involved spending a lot of time stuck in Port-au-Prince's traffic, then the escape to the mountains is simply divine. Most people choose to trek from Furcy to Seguin in the heart of the national park. It's a long half-day according to your fitness levels, and there's accommodation at the end of it. From Seguin, you can stay and explore on foot, retrace your steps to Furcy, or continue down the mountains to eventually finish in Jacmel.

It's best to start early from Furcy to avoid too much hiking in the heat of the day, as the sun is a lot stronger at this altitude. The path from Carrefour Badyo has uninterrupted views out across the **Massif de la Selle**. The terrain here is largely denuded of trees, but wherever the slopes give any sort of purchase, they've been intensively terraced. The red soil might look dry and dusty but it is incredibly fertile. As the path bends around the ridges, you'll encounter a continuous stream of people walking, particularly women carrying incredible loads of produce on their heads to take to market. It's tough work, and there's virtually no shade. Bring ample water, but also remember that clouds can roll in at any time, shrouding the views in mist and sending the temperature plummeting.

The path to Seguin is almost entirely uphill, but the views are constantly rewarding. As you near Seguin, the land begins to level out somewhat and trees start to reappear. This is the pine forest at the heart of the national park. Growing amid them are huge agave plants, and ferns that thrive on the cooler, damper atmosphere here.

Coming through the forest, there's a small turn-off (signed) that leads to the **Auberge la Visite** (*3 rooms;* ☎ *3464 6131/3851 0159;* e *aubergelavisite@gmail.com/winthropattie@hotmail.com;* **$$** *HB*), the only sleeping option. It's a lovely place, with great views to enjoy from a rocking chair on the porch, and a charming and knowledgeable host. The guesthouse is involved with the work of the local environmental organisation **Fondation Seguin** (*www.fondationseguin.org*), which works on reforestation and soil protection, as well as making sure that the local community can benefit from conserving the environment.

Swathes of the pine forest are fenced to prevent cutting for charcoal and grazing of livestock. Most of the forest is actually less than 100 years old, as it was commercially logged throughout the 20th century. The park was gazetted in 1983 and covers 30km². It's an important watershed and is rich in birdlife – twitchers could easily spend a day or more here. There's great potential in the area for mountain biking. Although portions of the route from Furcy are so rough as to demand you dismount and push, the area around Seguin has endless ribbons of single track and walking paths that should be enjoyable to even novice riders, with plenty of trails for the more dedicated. There's a lovely walk up to Rivière Blanche, with a tumbling waterfall.

As you descend from the *auberge* to Seguin proper, the plateau is littered with fields of weird rock formations jutting out from the ground. Made of limestone karst weathered into jagged shapes, their local name *kraze dan* (broken teeth) seems entirely appropriate. Once the early morning mist burns off the views stretch out to the Caribbean Sea.

It's all downhill from here. At Seguin you can find moto-taxis to take you down to the coast, or it's another half-day's walk. The path is cobbled and broken in some places, the remains of the old logging road built by the Americans in the 1920s. The further you descend, the landscape becomes a little more lush, until you eventually pop out at Savanne de Bois and then Marigot – small towns that were once clearing houses for coffee merchants. Marigot sits on the main road to Jacmel, 30 minutes away by *taptap*.

EAST OF PORT-AU-PRINCE

CROIX DES BOUQUETS One of the most popular forms of art in Haiti is the intricate flat metal sculptures known as *fer decoupé*. Although they're now made all over the country, the centre of production is Croix des Bouquets, where the art form was first created in the 1950s.

Croix des Bouquets is the first town you hit when you leave Port-au-Prince on Route National 3 towards the Dominican border, although you might be hard pressed to notice the transition as it's very much becoming part of the capital's concrete sprawl. Get away from the clogged main roads however and you're quickly reminded that you're on the edge of the countryside. This is the Plaine du Cul-de-Sac, once thick with sugar plantations that made the colonial capital boom (and which still provides the sugarcane to make Barbancourt rum). Croix des Bouquets was an important battleground in the revolutionary war – in 1792 its capture by the slave armies opened the door to Port-au-Prince.

The metal artisans keep their workshops in the district of **Noailles**, which they have taken care to sign from the main road (you can always ask for the *village artistique*). There are around 20 workshops in total, and the air rings with the sound of hammers on metal. Even the ground here can seem to be metal, since there are still the remnants of the old railways that served the sugar plantations until the

1960s. Visitors are welcomed and there's no hustle to buy (resisting temptation is another thing entirely).

The tradition of *fer decoupé* was started by local blacksmith George Liautaud, who made metal cemetery crosses adorned with Vodou flourishes. Encouraged by members of Port-au-Prince's Centre d'Art, he branched into freestanding sculptures and intricate two-dimensional figures. Although he died in 1992, his techniques still form the basis of today's art: a steel drum is cleaned by burning and hammered flat, then shapes are drawn or stencilled onto the metal with chalk, and cut out with chisels. The classic finish is to add a simple coat of varnish, although painting in bright colours is almost as popular. Vodou iconography is an important component, with representations of the *lwa* Lasiren (the mermaid) and the love heart of Ezili commonplace. Elsewhere, look for anything from angels and *rara* bands to trees of life and animals. Pieces range in size from palm-sized to taller than a person.

The atmosphere in Noailles is very laid-back, and it's fun to wander between the workshops talking to the artists and comparing their different styles. The first workshop in the village is that of Serge Jolimeau, Liautaud's most celebrated apprentice, whose pieces are sold internationally. A personal favourite is the quirky Jacques Eugene, who has started to subvert the style by introducing items like recycled cutlery into his sculptures to make bizarre and comic figures. Most of the workshops are along Route des Rails or Route Remy (the Jolimeau workshop is on the junction of the two). Prices are reasonable, starting at just a few dollars for something small, then leading up to several hundred for the large gallery-quality pieces.

Every October, the artisans hold a fair in Noailles to celebrate their work. The **Foire George Liautaud** commemorates the original master of the artform, and there are exhibitions, tours, sales and music. The fair normally coincides roughly with Croix des Bouquets's *fête patronale* on 7 October.

TROU CAÏMAN The small shallow lake of Trou Caïman offers some of the best birdwatching in Haiti. It's a marshy lake surrounded by saltbush flats, and takes its name from the caimans (American crocodiles) that were once found here until being hunted out. The main reason to come is to see the colony of greater flamingos that live and nest here. A rich orange pink with black-tipped wings, they look ungainly when wading but are strikingly elegant when taking flight.

As well as flamingos, there is usually plenty of waterfowl and small waders to spot, as well as raptors such as kestrels and merlin.

To get to Trou Caïman (also known as Eau Gallée by some locals), head from Port-au-Prince on Route National 3 toward Mirebalais. Soon after the road begins to climb up to the Central Plateau, turn right off the tarmac in the direction of Thomazeau. This road, in a bumpy condition, leads to the northern tip of the lake. To get to the flamingos, you'll need to hire a local fishing boat, which are mostly rickety affairs pushed through the water with poles.

ETANG SAUMÂTRE The largest lake in Haiti, Etang Saumâtre sits in the driest part of the Plaine du Cul-de-Sac. Its eastern shore borders the Dominican Republic and should you travel the main road from Port-au-Prince to Santo Domingo, its shores make up one of the striking sections of the drive. Its name means 'brackish pond', but it's also known locally as Lac Azueï.

The brackish nature of the water is due to the lake entirely lacking any outlet – it's fed by springs and loses water only by evaporation, which has led over the millennia to a build-up of salts. The lake used to be famous for its caimans, but the current health of the population – which has been endangered since the 1980s – is not known.

There are two approaches to Étang Saumâtre. The most common is to travel along Route 102 towards the Dominican border at Malpasse. The shore of the lake comes close to the road at Fonds-Parisien. You can get out here for views, but better to stop just before the town to visit the **Parc Naturel Quisqueya de Fonds-Parisien**, which is trying to develop visitor facilities. It has a botanic garden with a large number of the cacti that dominate the dry forest that is the trademark of the area. It should be possible to arrange a trip on the lake from here; the staff claim that it's possible to see caimans from relatively close to the edge of the park. They can also arrange walks into the nearby hills.

The road continues to closely track the lake until you reach Malpasse. If you're passing the lake at Easter, the town of Ganthier attracts large numbers of pilgrims every Good Friday, who recreate the Stations of the Cross by climbing the Kalvé Mirak (Calvary Miracle) hill here.

A rougher and slightly more remote option is to continue along the road past Trou Caïman, off the turning from Route National 3. Passing Thomazeau towards Manneville, you reach Font Pite, a marshy area good for birdwatching. The tracks along the northern edge of the lake are very pitted, so a good vehicle is essential.

FORET DES PINS The Massif de la Selle runs across the southeast corner of Haiti and into the Dominican Republic, where it turns into the Sierra de Bahoruco. The most common way to access it in Haiti is through Furcy and Seguin, and the Parc National la Visite, but it's also possible to visit from the east at Forêt des Pins, a large area of mountainous pine and mixed forest.

The area was once a commercial logging zone and is classified as a national reserve, with clearing no longer allowed. Most of the trees are actually younger, secondary forest but despite this it remains a beautiful area, cool and high and perfect for hiking.

To get to the forest, you must turn south off the main highway between Port-au-Prince and Malpasse (the Dominican border) at Fonds-Parisien. The road quality is mostly reasonable but poor in places, particularly after rain – a 4x4 will take between three and four hours to reach **Forêt des Pins**, a small mountain market town from where you can hike. It's also possible to continue south through the mountains to Thiotte, from where you can reach Belle Anse and Seguin and the main road to Jacmel, or the tiny border town of Anse-à-Pitre. For more information on this remote and adventurous route see *Towards the Dominican Republic border*, page 154. Forêt des Pins is a small place, but it has the only accommodation option, a cluster of restored and brightly painted **logging cabins** run by the Ministry of Agriculture, Natural Resources and Rural Development (MARNDR; ☎ *2510 8480/2250 0867; www.agriculture.gouv.ht*). In theory, these must be booked in advance, but in practice this often seems to be difficult and it's often possible to turn up on spec and ask for the *guardien*, who can give you the keys. As you enter Forêt des Pins, turn right at the ministry checkpoint; the cabins are a short way past this amid the trees. You'll need to be self-sufficient in terms of food and drinking water, as well as bringing bedding (be prepared for chilly nights). Each cabin is furnished in a basic style, with a bathroom and kitchen (no gas). The *guardien* can also arrange for someone to bring simple meals for you. The cost is around 1,000HTG per person.

The walking possibilities are almost endless – as well as the forest, the mountains open on to meadows that are often dotted with wild flowers, plus plenty of caves.

CLIMBING PIC LA SELLE

David Eisenbaum

For those seeking real adventure, a trip to Haiti's tallest peak, Pic la Selle (2,674m), is an absolute must. It offers a wonderful opportunity to see some of the most dramatic landscape in Hispaniola, taking you from forest to farm country, and along a dramatic pine-clad ridge line with stunning views of Haiti's south coast, over Port-au-Prince and across into the Dominican Republic. Some pre-planning is required, however, and taking a local guide is strongly recommended.

Getting to Pic la Selle's base is an adventure all its own; trucks and buses leaving Croix des Bouquets for Thiotte take you over the mountains to the market town of Forêt des Pins (four to six hours), in the centre of the protected pine forest. From there, a two-hour walk through the forest takes you to Gwo Cheval, a town at the mountain's base where you can try to hire a guide and stock up on food (dry/tinned goods and seasonal produce) and water. There are no formal guides available, but asking around you should find someone willing to take you for US$20–40. From Gwo Cheval it's more than ten miles to the peak, with no opportunities for resupply, so planning to camp along the way is a good idea. Water is scarce on the mountain in the dry season, and should be carried in volume, unless you want to catch rainwater or collect it from agave leaves. If you choose to attempt the hike without a guide, a map and compass (and ideally a GPS unit) will be a must, as there is no marked trail to follow. Along the way locals might point you in the right direction, but don't expect it to be easy to find.

After Gwo Cheval you follow a dirt road up the mountain. After about two hours, turn off the main road, following paths through farm fields and then entering a high valley. There's a small farming community here; just past it you enter a dry landscape dominated by tall grasses, scrub vegetation and clusters of pine saplings.

After about two hours in the valley, you begin going up more dramatically, eventually climbing up steep hillsides and arriving on the ridge trail. It's still forested, mostly with pine, but there is active logging in the area. This trail is marked (poorly) with yellow paint spots on trees and rocks, but many blazes are missing, and fallen trees often obscure the path. Once on the ridge trail, there are four false summits before you reach the actual highest point, which is marked with a small concrete pillar and a waterproof log book. Be sure to leave your name. The ridge trail section will take anywhere from two to four hours at least, and if visibility is poor, it might make navigation near-impossible.

It's important to note that the ridge trail has several sections where the path itself is faded or missing entirely. By following the peaks however, it's possible to find your way. There are several steep sections with loose rock – this is a challenging hike and not without risk, but it rewards visitors with spectacular views and a visit to one of Haiti's more remote places.

Turning around and heading back down right away might seem daunting – I found it more pleasurable to camp just below the summit; while the peaks are shrouded in cloud much of the day, sunrise often offers clear views as far as Port-au-Prince.

It may also be possible to find a guide in Fonds-Parisien to approach Pic la Selle from the north instead of from Forêt des Pins.

The birdlife is rich. The forest is inhabited, with grazing livestock and crops tended by farmers who can point out hikes. There's a walk of a couple of hours from Forêt des Pins up to Chapotin, with views south to the Caribbean Sea and across the Dominican border to Lake Enriquillo. The most dedicated may even attempt to trek to the summit of Pic la Selle, Haiti's highest mountain – see box, *Climbing Pic la Selle*, page 135.

NORTH OF PORT-AU-PRINCE

CÔTE DES ARCADINS As Route National 1 leaves Port-au-Prince on its northward slog to Cap-Haïtien, it tracks the long sweep of the Gulf of Gonâve. Leading all the way to Saint-Marc, this stretch of the coast is known as the Côtes des Arcadins, and is a popular weekend beach destination for Port-au-Prince residents. While most people head straight for the sun-loungers, the road has a couple of interesting sights, as well as Fort Drouet, a truly knockout historical site only recently discovered.

Despite what the maps will tell you, while Route National 1 leads straight out of the top of Grand Rue (Boulevard Jean-Jacques Dessalines) in Port-au-Prince, poor surfacing and congestion means that most traffic (including all public transport) actually leaves the city by skirting along the rural edge of Cité Soleil, a dusty shortcut that comes out on to the highway at **Zoranje**, home to a post-2010 model village. Soon after this, it's easy to zip past the small settlement of **Titanyen**. The name literally means 'a little bit of nothing' in Creole, something of an unfortunate name as it was used as a dumping ground for the victims of the Duvalier regime, and after 12 January 2010, as a mass burial site for the earthquake dead. A field of gravel and the massed ranks of simple crosses mark the spot, some way from the road, while nearby plots have been staked out for the resettlement of those internally displaced on that day.

The first town of any size is **Cabaret**. In 1961 it was renamed Duvalierville in honour of the dictator Papa Doc who had practised medicine near here in the 1940s. The project was to be a new Brasilia, funded entirely by shakedown: Duvalier's lieutenants tapped up everyone from rich businessmen to lowly government employees. The project's pretensions were cruelly lampooned by Graham Greene in *The Comedians*. When Jean-Claude Duvalier fled Haiti in 1986 Duvalierville became Cabaret once again; the only remaining monument to his father's ego is the futuristic cock-fighting arena with a winged roof, on the left side of the road as you drive through the centre, and now a nightclub. Soon after leaving Cabaret, a road turns right into the Chaîne des Matheux mountains and up to **Fort Drouet** (see page 138).

The road passes through rich mango and plantain country before quickly arriving at **Archahaie**, where the Haitian flag was created in 1803. Wherever the traffic slows, women approach selling bags of *tablet*, a sweet peanut brittle with a hint of ginger, that the town is also known for – be sure to pick up a bag for a few gourdes. Another thing worth buying around here are watermelons – the area immediately north of Archahaie, called Luly, produces them by the tonne, and roadside stalls are common.

Most of the beach hotels are concentrated in the stretch of coast between Luly and Montrouis. The **beaches** can't really compare to those in the south, but their access to the capital is their strong suit. Most are pebbly or have coarse sand, but the shallow clear water is good for swimming. If you don't fancy one of the resorts, the **Plage Publique** (Km 62) is open to all, and is a lively scene at the weekend with local families, food and drink sellers and sound systems at play. The Côte des

Arcadins also offers potential **scuba diving**, as it has some good coral in places, and a large sink-hole near Saint-Marc. There's just one operator, **Pegasus Diving** (☎ *3555 9633/3624 9486;* e *haitidivingpegasus@yahoo.com*), run by Jose Ed Roy, operating out of Kaliko Beach Club. They have a boat that can accommodate up to 12 divers, and provide PADI certification for new divers.

At Km 62, near Ouanga Bay Hotel, it's possible to get a ferry out to **Île la Gonâve**, which sits in the bay. It's Haiti's largest island, but is little visited. There's a chance of getting very basic accommodation at Anse-à-Galets, where the ferry lands (a one-hour voyage). If you have access to a boat, it's better to head to the western tip of the island and anchor at the lovely beach at **Pointe Ouest**. It's not unusual to see dolphins around here, and the diving and snorkelling is excellent – Pegasus Diving can arrange a trip. Somewhere in the waters near Île la Gonâve is the wreck of the ill-fated *Mary Celeste*. Having made her name as the archetypal ghost ship in 1872, she was wrecked here 13 years later in an attempted insurance scam.

At **Montrouis**, in the grounds of the Moulin-sur-Mer Hotel is the **Musée Colonial Ogier-Fombrun** (*admission free*). It sits in a restored French sugar plantation, and still has its aqueduct, waterwheel and sugar mills *in situ*. It's a rare opportunity to get an insight into the workings of a plantation – inside the museum proper there's a scale model of a working plantation, showing the factory and slave

THE HAITIAN FLAG

Much of the Haitian Revolution was a war of personal liberation, rather than national liberation: Toussaint, Dessalines, Christophe and Pétion all eventually threw their lot in with France once slavery was abolished. It was only relatively late when it was realised that only true independence guaranteed their freedoms. At Archahaie on 18 May 1803, the flag was created that first gave Haiti an ideal to aspire to.

At the Congress of Archahaie, as it was later called, Dessalines finally declared against France. The Tricolor, whose red, white and blue had represented the mulattoes, whites and blacks of the revolution was to be no more – Dessalines tore the white strip from the flag and ground it under his boot. His wife's god-daughter, Catherine Flon, then sewed the remaining red and blue together to create the new flag. The motto *Liberté ou mort* ('Freedom or Death') replaced the 'RF' of republican France. Soon after independence, the blue was replaced with black, making the link to Haiti's colour even more explicit.

The flag design has been updated regularly since then. Christophe's short-lived kingdom added his heraldic device to the red and black. Pétion kept the red and blue but made the stripes horizontal rather than vertical, as well as adding the current coat of arms of the palmiste tree with cannons and banners at its foot. The vertical stripes returned in the 20th century, but during the Duvalier period, blue was again replaced with black. This was a distinctly *noiriste* move: observers took the horizontal bands to indicate that mulattoes and black would share power equally; when black shifted to the mast, it was seemed to confirm who wanted to control the country. The current flag dates from 1987 – the year of the post-Duvalier constitution.

Archahaie is justifiably proud of its role in creating the flag, which can be seen everywhere in the town (the local football team is even called Catherine Flon). Flag Day – 18 May – is a national holiday, and it's become a tradition for the president to give a speech in the town on that day.

barracks surrounded by fields of cane. To throw the contrasts between master and slave into sharper relief, there's also a reconstruction of a colonist's fine room, and nearby a set of fearsome iron shackles to punish recalcitrant workers. Near the entrance to the museum, there's a framed letter from Toussaint Louverture to the ancestor of the current owner, granting him title of the land. The museum isn't always open – although it's by the entrance to the hotel grounds, you might have to go to reception to open it up.

Fort Drouet and Habitation Dion It would seem to beggar belief that in a country as small and densely populated as Haiti, a set of major historical sites could simply be lost, but this was the case with Fort Drouet and its surrounding colonial plantations, whose existence was only announced to the outside world in 2009. They sit near the newly constructed road leading from Cabaret over the Chaîne Matheux mountains to Deschappelles and the Artibonite river, and as such can easily be reached from Port-au-Prince in a couple of hours by car.

Fort Drouet is a splendidly preserved fortress with five strong bastions, part of the chain of defensive forts commissioned by Dessalines soon after independence. It has thick masonry walls pierced with loopholes and cannon emplacements, while inside is a powder magazine covered with red lichens and two water cisterns. The fort has a truly commanding mountaintop position (perhaps second only to that of the Citadelle in the north), atop a high ridge overseeing both the coast and back across the Artibonite Valley. As with the rest of the forts built at this time, it never saw a shot fired in anger.

A short walk downhill from the back of the fort are an intriguing cluster of ruins that make up the French Habitation Dion. This region was once thickly forested, providing the perfect shady high-altitude conditions for coffee growing (that the area has been long deforested and sparsely inhabited gives some indication as to how the site was largely forgotten to historians). There are several large stone buildings, the size of which give some indication as to how profitable the coffee trade was for Saint-Domingue. Although the roofs are gone, the imposing walls and staircases of the main coffee house, and pipes to feed rainwater into tanks, give an indication of its former grandeur.

More chilling are three low blocks that sit around a central courtyard – these were the slave quarters, each with seven cells of four metres square. On sugar plantations, slaves were frequently free to build their own rough housing and congregate with each other, but these coffee slaves were treated more like convicts. These masonry buildings are the only slave quarters known to still exist in Haiti.

The exact date of the plantation is unknown. Coffee was only introduced to Saint-Domingue in the 1740s, but was so successful that it quickly rivalled sugar in export value. An unidentified building near the coffee house has a plaque with an inscription bearing the name 'Lasaline'. If, as thought, this was the plantation owner, he might have reasoned that his investment had a long and prosperous future ahead of it, but the date on the plaque underpins a greater story. It's dated August 31 1791 – less than a fortnight after the slave uprising in the north that would eventually lead to the liberty of all the colony's slaves, those of Habitation Dion included.

BEACH HOTELS Hotels are presented in the order in which they are located on the road from Port-au-Prince. Although they are quiet in the week, they leap into life as soon as the weekend rolls around. Most have a day rate for non-guests who just want to soak up the sun, usually hovering around US$15–30, with some sort of refreshment included.

Club Indigo Km 78, Route National 1; 3441 1000/3650 1000; e reservations@clubindigo.net; www.clubindigo.net. Large & popular resort, at one time Haiti's Club Med. Bright & white with plenty of sporty beach activities & eating options. Expect to spend time outside – rooms are very small. Pool, Wi-Fi. Day rate available. **$$$**

Kaliko Beach Club Km 61, Route National 1; 2940 4609/2941 4609; e kalikobeachclub@hotmail.com; www.kalikobeachclub.com. Friendly resort made up of a series of bungalows with airy rooms among leafy grounds. Pool, bars & restaurants, Wi-Fi. Day rate available. **$$$**

Moulin-sur-Mer Km 77, Route National 1; 2222 1918/3701 1918; e info@moulinsurmer.com; www.moulinsurmer.com. Resort set in green, palmy grounds. Large, good rooms in a colonial-style main block, & smaller gingerbread-style chalets next to the beach. Various sports facilities & beachfront restaurant, plus the Musée Colonial Ogier-Fombrun at the entrance. Day rate available. **$$$**

Wahoo Bay Beach Club Km 62, Route National 1; 2514 2499/3735 2536; e wahoo@dadesky.com; www.wahoobaybeach.com. Great gardens & modern design at this resort. On a rise over the sea – the pool makes up for the walk to the beach. Good rooms & service. Wi-Fi. Day rate available. **$$$**

Xaragua Hotel Km 80, Route National 1; 2510 9559; e lexaraguahotel@yahoo.fr. An older hotel with all rooms in a giant block overlooking the sea. Occasionally a bit tired, but with a great terrace & pool along with access to the beach. Day rate available. **$$$**

Obama Beach Hotel Km 59, Route National 1; 3872 7584. A nice low-key hotel with simple rooms but a nice pebble beach & restaurant. **$$**

Ouanga Bay Km 63, Route National 1; 3756 5212/3932 5810; e ouangabay@hotmail.com. Hotel rather than resort, with a small but lovely beach. Rooms are fair & the air is relaxed; the thatched seafood restaurant on a small pier is a big plus point. **$$**

WEST OF PORT-AU-PRINCE

LEOGÂNE Léogâne is an old town. In 2013 it celebrates its 350th anniversary, but its roots go back beyond that, since it was founded on the site of an even older Taíno settlement called Yaguana, from which it takes its modern name. The ruler of Yaguana was the famed Anacaona, one of Haiti's true national heroines.

The town was very close to the epicentre of the 2010 earthquake, and suffered terribly as a result; it's estimated that nearly 80% of buildings in the town were

HAITI'S POLISH CONNECTION

When Dessalines ordered the massacre of whites following Haiti's independence, one group were given a notable exception to settle: the remains of Napoleon's Polish Legions. At the time, Poland was partitioned three ways between Russia, Prussia and Austria, and the Polish Legions were raised to fight for Napoleon in hope of French support for Polish independence. The Poles were unhappy to be shipped to Saint-Domingue to put down someone else's nationalist struggle instead. Horrified at the French brutality against the free black armies, they eventually defected and allied themselves to the Haitians.

In return, the Polish were granted land by Dessalines. Most of the thousand Poles settled in Canton de Plateau near Cabaret, now called Cazale – possibly a corruption of 'Zaleski', reputedly the name of the first soldier to settle there. The community still remains today – Haitian, but frequently with lighter skin and green or hazel eyes. A wider impact has been left through the Polish icon Our Lady of Czestochowska – a black Madonna subsequently adopted as an image of the Vodou Iwa Ezili Danto.

AN AMERICAN KING IN HAITI

The American occupation of Haiti at the time of the dime-store pulp novel provided plenty of opportunities for written accounts that projected both the fantasies and nightmares of the occupiers. Lurid accounts with titles like *Cannibal Cousins* abounded. Perhaps the strangest account to come out of the period was *The White King of La Gonâve* by Faustin Wirkus.

Wirkus was a marine sergeant who had several postings in Haiti. In 1920 he encountered a *mambo* called Ti Memmene from La Gonâve, arrested for illegally practising Vodou. A year later he requested a posting to La Gonâve, where he was made resident commander. He again encountered the mambo who led one of the Kongo Vodou societies on the island (Wirkus dubbed her the island's queen). Soon after his posting Ti Memmene advised Wirkus that the islanders had proclaimed him King of La Gonâve. By his account, he had been recognised as an incarnation of Faustin Soulouque, who reigned as emperor in the mid 19th century. Wirkus was *ti té pé vini* ('he who was to come'). Amid great ceremony a crown of bright feathers was placed on his head, and his majesty proclaimed to the beat of Vodou drumming.

The new king was the only American on La Gonâve, and by his own account was a good and fair administrator – Haitian voices are notably absent. His fame was spread by William Seabrooks' famous travelogue *Magic Island*, to the point where American schoolchildren would write to him as king. He 'reigned' for three years, until President Borno requested his removal in 1929, having piqued at the impropriety of a sergeant declaring himself monarch. Wirkus resigned his commission two years later and returned to New York, where he worked as a bond broker and wrote his memoirs – the last 'king' of Haiti.

damaged in some way, with a high proportion destroyed outright. Municipal authorities reportedly buried around 3,000 people in the aftermath. Reconstruction is slow but ongoing.

Léogâne's most famous landmark was the Church of St Rose of Lima, where another famous daughter of the town, Claire Heureuse, married Dessalines. It was tragically destroyed by the earthquake, but the saint is still commemorated on the town's *fête patronale* every 23 August, when the streets are lit with coloured lights, and there are processions and concerts. Even bigger celebrations are held between Carnival and the Easter weekend, when the town becomes a magnet for *rara* bands, with loud and raucous processions. There's much *klerin* rum drunk at this time, and the town has many stills – look out for the huge wooden vats visible from the main streets. Also worth noting are the carved stone souvenirs, for which Léogâne is renowned.

There's a small beach called **Jacksonville Plage** just outside the western outskirts of Léogâne. Owing to the large number of international aid workers and volunteers coming to the town post-quake, it's become a popular hangout, with people selling cold drinks and *fritay* at weekends, and fishermen happy to sell you their catch or hire their boats. There's an entrance fee of 50HTG. Also just outside the town limits is the **Grotte Anacaona**, a cave where the Taíno queen reputedly took shelter. It's covered in graffiti, left by visitors in apparent tribute to her.

Getting there and away Route National 2 bypasses Léogâne, which is off a slip-road. There are plentiful *taptaps* and buses throughout the day to Port-au-Prince (one hour), fewer to other destinations – if you want to get to Jacmel from here, it's easier to get a moto-taxi to Carrefour Dufort, where Route National 4 splits to head south, and pick up something from there. If you're headed to Léogâne by through public transport (say on a Jacmel to Port-au-Prince vehicle), make sure you get dropped at the turning, from where you can quickly grab a moto-taxi into town.

Where to stay and eat

Arawak Hotel 801 Rue de l'Hôpital; 3751 5531/3558 3922. Quake-resistant & eco-friendly hotel originally designed as a model for new housing in Léogâne. Compact but quiet & comfortable. Wi-Fi. **$$**

Hotel Taciana 47 Rue Chatuley; 3713 3009/3825 6674. Near the entrance to Léogâne, where the road splits off Route National 2. Mint-green hotel with simple clean rooms & restaurant/bar. Fair value. **$$**

Kiskeya Guest House Route Coloniale, Petite-Rivière; 3611 3619/3659 0325; e kiskeyaguesthouse@yahoo.com; www.kiskeyaguesthouse.com. Outside Léogâne & in the middle of a 10-acre organic farm in the country. Also offers intensive Creole & cross-cultural instruction for medics in the rural community. **$$**

Ocean Grill 252 Route National 2; 3666 0974/3606 6367; 11.00–23.00 daily. Not the cheapest place, but excellent fish, lobster & *lambi* in a rustic-style restaurant. **$$$**

Love Bambou Bar 22 Grand Rue; 08.00–23.00 daily. Pleasant bar-resto with open-slatted wooden walls. Simple breakfasts, seafood & chicken for lunch & dinner, & (pumpkin) *soup joumou* every Sun morning. **$$**

GRAND GOÂVE AND PETIT GOÂVE These twin coastal towns 10km apart more or less mark the destructive reach of the 2010 earthquake. They were settled in the mid 17th century, when the buccaneers were cleared out of Île de la Tortue by the French authorities, but under colonial rule soon fell into more prosaic livelihoods. That said, to this day both ports still carry something of a reputation for importing contraband from the United States. Most people pass through and stop only to buy a packet of *dous macoss*, the sugary brittle for which Petit Goâve is renowned.

Petit Goâve (usually shortened to Ti Goâve) is also famous as the birthplace of Faustin Soulouque, who fought in the revolutionary war and eventually crowned himself Emperor of Haiti in 1849, and whose courtly pretensions were widely lampooned abroad, yet reigned as an astute (if harsh ruler) until he came unstuck after trying to invade the Dominican Republic. His home in the town was much later converted into one of Haiti's great and eccentric hotels, the Relais de l'Empereur. In the tourist heyday of the 1970s, the owner kept pet leopards in the bar and hosted the international jetset. Sadly, it was completely destroyed in the earthquake.

There are a couple of beaches worth diverting for here. **Taíno Plage**, on the western edge of Grand Goâve, has the lovely **Hotel Taina** (*Rue Jeanty, Grand Goâve; 3720 6847; e tainarava@yahoo.fr;* **$$**). The restaurant is right on the beach and serves really excellent seafood; rooms are in a block at the back. To get here, turn right soon after leaving Grand Goâve (near the cemetery) it's a five-minute drive to the beach.

Alternatively, **Cocoyer Plage** is a boat ride from the wharf at Petit Goâve, between 30 minutes and an hour away depending on the horsepower of the engine. Secluded white sand with palms and azure sea, it feels like an exclusive getaway. Hiring a boat is pretty straightforward – alternatively you can arrange a round trip through the **Fort Royal Hotel** (*Rue des Roulottes, Av La Hatte, Petit Goâve; 3589 3223/3807 3030; e fortroyalhotel@yahoo.fr;* **$$$**), which is the only decent sleeping option in town, and has a restaurant, pool and Wi-Fi.

If you're looking for something a bit different, head inland to the **Hotel Villa Ban-Yen** (*Route de la Montagne, Vallue; 3420 2091/2941 2091; e absept60@yahoo.*

ANACAONA

Within just a few years of the Spanish arrival on Hispaniola, the native Taíno population was in a death spiral. Not just from the bloody treatment meted out to them by the new arrivals, but by epidemics of smallpox and consequent famine that swept through the population. Only one part of the island held out against Spanish rule, the *cacique* (chiefdom) of Xaragua in the south. Its ruler was Anacaona, whose name translates as 'Golden Flower'. She was celebrated not only for her inevitable beauty, but also her political nous and skill at composing ballads.

Her husband was the warrior-chief Caonabo, who the Spanish blamed for the destruction of their attempted colony at La Navidad in the north, and shipped off to die in slavery. On the death of her brother Bohechío, she assumed the leadership of Xaragua – apparently not an unusual situation in a strongly matrilineal society. While the rest of the island fell to the Spanish, Xaragua managed to repel them through continuous struggle and a refusal to provide labour for the colonists' quest for gold.

Anacaona was recognised as a force to be reckoned with. In 1502, the new Spanish governor Nicolás de Ovando invited her to peaceful negotiations, to which she fatally agreed. She brought with her 80 sub-chiefs from Xaragua and a feast was held in her honour. When the Taíno were dining, Spanish soldiers surrounded the building and set it ablaze, killing all who managed to flee. Anacaona herself survived, but was quickly placed in chains and hanged for treason against the Spanish crown. Her nephew Guarocuya also escaped, and was adopted as a child by missionaries and baptised as Enriquillo. Twenty years later, he would lead the last great Taíno revolt against the Spanish, which led to a treaty granting limited rights for the few Taíno left on the island.

fr; www.vallue.org; **$$**). This guesthouse 650m above sea level is run by the local L'Association des Paysans de Vallue, and really gives you the chance to get away from everything. There are some great hikes to do in the area, and the helpful staff can advise on walks, and visits to community projects. To get here, turn left uphill at Vallue (signed) as the road passes near Tapion Mountain halfway between Grand Goâve and Petit Goâve.

There's potential for more hiking a little further along the highway at **Étang de Miragoâne**, a small lake nestled in the folds of the mountains just before the town of the same name. Turn off Route National 2 at Morne Preval, which runs along the shore. It's possible to swim here – the water is very clean – although you'll have to go some way to get past the people washing clothes and motorbikes. It looks as if some business development is happening here, with possible bar-restos facing on to the lake. Alternatively, come off the road at Marché Mango (a roadside fruit market) and follow the short track until you reach a lagoon area. There are boatmen here who'll pole you to the far side of the lake for 10HTG, including a small village called Anous. It's a lovely slice of rural Haiti.

The town of Miragoâne itself sits in a small bay carved out of the hills. It has a busy harbour and attractive Gothic church.

5

Southern Haiti

Haiti's south is the lushest and prettiest part of the country. The two long ridges of the Massif de la Selle and Massif de la Hotte mountains run along the southern peninsula, and it seems that wherever they meet the Caribbean Sea they inevitably produce a coast of either dramatic cliffs or gentle sandy beaches.

The main draw here is Jacmel, just a few hours' drive from Port-au-Prince. The country's handicrafts capital, it has a tremendous historic quarter and holds famous Carnival celebrations every February. There are old forts near Les Cayes, miles of sand at Port Salut and several remarkable cave complexes such as the Grotte Marie Jeanne. At the end of the highway is Grand Anse, a green and thickly forested corner of the country that's little visited but which definitely deserves closer exploration.

JACMEL

Jacmel is probably the most visited town outside Port-au-Prince for foreigners. It's an easy sell – a renowned centre for arts and handicrafts, with some great architecture and easy access to some fine beaches. It's also just a few hours' drive from the capital on a scenic road over the mountains, and every February half of Haiti seems to descend for Jacmel Carnival, one of the biggest and best parties in the country. Jacmel is the sort of laid-back Caribbean town that it's hard not to be taken with.

Jacmel has always attracted tourists, but the biggest development in years may be the opening in 2013 of the four-star boutique hotel and resort in the heart of the old town, Le Village du Port Jacmel. Plans to restore part of the old town into the Haitian equivalent of New Orleans's French Quarter – with which it has many architectural similarities – have been on the drawing board for some time, but were put on hold after the earthquake. The municipal authorities seem to be pinning their hopes on this development as being the torchbearer for the regeneration of the old town.

HISTORY Jacmel was founded by the French in 1698 on the remains of a much older Taíno settlement, thought to have been called Yaquimel. It grew only modestly as a trading port until the 1770s when coffee was introduced to the area. For over a century, coffee was the crop that made Jacmel's fortunes. The city grew rich, and had a prosperous free black and mulatto population at the outbreak of the Haitian revolution. The town initially sided with the French colonists against the slave armies, and was a prize that much blood was spilled over until it finally settled for the revolution. Soon after independence, Jacmel hosted Simón Bolívar, en route to liberate Venezuela from the Spanish.

In the 19th century, Jacmel truly boomed. Coffee exports were high, and the city had direct trade links to France, Britain and the USA. In 1895, the town became the first in the Caribbean to be electrified, as well as having Haiti's first telephone

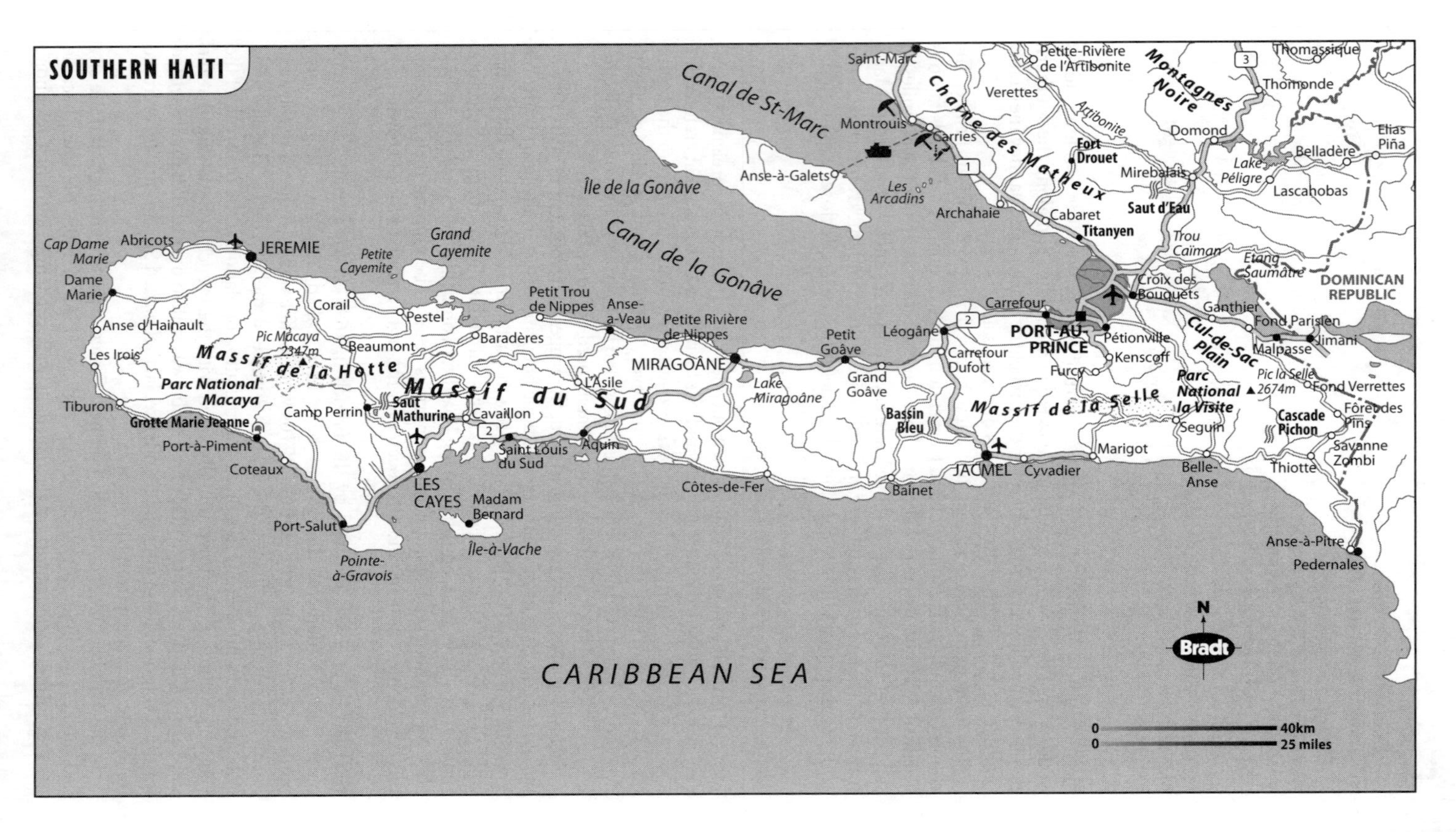

SOUTHERN HAITI
Canal de St-Marc
Île de la Gonâve
Canal de la Gonâve
CARIBBEAN SEA
DOMINICAN REPUBLIC
PORT-AU-PRINCE
JACMEL
MIRAGOÂNE
LES CAYES
JEREMIE
Massif de la Hotte
Massif du Sud
Massif de la Selle
Chaîne des Matheux
Montagnes Noire
Parc National Macaya
Parc National la Visite
Cul-de-Sac Plain
Pic Macaya 2347m
Pic la Selle 2674m
Saint-Marc
Montrouis
Carries
Archahaie
Cabaret
Titanyen
Fort Drouet
Saut d'Eau
Mirebalais
Verettes
Petite-Rivière de l'Artibonite
Artibonite
Domond
Thomonde
Thomassique
Lake Péligre
Lascahobas
Belladère
Elias Piña
Étang Saumâtre
Trou Caïman
Croix des Bouquets
Ganthier
Fond Parisien
Malpasse
Jimani
Fond Verrettes
Fôret des Pins
Savanne Zombi
Thiotte
Anse-à-Pitre
Pedernales
Cascade Pichon
Seguin
Belle-Anse
Marigot
Cyvadier
Kenscoff
Pétionville
Furcy
Carrefour
Carrefour Dufort
Léogâne
Grand Goâve
Petit Goâve
Bassin Bleu
Bainet
Lake Miragoâne
Côtes-de-Fer
Les Arcadins
Anse-à-Galets
Petite Rivière de Nippes
Anse-a-Veau
L'Asile
Aquin
Petit Trou de Nippes
Baradères
Saint Louis du Sud
Cavaillon
Madam Bernard
Île-à-Vache
Grand Cayemite
Petite Cayemite
Pestel
Beaumont
Saut Mathurine
Camp Perrin
Corail
Pointe-à-Gravois
Port-Salut
Coteaux
Port-à-Piment
Grotte Marie Jeanne
Tiburon
Les Irois
Anse d'Hainault
Dame Marie
Cap Dame Marie
Abricots
N
Bradt
0 40km
0 25 miles

exchange. Wealthy residents poured their money back into the city, ordering iron-framed prefabricated buildings from Europe – a style that became even more popular after a fire devastated much of the town centre in 1896. The mass rebuilding following the tragedy accounts for much of old Jacmel's architectural coherence today.

The boom period lasted until 1930. The American policy of centralisation during their occupation saw the port stagnate in favour of Port-au-Prince. As exports collapsed, so did the economy, setting the heart of the old town in aspic. In more recent years the city has fought hard to reclaim its old importance, now trading on its rich handicrafts tradition, and the annual Carnival – one of the biggest parties in the entire country.

GETTING THERE AND AROUND

By air Jacmel airport is east of the town centre. There are currently no scheduled flights, but at the time of writing, **Mission Aviation Fellowship** (e *flyhaiti@maf.org; www.mafhaiti.org*) were about to start a twice-weekly service, with flights to Port-au-Prince scheduled to take 15 minutes.

By road Transport to and from Port-au-Prince leaves from Portail Léogâne, a couple of miles outside Jacmel, near the large bridge on Route National 4. You can find the usual selection of buses, minibuses and *taptaps*. The trip to Port-au-Prince takes about 2½ hours. If you want to get off en route you'll still end up paying the full fare, but note that if you're heading to Léogâne, ask to be dropped at the turning for the town, as the main highway bypasses Léogâne proper. Route National 4 is very picturesque where it crosses the mountains – if you're travelling on a Saturday look out for the market at Fondwa, which stretches the length of the town, including a donkey park at both ends for villagers coming to buy and sell their wares. At Carrefour Dufort, the road joins Route National 2 to Port-au-Prince – get off here and flag down a bus if you want to head west (there are no direct options from Jacmel).

To head east from Jacmel, taptaps load up from near the Marché de Fer, although it's as easy to stand on the highway and flag them down as they're passing. The road continues all the way to the Dominican border at Anse-à-Pitre, but deteriorates significantly in quality once you get past Belle Anse. If you're feeling adventurous, there's also a rough road west, which eventually leads to Route National 2 and on to Les Cayes – see *Heading west from Jacmel*, page 155.

There are plentiful moto-taxis for trips within or outside town. A fare of 40HTG will get you as far as Cyvadier.

WHERE TO STAY Jacmel has a reasonable selection of accommodation, and finding a room isn't usually a problem. The one exception to this is Carnival weekend, when hotels get booked out far in advance, so you'll need to book ahead (also a good idea for the long holiday weekends around Easter and Fet Gede). Hotels are divided pretty evenly between those in Jacmel proper, and the beach hotels that stretch along the coast to as far as Ti Mouillage and Kabic. For the sake of the listings below, anything with direct access to a beach is listed separately.

In and around Jacmel

Moderate

Hotel Florita 29 Rue de Commerce; 3785 5154/3905 1732; e hotelflorita@yahoo.fr. In the heart of the old quarter, a 120-year-old merchant's house oozing with character. Decorated throughout with great art, charming rooms with mosquito nets (a couple at the rear are in a slightly cheaper price bracket). Great bar with bare brick & chilled atmosphere. Wi-Fi. **$$$**

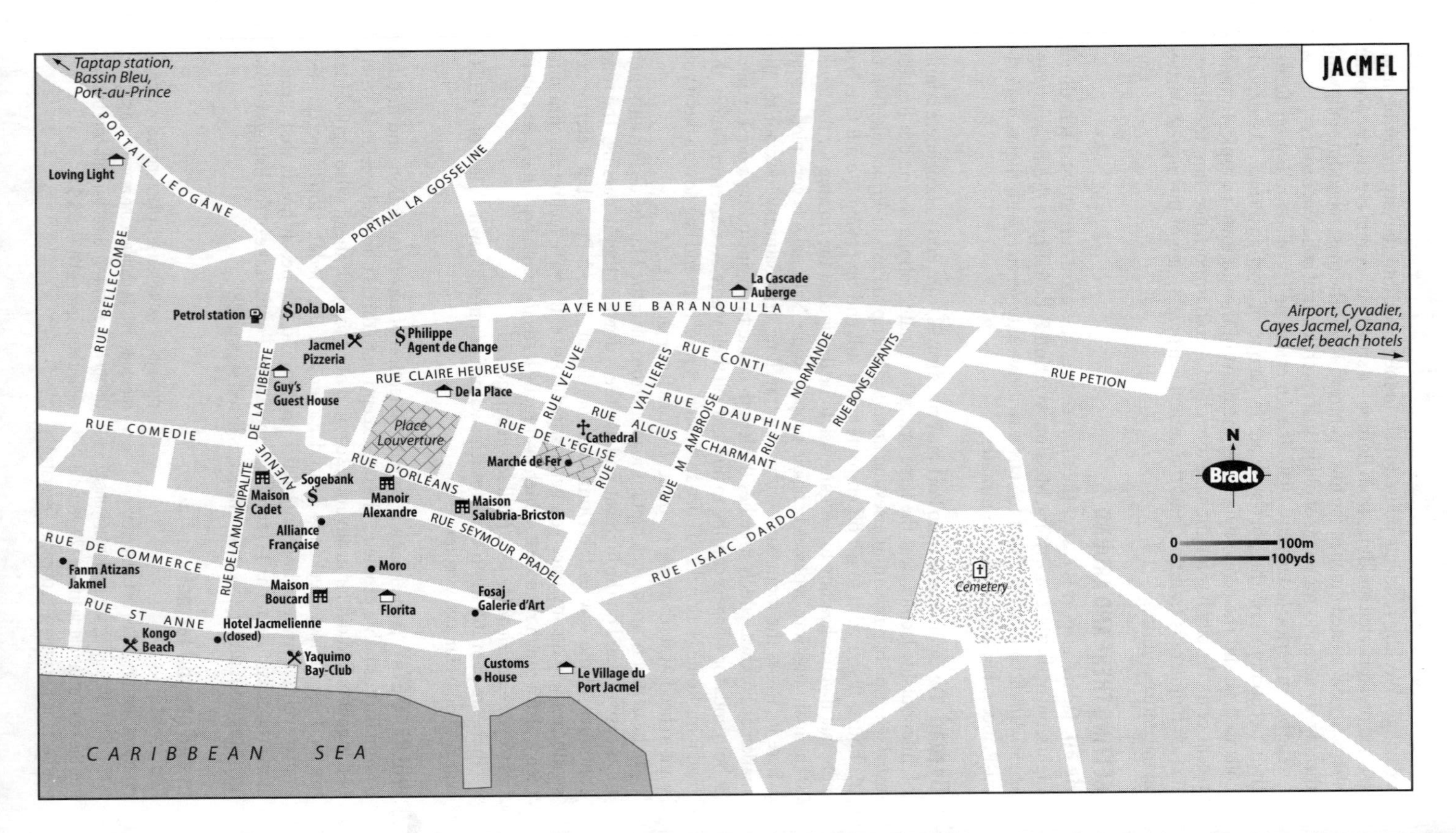
JACMEL
Taptap station, Bassin Bleu, Port-au-Prince
PORTAIL LEOGANE
Loving Light
PORTAIL LA GOSSELINE
RUE BELLECOMBE
Petrol station
Dola Dola
La Cascade Auberge
AVENUE BARANQUILLA
Airport, Cyvadier, Cayes Jacmel, Ozana, Jaclef, beach hotels
Jacmel Pizzeria
Philippe Agent de Change
Guy's Guest House
RUE CLAIRE HEUREUSE
De la Place
RUE DE LA LIBERTE
RUE VEUVE
RUE VALLIERES
RUE CONTI
NORMANDE
RUE BONS ENFANTS
RUE PETION
RUE DAUPHINE
RUE ALCIUS
RUE M AMBROISE
RUE CHARMANT
Cathedral
RUE COMEDIE
Place Louverture
RUE DE L'EGLISE
Marché de Fer
AVENUE DE LA MUNICIPALITE
RUE D'ORLÉANS
Sogebank
Maison Cadet
Manoir Alexandre
Maison Salubria-Bricston
N
Bradt
RUE SEYMOUR PRADEL
Alliance Française
RUE ISAAC DARDO
0 100m
0 100yds
RUE DE COMMERCE
Fanm Atizans Jakmel
Moro
Cemetery
Maison Boucard
Florita
Fosaj Galerie d'Art
RUE ST ANNE
Hotel Jacmelienne (closed)
Kongo Beach
Yaquimo Bay-Club
Customs House
Le Village du Port Jacmel
CARIBBEAN SEA

Loving Light Hotel 55 Portail Léogâne; 3887 9298/3750 8922; e info@lovinglighthotel.com; www.lovinglighthotel.com. Boxy, middle-of-the-road budget option on the road into Jacmel. Bland but reasonable rooms. **$$$**

Ozana Hotel Route de St Cyr; 3541 0247/3542 0497. Good modern hotel, grappling with the fact that it's quite a way off the main road outside Jacmel. Comfy, tidy rooms & food on demand. Wi-Fi. **$$$**

Budget

Hotel de la Place 3 Rue de l'Eglise; 2288 3769/3406 1123. One of Jacmel's older hotels, standing right on the edge of the town square. Rooms are fair if nothing special, some a little tired. Decent food at the restaurant out front. **$$**

Jaclef Plaza Hotel 97 Route de Cyvadier; 3605 0878/3757 6818; e jaclefhotel@yahoo.com. Fair but uninspiring hotel at the entrance to Cyvadier village on the main road. Large rooms fairly drown in chintz & over-dressed fabrics. Pool sometimes lacks water. Wi-Fi. **$$**

La Cascade Auberge 63 Av Baranquilla; 2942 7190/3695 0453; e cascadauberge@yahoo.fr. Compact guesthouse on the main road. Rooms are well sized & well kept, perfectly comfy but a few on the dark side due to small (or non-existent) external windows. **$$**

Shoestring

Guy's Guesthouse 52 Av de la Liberté; 3421 4597/3116 5909. Popular cheapie option, often busy with foreign volunteers. Fixtures & fittings are pretty stripped down, bathrooms are shared & electricity sometimes erratic, but friendly & good value. **$**

Le Rendez-Vous Hotel Route de Cyvadier; 2541 3044; e lerendez_voushotelrestobar@yahoo.fr. A series of chalets & bungalows in leafy surroundings opposite the airstrip. Rooms are slightly down at heel, but fair value for the price, & a chilled-out bar/restaurant area. **$**

Beach road hotels

Moderate

Cap Lamandou Hotel Route de Lamandou; 3944 4000/3720 1436; e caplamandouhotel@yahoo.fr. On the edge of Jacmel & down quite a long side road is Jacmel's fanciest hotel, soon to be rebranded as a Comfort Inn. Sat on a cliff, with steps down to the beach. Great views from well-appointed rooms. Pool, Wi-Fi. **$$$**

Kabic Beach Club 107 Ti Mouillage, Route Cayes Jacmel; 3780 6850/2940 1280; e kabicbeachclub@yahoo.com; www.kabicbeachclub.com. Immaculate Swiss-run hotel facing Ti Mouillage Beach. Clean & modern rooms, subtly decorated. Lawns & good open-side bar & restaurant. Pool, Wi-Fi. **$$$**

La Colline Enchantée Marigot; 3701 9697/2274 1464; e lacollineenchantee@gmail.com. Technically on the hill overlooking the sea rather than on the beach, but a good getaway. Charming thatched rooms painted in cheerful colours, great service & a nice restaurant. Be careful not to miss the sign for the turning on the main road. Pool, Wi-Fi. **$$$**

Budget

Hotel Cyvadier Plage Cyvadier; 3844 8264/8265; e contact@hotelcyvadier.com; www.hotelcyvadier.com. Perennially popular, due in part to its reliable service & good-quality rooms, but also for its beach contained in a very pretty circular bay. Excellent restaurant. Pool, Wi-Fi. **$$**

Hotel L'Amitié Hotel 120 Ti Mouillage, Route Cayes; 3888 9386/3812 3297; e patricelemaistre@yahoo.com. Slightly funky hotel, brightly decorated & very welcoming. Small shop, restaurant, decent rooms. Opens right on to the beach. **$$**

WHERE TO EAT

Hotel Cyvadier Plage Cyvadier; 3844 8264/8265; 11.00–22.00 daily. Hotel restaurant worth making a detour for. Menu strong on seafood; the sautéed lobster is renowned. Regular buffet nights, good rum cocktails. **$$$$**

Guy's Guesthouse 52 Av de la Liberté; 3818 0873; 09.00–22.00 daily. Small front-of-house restaurant for this hotel. Some good Creole standards, pizza, & reasonable sandwiches for a quick snack. **$$$**

Jacmel Pizzeria Av Baranquilla; 3818 0873; 12.00–22.00 daily. Not just a pizzeria, this blue-fronted place on the main drag is Haiti's sole Italian–Mexican restaurant. Against the odds, it seems to work. A plate of burritos is a change for the palate, amid decent pizzas & pasta. $$

✕ **Kongo Beach** Jacmel Beach; ☎ 3818 0873; ⌚ 11.00–23.00 daily. Right on the town beachfront, a large area lined on 3 sides with shacks turning out plates of chicken, meat & seafood. Great value, chilled atmosphere. Different restos open at different hours, but are mostly of a piece. Servings often come with hot lime-drenched pikliz; delicious. $$

✕ **Yaquimo Bay-Club** Av de la Liberté (beach end); ☎ 3818 0873/3102 2680; ⌚ 11.00–23.00 daily. Open-sided bar-resto-turned-club. Quiet in the day, very lively at night. Creole dishes, strong on seafood. $$

For eating by the sea, try the shacks at either the beaches at Raymond Les Bains or Ti Mouillage – simple Caribbean-style dining: seafood on the beach with a cold beer.

If you're just after a drink, the place to go is the bar at the historic Hotel Florita, with big tables and some deep sofas, surrounded by art and character. Alternatively, head for Kongo Beach, where the music pumps loud into the night.

ART AND CRAFT GALLERIES Pretty much wherever you go in Jacmel, you'll be offered art and handicrafts to buy. The most striking creations by some degree are the huge papier-mâché Carnival masks, animal and monster heads in the brightest

JACMEL CARNIVAL

When it comes to Carnival (*Kanaval*) every February, Port-au-Prince may lay claim to hosting the national celebrations, but Jacmel would argue that its own festivities offer the greatest spectacle. It's certainly the most visually appealing, and has become so popular that Jacmel now holds Kanaval a week before Port-au-Prince to avoid an unfortunate clash of dates.

Jacmel's parade is dizzying in its scope and variety. There are plenty of dancers and rara bands along the way, but at the centre of things are the bright papier-mâché creations that are the town's hallmark. Everything seems to be here, from colourful birds, dragons and giant rum bottles, to figures from the Bible and Haitian history. Political comment and social messages get thrown into the mix too – the 2012 procession had a giant cholera bacterium accompanied by a bar of soap and tap of clean water, followed soon after by a bobble-headed Minustah soldier with 'tourist' disparagingly painted on his blue helmet.

Some of the troupes take a bit of deciphering, particularly those in costumes that don't rely on papier-mâché. Scariest of all are the *Lanset Kod*, stern figures stripped to a pair of shorts and covered in a mix of charcoal and cane syrup, often topped off with a pair of horns. The ropes they carry symbolise the struggle against slavery, and they run the length of the crowd threatening to smear onlookers with their bodies. Other important grotesques are the *Chaloskas*, who wear parodies of military uniforms and buck teeth, marching up and down to mock Charles Oscar, a notoriously sadistic army officer who terrorised Jacmel in the 1900s. Clacking their wooden wings together are the *Mathurin* bat-devils, often locked in combat with the Archangel Michael. *Yawe* is a giant red cowhide that's beaten through the streets, possibly a symbolic recreation of a Taíno hunting scene (several other troupes dress as Taíno, too). Somewhere in the crowd, look out for the half-king, half-Santa Claus figure, actually Papa Jwif, the Haitian version of the Wandering Jew of Christian folklore. These strange vaudevillian characters are hugely popular staples of Jacmel Carnival, and give the proceedings a unique and unkempt character.

of colours. Painted wood is another feature of Jacmel, from carved animals and people waiting to dance across your table to place mats in the shape of fruit. As well as this, you can find the expected Haitian paintings and metal sculpture. Most of the artisan shops are around Rue de Commerce, particularly near the long-closed Hotel Jacmelienne. While browsing the streets is part of the fun, three worth noting are listed below:

Les Créations Moro (*40 Rue de Commerce;* ☎ *3864 3156/3613 7121;* e *moro_buruk@yahoo.com*) High-quality crafts – delightful painted wooden figures, elegant masks and the like. Situated across the street from the Hotel Florita.

Fosaj Galerie d'Art (*5–7 Rue St Anne;* ☎ *3642 9373;* e *fosajhaiti2003@hotmail.fr, lucknercandio@yahoo.fr*) An innovative artisan collective – the main gallery is full of canvases, while to the side there are more unusual pieces such as stylish papier-mâché vases, macramé wall hangings, strange baskets and painted lumps of concrete – repurposed rubble from the earthquake.

Fanm Atizans Jakmel (*Rue Maboir*) Run by Jacmel's only female artisans' co-operative, with painted wood, papier-mâché and a nice line in woven baskets.

PRACTICALITIES Carnival in Jacmel takes place two Sundays before Ash Wednesday, the start of Lent. This usually falls some time in February. This is the busiest tourist weekend in Jacmel's calendar, so hotel rooms are at an absolute premium. Book as far in advance as possible, but be aware that some hotels only accept bookings for three nights over the weekend, or add an extra surcharge.

The procession typically starts around midday in the centre of the old town, and proceeds up Avenue de la Liberté before turning onto Avenue Baranquilla. Temporary viewing platforms are erected the length of this road, and you'll be asked to pay a few dollars to gain access (the same goes for the houses and businesses along Baranquilla that rent out space on their balconies). The views from above are definitely worth it, and offer a bit of respite from the crush at street level – it's fun to mix the two. Front porches and side streets offer plenty of food and drink options, as well as the obligatory masks and straw hats. It takes about three hours for the parade to pass – there are plenty of jams and stoppages as dance troupes do their turn for the crowd, floats try to manoeuvre and the police attempt to keep everything under control. It's a strange mix of impressive logistics and the most joyful anarchy imaginable.

With the parade over, there are plenty of street-level sound systems to entertain the revellers, many large and loud enough to qualify as weapons of mass destruction. Clubs host live music, and the whole thing continues on into the small hours, or as long as you can keep going. A week later, when Carnival is celebrated nationwide, Jacmel reprises the festivities with a similar, but much smaller, parade.

Two great books to get you into the carnival mood are Edwidge Danticat's pocket-sized travelogue *After the Dance*, and photographer Leah Gordon's *Kanaval: Vodou, Politics and Revolution on the Streets of Haiti*, with its mesmerising portraits of the many Carnival troupes.

OTHER PRACTICALITIES There's an **ATM** at the Sogebank branch on Avenue de la Liberté, and several money-changing offices on Avenue Baranquilla, including **Dola Dola** and **Philippe Agent de Change**. **Alliance Française** (*37 Av de la Liberté;* ☎ *3812 7410/3626 0424;* e *diralliancefr.jacmel@gmail.com; www.alliancefrancaise-haiti.org/jacmel*) has regular film showings, concerts and courses.

WHAT TO SEE AND DO

Historic Jacmel When Jacmel boomed in the late 19th century, its wealthy coffee-merchant class put its money into property. Wood was the initial building material of choice, but after the city was ravaged by fire in 1896, brick became favoured, often hand-in-hand with prefabricated buildings with cast-iron skeletons imported from Europe. As a result, old Jacmel has an architectural coherence rare in Haiti. The area around Rue de Commerce is the best place to get an idea of this.

The **Hotel Florita** and surrounding buildings are typical of their type. The ground floor would have been reserved for export commodities, with the upper storeys kept residential. At the front, covered arches give a shaded gallery, while the high shuttered doors allow plenty of air inside during the day and protection against fire and hurricanes at other times. There was plenty of attention to detail with fine metalwork on the balconies, verandas and stairs. The Florita is worth exploring even if you're not a guest, for its art collections, original hardwood floors and elegant staircases (finish with a drink in the bar). It was partially damaged by the 2010 earthquake, but has undergone a sympathetic restoration. On the corner of Grand Rue is the fabulous **Maison Boucard** – a grand building with delicate filigree metalwork and cast-iron columns. At the other end the road leads to the port, where you'll find the old **customs house**, one of the best-preserved buildings.

Although much of Rue de Commerce is in a poor state of repair, it is at the heart of regional tourism plans to restore and revive the old centre. Behind the old customs house, the new boutique hotel Le Village du Port Jacmel is opening in 2013.

HADRIANA DREAMING

One of Jacmel's most famous sons is the writer René Depestre, author of the 1988 novel *Hadriana dans tous mes rêves* (*Hadriana In All My Dreams*).

Hadriana is the most beautiful woman in Jacmel, due to be married during Carnival season. On her wedding day she dies at the altar while reciting her vows, and her body is displayed at a public wake before burial, throwing the town into mourning. Yet she has not died at all but was poisoned by a *bokor* (witch doctor). After the funeral, he exhumes her body and turns her into a zombie. Hadriana manages to escape and runs away to the mountains above Jacmel. Here she is taken for Simbi Lasous, a spirit of freshwater springs, and joins a boat of migrants heading to Jamaica to start a new life.

Depestre paints Haiti with a magic realist brush, echoing the best of the Haitian painting masters. The first part of the book is a rich idealised description of Jacmel in the late 1930s; Hadriana's 'death' takes place much later, when evil has entered Jacmel – both states echoing the novelist's experience as an exile from Haiti since 1959 and writing in the closing days of the Duvalier period, when the whole country could be said to have been zombified. Although Depestre has never returned to live in Haiti, Hadriana's escape and rebirth at the novel's close points to a happier conclusion for both Jacmel and the country.

Walking up towards Avenue de la Liberté, there are many more good examples of Jacmel merchant architecture, including the imposing **Maison Cadet** on the corner, with its columns and balustrades and strange 'witch's hat' roof. On Rue Seymour Pradel, look for the delicate blue-and-white **Maison Salubria-Bricston**, occasionally open as a private art gallery displaying a fine collection of Haitian masters.

Between the old port and Avenue Baranquilla is the small but tightly packed Bel Air district. It's in roughly two halves, with Place Louverture to the west and the Marché de Fer (Iron Market) to the east. The streets between are a maze of street vendors, noise and colour. **Place Louverture** hosts the town hall, as well as the iconic **Manoir Alexandre**. Built during World War I as a private house and later turned into a hotel, it was home to the beautiful and ill-fated Hadriana in the Jacmel novel *Hadriana dans tous mes rêves* (for more details, see box, *Hadriana dreaming*, opposite). Today it's in need of love and money, its gleaming white façade dirty and cracked, and the high window shutters split and peeling.

Between the square and the market, look out for the plaque marking the site where Simón Bolívar lived in 1816 while mounting his expedition to liberate South America.

The heart of the centre of old Jacmel is undoubtedly the **Marché de Fer**, imported from Belgium in 1895 during the city's heyday. It's a grand ornamental structure, with no need for the minarets of its larger counterpart in Port-au-Prince. Market vendors spill out from its red-tiled roofs in every direction. It's the commercial hub of Jacmel, and throngs every day of the week except Sunday.

Facing the Marché de Fer is the **Cathédrale de Saint Phillipe et Saint Jacques**, built in 1859. The two saints it is dedicated to share the same saint's day (1 May), which appropriately enough is the date of Jacmel's *fête patronale*. The brick building is no stranger to catastrophe, having been severely damaged and rebuilt in the 1896 fire that destroyed much of the town centre, and then shaken again in the 2010 earthquake. For several months after the quake, the cathedral displayed a banner saying simply 'Lord, I am hurt but my faith is strong.'

Bassin Bleu Bassin Bleu is Jacmel's stand-out natural attraction, a series of three pools linked by waterfalls in the mountains above the town. It's an extraordinarily pretty spot and a must-see for any visitor.

Heading upstream from the village of Grand Fond (where you park), the three pools are Bassin Palmiste, Bassin Bleu and Bassin Clair. To get to the first, you have to cross the rushing river over a series of stepping stones. This is the most open and shallowest pool – from here the mountain walls close in, funnelling the river through an increasingly narrow gorge. To ascend it is a mix of walking and climbing. At one point you need to descend a series of steep ropes; a local 'rope man' dutifully appears to assist. The gorge twists past Bassin Bleu, which appears impressive enough until you reach the final pool. Bassin Clair is a truly gorgeous spot: a wide and deep pool of turquoise bound by sheer cliffs and huge boulders worn smooth by the passage of water. Ferns and subtropical plants fringe the rocks, and add to the cool green atmosphere. You'll be glad you brought your swimming costume (and footwear good enough for rock scrambling but which you don't mind getting wet). Once you've dived, it's such a magical spot you'll be prepared to believe local stories about the mermaids that allegedly live here. They only come out at night, except to catch those who try to dive to the bottom to find out how deep the pool is.

The pools are a 45-minute drive from Jacmel. Heading towards Port-au-Prince, turn off almost immediately after leaving the town at Carrefour La Vallée, where the road fords the shallows of the Jacmel River. Take the right-hand road and start the climb uphill. The views over the bay are lovely. A couple of impromptu road signs help at junctions. On entering Grand Fond, you should be shown to the office of the local tourist organisation, where you pay a 100HTG entrance fee. You'll be asked for a similar amount for a local guide, who will then walk you to the pools.

If you don't have transport, most hotels will be able to arrange an excursion to Bassin Bleu. It's also possible to do it by moto-taxi from Jacmel, or even by horse – local guides in Jacmel will be eager to arrange this for around US$20 per person.

Although Bassin Bleu can be visited year-round, the rainy season can make the approach road a bit tricky, while muddy run-off from the mountains makes the pools less *bleu* and rather more *brun* – not so good for swimming.

Beaches Jacmel town beach isn't up to much; its dirty grey sand is best enjoyed by sitting at the Kongo beach bars and enjoying the view of the bay. It's better to get out of town a little – if you head east along the highway you can find a handful of good options that easily meet most people's criteria of a picture-postcard Caribbean beach. In order from Jacmel, the main beaches are Cyvadier, Raymond Les Bains and Ti Mouillage.

The beach at **Cyvadier** is small but picturesque – a sliver of sand in a secluded circular bay almost totally surrounded by low green cliffs. Entrance is via the Cyvadier Plage Hotel, so is best combined with lunch or dinner. It's a tranquil scene, although rocky in places underfoot as you enter the water.

The beach at **Raymond Les Bains** is located down a turning off the main road on the edge of Cayes Jacmel. There are a few bar-restos selling cold drinks and grilled fish, lobster and *lambi*. It's very popular with locals at weekends. The beach is behind a small reef, making it very calm for a dip.

JACMEL'S CINE INSTITUTE

The Ciné Institute (*www.cineinstitute.com*) is Haiti's only professional film school, and is the lasting legacy of the city's *Festival Film Jakmèl* which ran from 2004 to 2007. Very active in Jacmel and beyond, it aims to encourage local talent by offering university-level film training through their *Ciné Lekòl* programme, a film production centre to generate income as well as connecting more widely with the community by running free educational film screenings in local schools and weekly public film screenings in its theatre – the only permanent cinema screen in Jacmel. The institute fosters connections beyond Haiti by regularly linking with foreign film-makers and festivals and welcoming visiting professionals from abroad.

In the aftermath of the earthquake, the 50 students from the Ciné Institute were the first to document the damage done in Jacmel, posting videos online while the international media were concentrating on Port-au-Prince. Films had to be cut and uploaded in temporary accommodation after the institute's main building was left flattened by the tremor.

The institute welcomes visitors, particularly film-makers, so get in touch before planning a visit. Their campus is outside of Jacmel proper, well signed on the main road running east to the beaches, roughly halfway between Jacmel and Cyvadier. Films by the students can be seen on the institute's website or the Ciné Institute channel on www.vimeo.com.

above Anse d'Azur, near Jérémie, is one of Haiti's best beaches, with sugar sand and a sunken German U-boat a short swim out in the bay (PC) page 172

below Once dubbed 'the Paris of the Antilles', Cap-Haïtien retains the street pattern laid out by the French, including a *corniche* that runs the length of the seafront (UIG/A) page 175

left **Bassin Bleu, a series of three pools linked by waterfalls, has inspired a number of local myths** (SS) page 151

below **The Artibonite Valley is Haiti's rice basket; its eponymous river is the longest in Hispaniola** (W) page 207

bottom **Peasant farmers all over Haiti keep small terraced plots focused on subsistence crops** (SS) page 23

Every July thousands of Vodou and Christian pilgrims visit the sacred waterfalls of Saut d'Eau to perform religious devotions (SS) page 216

above Dubbed 'the city of poets' in honour of its writers, Jérémie is the perfect base for exploring the isolated Grand Anse region (W) page 167

below left High shuttered doors, balconies and shaded walkways are typical of the old part of Les Cayes, where most buildings date from the early 20th century (KW) page 231

below right The small fishing island of Île-à-Vache, once the base of the famous Welsh pirate Henry Morgan, is today a quiet getaway with small resorts and homestays (AVZ) page 476

above Fort Dauphin, built in 1731 to celebrate the birth of the French king's son, commands the entrance to the circular bay of Fort Liberté (W) page 196

right Cap-Haïtien's cathedral is one of the last remaining colonial buildings in the city, once the richest in the Caribbean (JC/A) page 182

below A stilt-dancer leads a street band through an open-air market in a village near Les Cayes, to celebrate Easter Monday (BD) page 77

above left A gambling game in Hinche market: you're never far from an opportunity to gamble in Haiti, whether on the lottery, cockfighting or dominoes (JM/A) page 26

above right The village of Croix des Bouquets is an artisans' enclave, with countless workshops producing intricate metal sculptures (JL/VL) page 132

below Farmers in a *rara* band share a bottle of sugar cane alcohol they have been given while performing (MAU) page 238

top and above The carnival celebrations in Jacmel are famous for oversized papier-mâché masks, street theatre and exuberant dancing (PC) page 148

above right Vodou flags are adorned with the sacred symbols of the *Iwa* and their Catholic counterparts, and embellished with thousands of beads and sequins (SS) page 38

below *Rara* bands typically take to the streets in the run-up to Carnival and during Lent, but they are also closely associated with Vodou (BD) page 37

above **Townspeople boating off the coast of Saint-Marc; the port has a distinguished history as the embarkation point for 500 Haitians who set sail to fight in the American Revolution in 1779** (LS) page 211

below **The rich agricultural land of the mountainous Kenscoff region provides much fresh produce for the capital below** (SS) page 129

The beach at **Ti Mouillage** is right on the road, and is the closest that the Jacmel area gets to ticking off the Caribbean holiday checklist of sand, surf and palm trees. It's a delight, and as at Raymond Les Bains, there are shacks for a seafood lunch or dinner. Take care when swimming as there's a sharp undertow not too far from the shore.

An alternative in the opposite direction is **Baguette**, just across the bay from Jacmel wharf – you'll need to hire a local boat to get here (30 minutes), where you can haul up on a pretty pebble beach and explore the ruins of an old French fort.

Moulin Price Jacmel never had the large-scale sugar industry of the north, but sugar remained an important crop at independence. A forgotten slice of this history is a short drive from Jacmel airport at Moulin Price. Abandoned in a field is an English steam engine imported in 1818 from Liverpool, which would have powered the mill to crush the sugarcane, before the juice could be boiled in a giant kettle to produce refined sugar. Some of the original stonework of the mill also still stands, but it was partly damaged in the 2010 earthquake.

An early example of the Industrial Revolution played out in the Caribbean, the engine is one of only two of its type remaining in the world, and was brought to Jacmel by Hannibal Price, who settled in the area in 1806 (like the newly independent Haitians, he too had fought Napoleon, having served at the Battle of Trafalgar). A papier-mâché replica of the engine recently made its debut in the Jacmel Carnival parade.

To get to Moulin Price, turn left straight after the airport – from here it's ten minutes on a muddy track.

Fort Ogé Commanding the view out across Jacmel bay, Fort Ogé (locally also called Fort Cap-Rouge) is part of the chain of defensive forts built across Haiti by Dessalines in 1804. It has impressively high rampart walls with a couple of watchtowers and a wide courtyard. The site is partially overgrown, but look out for graffiti left by American soldiers during the occupation. The fort (which is on the back of the 10HTG note) is named after the mulatto leader Vincent Ogé, whose failed insurrection against the French in 1790 was an opener for the slave revolution a year later that ultimately led to independence.

You can reach Fort Ogé by taking the road that runs along the left side of the airport (Route des Orangers). Once in the village of Les Orangers, turn right uphill to Cap-Rouge. The road is pretty rough and takes the best part of an hour by car; the final approach must be done on foot.

Etang Bossier This small hillside lake is about an hour west of Jacmel, and makes a tranquil picnic and hiking spot. Drive east from Jacmel and turn off the highway at Carrefour Raymond near Cayes Jacmel. It's a short drive, but after 2km you must park and walk the remainder of the way (about 45 minutes). Locals will direct you. It's an interesting walk as the area has a couple of traditional animal (or human) powered sugar mills, with hand-carved wooden cogs and rollers to crush the cane. The surrounding hills are reasonably wooded for the area, and the lake itself attracts plenty of birdlife.

According to tradition, the lake was formed after an old man was repeatedly refused a drink of water by mean local villagers who lived on the hill where the lake now stands. Only one person offered the man charity, and was thus advised to leave his house for the night. When the villager returned the next morning, the man had turned the hill into a lake and drowned everyone as a punishment.

TOWARDS THE DOMINICAN REPUBLIC BORDER

Public transport starts to diminish after Marigot. The highway heads away from the sea and up towards the mountains of the Massif de la Selle. The road quality also decreases quite considerably, turning from tarmac to rough piste. After a couple of hours, passing through the village of Fond-Jean Noël (where you can turn to go towards Seguin and Parc National la Visite) you descend again to the coast at the remote but pretty coastal town of **Belle Anse**. There are long and gorgeous stretches of largely untouched beach here, the main attraction – the town was originally called Troue de Boue, but was apparently renamed to celebrate its beautiful setting. Fishing is the mainstay of the town, and it has an interesting market on Tuesdays. On other days it's possible to hire boats from local fishermen – two short trips worth making are east to the beach at **Lagon des Huîtres**, or west to the white monolithic rock **Le Colombier**, which juts dramatically out of the cliffs. If you're feeling extravagant, you might even try to arrange a trip back to Jacmel.

If you want to spend the night here, the **Cocky Hotel** (*Rue du Calvaire;* ☎ *2288 3269/3279;* **$$**) is a small and simple option.

Quite soon after leaving Belle Anse, the road turns sharply inland again and starts climbing back into the mountains. It's another rough road, demanding a 4x4 with a good driver. The big draw along this road is **Cascade Pichon** (also called Étang Pichon). In a country that abounds in waterfalls, this is possibly the most stunning – a good job considering the effort required in getting there. There's a village called Pichon en route, but the falls are nearly another hour's drive further on – locals will direct you. You can see the falls from the road, a bright veil of water playing in the sunlight, but you need to walk for about 30 minutes from where you park to actually reach them. They're quite incredible: a series of falls tumbling from a great height in a wide semi-circle through lush forest and over limestone boulders, meeting at a large clear pool at the bottom. The whole scene is simply idyllic, and given the time it takes to get here, you'd be foolish not to want to dive in.

The road continues through the mountains to **Thiotte**, perhaps another two hours' drive. The surrounding area is perfect coffee-growing country, and Thiotte is an important place for local wholesale merchants, who come to meet the peasant farmers who descend on the town every Monday and Friday for the big market (this is also the day that *taptaps* and passenger trucks ply the roads here). It's a fascinating place to observe traditional, rural Haiti. There's one adequate sleeping option here, the **Esperanza Guesthouse** (☎ *3634 2171*).

Thiotte is a junction town. As well as continuing to Anse-à-Pitre, there's the choice of heading north along the Dominican border. The road leads through Savanne Zombi to Forêt des Pins and Fond Verrettes, eventually joining the tarmac highway to Croix des Bouquets (and Port-au-Prince) at Fond Parisien. Passenger trucks also run this route. This is the area of Parc National Forêt des Pins – for more information see *Forêt des Pins*, page 134.

Turning southeast again, the road from Thiotte to Anse-à-Pitre is beautiful; farmland rolls towards the sea, and large cacti and scrub foliage dominate the terrain. It's an hour's drive (moto-taxis will take you, but ask up to 500HTG for the trip).

Anse-à-Pitre is a small neat town that lives off its position as a border town: across a small bridge over a river is the Dominican Republic, and Anse-à-Pitre's more prosperous twin, Pedernales. The border crossing is the most laid-back in the country, and immigration officials (look for their small blue building) will be genuinely interested (in a friendly way) in why you ended up in this remote corner of the country. There's rarely a wait, or even a crossing fee. Pedernales town is about

1km over the border. It has an ATM, onward transport connections (on paved roads) and a good sleeping option in the **Hostal Doña Chava** (*Calle PN Hugson;* *+809 524 0332; www.donachava.com;* **$**).

HEADING WEST FROM JACMEL

It's possible to drive directly from Jacmel to Les Cayes without having to backtrack along Route Nationale 4 to Carrefour Dufort. The road is slightly longer, taking perhaps around six hours, but it tracks through some truly beautiful mountain scenery. As with any trip off the main highways, a 4x4 is preferred due to the poor road quality.

On leaving Jacmel in the direction of Port-au-Prince, turn left at Carrefour La Vallée (this is the same turning for Bassin Bleu, at the river crossing). The way climbs steeply into the mountains, twisting for nearly an hour before you reach the market town of **La Vallée**. Its elevated position commands splendid views, and the scenery is a lot greener than expected. The red laterite soil in the area is ideal for coffee-growing, although the town is also known for its basket-making. The region cries out to be hiked through, and if you want to base yourself here there's a great sleeping option, the **Auberge Mont Saint-Jean** (*3702 0510/3753 6823;* e *aubergemontsaintjean@yahoo.fr;* **$$**). The *auberge* can even offer paragliding in the region.

From La Vallée, the road continues west following the spine of the mountains before suddenly switching down to the coast through the hamlet of Blockauss to emerge at the old port of **Bainet** (two hours from Jacmel), which sits in a wide bay with a lovely pebble beach. Bainet is three centuries old, founded around the same time as Jacmel – its name is from the French for 'clean bay', because of the lack of reefs. Like Jacmel it prospered through its coffee merchants, who left behind many fine old houses, but its port is long closed. Contemporary Bainet feels very isolated, although it spurs itself into life for its Wednesday and Saturday markets. The **Guest House Kanpanyol** (*3608 2445;* **$**) on the road out of town has reasonable rooms. A 90-minute hike uphill from Bainet by the Ti-Penn River is **Source Martino**, a narrow gorge that terminates in a cavernous waterfall where it's possible to swim. Ask locals for directions.

The road from Bainet tracks back up into the mountains. The landscape really opens out, and the stretch to Gris-Gris offers some of the best vistas of the drive (as well as some of the roughest sections of road). From Gris-Gris, you drive through Cavalier, a village that seems to have received an incongruous consignment of road signs, before ending up back on the coast road. As you approach Côtes de Fer there are several gorgeous white sandy beaches, but they can be hard to access as much of the landscape is simply covered with scrubby native acacia trees. There's speculation over developing it for hotel resorts, but any action is likely to be a long time in the future. The Côtes de Fer road is well graded (if muddy after rain), and continues west until it eventually joins Route Nationale 2 slightly east of Aquin.

AQUIN AND SAINT LOUIS DU SUD

If you've been heading out from Port-au-Prince on Route National 2, the stretch of road between Aquin and Saint Louis du Sud is where the charms of southwestern Haiti really start to reveal themselves. The scenery is lush, green and hilly, and there are long stretches where the road tracks the coast – miles of white sand and the clean turquoise waters of the Caribbean Sea. It's startlingly pretty.

The main towns are strung along the coast, although most of the action takes place off the highway. **Aquin** is the first place of any size. Every Easter weekend, the **Destination Aquin Festival** (*www.destinationaquin.org*) is held in the town, and seems to get bigger every year. It attracts major Haitian bands and others from neighbouring countries, and has dance shows, exhibitions and local handicrafts.

Just outside Aquin is the village of **Zanglais**, which has a lovely hotel in the **Jardins Sur Mer** (*Route National 2;* ✆ *3668 6147/3119 8686;* e *jardinsurmer@hotmail.com;* **$$**). Built on a hilly peninsula it has simple but charming rooms, and a lovely terrace surrounded by gardens and overlooking the sea. It's particularly popular on the weekends for its seafood buffet, which is worth a detour (**$$$$$**). The hotel can also arrange boat trips to the **Île de Trompeuse** in the bay, which is great for secluded swimming.

A further 15 minutes from Zanglais (or a 30-minute *taptap* ride from Les Cayes) is **Saint Louis du Sud**. It's worth a stop for its two colonial-era forts: Fort Olivier and Fort Anglais. To reach them stop just near the green sign for Saint Louis du Sud on the Les Cayes side of town. On the beach side of the road, steps lead down from behind a roadside barrier past a small compound to the beach – from here you can see Fort Olivier on its spit of land, and the island with Fort Anglais in the bay. (If you've stopped in the centre of Saint Louis du Sud, it's a 20-minute walk through town and fields to get to the same point).

Fort Olivier is the first fort. It's in undoubtedly poor condition, romantically crumbling at the end of the tiny peninsula. A solitary cannon still guards the approach to the bay. The views are better from the western side. It's a little unclear if there's an entrance fee – I was approached by a local 'guide' wearing a T-shirt with '*securité*' hand-written with marker pen, and slightly drunk on *klerin*. A tip seemed enough to be left alone to explore the ruins myself. The fort and beach is where Saint Louis du Sud's *fête patronale* is held every 25 August.

Better by far is **Fort Anglais**, which sits on a small island in the bay. There's no organised transport, but the local *lambi* fishermen seem game to take passengers (I went in what was essentially a dug-out canoe with a sail made from stitched-together bin liners. It was possibly the single most enjoyable form of transportation I used researching this guide). Under sail, it takes about 20 minutes to reach the island. The approach to the island is very shallow with plenty of coral, and a couple of small wrecks stick their ribs out of the sea to provide perches for local terns.

The fort is much larger than its mainland counterpart, and covers almost the entire island in a giant skewed pentagon. It's very overgrown – in several places there are mature *mapou* trees with great buttress roots slithering over the brickwork. It's possible to walk around the island if you don't mind getting your feet wet – the best views are of the bastions rising out of the water. Some fine stone detailing (imported specially from France) remains, just one sign that this fort was once the cutting edge of military architecture. Although tumbledown, it's very evocative and great fun – exactly the sort of place where you feel like searching for buried treasure with an old parchment map and 'X marks the spot'.

When the French built this fort in 1702 they called it Fort St Louis, and it was the most important defensive structure in the south. It needed to be, since it faced the busy passage to Jamaica, then a colony of the hated British. However, in 1748 it was bombarded and sacked by a squadron of ships from the Royal Navy, who made off with its 72 guns. The French tried to improve their defences with the construction of Fort Olivier a few years later, but Saint Louis du Sud never recovered its prestige, and Les Cayes soon took over as the south's most important city.

SOUTHERN BACKROADS

Halfway between Les Cayes and Saint Louis du Sud is the market town of **Cavaillon**. It's famous for *gelée*, its bright-red guava jam. As vehicles slow to pass through town, vendors press jars against the windows in hope of a sale.

Instead of motoring straight through to Les Cayes, it's possible to make an interesting diversion through the local backroads. Turn north in Cavaillon on the road to **Maniche**. It's a mostly earth/gravel piste, although during the rainy season it might be a challenge in some places. There's only one major junction en route, where you must turn left (to Dory) instead of right (to Piton). Its simple but attractive well-watered farmland was originally developed by the French, and it's not hard to find traces of old irrigation canals and sugar and fruit plantations. Some of the works were used until the early 20th century but are now abandoned, overgrown old buildings and factory chimneys poking out of the trees.

Maniche is a small and diverting market town. The road climbs from here, and eventually brings you out at Camp Perrin – if you stop and ask regularly for directions you'll pop out virtually in front of the Saut Mathurine waterfalls. The road leads from here straight to Les Cayes.

In 2012, plans were being promoted for a large tourist development on the nearby uninhabited island of Grosse Cayes, which had been leased tax-free by the Haitian government to a joint Haitian–Dominican company called San Aquino. The plans, called **Port Yaquimo**, aim to turn the island into a self-contained cruise-ship destination, with up to 1,000 hotel rooms, a shopping village, aquarium, marina and watersports. It was unclear how fully the project was funded at the time of going to press, but you can follow its progress at www.sanaquino.com.

LES CAYES

Les Cayes – more usually just referred to as 'Cayes' – is the largest city in the south, and feels a lot more prosperous than anywhere else south of the capital. It's not a great draw in and of itself, but has plenty of facilities and a laid-back atmosphere complemented by some attractive architecture. It's also a good place to base yourself to explore the region, and puts you within striking distance of Port Salut, Île-à-Vache and other attractions along the southern coast.

Despite its outwardly quiet air, Les Cayes's history is as turbulent as anywhere in Haiti. Its low-lying coastal position has made it prone to natural disasters, being regularly thrashed by hurricanes throughout its history, while the current city centre dates from 1885, when a torrid fire ripped through the heart of Les Cayes.

The city sits on the site of the Spanish settlement of Salvatierra de la Zabana, founded in 1503 but abandoned soon thereafter. The French returned in 1726, and threaded the surrounding plains with a network of irrigation canals, many of which are still in use today. Les Cayes soon became the third city of Saint-Domingue, exporting coffee and rum, but its proximity to the dangerous sea route to British-held Jamaica meant it never attained the grandeur of Port-au-Prince or Cap Français (modern Cap-Haïtien).

Les Cayes was the hometown of the accomplished mulatto general André Rigaud, and was regularly besieged during the revolutionary war. Rigaud was an independent-minded leader and even went as far as declaring the short-lived autonomous State of South Haiti in 1810 with Les Cayes as its capital, splitting himself from Pétion's republic, until being persuaded that unity was the better part of valour. A few years later, Pétion hosted Simón Bolívar here, when the latter was on his way to liberate Venezuela.

Much of Les Cayes was destroyed by fire in 1885, and most of the buildings in the city centre follow this period. The city's port infrastructure was heavily revamped in the 1920s during the American occupation, although by this time much international trade was already slipping away to the capital. Resentments were fuelled further in 1929 when the 'Cayes Massacre' left 12 dead from the guns of US marines, following nationwide strikes against the occupation. One of Les Cayes's most famous sons, Othello Bayard, wrote a poem against the occupation that when set to music became *Haïti cherie*, now the country's unofficial national anthem (the city's music institute remains named after him).

Attesting to Les Cayes's easy-going nature, one anecdote of dubious nature recounts that rum exported from here had its crates marked 'Aux Cayes', with hard-drinking American stevedores corrupting the name to 'OK' as a mark of quality and eventually spreading the slang through the world's shipping lanes. Whether you believe this or not may well depend on how many rum sours you've consumed while being told.

GETTING THERE AND AROUND

By air Antoine-Simon Airport is 20 minutes outside Les Cayes on the road to Camp Perrin. At the time of writing no commercial flights were running, but **Tortug'Air** (*Rue Stenio Vincent, next to Pen Doré; 2286-8600*) maintain an office in town anyway.

By road Route National 2 passes through Les Cayes, and commercial transport departs from around Carrefour Quatre Chemins, with its white traffic circle topped by a statue of the Crucifixion.

Les Cayes has several air-conditioned minibus companies running early-morning set departures to Port-au-Prince (four hours), including **Transport Voyageur** (*at Meridien Hotel; 2942 7025*) and **Transport Chic** (*227 Av des Quatre Chemins; 3630 2576*). These offer comfort virtually unheard of on Haitian public transport, and well worth the 400HTG fare. Buy a ticket the day before (take ID). **Cinq Etoile** (*3813 3149*) have identical minibuses which fill and go until early afternoon, leaving from the Texaco station at Quatre Chemins.

The more usual *taptaps* and brightly painted buses leave for Port-au-Prince throughout the day from an organised station on the highway, 500m west of the crossroads. Taptaps to Port Salut also depart from here – ludicrously over-filled open-top pick-ups, and easily the most overloaded and uncomfortable taptaps I've experienced in Haiti. The 45-minute drive may be better accomplished on the back of a moto-taxi; the road is particularly scenic.

On the Port-au-Prince side of Quatre Chemins, taptaps depart to Aquin (one hour), while slowly filling taptaps to Camp Perrin (45 minutes) leave from the northern side (pick up passing buses to Jérémie from here).

Within Les Cayes, moto-taxi fares shouldn't top 35HTG, while there are radio taxis operated by **Wuidny Taxis** (*3148 8283*).

By boat There are daily *bateaux-taxis* from Les Cayes wharf to Madame Bernard on Île-à-Vache, taking 30 minutes and operating to no particular schedule.

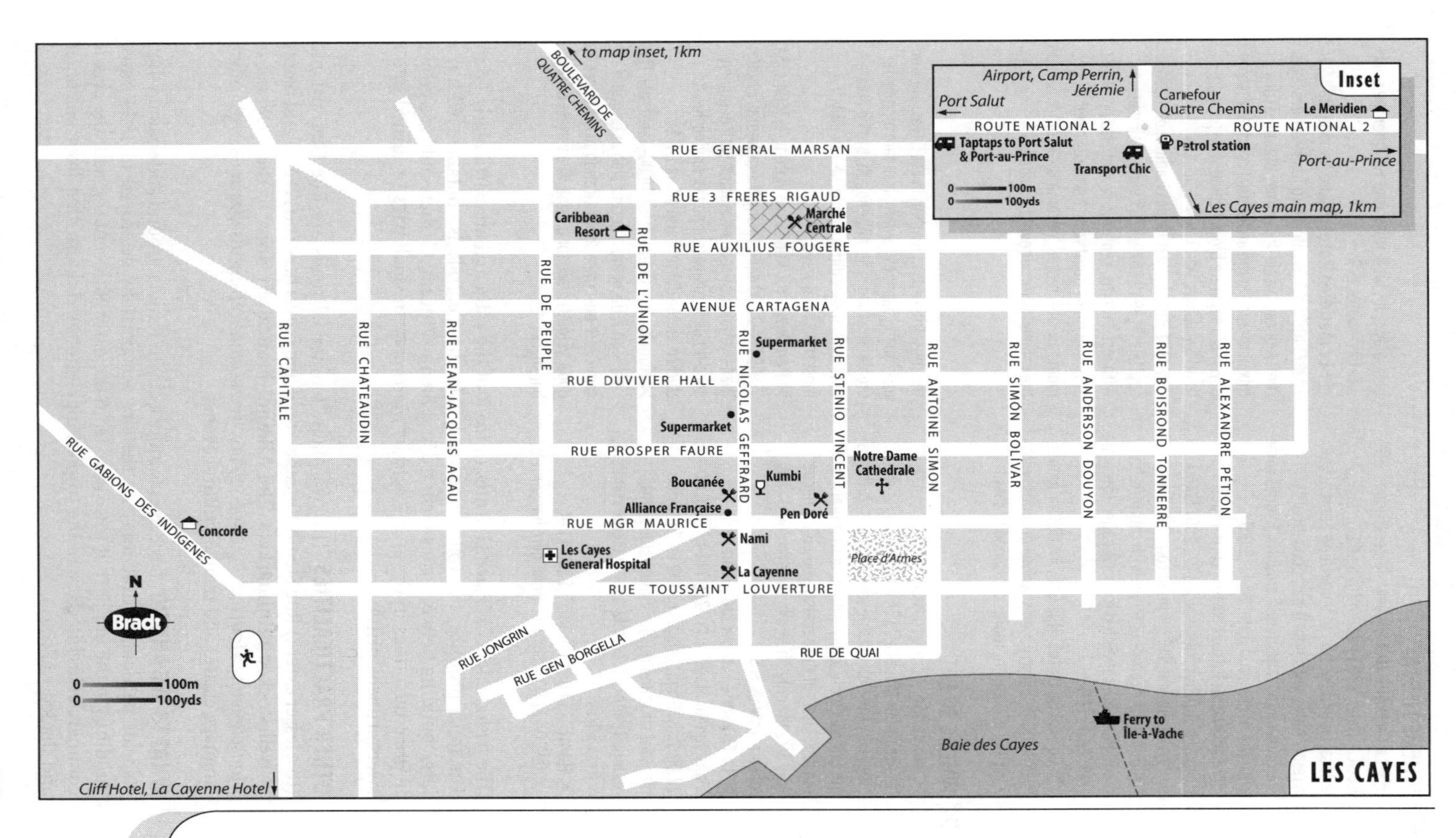
LES CAYES
Inset
Airport, Camp Perrin, Jérémie
Port Salut
Carrefour Quatre Chemins
Le Meridien
ROUTE NATIONAL 2
ROUTE NATIONAL 2
Taptaps to Port Salut & Port-au-Prince
Transport Chic
Petrol station
Port-au-Prince
0 100m
0 100yds
Les Cayes main map, 1km
to map inset, 1km
BOULEVARD DE QUATRE CHEMINS
RUE GENERAL MARSAN
RUE 3 FRERES RIGAUD
RUE AUXILIUS FOUGERE
AVENUE CARTAGENA
RUE DUVIVIER HALL
RUE PROSPER FAURE
RUE MGR MAURICE
RUE TOUSSAINT LOUVERTURE
RUE DE QUAI
RUE CAPITALE
RUE CHATEAUDIN
RUE JEAN-JACQUES ACAU
RUE DE PEUPLE
RUE DE L'UNION
RUE NICOLAS GEFFRARD
RUE STENIO VINCENT
RUE ANTOINE SIMON
RUE SIMÓN BOLÍVAR
RUE ANDERSON DOUYON
RUE BOISROND TONNERRE
RUE ALEXANDRE PÉTION
RUE GABIONS DES INDIGENES
RUE JONGRIN
RUE GEN BORGELLA
Caribbean Resort
Marché Centrale
Supermarket
Supermarket
Notre Dame Cathedrale
Boucanée
Kumbi
Pen Doré
Alliance Française
Nami
La Cayenne
Place d'Armes
Les Cayes General Hospital
Concorde
N
Bradt
0 100m
0 100yds
Ferry to Île-à-Vache
Baie des Cayes
Cliff Hotel, La Cayenne Hotel

WHERE TO STAY

La Cayenne Hotel Near Île des Icaques, off Rue Capitale; 3814 2594/3675 5615; e lacayenneht@yahoo.fr. Something approaching a resort hotel, with pool & bar, good-quality spacious rooms & gardened grounds. Fridges come with the higher room rate. Wi-Fi. **$$$**

Caribbean Resort Hotel Corner rues L'Union & Auxilius Fougere; 3498 2007/3460 9799; e caribbean5193@gmail.com. A tall new building in the centre of town, with comfortably bland but well-appointed rooms & eager-to-please staff. Wi-Fi. **$$**

Concorde Hotel Rue Gabions des Indigenes; 2286 0079. Set in green spacious grounds, with a variety of pleasant rooms contained in small bungalows. It's hit & miss as to whether the pool will have water. **$$**

Le Meridien Hotel Route National 2; 2942 7025/3408 7265; e info@hotelmeridiendescayes.com. A decent value-for-money option, with a mix of rooms around an internal courtyard (some noisy) & a separate block behind with parking. Good breakfasts. Wi-Fi. **$$**

Cliff Hotel Near Île des Icaques, off Rue Capitale; 3919 3679/3765 9966. A tiny place with just 4 rooms, kept spic-&-span. No breakfast, although many guests don't actually need it, as rooms are also rented for romantic 'moments' (note the ceiling mirrors above the beds). **$**

WHERE TO EAT

Boucanée Corner rues Geffrard & Monseigneur Maurice; 3449 2048; lunch–late daily. The sign outside says 'Kay Arts', & things get unexpectedly funky within, with murals, loud music & lasers in the evening. Food is barbecue only & really only offered in the evenings – fish, lobster & steak. **$$**

La Cayenne Corner rues Geffrard & Monseigneur Maurice; 2286 1114; 10.00–22.00 daily. Bright murals on the wall provide pleasant surroundings for dining, along with a menu offering a good selection of Creole standards & fresh juices. **$$**

Nami 15 Rue Geffrard; 2286 1114; 09.00–22.00 daily. The menu here has some of the most interesting reading in Les Cayes, offering up Chinese, Japanese & Jamaican fare alongside Creole. The food is decent enough, but be aware that some dishes differ from others in only the most superficial ways. **$$**

Pen Doré 166 Rue Stenio Vincent; 3604 3334; 08.00–22.00 daily. Facing the cathedral, a better-than-average fast-food restaurant, with genuinely good burgers, competent pizzas, sandwiches & chicken. Home delivery also offered. **$$**

Kumbi Rue Geffrard; 10.00–late daily. The 'cool' sign & décor are a decent stab at bringing some Port-au-Prince sophistication to Les Cayes. A good (if loud) place for a drink, & a variety of tasty bar snacks. **$**

The *fritay* sellers on Place D'Armes in front of the cathedral are particularly good. For fresh produce, the rough-and-ready Marché Centrale is contained within a large building between rues Geffrard and Stenio Vincent. Cashew nuts are grown in great quantities in the area – sold by *marchands* in small bags or turned into a sweet crunchy brittle.

OTHER PRACTICALITIES The two main commercial roads are Rue Geffrard and (to a lesser extent) Rue Stenio Vincent. You'll find banks here (no ATMs) and plenty of well-stocked **minimarkets**. The **Alliance Française** (*corner of rues Geffrard & Monseigneur Maurice; 3806 9766; www.alliancefrancaisedescayes.org*) offers language classes and regular cultural events.

WHAT TO SEE AND DO Les Cayes is more a city to wander around and soak up than visit for particular attractions. As the city was partially destroyed in 1885, most buildings in the old part of town date from the early 20th century, with the classic commercial architecture of the tropics: high-shuttered doors, first-floor balconies and shaded walkways.

Les Cayes's most important building is the **Notre Dame Cathedral**, built to commemorate the city's patron saint in 1908 and in need of a facelift. Opposite is the pleasant square of **Place D'Armes**. At the entrance you'll find a poorly painted bust of Boisrond Tonnere, who was born in nearby Torbeck. Boisrond was Dessalines's secretary and drew up Haiti's Declaration of Independence, famously declaring that to do the document justice he'd 'need the skin of a white man for parchment, his skull for an inkwell, his blood for ink, and a bayonet for a pen'. Also in the square is a memorial to President Geffrard, claiming to contain his mortal remains, and a simple memorial to the dead of the 12 January 2010 earthquake.

Les Cayes's beach is **Plage Gelée**, on the outskirts of the city in the direction of Port Salut. There are a few beach bars for food and drinks. Every 15 August it's crammed for the city's *fête patronale*, better known as Fet Gelée, one of the biggest summer festivals in the south, with big bands and DJs.

Adventurous travellers may consider hiring a moto-taxi for a trip to **Camp Gérard**, the ruins of an old French fort in the hills above Les Cayes. It's in a relatively poor condition, but the views over the plain below are lovely. The agricultural richness of the area is laid out before you, neatly divided into bright green plots, and still irrigated by a system of colonial-era canals.

ÎLE-À-VACHE

In 1816, Simón Bolívar departed from the wharf at Les Cayes to liberate Venezuela from the Spanish. Today, visitors set sail for the rather more relaxed pastime of enjoying the beaches and waters of Île-à-Vache. It's a small fishing island with a handful of good hotels, and a great place to get away from everything.

Throughout the years, others have been attracted to Île-à-Vache. It was originally inhabited by the Taíno, who left evidence of their civilisation in huge mounds of discarded conch shells that are still being excavated in some places. In the 17th century the island was used as a base by the famous Welsh pirate Henry Morgan, who acted as a privateer for the British government to harry the Spanish treasure ships. It's thought that the remains of his flagship, *The Oxford*, and several of his other ships, lie in the waters just off Île-à-Vache. It sank after an explosion in the powder room (killing Morgan in the process), and was located by divers in 2004, who found several cannons. Also in the waters off the island is the wreck of *Bluenose*, a celebrated Canadian racing schooner that sank on a reef here in 1946.

There are two villages on the island: Cay Coq and Madame Bernard.

GETTING THERE AND AWAY Port Morgan and Abaka Bay have boats to pick up guests from the wharf in Les Cayes, but there's also a ferry running a couple of times a day. Check times in advance if possible. The boat leaves from the public wharf, a short walk from the wharf where the private boats dock. A small boat transfers you to the ferry for about 10HTG. The voyage costs 100HTG and takes about an hour – pack sunscreen and a hat. You'll normally be deposited at Cay Coq, but it's possible to ask to be dropped at wherever you'll be staying.

WHERE TO STAY AND EAT There are three places to stay on Île-à-Vache, although quite a few villagers offer very basic homestays if your Creole is up to it and you don't mind roughing it. No addresses for these places – you get dropped off by boat and the island is tiny.

Abaka Bay 3721 3691/3683 6253; e info@abakabay.com; www.abakabay.com. High-quality resort (with attendant price tag), sat on a simply stunning curve of sandy beach. There's a main hotel & a series of bungalows along the sand. Activities include horseriding, boat trips, snorkelling & idling the time away over a rum punch. Meals included. Wi-Fi. **$$$$**

Port Morgan 3921 0000/3922 0000; e portmorgan@hughes.net; www.port-morgan.com. French-run hotel next to a small marina with facilities for visiting yachts. Bright airy chalets with verandas have a hint of gingerbread about them. Excellent food. Boat trips & massages can be arranged. **$$$**

Village Vacances 3637 4391; e vacation@ile-a-vache.com; www.haitivillagevacances.com. A relatively simple series of bungalows, next to a gorgeous beach. Good Creole seafood & a friendly welcome, although the nearby mangrove means that there are often plenty of mosquitoes. **$$$**

PORT SALUT

In recent years, Port Salut has become *the* place for weekend breaks from Port-au-Prince. One look at the long stretch of palm-fringed white sand and it's easy to see why. Hotels seem to be springing up all along the coast to satisfy demand – but since this is Haiti there's still some way to go before things reach the crush point of many other Caribbean beach destinations. Come during the week and you can still have the place pretty much to yourself.

Port Salut is neatly paved, and strung quite some way along the coast. The part most people are interested in is the beach at **Pointe Sable**. All your favourite Caribbean holiday clichés are here to be fulfilled – miles of clean white sand lapped by a shining blue sea, the occasional beach bar serving grilled fish, with the whole thing fringed with coconut palms. Pointe Sable is on the western edge of Port Salut – there's access via a slip-road (vehicle entrance 50HTG).

Most people will be rightly content with kicking back and spending their time here doing nothing more energetic than ordering another rum sour. If you want something a little more active, there's a small but pretty **waterfall** about half an hour's walk inland from near the turning for Pointe Sable – anyone will be able to direct you to the *cascade*. It's possible to swim in the pool beneath the 10m-high falls. With a vehicle, an ideal day trip is to Port-à-Piment, for a visit to the stunning Marie Jeanne Cave (for further details, see *Port-à-Piment*, page 164). A longer drive on a rougher road up into the hills would take you through the tiny hamlet of Douyon. It's a poor and very dry area, but when you approach the village, a gleaming new road appears as if by magic. Douyon was the home village of Jean-Bertrand Aristide. In his honour, the **Peasant's Museum** (Musée Paysan) was built here, a very grand building sitting incongruously in its surroundings. It was closed when I tried visiting, and in fact no-one around was able to tell me if it had ever opened at all. From the outside it looked something of a white elephant. If you carry on driving for another 15 minutes from Douyon, the road runs along a high ridge where, in a couple of places, it's possible to look north and south and see the sea on both sides of the southern peninsula – spectacular.

Port Salut's *fête patronale* is held on 4 August. Bullfights are held on Saturdays throughout the year, in the fields behind the police *commissariat*. It's not a bloody man-versus-bull competition, but a locked-horns pushing contest between bulls. It's a sport peculiar to the town, with plenty of betting on the side among spectators.

GETTING THERE AND AROUND A smooth highway runs to Port Salut from Les Cayes, at first following the green rice fields of the plain and then at L'Acul looping up and over the hills to cut across the headland to Port Salut. In a car, the trip

ABRAHAM LINCOLN AND THE ÎLE-À-VACHE 'COLONY'

In 1863, shortly after the USA had finally recognised Haitian independence, President Abraham Lincoln received an intriguing proposal from a New York businessman. The Haitian government had offered the then uninhabited Île-à-Vache for settlement by ex-slaves fleeing the US's southern states – this at the height of the American Civil War.

Haiti had long been a magnet for African-Americans freeing slavery, and an intrigued Lincoln signed off on the idea. A ship carrying over 450 ex-slaves was soon setting sail for Haiti. The expedition was headed by an entrepreneur, Bernard Kock, who would soon prove more interested in the American government's resettlement subsidy than assisting his charges towards a better life.

Kock's honorific was the 'King of Cow Island', and his first action was to get the colonists to sign a contract recognising him as the sole power on Île-à-Vache. The freed slaves were to be his indentured servants instead. The houses that were promised to be waiting for the colonists never materialised, there was a dearth of drinking water, and even a smallpox outbreak. The colonists arrived too late in the year to plant crops, and instead were made to labour for Kock and buy their provisions from him (Kock having taken the opportunity to print his own currency at a personally enriching exchange rate).

His 'subjects' eventually rebelled. Kock sought soldiers from the governor at Les Cayes, who arrested a few of the colonists, only to later release them without charge. Undaunted, Kock even threatened to arrest the American consul who sought to investigate rumours of mistreatment, claiming the diplomat had no jurisdiction over his newly naturalised Haitians. Eventually the US government sent a formal investigator, who found the remaining colonists in a desperate condition, with nearly 100 having died of disease and privation. After a flurry of outraged diplomatic communiqués, the US navy sent a ship to repatriate the colonists to the States, less than a year after the colony's supposed bright start.

By this time, Kock (with the money) had long fled the scene, fearful of the colonists' threats of violence against him. But his name lives on through the geography of Île-à-Vache, at Cay Coq, and the main village of Madam Bernard.

takes about 30 minutes. There are *taptaps* throughout the day (back to Les Cayes, they leave from near the police *commissariat*, and cost about 50HTG. Alternatively, there are plenty of moto-drivers who'll also make the ride. They're also the best option if you're without transport and want to go to Port-à-Piment.

WHERE TO STAY Hotels are listed in order from arrival into Port Salut from Les Cayes. Unless noted, all are either on the main road through the town or on Pointe Sable. Note that whenever there's a public holiday or long weekend, accommodation in Port Salut can book up some time in advance.

Au Beau Lambi Hotel Port Salut; 3860 4278/4280; e aubeaulambiportsalut@yahoo.fr. Pretty blue gingerbread-style house. Some way from Pointe Sable, but a good option at the cheaper end of the budget scale. **$$**

Relais du Boucanier Port Salut; 3558 1806/3702 1066; e lerelaisboucanier@hotmail.com; www.lebouknier.com. Unmissable bright lobster-pink hotel. Charming rooms look over the sea, & the restaurant opens practically onto the surf. Good service. No beach, but a pool (& a pool table). Wi-Fi. **$$**

Naz Inn Hotel Port Salut; 3797 6737; e infonazinn@yahoo.fr. Bling is the key word here, from the metal giraffes guarding the pool to the giant gold fountain of Dessalines. Curiously, rooms are a picture of spartan white – pleasant but confusing. A walkway over the road leads to a private 'beach' above the sea. Wi-Fi. **$$**

Hotel du Village Pointe Sable; 3713 9035; e portsaluthotelduvillage@yahoo.fr. Literally on the beach, at the start of Pointe Sable. Small but attractive chalets, a good thatched bar on the sand – a lazy holiday vibe. **$$**

Auberge du Rayon Vert Pointe Sable; 3713 9035/3779 1728; e aubergedurayonvert@yahoo.fr; www.aubergedurayonvert.com. On the other side of the road to the beach, a small guesthouse with a handful of large rooms in a rugged stone-clad building with crazy wooden furniture. French-run, with an excellent restaurant. **$$$**

Coconut Breeze Hotel Pointe Sable; 3727 4885/3692 4946. Small, chilled-out hotel opposite the beach bar-restos. The rooms are fine but nothing special, but you're more likely to be chilling at the bar or on the sand out front. **$$**

Dan's Creek Hotel Route National 2; 3614 8143/3664 0404; e danscreekhotel@gmail.com; www.danscreekhotel.com. Lovely green-&-white gingerbread-style hotel just outside Port Salut, built around a tiny cove with its own private beach. Great rooms in different shapes & styles, a restaurant, & top service. Satellite TV & Wi-Fi. **$$$**

WHERE TO EAT Hotels all have their own restaurants, which are open to non-guests. Of these, the **Auberge du Rayon Vert** (**$$$$**) probably offers the finest dining in Port Salut, while the **Hotel du Village** does a particularly good line in rum sours, to be enjoyed at sunset while waggling your toes in the sand. **Dan's Creek Hotel** has a good evening buffet at weekends (**$$$$**), and à la carte during the week. If you just want to fill up with a few supplies, there's a small supermarket next door to Naz Inn, and another at the petrol station just outside Port Salut on the way to Port-à-Piment.

Les Trois Tables Route de Port-à-Piment; 3652 2115; open daily, but call ahead for a table. Named for its small size, a gourmet restaurant a short drive outside Port Salut. Everything is deliberately low-key, allowing all the focus to go on the food, a careful mix of French & Caribbean, strong on seafood. Intimate, excellent. **$$$$**

Beach bar-restos Pointe Sable; 10.00–late daily. Near the end of the slip-road running the length of Pointe Sable, there's a cluster of bar-restos on the beach, painted in bright colours. They're all eager to serve you freshly caught & grilled seafood, & a few cold beers to wash it down with. Good fun. **$$$**

PORT-À-PIMENT

The good tarmac road that runs all the way from Port-au-Prince through the south ends abruptly at the small town of Port-à-Piment. Founded around 1700, locals say the town has a fiery rather than peppery origin for its name, with passing French mariners apparently noting the many red-flowered flamboyant trees that were common in the area. Port-à-Piment was a coffee port and its merchants built some fine houses here, although many are now in a sorry state of repair. The town has always had close trade connections with nearby Jamaica, exporting coffee and importing labour; boats passing between the two nowadays are likely to be carrying rather more illicit cargoes.

Port-à-Piment is home to one of Haiti's greatest natural wonders, the Marie Jeanne Cave – more than worth the short trip from Port Salut.

GETTING THERE AND AWAY There are no accommodation options in Port-à-Piment, but the town is only about 40 minutes by road from Port Salut. There are a few *taptaps* running between the two, but the quickest option is by moto-taxi. Most maps suggest that it's possible to continue west from Port-à-Piment all the way to Anse d'Hainault, and from there to continue to Jérémie. In practice, the unmade road continues along the coast through Tiburon in a reasonable condition. At Les Irois (apparently named for Catholic Irish who fled here in the 17th century to escape Oliver Cromwell's military campaigns), it cuts inland through the mountains and deteriorates significantly in quality. The most experienced 4x4 drivers would find this challenging and dangerous in the dry season; in the rainy season it is completely impassable.

WHERE TO STAY AND EAT The only accommodation near the cave is at Coteaux:

Hotel Somando 149 Bd St Pierre, Coteaux; 3667 0985/3617 4689; e hotelsomando@gmail.com. An imposing building with an abundance of capacity for such modest surroundings. Generously sized & whitewashed clean rooms with AC & breakfast. Dinner on request in restaurant. **$$**

THE MARIE JEANNE CAVE The Marie Jeanne Cave (Grotte Marie Jeanne) is the largest cave system in Haiti, and one of the largest in the entire Caribbean. Located on a hill 20 minutes' walk above Port-à-Piment, its galleries extend 4km below the surface.

The cave entrance is kept locked. To arrange a visit, call local guide Jean-Baptiste Eliovil (*3638 2292/3782 3275*), who helped map the cave with a speleological survey team from West Kentucky University. He can provide hard hats, but you should bring your own torches.

At the gate, there's an impressive information board with a map and caving safety information in multiple languages. Metal steps lead down into the cave. The entrance was revealed by the collapse of the ceiling of a central gallery, now long overgrown with trees. Three cave galleries lead off this bowl. The first you're taken to is the most open of the three. The floor is covered in bat guano, while roots extend into the mouth – all rich environments for cave fauna. Most notable are the impressively large Amblypigids (whip spiders, or whip scorpions), with wiry legs that extend up to 40cm from their bodies. Their mandibles look scary, but arachnophobes should take heart that they are in fact quite harmless.

The most impressive of the three galleries is full of beautiful formations, each with their own names. The pachyderm-like 'Elephant' has a beautiful quartz glint, while the twin stalagmites of the 'Two Candles' tower over you at 3m high. Near the top of the gallery is a narrow chamber with overhead 'cathedral bells' and the 'robes of Marie-Jeanne', hanging down in smooth stony folds.

The final gallery is the deepest, and has its own metal staircase descending into the mouth. Near the entrance there's a small reflecting pool contained by a travertine dam. Casual visitors will probably be happy with this but for avid spelunkers there's the potential to explore much further – the passages from here lead deep into the hill.

500 STEPS If your interests lie more in viewing the world from the top of a hill rather than from within, Coteaux has its own attraction with its 500 Steps (Cinq Cent Marches). In 2000, a vision of the Virgin Mary inspired a local priest to build a shrine on the hill overlooking Coteaux. Its name indicates how many steps you need to climb to reach the shrine (if you want to count them out, every tenth step is painted blue). Signs along the way offer Biblical encouragement and admonishment. The walk is best early in the morning.

CAMP PERRIN

On the road north from Les Cayes en route to Jérémie is the pretty town of Camp Perrin. It sits where the road starts to climb up into the Massif de la Hotte, giving it a slightly cooler air than the plain below. The town is divided into a lower and upper part – Quartier Merson at the bottom of the hill and Camp Perrin proper uphill with its attractive streets and paved main road. There are a number of natural attractions in the area, not least the **Saut Mathurine** waterfalls, which are arguably the most spectacular in the country.

Camp Perrin was founded under the French, who built an extensive irrigation system in the area. The **Canal d'Avezac** is still in operation, and can be traced in the lower part of Camp Perrin, a pleasant way to explore behind the town. Such irrigation canals have become an important feature of farming in the area, and are found throughout the *département*. During the Haitian Revolution and throughout the 19th century, Camp Perrin was an important source of *piquets* (peasant armies), raised during periodic disturbances to support one leader or their opponent.

On the opposite side of the river to Quartier Merson is the **Grotte Kounoubwa**, a large cave with several chambers with high vaulted ceilings dripping with stalactites. It has been used as a Vodou site, and long before that, by the Taíno, who left behind symbolic petroglyphs etched into the walls. A guide is required – call Fresnel or Joel Constant (*3669 5458/3810 5075*) to arrange a visit.

Camp Perrin has an important *fête patronale* every 26 July, dedicated to St Anne, which kicks off the summer season of local fêtes patronales.

GETTING THERE AND AROUND *Taptaps* to Les Cayes leave from the lower part of town, near where the road switches uphill. There are no scheduled departures to Jérémie – buses en route from Port-au-Prince tend to pass through around the middle of the day. At the time of research, Route National 7 to Jérémie was still under improvement, and it wasn't clear whether the entire route would be paved. There are plentiful moto-taxis around town.

WHERE TO STAY AND EAT

Auberge du Canal Quartier Merson; 3739 2800. Tucked off the main road next to the canal. Several red & white buildings, with fair rooms & a restaurant. Unusual in having its own football pitch. **$$**

Kamp Inn Bar & Grill Upper Camp Perrin; 2775 6770. Good modern restaurant. Well signed on the main road. **$$**

Le Recul Hotel Route de Merson; 3454 0027/3727 3589; e valnuma@yahoo.fr; www.lereculhotel.ht. A tangerine- & purple-fronted hotel with a hint of gingerbread style & the best accommodation option. Good rooms, restaurant & pool. Arriving from Les Cayes, turn left at the Recul junction opposite the Latino Bar-Resto. **$$**

SAUT MATHURINE WATERFALL Haiti is blessed with abundant waterfalls, but of all of them Saut Mathurine is probably the most spectacular. Water cascades over a wide limestone dome from a height of 30m, set into an even higher lush green mountain face. At the base of the falls there's an Olympic swimming pool-sized basin of a rich turquoise colour. Take your swimsuit, as it's almost impossible not to want to dive into such a gorgeous swimming hole.

Saut Mathurine is about 11km northeast of Camp Perrin – there's a large turning on the right as you head past the northern outskirts of town. The road is a trifle rough, and there are a couple of minor turns as you twist up the mountains, but any local passing will automatically know where you're heading. The entrance to the falls is gated, and the guardian will want around 100HTG per vehicle to unlock it. Be careful if it's been raining recently – the parking area is quite steep, and the grass and mud can be quite slick under the wheels. Local kids will invariably turn up to impress you by climbing to the top of the falls to dive into the pool below (and then expect a gratuity for the show).

One word of warning – on one visit I made during the dry season, the local river had been temporarily diverted for hydro-electric power, turning off the falls completely. It was quite a surreal sight, with the pool minus the main attraction. Apparently this is a rare occurrence, but if you're visiting between November and March it might not be a bad idea to check in advance if the falls are indeed falling.

MACAYA NATIONAL PARK

Sat astride the Massif de la Hotte mountain range in Grand Anse, the Parc National Macaya is the remotest corner of the country. Barely touched by roads, it is rarely visited by outsiders, and even then mostly field biologists. They're drawn by the amazing biodiversity of the area. It's Haiti's only remaining cloudforest and is rich in animal and plant life. Over 114 species of orchids have been inventoried in the park, which also abounds in endemic bird and amphibian species. The park receives nearly 4m of rain per year, making it the key watershed for the intensive agriculture on the southern plains below its slopes. Unfortunately, like almost everywhere else in Haiti, the park is prone to charcoal burning, and it's feared that the newly resurfaced highway to Jérémie will prompt increased incursions into the park.

Anyone planning a trip must be completely self-sufficient. A 4x4 will only get you so far, from Camp Perrin east to Formonde on the park boundary. It may just be possible from here to reach the **Citadelle des Platons**, a revolutionary-era fort. It was from here that the independent black slave leader Goman harried the French, and after independence, the forces of Pétion. From here, the most adventurous might attempt to hike to the summit of Pic Macaya, Haiti's second-highest mountain (2,347m). Anticipate a three-day hike, with frequent cutting of your own paths. Bring food, camping gear for the wet and cold, and a Shackleton-like sense of perseverance.

JEREMIE

Jérémie is one of those places in Haiti that feels like a long way from anywhere. Relatively few people seem to make it here, which is a shame, because it's a charming and relaxed little city, smack in the middle of the greenest and most lush corner of the country.

Self-styled as the 'City of Poets', Jérémie's recent isolation has been in great part due to the terrible transport links, but the new road to Port-au-Prince is slowly improving things. As well as the city to explore, Jérémie is the base for wider discovery of the Grand Anse, with towns such as Dame Marie and Abricots to visit, and beautiful beaches to have pretty much to yourself. The region is heavily agricultural, and the fertile mountains produce avocadoes, coffee, cacao and a dozen other crops. Jérémie is also famous for *komparet*, a deliciously heavy cake-bread, sweetened with coconut, ginger and many other good things.

Jérémie sits next to the Grand Anse River – the views in the morning are particularly lovely when the mist seems to smoke off the valley. Fishermen stand waist-high with throw nets to catch fish, particularly the tiny anchovy-like *piskit*,

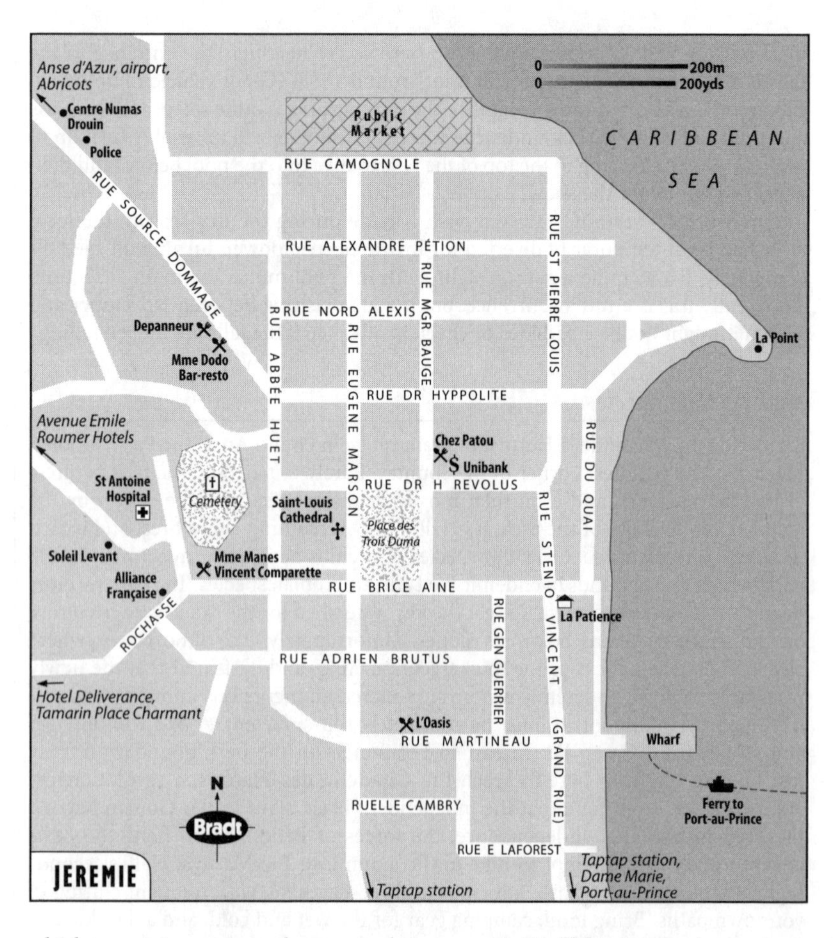

which swarm in great numbers several times a year. You'll frequently also see long bamboo rafts called *pipirit* (after the trilling song of the tropical kingbird), which villagers upstream build in a day to bring their produce to market.

HISTORY The first French settlers came to this stretch of Grand Anse in the late 17th century, an unlikely mix of buccaneers and Carmelite monks. Jérémie was formally settled in 1720, with the foundation of its first church. The centre of the town still follows the old colonial layout. The land was too hilly for sugar production, so the population – a roughly equal mix of French and free blacks – traded in cocoa, coffee and hardwood, all products that remain important today.

Slaves outnumbered their masters roughly eight to one, so it's unsurprising that the bourgeoisie didn't take well to the abolition of slavery during the revolution. Seeing no place for themselves in a free French republic, they threw their lot in with the English, who landed a force here in 1793. The occupation lasted four years, before the English surrendered to Toussaint Louverture and slunk out of the south. On independence in 1804, the town was the first to feel Dessalines's wrath against the whites, and over 1,500 French were massacred here.

The mulatto class prospered in the 19th century through coffee exports, despite being occasional targets for local resentments – in 1847 the newly crowned emperor Soulouque led a peasant army here, over fears of mulatto dominance of Haitian politics. But Jérémie boomed. The second half of the century was a golden era. Direct trade to Europe led to a building boom, and many European and Latin American countries maintained consulates at the port. Rich Jérémiennes looked to Paris, rather than Port-au-Prince for their cultural links. The city eventually became known as the 'City of Poets', the hometown of celebrated writers like Etzer Vilaire and Eric Roumer, as well as the birthplace of Thomas-Alexandre Dumas, the father of *Three Musketeers* author Alexandre Dumas.

Centralisation was the curse of Jérémie. Beginning during the US occupation, more and more trade was diverted from the town to Port-au-Prince. Hurricane Hazel devastated Jérémie in 1954 and, ten years later, François Duvalier dealt the town a double blow. The bloody events of the 'Jérémie Vespers' (see box, *Jeune Haïti and the Jérémie Vespers*, page 171) marked the end of Jérémie's mulatto middle and upper class, and punitive closure of the port to international trade brought economic stagnation and isolation. Even today, Jérémie feels some way from the mainstream of Haitian life.

GETTING THERE AND AROUND

By air There's a daily flight with **Tortug'Air** (*Rue Dr Hyppolite; 3610 0520*) between Jérémie and Port-au-Prince. The tiny airport is 15 minutes west of town, past Rue Source Dommage. If you don't arrange a pickup, you'll be reliant on flagging down a passing moto-taxi en route to town.

By road Road transport leaves from Carrefour du Bac, near the river. A couple of daily big buses do the run to Port-au-Prince (and points en route), leaving in the early morning and taking around nine hours. Note that the full 500HTG fare applies even if you want to get off halfway at, say, Les Cayes.

The road out of Jérémie is currently being upgraded, and may shave another hour off the time when finished (the trip to Port-au-Prince used to take 14 hours). The stretch between Beaumont and Camp Perrin was still particularly rough at the time of research. While improving Jérémie's connections is undoubtedly a good thing, many fear that increased charcoal truck access will further drive deforestation into the last truly green corner of the country.

There are daily *taptaps* to Dame Marie and Abricots, and most days on the appalling road to Pestel – if you're driving, turn off the main road at Carrefour Zaboka, just before Beaumont. Moto-taxis to Dame Marie and Abricots are bumpy affairs, but the fastest option, getting you to both destinations in a couple of hours.

Getting around Jérémie is quickest by moto-taxi. You'll rarely pay more than 30HTG for a fare.

By boat A shallow-draft ferry sails to Port-au-Prince every Tuesday, returning on Saturday and costing the same as the bus. The 12-hour voyage is overnight each way, although several locals advised against taking it – more for safety than time issues.

WHERE TO STAY

Budget

Auberge Inn 6 Av Emile Roumer; 3727 9678/3465 2207; e aubergeinn@netscape.net. A charming guesthouse with a clutch of sweet rooms (soon all to be en suite), decorated with local handicrafts from Abricots – examples of which are for sale in the small shop. Meals are available on request & are well worth ordering. Wi-Fi. **$$**

Hotel La Cabane Av Emile Roumer; 2284 5128. Efficiently run hotel, with a mix of fan or ACcooled rooms, packed with over-sized furniture & held together throughout by an over-enthusiasm for candy-pink paint. Wi-Fi. **$$**

Hotel Le Bon Temps 8 Av Emile Roumer; 2943 5030; e hotelbontemps@yahoo.fr. Next door to the Auberge Inn, a reasonable value if unexciting hotel option, with rooms varying from the cramped to the airy. Wi-Fi. **$$**

Tamarin Place Charmant 2 Calasse; 3722 5222; e tamarin_jeremie@hotmail.com. Rambling & homely place with great views over Jérémie's coastline, run by an American health worker who came to Haiti in the mid 80s & never left. Rooms vary from hotel-style to bungalow, & generous servings are included in the half-board rate. Popular with NGO workers (there are usually a few long-term rentals). Wi-Fi. **$$**

Shoestring

Hotel Deliverance Caracolie; 2284 5517. A simple but friendly place, slightly away from the bustle. Beds & bathrooms aren't fancy but are clean & perfectly decent. Meals available on request. **$**

La Patience Hotel Corner rues Stenio Vincent & Brice Ainé; 2284 6290. As basic a downtown cheapie as you can find in Jérémie, where you get what you pay for (or rather, feel its absence). Just about tolerable. **$**

Hotel Trois Dumas Av Emile Roumer. Every time I've gone past this hotel in the past 4 years it's been 'under restoration' – it's listed here in the hope that one day it might even reopen. From the outside at least, cut from the same cloth as Hotel La Cabane.

WHERE TO EAT

L'Oasis Rue Martineay; 11.00–23.00. Popular restaurant with a good atmosphere in the evenings & a slight *cabaña* feeling, as much a bar & dancing spot as a restaurant. Food is standard Creole fare. **$$$**

Chez Patou Rue Monseigneur Boge; 08.00–15.00 & 18.00–21.00. Near the main square, with bright red doors. Good for snack meals – sandwiches, burgers, pasta & unexpectedly good ice cream. **$$**

Choucoune Corner Av Emile Roumer & Rochasse (inside Alliance Française); Mon–Sat. Simple café set-up run by Alliance Française, with sandwiches, rice & beans, pasta & the like. Pleasant atmosphere, & often interesting conversation with local students. **$$**

Depanneur Rue Source Dommage; 11.00–23.00. Above the supermarket of the same name. A slight cut above the usual bar-resto in terms of décor, with decent if unsurprising Haitian fare. The *plat du jour* is usually a reliable option. **$$**

Mme Dodo Bar-Resto Rue Source Dommage. A bright red-&-yellow bar-resto, a couple of doors down from Depanneur. Good food, the sort of place where you ask what they're serving rather than say what you actually want. **$$**

Mme Manes Vincent Comparette Av Brice Ainé; Mon–Sat. A small green-&-red bakery on the road uphill from the centre of Jérémie, & a great place to get your fix of *komparet*, fresh from the oven & individually wrapped to take away. **$**

OTHER PRACTICALITIES The **Alliance Française** (*corner of Av Emile Roumer & Rochasse; 2284 6573; e alliancefrjeremie@hotmail.com; Mon–Sat*) has regular courses, cultural events as well as a cybercafé. Other cultural events are sometimes also held at the **Centre Numas Drouin** (*Rue Source Dommage*), which has an interesting library.

The **Unibank** (*corner of Pl Dumas*) will change money, although queues can be beaten by going to the **Soleil Levant shop** (*Av Emile Roumer*) or **Deppaneur** (*Rue Source Dommage*), Jérémie's best supermarket. The Minustah base is near the airport.

WHAT TO SEE AND DO The centre of Jérémie is **Place des Trois Duma**, bordered on its western side by the terracotta-red **Saint-Louis Cathedral**, built in 1877. There's a bust of Thomas-Alexandre Dumas, as well as a plinth and the broken remains of a giant statue of the local revolutionary slave leader Goman, who made Grand Anse his fiefdom and fought Pétion to a standstill. At the time of

JEUNE HAÏTI AND THE JEREMIE VESPERS

François Duvalier faced several attempts to overthrow him throughout his rule, but none was as dramatic or as bloodily suppressed as the campaign by the group *Jeune Haïti* around Jérémie in 1964. Jeune Haïti were a group of 13 mostly mulatto Haitian exiles from Jérémie based in the USA, and possibly given military training from the CIA. In August 1964 they landed at Dame Marie and attempted to start a guerrilla uprising against the regime, through direct military action and winning over the support of the local populace.

The group's campaign lasted nearly three months. Against the backdrop of hurricane season they trekked through the rugged Grand Anse country, fighting ten serious engagements with the Haitian army. It was such a tough fight that Duvalier tried to block off the entire southern peninsula at Miragoâne and raise local militias. The result was inevitable. When three of the group were cornered, they were beheaded with the resulting photos printed on the front page of the newspapers.

The reprisals were even bloodier. The *noiriste* dictator had long mistrusted Haiti's pale-skinned elite, and so Jérémie's mulatto population was to be subjected to a terrible communal punishment. The Tonton Macoute militias were unleashed on the city, and whole families were rounded up and their houses looted. Then they were killed, irrespective of age or connection to the rebels, from two-year-old children to a handicapped grandmother. Somewhere between 100 and 300 people were killed in the reprisals. Collectively the massacres are known as the Jérémie Vespers, for the 'vesper' country picnics that Jérémie's elite would take at weekends.

Jeune Haïti's campaign came to an end on 12 November. The last two of the group to be captured, Marcel Numa and Louis Drouin, were executed by firing squad in Port-au-Prince's national cemetery. A public holiday was declared, shops were closed and schoolchildren bussed in to watch. The event was broadcast on television for a week as Duvalier's warning: 'Here is the fate awaiting you and your kind.'

The executed two are currently remembered through Jérémie's Numa Drouin library and cultural centre.

writing a huge brand-new Catholic cathedral was under construction on a rise near the city cemetery.

East of the square, Rue Stenio Vincent runs the length of the harbour. The beachfront itself is a grubby nothing, mainly populated by scavenging pigs. In the water, several wrecks testify to the difficult approach to the harbour. Instead, walk up to **La Pointe**, a breezy finger of land offering the best views back to Haiti. The main market area is north of Rue Nord Alexis.

The ruins of **Fort Télémaque** (sometimes called Fort Marfranc), built soon after independence are on heights of the Sainte Hélène district in the southeast of town.

Jérémie has some fine architecture, although much in disrepair. Rue Stenio Vincent is packed with late-19th-century coffee warehouses, with high-shuttered hurricane doors and arched verandas. The old customs house adds a long overhanging balcony. Also speaking to Jérémie's former glory are the Hôtel de Ville on Rue Destinville-Martineau and the even-grander L'Ecole de Frères de l'Instruction Chrétienne, on the corners of rues Moussignac Warrior and Adrien Brutus. Most notable are the many wood-framed houses with extending dormer windows, their upper floors resting on some precarious wooden columns.

Little more than a ten-minute drive out of Jérémie on the airport road is **Anse d'Azur**, for my money one of the best beaches in Haiti. The turning is unsigned – if you pass Becs' Bakery & Patisserie (selling *paté*, *plat du jour* with lots of fish, and pizza by the slice at weekends), you've just overshot it. Park your vehicle and walk down the narrow path past the ruins of an old fort, and the cove is revealed to you – bound by cliffs on one side, and curving around with sugary sand. Jacmel wishes it had a beach so pretty, but bizarrely the beach is often empty – make the most of it! If you have a snorkel and fins, there's the added attraction of a German U-boat sunk in the bay, and an easy swim out. Local stories differ as to how the ship came to be here. The most colourful version has the submarine running aground during World War II and the crew living in Jérémie relatively freely under the watchful eyes of the authorities, before returning to Germany at the end of the war.

ABRICOTS

Two roads head west from Jérémie: the one to Abricots leaves town past Anse d'Azur and the airport, and sticks closely to the coast. It's a rough and muddy affair during the rainy season.

The first place you reach after passing the airport is the tiny but sweet town of **Bonbon**. It has an attractive pebble beach, with skiffs and rowing boats hauled up after landing the catch of the day, and views back into the town. To get to the beach, turn right where the road fords the river – a busy spot with market stalls and women washing clothes.

The road continues to **Anse du Clerc**. Bound by steep hills (there are dramatic views as you both approach and leave the town), it's another small town on a very pretty bay. The road into town is in a poor state. On the pebble beach you can often see traditional wooden boats being made. If you ford a small inlet on the beach, you'll find the **Anse du Clerc Beach Hotel** (☎ *3647 5662*), a place groaning under its own potential: charming thatched cottages set in lawns under shady palms. It was technically closed when I visited, but they were happy to take guests in for US$50 a head: you'll need them to arrange all meals and attend to a thorough clean beforehand, though.

Abricots sits at the end of a bumpy road, although the town itself is paved and feels relatively prosperous given its isolation. The big draw is the long stretch of palm-fringed sandy beach that shelves very gently so you can walk far into the sea. It's a lovely, laid-back place. The local NGO **Fondation Paradis des Indiens** (FPDI; e *mdeverteuil@fondationpdi.org*) has an extensive education and alternative income here. An example of long-term community development, it was established by a French woman, Michaëlle de Verteuil ('Madam Mika') who came to Abricots in 1975 and has remained ever since. FPDI also employs many women making the fine embroidery for which Abricots is renowned – which can be purchased in the town (advance appointments preferred).

There's one place to stay, the **Paradis des Indiens** (☎ *3783 5349*; **$$**). Next to Abricots cemetery and operated by the owner of the Auberge Inn in Jérémie, it's a tiny two-room guesthouse (shared bathroom) facing the sea. It's simple but very cute, with meals on request. Next door is **Mi Jean Restaurant** (**$$**), Abricot's only bar-resto, with shady tables freshened by a sea breeze. It has great local seafood, but you must order as far in advance as possible – walk-in customers can expect at least an hour's wait.

Near where the road approaches Abricots, there is a rough road – more a track really, and impassable by vehicle – that allows you to hike over the mountain to Dame Marie.

DAME MARIE AND ANSE D'HAINAULT

The road to Dame Marie cuts inland from Jérémie at Carrefour de Bac, and follows the broad sweep of the Grand Anse River. It's a rough piste, which steadily decreases in quality the further you get from Jérémie. The river is shallow, but its wide gravel shores suggest a livelier prospect when in its rainy season spate. It's a constantly busy place, with laundry women, people washing or tending their mules and donkeys. On market days, *pipirit* bamboo rafts are a common sight, as villagers float their goods downstream for sale.

The road first passes through **Marfranc**, a long lick of a town 20 minutes from Jérémie, with a large municipal marketplace (market day on Wednesday), then **Moron**, the biggest town en route to Dame Marie. Moron has paved roads and a grand church painted bright blue, as well as the first signs in the markets that the road is entering cacao-producing country.

From here, the road leaves the river and climbs into the mountains to be had here. It's worth noting that although the region is still heavily forested, it's also in part a manmade landscape – look for the tall breadfruit and mango trees, and by the side of the road, coffee bushes and manioc.

Your arrival into **Dame Marie** is marked by a roadside statue of the Virgin Mary. It's a reasonable-sized place, with wholesale merchants' stores buying cacao from local farmers. The beans are frequently raked out to dry in the street – on hot days their concentration gives a faintly sweet, narcotic aroma. Every year, Dame Marie celebrates its Fête du Cacao at the end of the third week of April.

There is a long seafront with a few seats and palms, although not much beach to speak of – mostly grey sand with rubbish, discarded conch shells, and pigs truffling around in the waves. It's more pleasant if you continue to the edge of town, where you can find **Le Bon Coin Hotel** (*Route d'Anse d'Hainault;* ☎ *2772 6826;* **$$**) a simple shore-side hotel surrounded by a pink-and-white picket fence, looking back across the bay to Dame Marie. It has plain en-suite rooms, each with TV and a selection of evangelical and Justin Bieber DVDs. Meals – mostly seafood – must be ordered in advance. There are also a couple of eating places in town: Alice and Bon Bagay bar-restos.

A very rough earth road continues to **Anse d'Hainault**, half an hour's drive from Dame Marie. It's an interesting though very poor fishing town, with a real feeling of having reached the end of the road. The wharf area is usually deep with fishing boats, and when they're not at sea, the fishermen are working in the area, making and repairing their fish traps. These are beautiful lattice affairs made from strips of palm frond and weighted with rocks – each takes a week to make, and lasts for about three months. There's a weekly market every Wednesday; otherwise not much seems to happen here.

Despite what the maps suggest, it's not possible to continue on towards Port-à-Piment (see page 164) from here. The road has been as good as impassable for several years due to road slips and rock falls. In the dry season, it's possible that an experienced 4x4 driver *might* make it, but it's a dangerous route and not recommended.

PESTEL

Pestel is a small port town east of Jérémie with a pretty harbour full of wooden fishing boats under sail. The main business here is fishing and charcoal export to Port-au-Prince. It's also pretty remote, down a rough road from Jérémie (about three hours by 4x4). The town is more or less self-contained and economically depressed, and even the town's one sleeping option, the Hotel Louis & Louise, no longer seems to be in operation. The town is busiest for the Wednesday and Saturday markets at the port, when you can also find most transport to and from Jérémie.

While the town is charming enough, a big draw for those that want to really get off the beaten track is the chance to get out to the **Cayemite Islands** just off the coast. People with boats readily approach you at Pestel harbour offering themselves for hire. There are two islands: Grand Cayemite and Petit Cayemite. The larger has its main village, Anse-à-Macon, on the southern side facing Pestel, but there are tremendous, magical beaches on the northern side, which feel like your own private Caribbean getaway. The Anse-Blanche Beach of Petit-Cayemite is the same – about 30 minutes by motorboat through the bay; a lovely trip.

Every Easter Monday, Pestel has traditionally held its **Fête de la Mer** (Festival of the Sea), with *rara* bands and a regatta of fishing boats of all sizes. Check in advance before planning a trip, as the festival has not taken place in the last couple of years, although plans are apparently afoot to restart it.

Just outside Pestel (a 15-minute drive followed by a half-hour walk) is the **Bellony Cave**. Its large central cavern full of dramatic formations is well worth a visit. The entrance is kept locked, so you need to call the Pestel town hall (☎ *3767 1587*) to get the guide with the key.

The best road between Pestel and Jérémie is via Beaumont, turning off the main road at Carrefour Zaboka. There's a second road via Corail on the coast, but it's not maintained and is absolutely appalling. Enterprising travellers might try to hire a boat from Pestel back to Jérémie.

6

Northern Haiti

History is everywhere in north Haiti. It was where Columbus made his first landfall in the Americas, the powerhouse of the French colonial slave plantations, and then the crucible of the heroic revolution that gave birth to the free black republic. For many visitors, this history is most neatly encapsulated in the form of the Citadelle la Ferrière, the immense fort near Cap-Haïtien that's a rare match for its 'eighth wonder of the world' hype.

Northern Haiti is more than just the Citadelle, however. Cap-Haïtien is a fascinating destination in its own right, as well as being close to some great beaches along the Atlantic coast. It is less densely populated than southern Haiti, but the scope for exploration is enormous, from the colonial and Vodou sites leading from the Plaine du Nord to Fort Liberté and the Dominican Republic border, to the little-visited gem of Môle Saint-Nicholas in the far northeast, a truly underrated corner of the country.

CAP-HAÏTIEN

Cap-Haïtien is Haiti's second city and the crucible for many of the great acts of Haitian history. Under French colonial rule it was the richest and grandest city in the Caribbean, running to fat on its sugar plantations. It has been the centre of revolution, and razed to the ground and renamed several times over. Today, Cap-Haïtien (often simply referred to as Cap or O'Kap) is a much quieter place, and a big step down from the frenetic pace and crush of Port-au-Prince.

Cap-Haïtien is a pretty compact city. The centre follows the gridded street pattern originally laid out by the French, with a long *corniche* stretching along the seafront to the port. At its northern end, the city runs into the hilly district of Carrenage, petering out in a string of old defensive forts that are worth visiting. To the south, a bridge crosses a stream at Pont Neuf and the road leads off towards the Dominican border – as well as to nearby Milot and the Citadelle la Ferrière, north Haiti's biggest tourist draw. In the other direction, a rougher road leads along the dramatic Atlantic coast to the beaches of Cormier and Labadie, both deservedly popular with visitors. The city itself has few 'attractions', although it is a pleasant place to walk around. The old part of Cap-Haïtien has an interesting selection of architecture on show, from mid-19th-century houses to gingerbreads, bookended by a grand cathedral at one end and a busy Iron Market at the other.

One of Cap-Haïtien's biggest annual events is its *fête patronale* in honour of Our Lady of the Assumption. It falls on 15 August, which is also the date when the Haitian Revolution started nearby, following Boukman's great Vodou ceremony of Boïs Caiman. This has led many to believe that the Virgin Mary blessed the revolution herself. In the 19th century, the fête was a big pilgrimage date, and although this is no longer the case, the festival is still celebrated with great gusto.

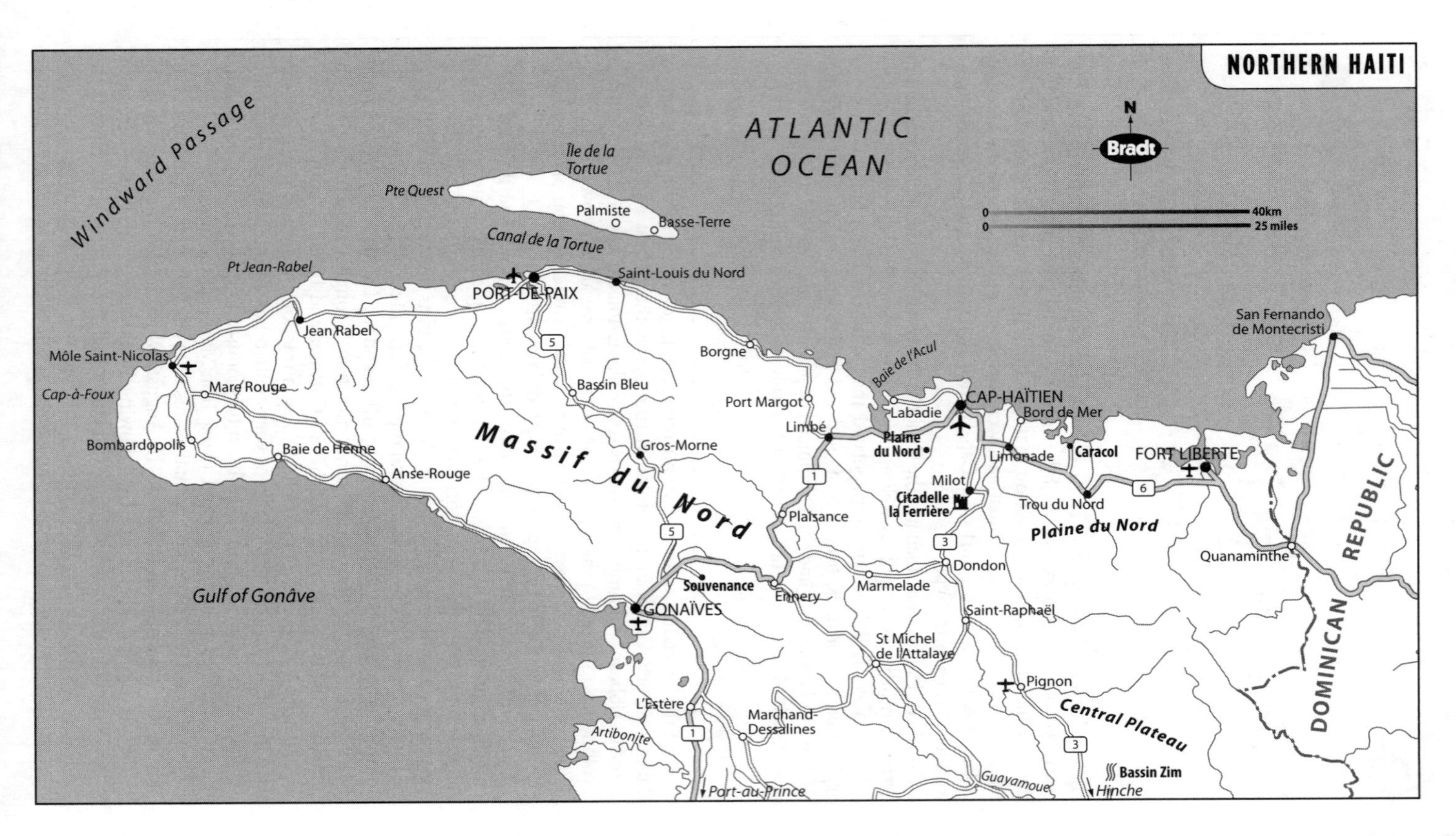
NORTHERN HAITI
N
Bradt
0 40km
0 25 miles
ATLANTIC OCEAN
Windward Passage
Gulf of Gonâve
Île de la Tortue
Pte Ouest
Palmiste
Basse-Terre
Canal de la Tortue
Pt Jean-Rabel
PORT-DE-PAIX
Saint-Louis du Nord
Jean Rabel
Môle Saint-Nicolas
Cap-à-Foux
Mare Rouge
Bombardopolis
Baie de Henne
Anse-Rouge
Bassin Bleu
Gros-Morne
Massif du Nord
Borgne
Port Margot
Limbé
Baie de l'Acul
Labadie
CAP-HAÏTIEN
Bord de Mer
Plaine du Nord
Limonade
Caracol
FORT LIBERTÉ
Milot
Citadelle la Ferrière
Trou du Nord
Plaine du Nord
Plaisance
Dondon
Marmelade
Souvenance
Ennery
GONAÏVES
Saint-Raphaël
St Michel de l'Attalaye
Pignon
Central Plateau
L'Estère
Marchand-Dessalines
Artibonite
Port-au-Prince
Guayamoue
Bassin Zim
Hinche
San Fernando de Montecristi
Quanaminthe
DOMINICAN REPUBLIC
1
3
5
6

HISTORY The founding of Cap-Haïtien in 1670 was a definitive move for French interests in Hispaniola, away from a tradition of semi-licensed piracy against European rivals and towards the development of a fully fledged colony. Its original name was Cap-François, and its location was well chosen by the French governor Bertrand Ogeron: its wide bay could not only host a deepwater port, but a series of reefs on its approach also made it easily defensible against foreign powers. To its rear spread the well-watered expanse of the Plaine du Nord, which the French turned into the plantations that would generate the colony's wealth.

That wealth was well reflected in Le Cap, as it was popularly known (it was subsequently renamed Cap Français during its boom years). Expensive stone buildings and fine gardens were the order of the day for its rich white inhabitants, who enjoyed theatres, debating houses and even a waxwork museum. On the outskirts was Petite Guinée, home to the free blacks and mulattoes, and beyond that the rough slave barracks, whose inhabitants outnumbered their masters ten to one.

Such a disparity was ultimately untenable. After rebellions led by the slave Mackandal in 1758, and the attempted uprising by mulatto leader Vincent Ogé in 1790, Le Cap was a focus for the great revolutionary conflagration that followed. It was besieged, captured and in 1803 completely torched by Henri Christophe, lest it fall back into French hands. In November of that year, Dessalines's free slave army won its final victory on the outskirts of the city at Vertières. On independence the city was given its modern name, Cap-Haïtien, although when the country later split, the city became Cap-Henri, to flatter the vanity of Christophe's short-lived kingdom.

Cap-Haïtien was almost completely destroyed again in the terrible earthquake of 1842. By this time, political and economic power had long been removed to Port-au-Prince, although the port remained an important player in the internecine conflicts of the 19th century. During the US occupation, Cap-Haïtien suffered a further blow when revenues from its port were sent straight to the capital.

Today, the fortunes of Cap-Haïtien seem to be on the up. A joint project with Cuba and Venezuela has built a large gas storage facility by the port and improved the city's power supply; Venezuelan money is also funding large-scale improvements to the airport. The planned Caracol industrial park is close, and the city is banking on economic spin-offs. The centre is being repaved, its roads upgraded, and improved rubbish collection has made the city the cleanest it's been in years.

GETTING THERE AND AWAY

By air Cap-Haïtien airport is on the southern outskirts of the city, on the road to the Dominican border. There are four daily flights to Port-au-Prince with **Tortug'Air** (✆ *2262 2127/3454 8173*) and one flight with **Salsa** (✆ *2813 1223*). **IBC Air** (*www.flyibcair.com*) have direct flights to Miami and Fort Lauderdale, and Marsh Harbour in the Bahamas. **Air Turks and Caicos** (✆ *2942 6711; www.airturksandcaicos.com*) have direct flights to Providenciales. All airline offices are at the airport. There are plans to renovate the terminal and extend the runway to allow more direct international flights from the US to Cap – the project is scheduled to finish in 2013.

By road The main road transport hub is **Barrière Bouteille** (the old city gates). Big buses leave throughout the day to Port-au-Prince, taking seven hours. *Taptaps* and minibuses head for points in between such as Gonaïves (if you're going to Port-de-Paix, it can be quicker to head here and change). Between Cap and Gonaïves, Route National 1 crosses the Chaîne du Bonnet Mountains. The road has great views, although the tarmac is very pot-holed.

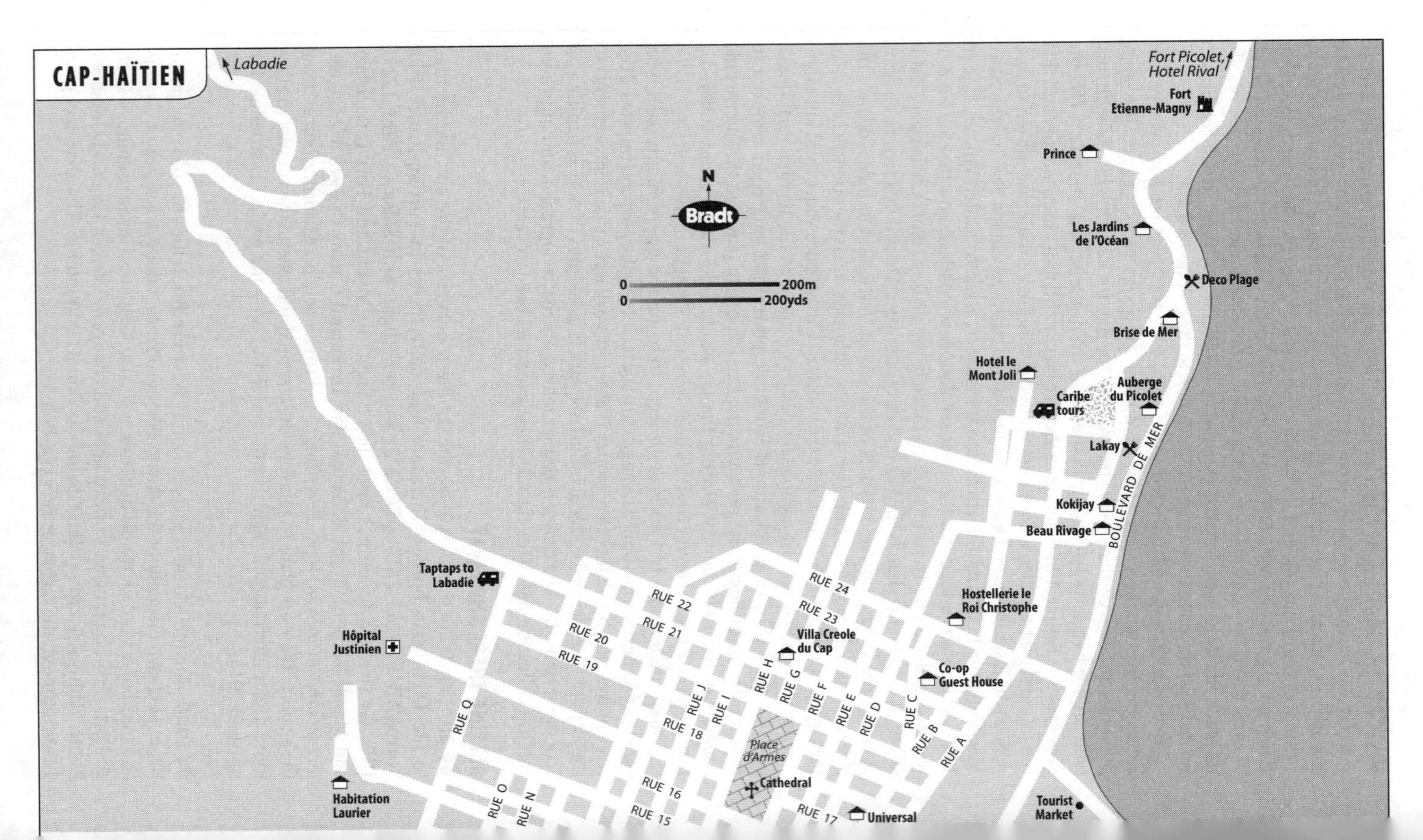
CAP-HAÏTIEN
Labadie
Fort Picolet, Hotel Rival
Fort Etienne-Magny
Prince
Les Jardins de l'Océan
Deco Plage
Brise de Mer
Hotel le Mont Joli
Auberge du Picolet
Caribe tours
Lakay
BOULEVARD DE MER
Kokijay
Beau Rivage
N
Bradt
0 200m
0 200yds
Taptaps to Labadie
Hôpital Justinien
Habitation Laurier
Hostellerie le Roi Christophe
Villa Creole du Cap
Co-op Guest House
Place d'Armes
Cathedral
Universal
Tourist Market
RUE 24
RUE 23
RUE 22
RUE 21
RUE 20
RUE 19
RUE 18
RUE 17
RUE 16
RUE 15
RUE Q
RUE O
RUE N
RUE J
RUE I
RUE H
RUE G
RUE F
RUE E
RUE D
RUE C
RUE B
RUE A

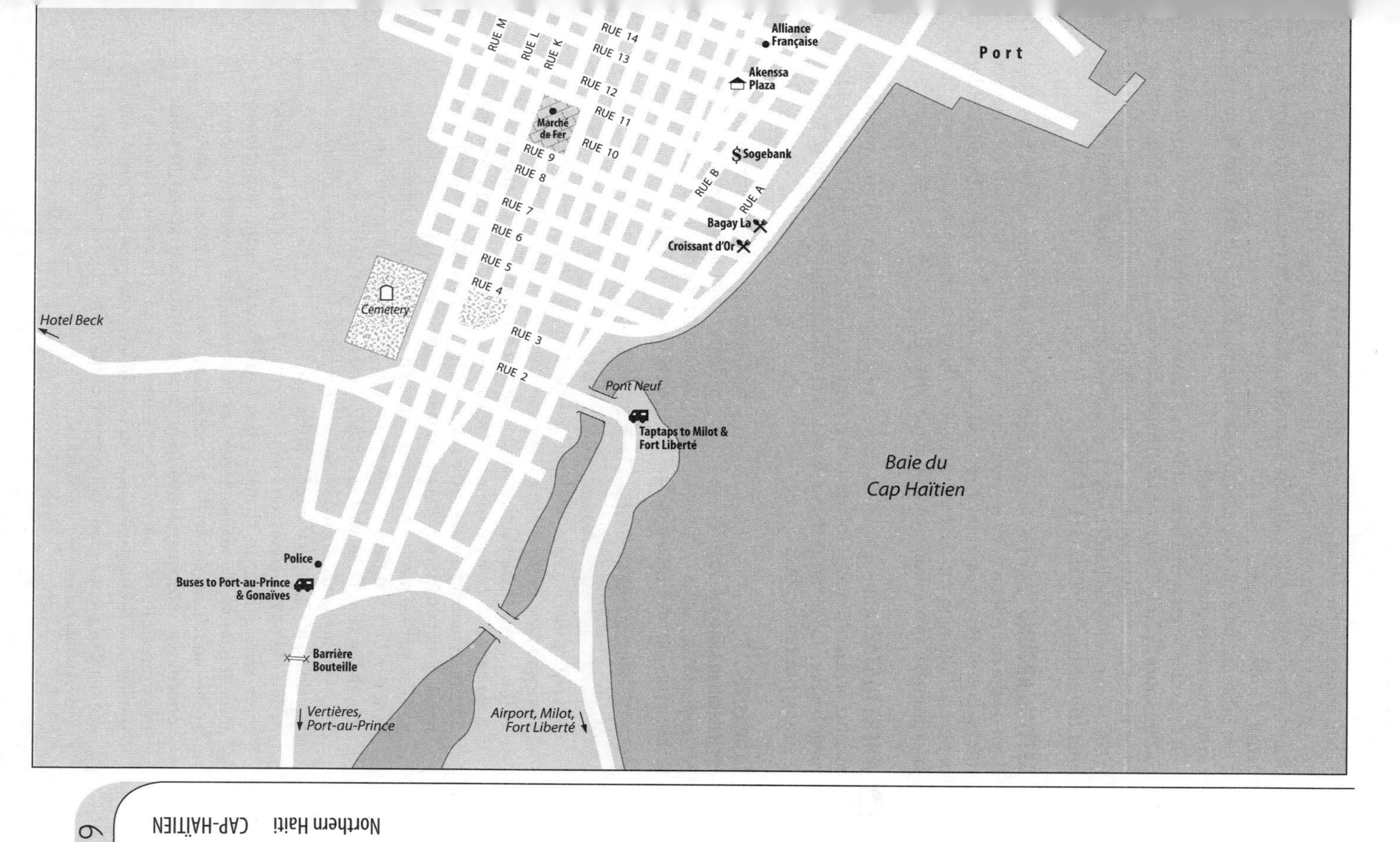
Port
Alliance Française
Akenssa Plaza
Sogebank
RUE A
RUE B
Bagay La
Croissant d'Or
RUE M
RUE L
RUE K
RUE 14
RUE 13
RUE 12
RUE 11
RUE 10
RUE 9
RUE 8
RUE 7
RUE 6
RUE 5
RUE 4
RUE 3
RUE 2
Marché de Fer
Cemetery
Hotel Beck
Pont Neuf
Taptaps to Milot & Fort Liberté
Baie du Cap Haïtien
Police
Buses to Port-au-Prince & Gonaïves
Barrière Bouteille
Vertières, Port-au-Prince
Airport, Milot, Fort Liberté

For points on the good road east, including Milot (45 minutes), Fort Liberté (90 minutes) and Ouanaminthe (2½ hours), taptaps leave from Stasyon Pon, near the town bridge. It's a slightly anarchic mishmash of vehicles parked near a petrol station.

To get to Labadie, pick-up taptaps run when full from Rue 21Q. The 30-minute coastal road is rough, but beautiful.

It's possible to get a coach direct to the Dominican Republic from Cap-Haïtien. **Caribe Tours** (*2260 1258/3614 0264*) have a daily coach service to Santiago, leaving from their bright yellow building on Rue 24B. The six-hour trip costs 1,000HTG (US$25) one-way plus border fees. The coach continues to Santo Domingo, an 11-hour trip costing 1,200HTG (US$30).

GETTING AROUND Cap-Haïtien is a rarity in having *publiques* – public taxis. Spot them by the red ribbon hanging from the rear-view mirror. Although they run set routes, they're always eager for fares, and can be hired for as far as Labadie, Milot or beyond, although you'll have to haggle for the price. Otherwise, most moto-taxi fares around Cap are unlikely to top about 40HTG.

WHERE TO STAY Although on first glance Cap-Haïtien appears to have a reasonable number of places to stay, it suffers from a shortage of hotel rooms in the upper/mid-range bracket. Even during the week, places can fill up quickly, so advance booking is strongly recommended.

Expensive

Habitation Jouissant 202 Habitation Jouissant; 2943 7317; www.habitationjouissant.com. Brand new boutique hotel, raised above Cap-Haïtien in green surroundings with lovely views out to sea. Charming rooms with good service & attention to detail. Pool & Wi-Fi. **$$$$**

THE ABC OF CAP-HAÏTIEN'S STREET NAMES

Just as Cap-Haïtien has undergone several changes of name throughout its history, so have its street names.

The current alpha-numeric naming system dates from the US occupation in the early 20th century. For ease of military reference, the US army renamed the streets running parallel to the seafront A to Q, and numbered them 1 to 24 running south to north. After the Americans left, the names stuck, although you can still see plenty of old street signs on the corners of buildings in the centre of Cap. You have to look for them as they're often painted over, but they're fun to spot, as well as revealing another layer of the city's history. The signs are usually dated – the oldest are from 1849, erected during the rebuilding of Cap after the 1842 earthquake.

The old names correspond to the original French street plan, but even these were subject to change: when Cap Français caught revolutionary fever, it patriotically renamed many of its streets. There were rues Liberté, Egalité and Fraternité, while the waterfront became Quai Sans Culottes – formerly and subsequently Quai Saint-Louis, and today just named the rather more prosaic Rue A. That this street is one block back from the seafront is a testament to land reclamation over the years, extending the port further into the sea. The avenue running the length of the seafront is relatively modern, and is simply called the Boulevard.

Moderate

Auberge du Picolet Bd de Mer; 2262 5595/5566; e aubergedupicolet@yahoo.com. Popular guesthouse, with a hint of colonial architecture about the place. Good-sized rooms, well appointed, & a very good restaurant. Wi-Fi. **$$$**

Habitation Des Lauriers Rue 13Q; 3836 0885; e habitationdeslauriers@yahoo.com. A new guesthouse with a clutch of rooms in a lovely converted late-19th-century house, quite some way uphill from the turning on Rue 13Q. Pretty rooms & strong on attention to detail in service. Good food. Wi-Fi. **$$$**

Hostellerie du Roi Christophe Rue 24B; 2262 0414/3687 8915; e hotroi24b@yahoo.com. Recently extended to add a completely new block, this is Cap's oldest hotel – parts date from the early 18th century. Terrace restaurant & leafy grounds, good-quality rooms. Wi-Fi. **$$$**

Hotel Le Mont Joli Rue 29B; 2943 1110/2942 6975; e hotelmontjoli@gmail.com; www.hotelmontjoli.net. On a hill with views over Cap-Haïtien, this is a hotel also looking back to its part in the 1950s tourism heyday. Large rooms, decent service & a nice restaurant & bar. Hillside terrace with pool. **$$$**

Hotel Rival Rue 90, Carrenage; 2262 6418/6419; e hotelrival@hotmail.com. Follow the path through Carrenage until it hits the beach to find this edge-of-town hotel. Large concrete hotel, well-sized rooms with spacious bathrooms. Poor service, curiously priced; while breakfast is included, a cup of coffee on the side attracts an extra charge. Wi-Fi. **$$$**

Les Jardins de l'Océan 90 Carrenage; 2260 1655/3446 1611; e jardindelocean3@yahoo.fr. Full of great art, a French-run hotel with several levels & annexes, seeming to climb up the hill. Rooms of all shapes & sizes, uniformly good. Decent restaurant plus terrace bar overlooking the sea. Wi-Fi. **$$$**

Budget

Akenssa Plaza Hotel Rue 14B; 2262 4354/1808. Profoundly grim & off-putting entrance, but rooms upstairs are surprisingly decent – well-sized with working features & verging on the comfortable; a few rooms even have fridges. Unexpected. **$$**

Beau Rivage Hotel 25 Bd de Mer; 2816 2123/3682 5583; e beaurivage.hotel@yahoo.fr. Bright & friendly modern hotel with good service. Ideally located on the seafront, though few rooms (some of which can be boxy) have views. Wi-Fi. **$$**

Brise de Mer 4 Carrenage; 2262 0821/3733 1741. A low-lying period house with garden facing the sea (entrance on the street behind). Should be lovely but run slightly into the buffers. Rooms are spartan, though staff are friendly & show willing. (Prices should be negotiable, as it's over-priced & generally empty.) **$$**

Prince Hotel Rue 90, Residence Pauline Bonaparte; 3768 8888/2949 8888; e princehotelj90@gmail.com. Uphill where the rough road through Carrenage begins. An old 19th-century *habitation*, surrounded by greenery. Rooms are fair; those in the new block are much better, despite the decision to have windows facing away from the sea. Restaurant, pool, Wi-Fi. **$$**

Universal Hotel Rue 17B; 3449 8540/3474 8220. Slightly knocked-about hotel with dreary fittings. Average rooms; mirrored bedheads & ceiling suggest a clientele not easily put off by the religious exhortations on the door. A cheapie with a cheeky price tag. **$$**

Villa Creole Du Cap Hotel Rue 21G; 3939 6830/4601 4469; http://villacreoleducap.e-monsite.com. Average city-centre option. Friendly staff, & bright murals on almost every wall, but very cramped rooms. **$$**

Shoestring

Co-op Guest House Rue 22C; 3754 5743; e pcs1@2346.net; http://thecoopguesthouse.yolasite.com. Tiny guesthouse on several levels, with just a few rooms. Caters mainly to foreign volunteers (long-term rates available). 1 room with bathroom; others share facilities. Kitchen available for cooking. **$**

WHERE TO EAT

Mid range

Auberge du Picolet (Les Amandiers) Bd de Mer; 2262 5595/5566; 18.00–22.00 daily. Classy restaurant with terrace garden area, & menu aspiring to fine French-style dining & mostly pulling it off. Relaxed experience, good service. **$$$**

Hostellerie Le Roi Christophe Rue 24B; 2262 0414/3687 8915; 10.00–22.00 daily. Hotel restaurant, with terrace & off-courtyard dining. Good for light lunches, or evenings out with excellent-quality Continental & Creole dishes in charming surroundings. $$$

Les Jardins de l'Océan 90 Carrenage; 2260 1655/3446 1611; 12.00–14.00 & 17.00–22.00 daily. Excellent French-styled food in this French-run hotel, plus a few pizzas & Creole dishes. Worth the price tag. $$$

Cheap and cheerful

Bagay La 10 Bd de Mer; 11.00–midnight daily. Brightly fronted bar-resto, unpretentious inside but with hearty servings of Creole food. $$

Croissant d'Or 8 Bd de Mer; 07.00–17.00 Mon–Sat. Excellent bakery, with savoury & sweet pastries, sandwiches, quiches & pizza slices. Eat in or take-away. $$

Deco Plage Bar-Resto 90 Bd de Mer; 11.00–23.00 daily. Decent seafront bar-resto, where you can chow down on fish, chicken, *griot* & the rest with plates of rice & beans. More of a bar-feeling in the evening, but always good for a drink & sea breeze. $$

Kokiyaj 26 Bd de Mer; 11.00–23.00 daily. Sports-bar-meets-restaurant, sat atop a supermarket of the same name. On the breezy seafront, best for well-turned-out Haitian standards, but with a decent line in American & Continental dishes. Good bar, huge TV screens. $$

Lakay Bd de Mer; 2942 7725; 12.00–03.00 Mon–Sat, 18.00–03.00 Sun. Perennially popular bar & restaurant facing the ocean. Thatched interior & bar, with Creole dishes strong on seafood, but a few salads & American dishes. Swift service & lively atmosphere, frequent live music. $$

OTHER PRACTICALITIES Sogebank (*Rue 11A*) currently has north Haiti's only **ATM**. Unibank (*Rue 11A*) can also change money; there are plenty of street money-changers around rues B and 14–17. **Cybercafés** are everywhere in central Cap. **Alliance Française** (*Rue 15B; 2262 0132; e af.caphaitien@yahoo.fr; www.alliance-cap-haitien.org*) has regular film showings, concerts and courses. There's a Dominican Republic consulate on Rue 24C.

For medical care, go to **Hôpital Justinien** (*Rue 17Q; 2262 0512*).

WHAT TO SEE AND DO

Central Cap-Haïtien

Cap-Haïtien may no longer be the 'Paris of the Antilles', but it's a pleasant and relaxed place to explore on foot, looking for traces of its history.

Start your visit at **Place d'Armes**, the wide square near the northern end of the city grid, between rues 18 and 20. The square was laid out by the French, and has hosted many momentous events in Haitian history. In January 1758, the slave revolutionary Mackandal was burnt at the stake here. The execution took two attempts, as Mackandal managed initially to break free from the flames before being secured for his definitive roasting, an act of defiance still celebrated. The mulatto revolutionaries Ogé and Chavannes were also broken on the wheel here in 1790, their rebellion the opening act for the following year's slave uprising. In 1793, the general proclamation of slave emancipation was announced on the square.

The **Notre Dame Cathedral** was witness to the last of these acts, having been built by the French in 1774. It remains one of the few colonial buildings to survive in Cap-Haïtien. It has a high and calming whitewashed basilica topped with a fine dome, abstract stained glass and a fascinating series of panels of the Stations of the Cross by local artists. Opposite the cathedral is a **statue of Dessalines**. The square is a popular meeting place, particularly for students hanging out from the nearby Roi Christophe University.

Heading south down Cap-Haïtien's grid (as the street numbers decrease), there is quite a mishmash of architectural styles. The predominant forms are the commercial buildings of the late 19th century, which have high arched arcades giving plenty of shade and tall shuttered doors and windows. The first floors were designed to be residential, and typically have wide balconies, often decorated with fancy railings. Dotted among these are the few buildings to have survived the 1842 earthquake – easily picked out by their sharply pitched roofs with stone or terracotta tiles. They're mostly in a sad state of repair, holding on against a tide of new, concrete construction. One of the oldest buildings in Cap-Haïtien is the **Hostellerie du Roi Christophe**, now a hotel. Although much-restored, parts date from 1724 (an apocryphal tale has Henri Christophe working as a waiter here before the revolution). Cap-Haïtien wasn't immune to the fashion for gingerbread houses – look for some good examples behind the cathedral, particularly the Gothic mansion on Rue 16F.

Covering two square blocks between rues 9 and 11 is the **Marché de Fer** (Iron Market), inspired by the more famous Port-au-Prince namesake erected in 1891. As you get closer to the market, the streets get busier and more crowded with street vendors – even the most persistent moto-taxi would have trouble navigating here. Under the market proper, there is meat, vegetables, dry goods and kitchenware for sale, surrounded by no small degree of clamour.

By comparison, the **port** area seems staid and quiet, with the incongruous sight of wooden fishing boats under sail moored close to the bigger cargo ships. Just north of the port on Boulevard de Mer, there's a small **tourist market**, selling paintings, metal art, woodcarvings and the like. It's been a long time since passengers disembarked from a cruise ship to buy from them, so walk-ins will certainly attract the attention of vendors. The whole of the Boulevard seems curiously under-used. There's no beach here, just waves crashing up against the sea wall – the closest you'll get is Plage Rivál, a stony beach north of Carrenage, which you'll pass en route to Fort Picolet (see the following section).

Forts By 1740, Saint-Domingue was already the world's largest single sugar producer, and Cap Français needed to be protected from the jealous eyes of colonial rivals. To this end, the French built a series of forts along the cliffs outside the city, lined up to target any ship trying to delicately navigate the reef-protected entrance to the harbour. The forts can be reached by continuing on the rough road past the Jardins de l'Océan Hotel at the end of Carrenage.

The first fortification is **Fort Etienne-Magny**, also known as **Batterie du Gris-Gris**. It's a five-minute walk from the turning on Carrenage. This was a simple gun emplacement dating from 1758, and several of the original mortars remain. There's little else to see besides, to be honest, apart from some old worked stone walls. Continue walking for another ten minutes and you'll reach **Fort Saint-Joseph**, another walled area hanging on the edge of the cliffs, although only the most ardent military historians are likely to get much out of the site.

Fort Picolet is the real prize, with some great exploring to be had. It covers the most strategic part of the channel through the reefs. The road ends by the Hotel Rival, so head onto the beach (Rivál Plage) and follow the path along the bottom of the cliffs. The fort is clearly visible on the headland. Be careful here – the path can involve a bit of scrambling along the shore, and although locals say that the fort is accessible any time of day, it would still be sensible to be wary of high tides. It's about half an hour's walk from Carrenage.

Built around 1740, the fort has two batteries. Several cannons litter the lower battery, looking out to the reefs and back to Cap. The upper battery has high parapet walls. Stairs lead between the two, while a high-walled walkway protected troops from

THE BATTLE OF VERTIERES

The final and decisive battle of the Haitian Revolution took place at Vertières on the southern outskirts of Cap-Haïtien on 18 November 1803. The French, under General Rochambeau, were in control of the last fort guarding the approach to Cap – the final bastion of French colonial control. He was faced by Dessalines's army of some 16,000, but the elevated setting of the fort gave him a strong defensive position.

In charge of the assault was François Capois, also known as Capoix-la-Mort, who led his Haitian 9th Demibrigade in a bloody full-frontal assault on the French positions. Capois had a near foolhardy sense of bravery – he led his troops from the front, taking a bullet through his hat and, when his horse was shot from under him, he continued on foot, flourishing his sabre to encourage his troops. He cut such an inspiring figure that halfway through the battle the French called a brief ceasefire to allow Rochambeau to send a messenger to pay compliments to the Haitian officer who had covered himself with such glory. The tribute paid, the fighting then recommenced. After a day's combat, the fort's magazine was destroyed and two-thirds of the French were dead and wounded. Rochambeau withdrew the remains of his forces, and the next day sued for peace with Dessalines, bringing a final close to the fighting that had raged since the summer of 1791. The French general even presented a stallion to Capois, to replace the slain mount.

Battle of Vertières Day (Armed Forces Day until the abolition of the Haitian army) is celebrated as a national holiday every November, and Capois is remembered on the 50HTG note. When Haiti marked its 150th anniversary, the battle was famously re-enacted on the site, with the assembled audience even taking part in the final assault, to make sure of a home win (despite the use of blank cartridges, Capois's unfortunate mount was still shot dead for extra realism). Vertières has now been subsumed into the suburbs of Cap-Haïtien, but the spot is marked by an impressive monument, with Capois and his exhausted soldiers cast in bronze looking proudly forward to independence. The monument is easily visible from the main road south out of town.

potential attack from the rear. Unfortunately for the French, the excellent defensive position was turned against them in the revolutionary war, when Christophe used the battery to fire on ships trying to reinforce the French positions in Cap.

Today, Fort Picolet is possibly the most important Vodou site in the Cap-Haïtien area. It has a rough peristyle, with *lwa* and *vévé* painted on the walls. Wednesday and Thursday are popular for services – the lwa Ogue Feray is particularly celebrated here. If you're lucky enough to meet any Vodouisants here, they may show you some of the other sites near the fort, from lwa carvings on the rocks at the bottom of the cliffs, to trees tied with votive tokens and secret caves.

MILOT

A small town nestled into the green folds of the Bonnet à l'Evêque Mountain, Milot is the entry point for the Citadelle la Ferrière and Sans Souci Palace – collectively Haiti's most impressive historical site as well as being the country's first UNESCO World Heritage Site. Sans Souci is on the edge of town, but the Citadelle is hidden from view on the peak of a nearby mountain. If you're going to visit one obvious tourist site in Haiti, it really should be this one.

Milot itself is a small farming community. As well as its obvious historical attractions, Milot is also the proud home to the Hôpital Sacré Cœur, the largest private hospital in northern Haiti and regional centre of excellence. It's run by the CRUDEM Foundation (Center for the Rural Development of Milot; *www.crudem.org*), who also produce an interesting online magazine twice-yearly about the hospital and Milot.

The area containing the Citadelle was made a national park in 1982 – the limits stretch from the entrance to Sans Souci at the edge of Milot, to Morne Bellevue in the south on the cusp of the town of Dondon.

GETTING THERE AND AWAY Milot is just under an hour from Cap-Haïtien by *taptap*. The road is paved most of the way, but becomes unsealed shortly after the worryingly named Carrefour La Mort, where the highway turns towards Fort Liberté and the Dominican border. Taptaps back to Cap patrol Milot's main street looking for fares – a good place to flag them down is outside the hospital.

THE NIGHT OF FIRE – HAITI'S PACT WITH THE DEVIL?

Small-scale slave revolts were part and parcel of colonial life in Saint-Domingue. But it was at Boïs Caiman in 1791, just outside Cap-Haïtien, where the slaves became truly organised. A meeting of slaves was called on 14 August, presided over by the *houngan* Boukman, a Jamaican coachman from a local plantation. Toussaint Louverture was also in attendance. A Vodou ceremony took place and a pig was sacrificed, accompanied by Boukman's famous exhortation:

> The God who created the sun that gives us light, who rouses the waves and rules the storm, though hidden in the clouds, He watches us. He sees all that the white man does. The God of the white man inspires him with crime, but our God calls upon us to do good works. Our God who is good to us orders us to revenge our wrongs. He will direct our arms and aid us. Throw away the symbol of the God of the whites who has so often caused us to weep, and listen to the voice of liberty, which speaks to the hearts of us all.

Hand in hand with the ritual, Boukman had worked with fellow conspirators to launch a mass uprising across the plantations of the north. Sworn to secrecy and bound by ritual, the slaves melted away to their plantations. Within a week, the north was on fire, and the path to freedom was set, with Vodou an integral part of the rebellion.

Just as the Boukman ritual has provided inspiration for Haitians, it has proved an equally pernicious currency for Haiti's detractors. The apparently diabolical nature of the ritual provided French writers of the 19th century easy cover for the inexplicable loss of Saint-Domingue, while some modern Christian missionaries have laid the centrality of Vodou in Haiti's founding moments to be the root of many of the country's problems. Notorious American televangelist Pat Robertson even went as far as saying the 2010 earthquake was a direct result of the ritual – a divine comeuppance for the slaves making a pact with the devil to win their freedom.

WHERE TO STAY There's one accommodation option:

Lakou Lakay Milot; 3667 6070/3614 2485; e lakoulakaymilot@aol.com. A community centre in green surroundings with simple attached rooms, run by local guide Maurice Etienne. Friendly welcome. Lunch or dinner is available for US$10, frequently accompanied by a drumming & dance show (arrange in advance). **$**

OTHER PRACTICALITIES

Entry to Sans Souci and the Citadelle la Ferrière The ticket office for entry to the historic sites is opposite the cathedral at the foot of Sans Souci. Prices are 500HTG for Sans Souci, or 1,000HTG for Sans Souci and the Citadelle. Local guides are of varying quality; English-speaking Maurice Etienne (*3667 6070/3614 2485; e lakoulakaymilot@aol.com*) is a font of historical and local knowledge.

While entering Sans Souci is a simple matter of walking through the gates, getting to the Citadelle involves getting to the top of a mountain, so you have a few choices. If you have your own vehicle, you can drive on the cobbled road to the village of Choiseul, also known as 'second parking' ('first parking' being at the entrance to the palace). It's a 20-minute drive. From here, it's a further half-hour walk to the actual Citadelle.

A common way of climbing the mountain is by mule, and at the ticket office you'll undoubtedly be accosted by mule-handlers offering themselves for hire. The usual fee is about US$15, although tips are always requested. Unfortunately, some mule handlers can be incredibly pushy, so stand your ground. There may be a fee for a second handler, who 'encourages' the mules' ascent. Some people may be uncomfortable with this as not all the mules look in great shape. If you do ride, expect the climb to take about 90 minutes to Choiseul.

The third option is simply to walk. Allow a couple of hours. If you don't have a guide however, you can expect to be repeatedly approached by more mule handlers and would-be guides, although once you're clear of Sans Souci this tends to drop off. At Choiseul, they start over again, charging US$10 per mule for the final climb.

SANS SOUCI The magnificent remains of Sans Souci Palace, toppled by the great earthquake of 1842, are at the far end of Milot, a testament to the vision of Henri Christophe. Within days of crowning himself King of Haiti in 1811, construction started on a suitably regal palace. Milot was chosen over Cap-Haïtien, a secure location far from potential bombardment from the French navy.

Sans Souci was a vision of Christophe's over-arching ambition, its design straight out of classical European tradition, allegedly modelled on the palace of Frederick II of Prussia. Its heyday lasted just a handful of years. When Christophe was laid low by a stroke and surrounded by rebellious subjects in late 1820, it was to here that he retreated and took his own life. Today, the ruined façade makes it appear like a crumbled Versailles of the Caribbean, a vision of a Haiti that almost was.

You enter by a sweeping double staircase. Huge picture windows overlook the scene. Only traces of the original stucco decoration remain today. A fountain halfway up the stairs was once flanked by a pair of bronze lions, Christophe's regal emblem. On entering the building proper, the scope of the palace is astounding. The four storeys are now open to the sky, but you walk through a series of grand reception salons, once finely dressed with carpets, paintings and mahogany flooring. The fine stone detailing on the window casements demonstrates the attention to detail. The king, queen and princess all had private apartments.

CHRISTOPHE'S INSTANT NOBILITY

Any new ruler needs symbols to assert their power and legitimacy, and this applied doubly to Henri Christophe following the trauma of both the epic revolutionary war and the splitting in half of the country following the assassination of Dessalines. When he crowned himself king in 1811, the Citadelle was some way from completion, and barely a brick laid at Sans Souci, so he did the next-best thing and created an instant class of nobles, modelled firmly on the European tradition.

As well as king, Christophe's other titles were modestly listed as Sovereign of Tortuga, Gonâve and other adjacent islands, Destroyer of Tyranny, Regenerator and Benefactor of the Haitian Nation, Creator of her Moral, Political and Martial Institutions, First Crowned Monarch of the New World, Defender of the Faith, and Founder of the Royal and Military Order of St Henry. The newly created College of Arms provided the heraldry: two crowned ermine lions flanking a shield bearing a phoenix rising from the flames. Ex-slaves who had served as his officers were enobled – 'Congo-born' general Jean-Pierre Richard became the splendidly titled Duke of Marmelade, while Christophe even claimed those far from the kingdom as his subjects, such as the rebel leader Goman, fighting Pétion in the Grand Anse, who suddenly (and probably unbeknownst to himself) became the Count of Jérémie.

In total, Christophe created four princes, eight dukes, 22 counts and 37 barons – each with their own intricate coats of arms. Traditional pageantry butted up against African and Caribbean imagery – creatures from Greek mythology easily co-mingling with elephants and flamingos. Surrounded by pomp, Christophe would set about building the kingdom in his image.

The spectacle was short-lived. Many viewed Christophe's reign as tyrannical, and it was the Duke of Marmelade himself who led the uprising against the stroke-debilitated king, closing the page on this colourful chapter of Haitian history.

Outside are the remains of the rest of the palace complex. There was a hospital and school, staffed by Scottish doctors and English tutors. Christophe was a keen Anglophile and regularly corresponded with the abolitionist William Wilberforce, and imported his royal carriage from London for £700. Next to the hospital stands the old printing press, and behind these the barracks of the Royal Corps of Dahomets, Christophe's fierce personal regiment. There are also the remains of brick channels that drew cooling water from the hills under the palace floors, for an early form of air conditioning. At the centre of the grassy clearing right of the stairs is a star apple tree, where Christophe would sit and hear plaintiffs to the court. An Italianate bust sits nearby on a plinth (it's not Queen Marie-Louise, despite what some guides may tell you).

Next to the gates of Sans Souci is **Milot Cathedral**, a striking round white building topped by an enormous dome, with a separate bell tower. It was built by Christophe at the same time as the palace, and also devastated in the 1842 earthquake. It was heavily restored in 1933. The cathedral is dedicated to the Virgin Mary, and Milot teems with visitors every 8 December for the *fête patronale* of the Immaculate Conception.

CITADELLE LA FERRIERE Even before you reach it, the statistics about the Citadelle demand that you be impressed. On top of a mountain 900m above sea level, 14 years to build with the labour of 20,000 people and with walls 4m thick and 40m high. By some way the biggest fort in the Caribbean, it could hold a garrison of 5,000 people for a year, and yet it never saw its guns fired in conflict.

Visitors get their first glimpse of the Citadelle soon after leaving the village of Choiseul. The landscape suddenly opens up and there it sits above you, its massive scale designed to humble anyone approaching. The sharp wedge of its forward bastion sits high out of the vegetation, 'the prow of a ship breasting a green wave,' in the words of one observer. Anyone attempting to lay siege here would surely have their work cut out.

Construction began in 1804, when Dessalines ordered the fortification of Haiti against future invasion. Larger than anything previously constructed, it was to be a final redoubt and seat of power in the north. Its radical design more closely echoes the castles of Europe than any contemporary military forts, but who its architects were remains unclear. When Christophe took over its construction he famously banned any Europeans from approaching the Citadelle, nervous of prying eyes.

There's one small entrance gate, outside which sit a row of impressive mortars (if you've walked up, you might be pleased to see the cold drinks seller too). The nail-studded door is a modern replacement dating from a large restoration project in the 1970s; the original sits off its hinges just inside. The entrance corridor twists in several places, with blind corners and loopholes to aid defenders. The entry point to the forward bastion, the oldest part of the fortress, is also here.

To get further you need to cross a small drawbridge – the Citadelle even has its own internal moat, fed by an ingenious rooftop water-capture system that drained into eight large cisterns. The walls here are north-facing and covered

CANNONS OF THE CITADELLE

There are 163 pieces of artillery *in situ* at the Citadelle, from the ranks of mortars arrayed in front of the entrance to the two grand galleries of cannon guarding the main approaches to the fortress. Taken together, they give not only a picture of state-of-the-art 18th-century weaponry, but also a snapshot of the way that Haiti was linked to the pan-European wars of the same period.

The first gallery of the Royal Battery contains several treasures, still mounted on their original mahogany carriages. The cannons were so valuable they were given names, inscribed on their barrels when originally cast. 'The Mercury', dating from 1744 was brought to Haiti by General Leclerc's army, its republican nature revealed by the defaced French royal crest (elsewhere, revolutionary cannons bear the slogan 'Liberté, Egalité, Fraternité'). 'The Defender' and 'The Great' have handles of stylised dolphins, and a monstrous face at the base of each barrel. A little further down the gallery are British cannons: the Duke of Marlborough's cannon and the Duke of Montagu's cannon, bearing the coat of arms of King George I and in service for 80 years before their capture by Toussaint Louverture at Môle Saint-Nicholas in 1798.

In the small museum in the Officer's Quarters, is the Spanish howitzer 'Cayem', captured by the French in Catalonia in 1802, and shipped to Saint-Domingue just a year later. Also here is the so-called 'Napoleon' howitzer, bearing the image of the emperor wearing laurel leaves. Cast a full year after Haitian independence, its presence in the Citadelle remains a mystery.

with deep orange lichen known locally as *sang de Christophe* (the blood of Christopher). Turning inside again, you proceed through a long gallery filled with cannons, the first of two royal batteries, before popping out in the courtyard and parade ground.

There's a small museum here in the restored Officer's Quarters, but you'll need to ask for it to be opened – it contains a few particularly treasured pieces of artillery, and plans and information about the modern restoration. The key holder may also offer you some souvenirs. In keeping with the currently modest state of Haitian tourism, these run to some ancient posters and (bizarrely) a book of Citadelle-inspired Haiku. Across the square are the remains of the powder magazine, as well as the whitewashed tomb of Prince Noel, who died when the magazine exploded in an accident. In the centre of the square, a piece of the mountain that forms the Citadelle's foundation juts proudly out, with a small plaque explaining that Christophe was secretly buried here after his suicide.

It's possible to climb the walls, and doing so gives you an incredible impression of the Citadelle's strategic location. From here you can see as far as Cap-Haïtien, and Christophe could look out with his spyglass to observe what ships were arriving in port. The whole of the Plaine du Nord is laid out before you, with the ranks of the Massif du Nord queuing up behind. On every side there are some frighteningly sheer drops, but be advised that there are absolutely no safety rails whatsoever on any part of the walls or roof. It's at this point that guides often tell the story of Christophe demonstrating the fanatical loyalty of his soldiers by ordering an entire company to march off the walls. It's apocryphal, but you can well imagine the messy end – it's a long way down indeed.

The back of the Citadelle looks back to a smaller secondary fort called **Ramiers**. This guards the only exposed flank of the Citadelle as well as overlooking the road south to Dondon. It's a short walk to there, past massed piles of cannonballs and ranks of mortars – leave the Citadelle and track along its base past where the mule handlers park their mounts, and the path quickly opens up to another old powder magazine.

LABADIE

The road from Cap-Haïtien to Labadie hugs the cliffs of the coast, repeatedly offering great vistas of the rough Atlantic coast. The road is poor, which makes the destination – Haiti's single biggest tourist draw – seem even more unusual. Labadie is the one place in Haiti where the cruise ships bring their passengers to play.

In reality, there are two Labadies. The village proper, and 'Labadee', the name given by the cruise company Royal Caribbean to its private resort. Sadly, entry to the resort is not generally allowed, but the relaxed charm of Labadie still has plenty of drawcards, with some good nearby beaches and boat trips along the coast.

GETTING THERE AND AROUND Labadie is 30 minutes from Cap-Haïtien, leaving town from the end of Rue 21 (there is a *taptap* station at Rue 21Q; a moto-taxi will set you back 100HTG). Soon after leaving Cap-Haïtien, the road climbs stiffly to Fort Bourgeois, which has a good view back across the city and bay. The road terminates behind the high fences of the Royal Caribbean complex – to get to Labadie you have to catch a shared *bateau-taxi* (taxi-boat) around the headland, which takes ten minutes. The fare should be 10HTG, dropping you in the village, but if you ask the boat to divert to take you to one of the two hotels, the fare shoots up five-fold (even if you're already sharing the boat with other passengers).

WHERE TO STAY AND EAT

Cormier Plage Route de Labadie; 3702 0210/3804 6673; e cormier@hughes.net. Two-thirds of the way from Cap-Haïtien to Labadie, a relaxing hotel with big rooms, shady gardens & plenty of beachfront. The seafood at the restaurant is excellent although sometimes slow in delivery. Boat trips & snorkelling available on the reef. Wi-Fi. **$$$**

Norm's Place Kay Norm; 3425 8127/3810 5988; e normsplacelabadie@yahoo.com. A quiet & tranquil waterfront retreat on the edge of the village, with rooms in stone bungalows loaded with character (including four-poster beds with mosquito nets). Superb food, Wi-Fi. **$$**

Belly Beach Hotel Plage Belly; 3610 3043; e admajor@hotmail.com. Immediately after the headland when coming to Labadie by *bateau-taxi*. Pleasant beach & restaurant (plus a few oddities like an outdoor gym), although rooms themselves are pretty dark & basic. **$**

Most people eat in their hotels. Jessie's Bar-Resto in Labadie village is a very simple place serving up rice and beans with sauce, and there are other *marchands* selling *fritay*, but otherwise options are limited. There are plenty of small bars in the village – as well as a cold Prestige you can often pick up cheap Budweiser, Corona and other international brands, all presumably having made their way off the cruise ships.

OTHER PRACTICALITIES Long-term Labadie resident **Tim Mangs** (*3999 9711; e info@gohaititours.com*), who arrived in the 1970s and never quite left, has a catamaran and runs snorkelling and beach trips along the coast, as well as tours to Cap-Haïtien, the Citadelle, and local cacao plantations and rum distilleries. His cliff-side bungalows are being converted to offer accommodation, to be ready in 2013.

Labadie's mobile-phone reception is quixotic – you tend to either get no signal or prefect reception, depending on whether the cruise ship is in dock. At the time of writing the only solution was to take a boat into the bay and tell the skipper to keep going until you get reception – it's probably easier to switch the thing off altogether and enjoy being out of touch.

BEACHES NEAR LABADIE There's not much of a beach at Labadie village, but it's possible to take boat trips out to a couple of decent spots fairly close by – you'll be approached by boat owners eager to take you. Expect to pay about 2,000HTG (US$50) for a day trip, and 250HTG if you want them to throw in a mask, snorkel and fins.

The closest option is **Paradise Beach**, 20 minutes' sail around the headland west of Labadie. It's a sheltered cove surrounded by green wooded hills. The sand is creamy white and there's a natural spring running into the sea, turning the shallows a pretty turquoise where the waters mingle. If you walk up past the spring, you'll find a neat tourist 'village' laid out for passengers from the cruise ship. On days when the ship visits, the village has artisan stalls, Haitian food cooked in thatched huts and even a 'voodoo' area where there's drumming and dancing. It feels a bit twee, but is still oddly fascinating, as this is a rare part of Haiti that the cruise passengers get to experience outside the perimeter of their compound. On other days of the week, you'll almost certainly have the beach to yourself.

An hour's sail out of Labadie is **Amiga Island**. It's picture-postcard stuff – a tiny island fringed with sandy beaches that takes just five minutes to walk around, and the sort of place you might expect Robinson Crusoe to have been stranded. It's perfect for sun lounging with a picnic. The island sits just behind a large barrier reef (complete with stranded ship), and you can snorkel amid the coral. It's quite denuded in places, but there are still plenty of bright tropical fish to spot. Several people in Labadie told me that the island takes its name (Spanish for 'friend') from when Columbus sailed by in 1492, with local tradition claiming that this is where he bedded a local Taíno woman, surely a made-for-tourists story if there ever was one.

A third beach is the one you pass at **Cormier** between Labadie and Cap-Haïtien. You can enter at Cormier Plage Hotel but non-guests must pay a 200HTG entry fee. The sand is particularly golden here, and the shelving of the beach can produce some good surf.

THE PLAINE DU NORD

The large Plaine du Nord runs from the Chaîne de Bonnet Mountains to the sea. Fertile and well watered, it was an obvious place for French colonists to settle, where it became the powerhouse of the plantation economy. The whole area is littered with interesting sights, although many of them are hard to find or abandoned. This is rich pickings for history and Vodou buffs, although the casual visitor may be content with a visit to the more obvious (and spectacular) Citadelle.

The town of **Limonade** sits at the heart of the plain, less than 20km east of Cap-Haïtien. It's one of the oldest parishes in Haiti and under French rule was a major centre of sugar production. At the centre of Limonade is the colonial-era **St Anne's**

CRUISING TO 'LABADEE'

Royal Caribbean has leased Coco Plage, on the headland outside Labadie, from the Haitian government since 1986, and developed it into 'Labadee®', one of its favoured resorts on its Caribbean itineraries. Labadee usually receives ships three times a week, including the *Oasis of the Seas*, which was the largest cruise ship in the world when launched in 2009, capable of carrying 5,400 passengers. In recent years, 450,000 tourists per year have visited Labadee. For every tourist arriving at the resort, the Haitian government is paid a landing tax of US$10. The resort is a big earner for Royal Caribbean, who have invested US$55 million in the facility since 2009 alone. About 230 locals are employed at the site.

The resort is completely self-contained, and tourists are not allowed to leave the compound. The opposite applies to non-guests – the closest you're likely to get is when taking the *bateau-taxi* to Labadie and you chug past the giant inflatables of the 'Arawak Aqua Park'. Although it's just a resort like any other in the Caribbean, the contrast with the under-developed outside (not least the terrible state of the road to Cap-Haïtien) feels instructive, not least on the days when the gleaming white ships are in dock, dwarfing everything around.

Aside from the embargo years of 1991–94, Royal Caribbean has stuck with Haiti throughout its recent history, even continuing to visit straight after the 2010 earthquake (for which it received some negative publicity, although the company donated around US$2 million to relief efforts). In the past, the company seemed to want to hide the fact that Labadee was actually in Haiti at all, with promotional material simply referring to a secluded paradise off the island of Hispaniola, although current cruise passengers can hardly miss the batteries of Haitian flags that now fly in the resort. With the hope of getting cruise passengers outside the wire and experiencing more of Haiti than their 'Labaduzee' cocktails, there are currently much-talked-about plans on the table to build a road direct from Labadie to Milot to allow day trips to the Citadelle.

Church, a simple white-and-blue building with a red tin roof sat opposite the town square. It was during a service here in 1820 that Christophe suffered the stroke that doomed him and his kingdom. A popular story tells how he received an angelic visitation just before his death on the road junction near Milot – still today named Carrefour La Mort ('Crossroads of Death'). Within a week of his stroke, his army mutinied, and Christophe took his own life with a silver bullet.

In the centre of the town square is a large plinth, repeatedly restored, dating from the French period. It was used for public pronouncements and the sale of slaves. South of Limonade, the fields contain many further relics of the plantation system, including some well-preserved irrigation canals (over-enthusiastic local rumours that these are the remains of a secret tunnel to Limonade built by Christophe from Sans Souci Palace at Milot can probably be safely discounted).

Limonade remains an agricultural area. An enterprising project is the production of drinking chocolate by RAFAVAL (Rasambleman de Femme Voyantes de Limonade), a women's co-operative supported by **Sonje Ayiti** (*www.sonjeayiti.com*), a locally based community development and micro-credit NGO. If you want to base yourself here, the town has one hotel, the surprisingly good **Puissance Divine Hotel** (*Bohama, Route National 6;* ☎ *3732 4516;* **$$**), a large olive-green building on the left as you enter Limonade from Cap-Haïtien.

The village of **Bord de Mer** (sometimes called Bord de Mer de Limonade) is on the opposite side of the highway, down an earth road leading to the sea, through fields of beans and plantain trees. It's a struggling fishing village hauled up on a black sandy beach, and a thoroughly unremarkable place but for its history, as archaeologists believe that it is the site of La Navidad, the first European settlement in the Americas (see box, *La Navidad*, page 194). The village also contains the **Church of St Philomena**, which has been an important pilgrimage site since a vision of the saint here in 1950. The site is venerated by Catholics and Vodouisants alike, who see the *lwa* Lasiren (the mermaid) as the saint's counterpart. It throngs with celebrants every 7 September, who bathe in the freshwater lagoon behind the shrine. Celebrations spill over into Limonade, which holds its own large *fête patronale* on 26 July for St Anne.

Near the church, but now returned to farmland, are the remains of **Puerto Real**, a Spanish town excavated by archaeologists in the 1980s. The town was established in 1503 for the purposes of cattle ranching and copper mining. At its height, it had a population of around 250 Spanish colonists, many of whom intermarried with the Taíno. Puerto Real was one of the first places to import African slaves to Hispaniola. Its inhabitants repeatedly incurred the displeasure of Spain by illegally trading with foreign ships, which led to its forced abandonment in 1578, with its inhabitants moved to Bayaha (modern-day Fort Liberté).

There are much more modern developments nearby. On the road from Limonade to the Dominican border, you quickly pass the brand-new University Roi Henri Christophe, a gift of the Dominican Republic, and opened in 2012. It's one of those rare buildings that actually looks like an architectural model blown up to life-size. A little further east along the coast is the site of **Caracol**, the giant industrial park that forms the centrepiece of the government's economic development plan. Budgeted at nearly US$260 million, it proposes to ultimately create as many as 20,000 jobs, concentrating on garment assembly for the US market.

There is an important Vodou site at the village of **Plaine du Nord**, a few miles south of Cap-Haïtien. In the run-up to 25 July, thousands of people mass here for a week-long festival. It centres on a muddy pool called Trou Sèn Jak (St Jacques' Hole), used for ritual bathing. The festival is dedicated to Ogue Feray, the warrior *lwa*, who is celebrated for his inspirational role to slaves during the revolution. It's an amazing and heady spectacle, with baptisms, healings, sacrifices and music, with trees decked out in red and blue for Ogue, and adherents covered from head to toe in the sacred mud.

Between Plaine du Nord and Limonade is the district of **Quartier Morin**. If you want to explore off the beaten track, you can still find the remains of two French plantations here – Habitation Duplat and Habitation Detreille. You'll have to ask locally for exact directions.

Habitation Duplat is a jumble of colonial buildings, the white brick of a sugarcane factory still impressive in its ruins. There is a tall chimney, and a jumble of lower buildings, including one impressively overgrown and buttressed old *mapou* tree. The main building contains tunnels and a flooded basin. Like many historical sites, it has long has been appropriated by Vodou, and you can see the *vèvè* markings on the floors and walls, and other remnants of the ceremonies that still take place here. A magical fish with silver earrings (the Lovanna aux Pierres) reputedly lives in the waters of the basin, granting wishes to those believers lucky enough to see it.

Further south in Quartier Morin off Route National 6 is **Habitation Detreille**. Still partly inhabited by local farmers (ask permission to enter), it has a similar but smaller selection of buildings. A chilling reminder of slavery remains on one of the plaques at the entrance to the habitation, with its cruel slogan *La travail est mon bonheur* ('Work is my joy').

LIMBE

Limbé is the first town of any note when you head south from Cap-Haïtien on Route National 1 towards Port-au-Prince. The road climbs up and over the Chaîne de Bonnet Mountains and affords constantly impressive views. All the better to take your mind off the dire state of the road which, though tarmac, is dotted with potholes almost continuously until you reach Gonaïves.

There would be little reason to stop in Limbé were it not for the small but surprisingly good **Musée de Guahaba** (*Rue Paul Magloire*). The museum was founded by William Hodges, an American medical missionary who settled in Limbé in 1953 and lived here until his death in 1995. He was an amateur archaeologist who became a leading expert on Taíno history and culture (Guahaba is the Taíno name for Limbé). The museum is full of his finds, not least several items found during the excavation of a Taíno town at En Bas Saline near Limonade. There are also exhibits representing the colonial and revolutionary period, all well labelled with plenty of information. Donations are welcome. The museum is set in leafy grounds and is part of (and run by) the **Hôpital Bon Samaritain** (*www.hbslimbe.org*), one of the largest hospitals in the region, also founded by Dr Hodges in the 1950s.

Limbé is said to have been where the slave and Vodou priest Boukman lived – it was he who organised the famous Boïs Caiman ritual in August 1793 that sparked the revolution, and the plantations around Limbé were some of the first to go up in smoke. Appropriately, Limbé has a large **peristyle** on the main road, covered in beautiful murals of the *lwa*. Just off the main road, the town square is called Nan Canno ('In Cannons'), and is celebrated as a gathering place for the Haitian army on the eve of the Battle of Vertières that finally routed the French from the island.

If you find yourself looking for accommodation in Limbé, the **Chez Mama Yoyo Hotel** (*Route National 1,* **$**) is a reasonable bet in a pinch. A newer, plusher-looking place, **Sunshine Inn** (*Rue Simonette; 3705 5519; www.sunshinelimbe.com;* **$$**) was due to open at the end of 2012. A decent eating place is **Le Voyageur Bar-Resto**

(*Route National 1*) – both it and Chez Mama are on the main road in the centre of town, near where *taptaps* and buses leave for Cap-Haïtien and Port-au-Prince.

FORT LIBERTE

Fort Liberté is the largest town between Cap-Haïtien and the Dominican border at Ouanaminthe. It was founded in 1578 as Bahaya by the Spanish, but despite a strong claim to be one of the oldest towns in the country, these days it feels more like an overlooked footnote – off the main highway, little visited and economically depressed. However, it's still worth a visit for Fort Dauphin, a French fort commanding the entrance to its wide circular bay, the largest in the country.

LA NAVIDAD

On his first voyage of discovery in 1492, Columbus famously sailed in the *Niña*, the *Pinta* and the *Santa María*. It was the last of these ships that ran aground on a reef at Bord de Mer on Christmas Day, the event that led to the founding of La Navidad. Bord de Mer was near a large Taíno town ruled by a chief named Guacanacaric, thought to be one of the paramount chiefs (*caciques*) of Taíno Hispaniola. Guacanacaric put his men to work aiding the Spaniards to salvage what they could from the ship. Columbus stayed with the Taíno here for three weeks, during which time they built a fort on the site, which they called La Navidad. Despite undoubtedly being the first European settlement in the Western hemisphere, many archaeologists believe that the fort was actually built within the Taíno village.

Columbus left 39 of his men at La Navidad, with instructions to trade and explore for gold. He wrote to his royal patrons in Spain:

> I commanded a fort to be built there forthwith, which must be completed by this time, in which I left many men as seemed necessary, with all kinds of arms, and plenty of food for more than a year … and also the extraordinary good will and friendship of the king of this island toward us. For those people are very amiable and kind, to such a degree that the said king gloried in calling me his brother. And if they should change their minds, and should wish to hurt those who remained in the fort, they would not be able, because they lack weapons, they go naked, and are too cowardly. For that reason those who hold the said fort are at least able to resist easily this whole island, without any imminent danger to themselves.

These were words of hubris. When Columbus returned in November 1493, La Navidad had been burnt to ash, and the bodies of 11 of the colonists were scattered on the beach. Questioning the locals, they said that they had retaliated against their cruel treatment by the Spanish, while others said that the settlers had quarrelled and fought among themselves, possibly over gold. Either way, Columbus chose not to press the point, and simply abandoned the project and sailed east along the coast. It wasn't until the founding of Santo Domingo, still capital of the Dominican Republic, that Europe finally got a permanent foothold in the Americas.

In the late 19th century, the anchor of the *Santa María* was found by local fishermen, and is now on permanent display at MUPANAH, the national museum in Port-au-Prince.

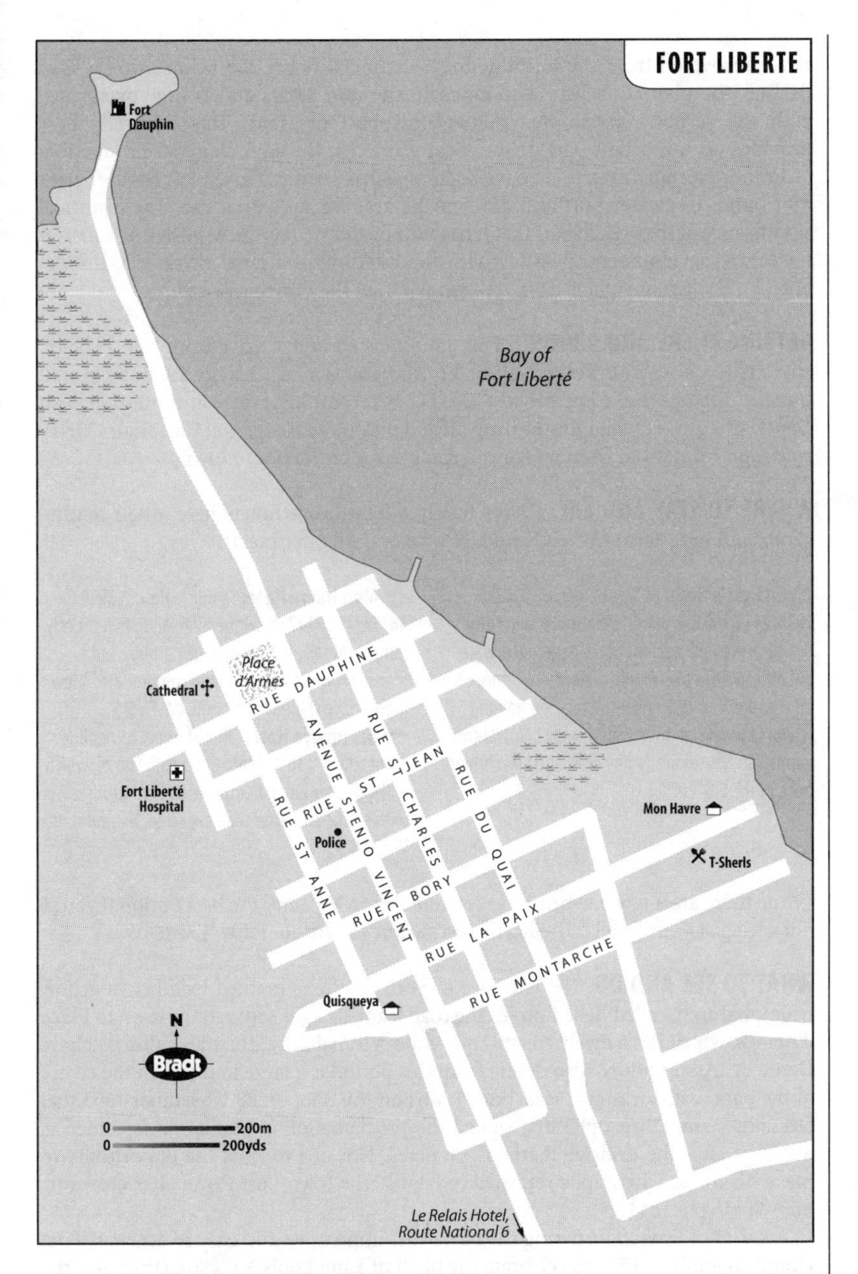

The relatively dry nature of the landscape meant that Fort Liberté never boomed in the same way as Cap-Haïtien and its surrounding plantations; the town's importance was strategic. It wasn't until the 1920s that agriculture really boomed here, when it was developed for sisal production. The American-run Dauphine Sisal Plantation spread across 25,000 acres, with its own light railway. At its height during World War II, it was a major supplier of rope to the US navy and one of the largest employers in the country, but production never recovered from the introduction of artificial fibres like nylon. After a slow decline, the plantation was abandoned in the mid 1980s and is now overgrown with the scrubby acacia that defines this part of Haiti. This ironically now provides an important part of the local economy, through charcoal production.

In more recent years, there have been repeated attempts to exploit Fort Liberté's moribund deepwater port and develop the area for industrial use. The historical significance of the area means that it has now been listed by the Ministry of Tourism for future development, possibly with the building of a large marina and resort hotels, although any plans have yet to make it off the drawing board.

GETTING THERE AND AROUND Fort-Liberté is an hour's drive from Cap-Haitïen, and sits some way off Route National 6 (the junction at Carrefour Chivry is well signed). *Taptaps* (Belle Entrée) cost 75HTG. Alternatively, taptaps running between Cap-Haïtien and Ouanaminthe drop off and pick up passengers at Carrefour Chivry by the petrol station, from where you can get a moto-taxi into town.

WHERE TO STAY AND EAT There's barely a handful of hotels here, often renting rooms out long-term to NGO and UN workers. All offer meals.

Le Relais Hotel 1 Rue Boukman; 3658 1035/2512 9601; e info@lerelaishotel.net. Large & well-presented modern hotel, next to the water but otherwise in the middle of nowhere – turn off the road into town near the teacher-training school (a hotel sign here would really help). Comfy rooms, bar & a comically phallic-shaped swimming pool. Wi-Fi. **$$**

Mon Havre Hotel 4 Rue la Paix; 3819 4613/3711 8127; e seignemd@yahoo.fr. A slightly ramshackle affair & occasionally grubby, but friendly owners & decent food compensate. A few rooms have shared bathrooms. Wi-Fi. **$$**

Quisqueya Hotel Rue St Anne, corner Rue Montacher; 3650 9965. Good-value hotel, which looks gloomy on first entrance & then surprises with rooms far better than expected. Helpful staff. Wi-Fi. **$$**

While there are a few bar-restos on Avenue Stenio Vincent, the best option if you're not eating at your hotel is **T-Sherls Restaurant** (*23 Rue la Paix; 3716 6927*).

WHAT TO SEE AND DO The entrance to Fort Liberté is marked by a bright yellow triumphal arch, called Belle Entrée. The road leads straight through the town to **Place d'Armes**, which has a lovely cream-and-white colonial-era cathedral, Église de Notre Dame de l'Assomption. Also dating from this period is a large fountain in the centre of the park, with a cannon at its base. It was on this spot on 28 November 1803 that Dessalines and Christophe first signed the proclamation of Haitian independence, five days after the decisive Battle of Vertières. Not one to miss the opportunity to make his mark, Christophe returned to baptise the town Fort Royal after crowning himself king in 1811.

A series of French forts ring the bay. Most impressive and easy to access is **Fort Dauphin**, built in 1731 to celebrate the birth of King Louis XV's son (then also the name of the town, which took its current name during the revolution). It sits on a thin spit of land guarding the west side of the bay, a ten-minute walk (also accessible by car) from the town square. There's a bit of clambering to be done – the initial section protects the entrance to the fort, rather than the fort proper, so be sure to go via the narrow gate slightly below ground level. Despite some restoration work in the 1990s, the interior of the fort is quite overgrown, but you can make your way past the old barracks (which could house 200 men) along the ramparts to the end of the fort, where it dramatically sticks out into the bay as the sharp point of a triangle. When you get here, the fort's strategic location becomes instantly apparent.

There is no entrance fee, and barring the occasional fishermen hauled up on the nearby beach mending their nets, you'll most likely have the fort to yourself.

There are several other forts guarding the opposite (eastern) side of the bay, built by the French during the same period. Best preserved is **Fort Labouque**, which sits on the beach at the narrow inlet to the bay. You have two options to get there: by road or boat. If you have a vehicle, turn right at the road leading through the hamlet of Dirac, shortly after Carrefour Chivry. It's a very rough track, and floods readily during the rainy season. A more interesting alternative is to approach a fisherman at the port and hire a boat. Fort Labouque has an intriguing design, with a curved defensive wall with two round bastions at each end, with a magazine and barracks behind, and abandoned cannons. Also on this side of the bay are the smaller forts of **Fort St Charles** and **Fort Saint Frédérique**, both in some state of disrepair but rife for exploration (by boat).

OUANAMINTHE

Route National 6 ends at Ouanaminthe, Haiti's northern border with the Dominican Republic. The border is marked by the Rivière du Massacre; on the other side is Ouanaminthe's Dominican twin, the town of Dajabón. For its size, Ouanaminthe is a prosperous town. There's the air of a lot of business being done, and shops are full of goods brought over from the Dominican Republic, with things especially busy on the market days of Monday and Friday. Ouanaminthe has a huge *fête patronale* every 15 August (Our Lady of the Assumption), when the town overflows with visitors from both Haiti and the DR, and the border seems to temporarily dissolve for the day.

Although it looks more a muddy stream today, Rivière du Massacre does indeed live up to its melodramatic name. It was so dubbed in 1728 after a bloody raid by French buccaneers on a Spanish settlement here. However, the river is more infamous today for the so-called 'Parsley Massacres' of 1937. The Dominican dictator Rafael Trujillo gave a speech in Dajabón demonising Haitian immigrants to the DR – the next day his army started to round up Haitians living along the border, killing indiscriminately as they went. Their test was to ask people to pronounce the Spanish word for Parsley (*perejil*), a tricky task for Creole-speakers who naturally flatten the latter 'R' when speaking. Up to 30,000 Haitians were killed, mostly hacked to death with machetes. Little known by the outside world, the massacres are memorialised in Edwidge Danticat's heartbreaking historical novel *The Farming of Bones*.

There's little reason to stay in Ouanaminthe overnight; it's very much a place to transit. There are a handful of grotty cheap places, but the best of the bunch if you're in need is **Ideal Hotel** (*Rue Espagnole;* ☎ *3475 7528/3946 4037;* **e** *idealhotelwanament@yahoo.fr;* **$$$**), at the end of the town, where Route National 6 turns for the border. It's got nice simple rooms, a restaurant and Wi-Fi. For food, **Plaisir Gourmande** (*Rue St Pierre*) is a good option – the road runs parallel to Rue Espagnole, one block to the south. Road transport is plentiful to Cap-Haïtien, taking just under 90 minutes by private car and slightly longer by *taptap* (100HTG).

PORT-DE-PAIX

Port-de-Paix is the provincial capital of Haiti's Nord-Ouest *département*, although not many people visit, since it has the worst road connections of any of Haiti's cities,

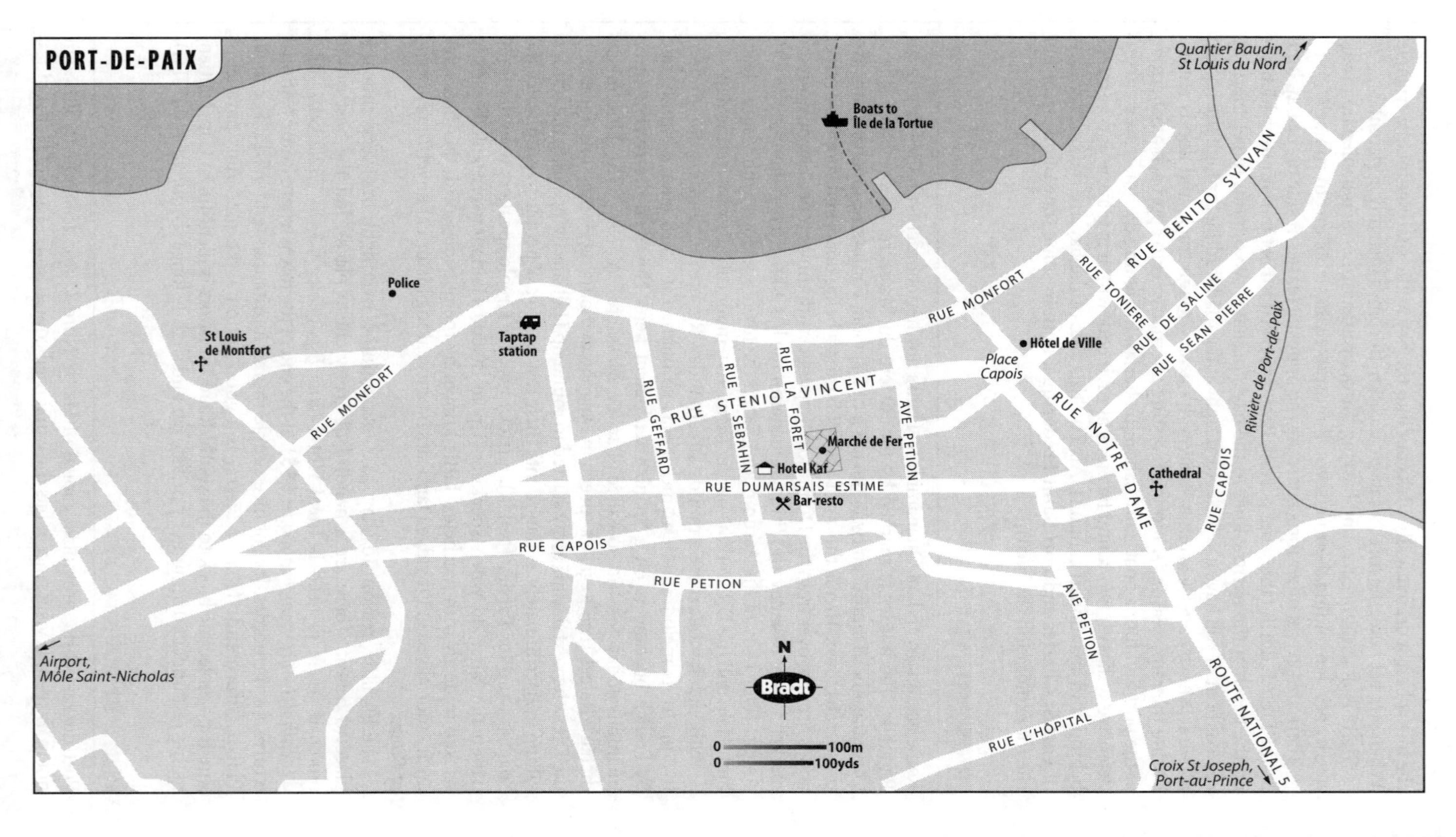
PORT-DE-PAIX
Boats to Île de la Tortue
Quartier Baudin, St Louis du Nord
Police
St Louis de Montfort
Taptap station
RUE MONFORT
RUE MONFORT
RUE BENITO SYLVAIN
RUE TONIERE
RUE DE SALINE
RUE SEAN PIERRE
Hôtel de Ville
Place Capois
Rivière de Port-de-Paix
RUE STENIO VINCENT
RUE GEFFARD
RUE SEBAHIN
RUE LA FORET
AVE PETION
Marché de Fer
Hotel Kaf
RUE NOTRE DAME
Cathedral
RUE CAPOIS
RUE DUMARSAIS ESTIME
Bar-resto
RUE CAPOIS
RUE PETION
AVE PETION
Airport, Môle Saint-Nicholas
N
Bradt
ROUTE NATIONAL 5
RUE L'HÔPITAL
0 100m
0 100yds
Croix St Joseph, Port-au-Prince

giving it something of the air of an unloved backwater. Once a major export centre for coffee and bananas, today it's best known as a jumping-off point for Île de la Tortue which sits across a narrow strait of water. Together, they form the smuggling centre of Haiti – mostly bringing in duty-free goods from Miami, but also serving as a trans-shipment point for drugs heading to the States. It's an inauspicious position for a place dubbed Valparaíso ('Valley of Paradise'), by Christopher Columbus when he made landfall here in 1492.

French buccaneers founded the town in 1665, and it served as the capital of Saint-Domingue for 50 years until the expansion of Cap Français (Cap-Haïtien). It remains proud that it was the site of the first general slave uprising against the French, in 1679, when plantation slavery was still getting on its feet. Port-de-Paix was an important but confusing battleground between the French, Haitian and British armies. Like much of the north it was levelled in the 1842 earthquake, and then razed by a terrible fire in 1902.

There's little compelling reason to visit Port-de-Paix today except on business, or transiting through to Môle Saint-Nicholas, but it's still a diverting place for a day. It's a long drawn-out town – the bumpy Route National 5 pulls into town and turns into Rue Notre Dame, where it passes the blue-and-white **cathedral** (which was having

CROSSING INTO THE DOMINICAN REPUBLIC

Entering Ouanaminthe, Route National 6 turns into Rue Espagnole, and at the end of town takes an unexpected turn right into a muddy field-cum-marketplace. It's all a bit rough and ready, a cluster of stalls, money-changers (more than on the Dominican side), mobile-phone guys and *marchands*. At the edge of the field is a girder bridge marking the official border crossing. Immigration is on the right at the start of the bridge. There's a US$10 departure tax, and you'll also need the green card you got when you arrived in Haiti. When your passport is stamped, walk through the gate into the DR.

Immigration is on the right, in an office under the imposing archway. You'll be asked your destination in the DR and charged an entry tax of US$5. Dajabón town starts immediately after the gates – the street leads towards the Parque Central, around which you can find several places to get food, as well as a couple of ATMs if you'd like to buy any Dominican pesos at the border. Continue five blocks from the border to reach the bus station (*estación de autobuses*), from where you can get buses to Santiago and Santo Domingo, or to Monte Christi for connections to the northern coast.

The process is much the same coming in the other direction – there's another US$10 departure tax on the Dajabón side. The Haitian authorities charge just a dollar for the privilege of entering the country.

It should be pointed out given the nature of the border, there are plenty of people who charge a small fee to simply carry you across the river, bypassing immigration completely. When I made an afternoon trip to Dajabón for the book, the Dominican border guards even joked as to why I'd bothered with the rigmarole of getting stamped in and out!

The border is open from 08.00 to 18.00. Note that if you have a vehicle with Haitian plates, it needs special permission to cross the border. **Caribe Tours** (*Rue 24B, Cap-Haïtien; 2260 1258/3614 0264*) also operate direct buses from Cap-Haïtien to Santiago (six hours, 1,000HTG (US$25) plus border fees), and Santo Domingo (11 hours, 1,200HTG; fares include all border fees).

two new towers added to its front in late 2011). The road splits at Place Capois in front of the Hotel de Ville – turn left for a small **Marché de Fer** (Iron Market; *Rue la Fôret*). To the right, the road leads to the outskirts of Quartier Baudin, where the two main hotels are, a ten-minute drive from the centre.

The open-air market along Rue du Quai is an interesting place to walk through, as far as the wharf. It's a bustling and fascinating place, full of sailing boats to Île de la Tortue – lovely tall-masted wooden ships – although given that the port is such a large centre for smuggling, asking too many probing questions and getting your camera out won't make you hugely popular.

A few kilometres south of Port-de-Paix (off Route National 5), a road climbs into the mountains at **Croix St Joseph**. Here you can find the remains of **Fort des Trois Pavillons**, one of the many built on the orders of Dessalines after independence. The air is cool, and the height affords good views over Port-de-Paix and out to sea.

GETTING THERE AND AWAY

By air There is a daily 40-minute flight to Port-au-Prince with **Tortug'Air** (*office at airport;* ☎ *2812 8000*). The airport is on the western outskirts of the city, near Trois Rivières.

By road Buses and *taptaps* leave for Gonaïves (six hours) via Gros Morne, and on to Port-au-Prince from Rue du Quai, near the attractively domed Église St Louis de Montfort. Taptaps run most days to Môle Saint-Nicholas, and more frequently east to Saint Louis du Nord. This road is particularly bad – it's just about possible to reach Cap-Haïtien, via Le Borgne and cutting through to Limbé, but you need a well-maintained 4x4, a good driver and potentially a couple of spare tyres. If you can do it, it's very beautiful – Chouchou Bay just past Le Borgne is a divine 6km stretch of white sand, sheltered from the waves.

By boat Ferries travel throughout the day to Île de la Tortue for as little as 100HTG, landing at the port-village of Basse-Terre.

WHERE TO STAY AND EAT

Breeze Marina Star Hotel Route St Louis du Nord, Quartier Baudin; ☎ 3732 3185/3892 0610; e breezemarinahotel@yahoo.fr; www.breezemarinastarhotel.com. Huge white blocky hotel, with improbably large 5-storey annexe at the rear. Average rooms for the price, & strangely laid-out, with many locked entrance gates & a walk through the car park from reception to the restaurant, despite being next to each other. Empty pool, but views to Île de la Tortue. **$$**

Lorina Hotel Route St Louis du Nord, Quartier Baudin; ☎ 3749 4528/3747 8444. New hotel with standard but comfy rooms, some with overly chintzy decoration. Friendly staff. Despite being next to the sea, rooms face inward to the courtyard (avoid those near the generator). Restaurant, Wi-Fi. **$$**

Kaf Hotel 277 Rue Estimé; ☎ 3747 4738/3711 2232. A reasonable budget option in the centre of town, well located for bar-restos & the like. Averagely clean rooms. **$**

There are several bar-restos along Rue Estimé, and Rue Benito Sylvain on leaving the main square – you'll also find the reasonably stocked NY Supermarket here.

ÎLE DE LA TORTUE

Named Tortuga by Christopher Columbus after its supposed turtle-like shape, Île de la Tortue is Haiti's second-largest island, stretching out along the coast opposite Port-de-Paix. It's dry and mountainous with only a few roads and settlements. The main town is Palmiste, a short ride from Basse-Terre, where boats leave for Port-de-Paix. There are no hotels.

If Île de la Tortue is little visited, the main reason is that the island is a smuggling point between the mainland and Miami. In this respect, islanders are simply carrying on the traditions of their 17th-century forebears, when the island was a hotbed of Caribbean piracy. Even today, it can be best to visit with a local guide – not that it's necessarily dangerous, but that people can be suspicious of foreigners here. In many ways, the short voyage by wooden sailing ship from Port-de-Paix is the most enjoyable aspect of a trip, and if you can haggle a decent price, a day's hire could be great fun.

From time to time, Île de la Tortue gets touted as the next big thing in Haitian tourism, although it continues to resist any development plans. Pointe Ouest, on the tip of the island, was once touted by *Condé Nast Traveler* as one of the ten best beaches in the Caribbean. Whether that's true or not, its creamy sand, turquoise sea and total isolation are certainly fabulous. You'll need your own boat to get there however.

MÔLE SAINT-NICHOLAS

Getting to Môle Saint-Nicholas can feel like getting to the end of Haiti. Unless you're flying in on a private plane, you'll have endured some of the bumpiest roads in the country and its most arid landscapes, seemingly populated by little more than cactus, agave and a few scrubby trees. It's ironic, because in some ways, the town could be called the start of Haiti: it was here, on 6 December 1492, that Christopher Columbus first made landfall in the country.

Môle Saint-Nicholas sits in a large bay enclosed by a narrow peninsula. The land is particularly rocky and barren and littered with fossils – this part of Haiti was formed by marine uplift of ancient coral terraces, and there are hundreds of caves between here and Jean Rabel that are only now beginning to be surveyed by speleologists. There's little agriculture here, and for those not involved in fishing, charcoal production and export to the capital is an economic mainstay.

For a town so far out of the way, Môle Saint-Nicholas punches well above its weight in terms of reasons to visit. It has a fabulous beach that offers great snorkelling, and its past has bequeathed it a good selection of colonial forts. The whole coast is riddled with caves that have yet to be surveyed. If you had your own mountain bike, trails abound. But better yet, the municipality seem to be trying very hard to develop tourism in the area, and produces a good map for visitors, a list of local guides and even information boards at the different historical sites. If Môle Saint-Nicholas were a couple of hours' drive from Port-au-Prince, it would be a popular weekend destination. As it is, those making it here can get a real sense of discovering an unknown corner of the country.

HISTORY Columbus spotted the large bay 'of beauty and graciousness' on the feast of St Nicholas, immediately coming up with its name. He noted the hard, rocky landscape, but failing to find any Indians to make contact with, he continued eastwards. The real significance of Môle Saint-Nicholas was less its surroundings than its location at the entrance of the Windward Passage to Cuba and Jamaica. Within a century, it was being used by French and British pirates to harass the Spanish. The French themselves failed to successfully colonise Môle Saint-Nicholas, but in the 18th century their fear of the British navy prompted them to heavily fortify the bay. This didn't stop the British capturing it in 1793 and using it as a beach-head for their invasion of Saint-Domingue. They managed to hold it for five years, safe in the captured forts but unable to do much else, before surrendering to Toussaint Louverture in 1798.

Môle Saint-Nicholas has always been a remote spot from Port-au-Prince. Several times from the mid 19th century onwards Haiti has tried to take advantage of its strategic location as the 'Gibraltar of the Caribbean', and offload it to foreign powers as a naval base. During the civil war of the 1860s, different factions offered it to the French and British in return for their support, while 30 years later American warships appeared at the Môle in a hard-handed attempt at negotiations. By the time Haiti made a serious offer to the USA during World War II, the Americans turned it down, having decided they preferred Guantánamo Bay instead. The US Coast Guard does still maintain an interest, and flies helicopter patrols here, as the region is a popular embarkation point for over-loaded vessels smuggling people to the States.

GETTING THERE AND AWAY

By air There's an airstrip on the eastern outskirts of town. **MAF** (e *flyhaiti@maf.org; www.mafhaiti.org*) offer a charter flight in a six-seater Cessna from Port-au-Prince, costing around US$600 one-way.

By road Môle Saint-Nicholas is linked by road to Port-de-Paix. *Taptaps* run early in the morning most days, so it's essential to check times well in advance of travelling. The journey takes around five hours, and the road is hard. During the rainy season,

THE REAL PIRATES OF THE CARIBBEAN

It took a century from Christopher Columbus naming Tortuga for the Spanish to make a go of colonising the island, but their attempts at tobacco and sugar cultivation never really took off. The island was too dry and rocky for sustained agriculture. In 1605, French settlers appeared on the scene, chased off the Spanish planters, and decided to make a living from hunting the cattle and boar that were now running free on the island. They sold hides and meat to passing traders, and with each sale they passed new words into English: the meat was dried over a low fire that the Taíno had called a *barbecu*. The Taíno called the process *boucaoui*; those who sold the dried meat were dubbed *boucaniers* – subsequently anglicised to buccaneers.

Trading was slow work with little reward. In the late 1620s, an enterprising French captain called Pierre le Grande decided that marauding against the Spanish was a better get-rich-quick scheme. On sighting a flagging Spanish treasure galleon, he motivated his crew by cutting holes in the bottom of his own ship. In what would later become true pirate fashion, they drew alongside, swarmed up the rigging and surprised the captain, who was in his cabin playing cards. Le Grande's outrageous success prompted a literal gold-rush among the buccaneers of Tortuga, who spent the next decade happily sallying forth to attack whatever ships were foolish enough to sail too close to the island.

The Spanish weren't too keen on such piracy on their doorstep, and repeatedly sent ships to sack Tortuga, but the buccaneers would simply melt into the hills and return when the coast was clear. By 1640, they were calling themselves the 'Brothers of the Coast', and operated a piratical quasi-democracy, with strict rules about which ships could be attacked and when. There was an insurance scheme, paying out in the case of the loss of a leg or eye. Many pirates even entered informal same-sex marriages with each other, a practice known as *matelotage*.

Môle can be cut off altogether, as the road fords the swollen waters of Trois Rivières outside Port-de-Paix. A bridge is currently under construction, which should allow year-round access when it is operational. If you have your own vehicle, there is a nice pebble beach at Bord de Mer de Jean Rabel, roughly halfway to Port-de-Paix. After this, the frequently dramatic coast road switches inland and becomes greener and more mountainous, before descending again to Port-de-Paix.

TOURIST INFORMATION Local guides have formed the Association des Guides Touristiques du Bas Nord Ouest to offer services. Try Jean Rinel (*3680 4471*) for historic or boat trips, or Pinchinat (*3606 2673*) for caves and 'back-country' Vodou sites.

WHERE TO STAY AND EAT

Boukan Guingette Rue de la Plage Raisinier; 3845 2874; www.boukanguinguette.com. A picture-perfect Caribbean beach-bar & campsite, next to Batterie de Vallière. Facilities are simple – tents with bedding or bring your own; a small number of bungalows are also planned. Hosts are full of local knowledge & there's snorkelling gear to hire. The restaurant is excellent, but order well in advance if you don't want seafood (a pizza oven is periodically fired up). **$**

Hotel Beau Rivage Rue de Cimetière; 3774 0825; e djoel@att.net. This new beachfront hotel wasn't quite open at the time of research, but looked an impressive construction opening straight onto the sand.

The French authorities formalised things even further by sending a governor to fortify the island and increase raiding against the Spanish.

Tortuga's most infamous pirate was François L'Ollonais, who had originally arrived in the Caribbean as an indentured servant and had a terrible reputation for violence and torture. He led an expedition against Spanish Venezuela and held entire cities to ransom. Hundreds were killed in his raids. But pirates never managed to stay rich for long. According to one contemporary account, once back in Tortuga with their spoils, 'the tavern keepers got part of their money, and the whores took the rest.' L'Ollonais finally came to a sticky end on the coast of Panama, when his ship ran aground and he was captured and eaten by a local tribe.

The pirate colony's days were also numbered. By the 1660s, the Spanish had stopped trying to capture Tortuga, and French settlement on the mainland was encouraged. The governor Bertrand Ogeron didn't try to rein in the pirates forcefully, but took the more subtle approach of importing prostitutes from Paris, who were apparently encouraged to emigrate by the promise of respectable overseas marriages. By simultaneously trebling the number of settlers, Ogeron tamed the colony by demographics. In 1670, the Welsh pirate captain Henry Morgan stopped briefly at Tortuga and shipped out most of the remaining buccaneers. Piracy moved south to Petit Goâve and Île-à-Vache.

When Ogeron encouraged the founding of Cap Français (modern Cap-Haïtien) in the same year, Saint-Domingue's future as an exporting colony was assured. Tortuga – now Île de la Tortue – slipped into obscurity. It re-entered the popular imagination in the early 20th century with the pirate-romance novels of Rafael Sabatini, most famously adapted in the Hollywood swashbucklers *Captain Blood* and *The Sea Hawk*, starring Errol Flynn. More recently, it has taken a starring role in the *Pirates of the Caribbean* films. None of the movies was filmed on location in Haiti.

BACKROADS TO MÔLE SAINT-NICHOLAS

The main ways of getting to Môle Saint-Nicholas are either by road from Port-de-Paix or flying in on a chartered plane, but a third and distinctly more rugged option exists – cutting directly across the northwest peninsula from Gonaïves. With a good 4x4 you can do this in a day, allowing plenty of time for puncture-repair stops en route.

In Gonaïves, turn off Route National 1 onto Route de Bienac at Place Carrefour Turene (near the BS Resto and Gonaibo Supermarket). The road becomes a dusty gravel piste almost immediately, and climbs into the hills above town, but always hugging the coast as you head west. As you proceed, the landscape becomes increasingly dry with bare limestone dotted about with thorny scrub and cactus. Yet wherever there's water there's life – secluded valleys occasionally burst into green, with villages surrounded by plantains and fruit trees.

After a couple of hours, you're back down on the parched coast and at the town of **Anse Rouge**, the only place of any size on this route. There are small fishing boats on the beach, and a tiny market, but not much else – the two largest buildings are a grand church in dressed stone, and a nightclub on a promontory overlooking the sea, where you can get a beer.

Anse Rouge suffers frequent water shortages, and with little opportunity for agriculture, one of the town's traditional industries is salt production. There are large evaporation ponds on the outskirts of town. Salt is women's business here, and the local NGO Article 29 (*www.article29organization.org*) works in the commune on capacity-building and improving economic opportunities.

Soon after Anse Rouge, the road splits, presenting you with two choices. In the dry season you can head inland and through the mountains towards Mare Rouge. During the rainy season, this road becomes difficult, so you should instead opt for the rockier road via Bombardopolis.

Heading towards Mare Rouge, the road rises to a high plain. The views are frequently stunning, particularly when the many agave plants are in flower, sending up tall flower spikes topped with bright orange pom-poms. The landscape greens considerably in the Petite-Rivière area, as you climb towards Mare Rouge, which feels positively lush. From Mare Rouge, turn at the *commissariat* to start the descent to Môle.

The alternative road hugs the coast from Anse Rouge through Petit-Anse until you hit the small fishing village of Baie de Henne. There are some beautiful, virtually unvisited beaches en route, and a piste of decent quality. After leaving Baie de Henne, the road follows a green river valley up and inland before turning west again until it reaches the farming town of **Bombardopolis**. This is the toughest section of the road, with plenty of steep rocky switchbacks. The town's unusual name dates from its settlement by Germans in 1765, sent there by the French. It was originally simply called Bombarde, but the Greek suffix was added by their colonial administrator as a classical affectation.The town is famous for its *fête patronale*, held every 4 October in honour of St Francis. The festivities also attract many Vodou worshippers.

From Bombardopolis, the road leads north over Morne Blanc before descending to Môle Saint-Nicholas, about an hour away.

There are a couple of bar-restos in Môle proper – by far the best is **Lauriers Flamme Cache** (*Rue Henri Christophe;* ☎ *3883 0920/3168 3146*), which has great seafood and exemplary, friendly service. Another option is **Chez Milot** (*Av de la Liberté*).

WHAT TO SEE AND DO Easily the most photogenic attraction in Môle Saint-Nicholas is **Plage Raisinier**, a stretch of palm-fringed sugary sand on the western outskirts of town. It's gratifying to see signs (and bins) encouraging the community to keep the beach rubbish-free, exhortations that actually seem to work. There is plenty of coral close to shore – the lack of soil run-off associated with agricultural clearance means that it is relatively pristine, with plenty of interesting fish life. There's a small wreck that's worth looking at if you have a mask and fins.

The French built a series of forts to protect the entrance to Môle Saint-Nicholas, giving defenders a continuous field of fire against potential attackers. Collectively they were designated national monuments in 1995, and the local authorities have worked hard to erect information boards at each site.

The largest fort built by the French in Môle Saint-Nicholas is the **Batterie de Vallière**, just past the cemetery. Its imposing gate is the emblematic symbol of the town, while the fort takes its name from the colonial governor at the time. The walls stretch an impressive 196m along the coast, its length demanded to cover any possible landing sites for invaders along the beach. The fort consists of two platforms (now partly overgrown), pierced with loopholes for muskets and cannon embrasures. The large courtyard contains the remains of a couple of buildings, although part of it is currently fenced off and appears to be being used to keep goats. Only one cannon remains – an abandoned barrel on the lower platform. The rest of the cannons were taken by Christophe during the building of the Citadelle.

Nearly an hour's walk west of the Batterie de Vallière is **Batterie de Grasse** (Grace). The path is reasonably well broken but splits confusingly at the information board, which is bizarrely placed at the start of the walk rather than next to the fort. Take the right-hand fork closer to the sea. The fort has thick parapet walls, and the outlines of several gun emplacements are laid on a finely dressed pavement. A few unexpected original features remain, including traces of the terracotta roof tiles and broken bottles cemented into the back walls to deter entry: a practice still common in Haitian construction. The views from the fort back to the town and beach are superb and well worth the walk.

The **Batterie d'Orléans**, better known locally as Fort George, hugs the coastline at the northern tip of the town, next to the river. When Haiti split in two soon after independence, Môle Saint-Nicholas was a republican stronghold that withheld a three-year siege by the newly crowned King Christophe. Its current smashed-up appearance dates from this time. At the end of the siege, Christophe saluted the bravery of his foes, before sending the heart of the slain General Lamarre to President Pétion as a victory token.

Uphill from the harbour on the eastern edge of town is **Le Vieux-Quartier**, with its thick-walled bastions and single forlorn cannon barrel. The fort is in bad condition, but worth clambering onto the ramparts to give an idea of how it once looked. Behind the fort, houses now stand where the soldiers' quarters would have been, but the finely dressed entrance portals still (just) remain.

If you continue through the old gates, you soon come to **La Poudrière** – the powder store or magazine that was built to serve the entire garrison. It's an impressive structure, over 25m long, with a pointed roof and thick walls supporting an internal barrel roof. The musket loopholes were added by the British, who used the building as a barracks. The enclosing wall was added soon after independence.

The interior is much graffitied, but the building actually remains in occasional use by locals, as a site for both Christian and Vodou services.

A stiff couple of hours' walk on a rough trail from the town centre are the overgrown remains of **Batterie du Morne-à-Cabris**. The fort is thought to have been built by Christophe when he was laying siege to Môle Saint-Nicholas. The battery itself is nothing special, but the hike is enjoyable. It sits 180m above sea level, and has commanding views of both the bay and roads approaching the town. On particularly clear days, locals claim that the tip of Cuba, 85km distant, can even be seen. To get here, leave town on Avenue de la Liberté, just before Le Vieux-Quartier. The route is hard to find, so be prepared to ask for guidance. Of similar nature, although closer to town and not offering quite such extravagant views, is the small **Batterie du Ralliement**.

7

The Artibonite Valley and Central Plateau

Central Haiti is the least-visited part of the country. While it's common for people to zip through the cities of Gonaïves and Saint-Marc, the rest of it is largely rural and quite some degree removed from metropolitan concerns. But if you've got the time to change down a few gears, it's a fascinating place to explore.

Tracking up the coast from Port-au-Prince, the landscape is relentlessly arid until you reach the broad sweep of the Artibonite Valley. Criss-crossed with irrigation canals, it's Haiti's breadbasket. As you explore inland, the region's historical importance reveals itself, with old forts amid the farming landscape from Marchand Dessalines to Petite Rivière de l'Artibonite. The Artibonite River climbs into the mountains until it reaches the Central Plateau, the most sparsely populated part of Haiti. Natural wonders are more the order of the day here, with the sacred waterfalls of Saut d'Eau and the no less spectacular Bassin Zim. The landscape is full of potential for hikes as well as cave exploration – there are many sites where the original Taíno inhabitants left their mark with mysterious petroglyphs.

GONAÏVES

Gonaïves is proud to be Haiti's City of Independence – it was here on New Year's Day 1804 that Dessalines, Christophe and Pétion signed the declaration that gave birth to the world's first black republic. It was an appropriate location since it was here that Toussaint Louverture was arrested and sent to die in exile, while the old Taíno name *Ayiti* was resurrected in a town that itself took its title from the region's original inhabitants, the Gonaibo. The town played a further part in advancing the cause of Haiti's people in 1985, when it was the epicentre for the protests that eventually brought down the rule of Jean-Claude Duvalier. It was also the capture of Gonaïves by rebels in 2004 that brought into play the end-game for President Aristide's second term as president.

It has to be said that modern Gonaïves isn't a particularly pretty place. It's flat, low-lying and dusty, surrounded by barren hills. This setting paid out an exacting toll on the city in 2008, when it was hit by the full force of Hurricane Hanna. Through a combination of high waves and torrential water run-off from the hills, Gonaïves was submerged almost completely by mud. Around 450 people lost their lives, a disaster that has taken the city a long time to recover from.

Gonaïves's main sight is **Place de l'Indépendence**. At its centre is a giant **monument to Dessalines**, standing on the prow of a ship raising the Haitian flag aloft. On either side he is flanked by the soldiers and free slaves he has led to freedom. Behind the monument is the striking triangle-shaped **cathedral**, looking like a gleaming white tent. On the other side of the square, two simple pavilions are decorated with murals of Haitian heroes from independence onwards. There's a

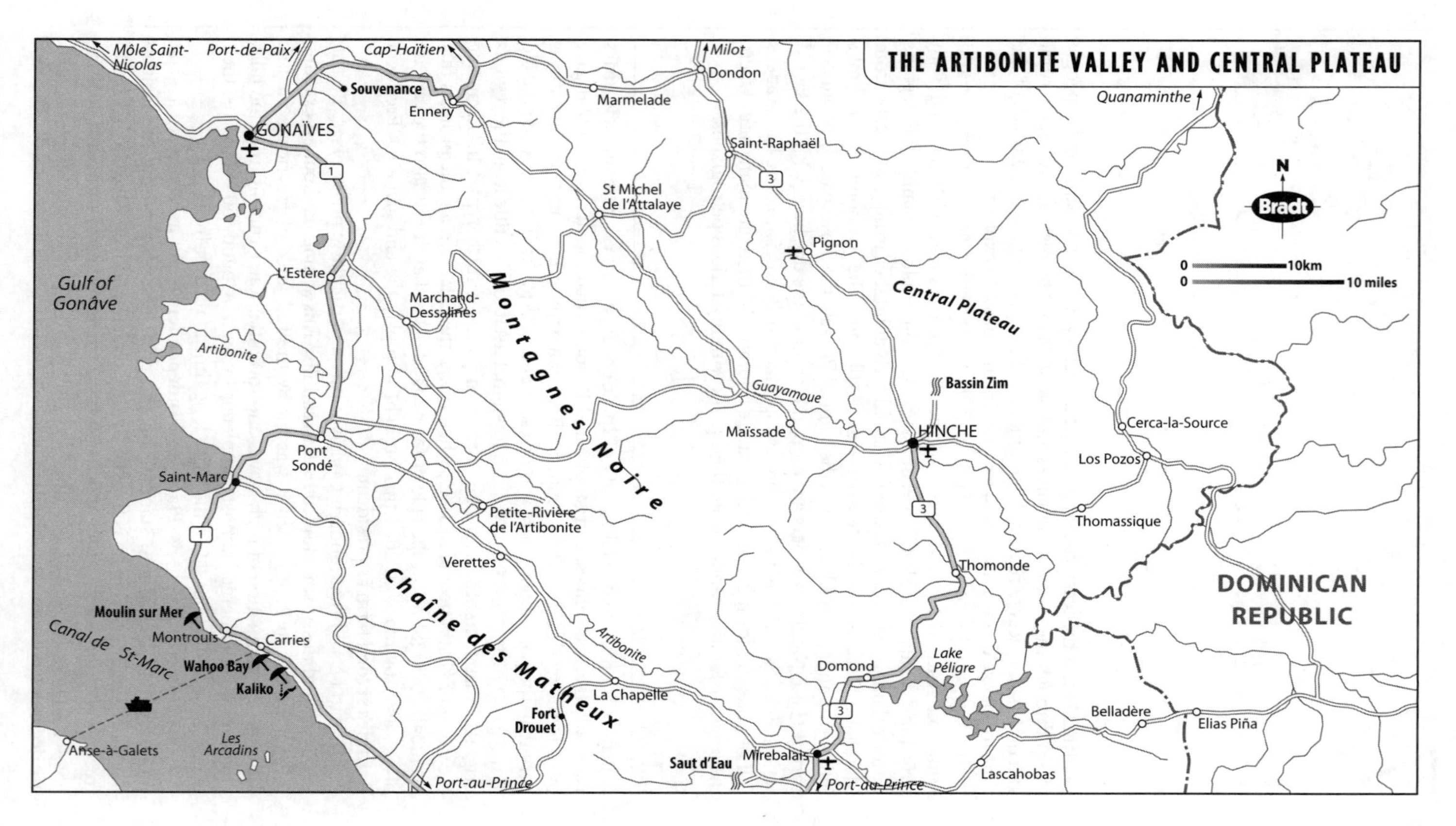
THE ARTIBONITE VALLEY AND CENTRAL PLATEAU
N
Bradt
0 10km
0 10 miles
Môle Saint-Nicolas
Port-de-Paix
Cap-Haïtien
Milot
Dondon
Souvenance
Ennery
Marmelade
Quanaminthe
GONAÏVES
1
Saint-Raphaël
3
St Michel de l'Attalaye
Pignon
L'Estère
Gulf of Gonâve
Marchand-Dessalines
Montagnes Noire
Central Plateau
Artibonite
Guayamoue
Bassin Zim
Maïssade
HINCHE
Cerca-la-Source
Los Pozos
Pont Sondé
Saint-Marc
Petite-Rivière de l'Artibonite
Thomassique
Verettes
Thomonde
Chaîne des Matheux
DOMINICAN REPUBLIC
Moulin sur Mer
Montrouis
Carries
Canal de St-Marc
Wahoo Bay
Kaliko
Artibonite
Domond
Lake Péligre
La Chapelle
Fort Drouet
Belladère
Elias Piña
Anse-à-Galets
Les Arcadins
Saut d'Eau
Mirebalais
Lascahobas
Port-au-Prince
Port-au-Prince

memorial plaque with part of the act of independence on Rue Louverture, which also has some fine old brick buildings from the late 19th and early 20th centuries.

A block behind the cathedral is the large concrete **Marché Communale**, with its stalls spilling out into the road, after which the streets get busier and more packed until you reach the dock. It's organised chaos here, with stalls selling everything from live crabs and smoked fish to cassava bread and cheap Chinese goods, with plenty of scrawny dogs and contented-looking pigs underfoot. Near the entrance to the wharf, there's a monument to **Admiral Killick**, who famously blew up his flagship (and himself) rather than surrender to a German blockade in 1902 (for further details, see box, *The sinking of Haiti's navy*, page 15).

GETTING THERE AND AWAY Gonaïves is the capital of Artibonite, and an important junction. Road transport departs from a station in Bigot, on the outskirts of Gonaïves on the Port-au-Prince side of the city. By *taptap*, the capital is just under three hours away, Saint-Marc just over an hour. You can also find transport north to Cap-Haïtien and Port-de-Paix (via Gros Morne) here. Note that if you're heading north, the smooth tarmac gives out soon after leaving Gonaïves – becoming heavily pot-holed towards Cap-Haïtien or reverting to piste en route to Port-de-Paix. There's also a rough road to Môle Saint-Nicholas – for more information on this route, see box, *Backroads to Môle Saint-Nicholas*, page 204.

WHERE TO STAY

Moderate

Complexe le Domaine 156 Av des Dattes; 3644 1790/3445 6598; e jeanosnel@yahoo.fr. This fancy-looking hotel was still under construction when I visited – open mainly for wedding parties – but looked a potentially good option if & when it finishes. **$$$**

Budget

Herberson Paradis Hotel Detour Laborde, Av des Dattes; 2515 6893/3924 5975. Set back but visible from the main road, this is a reliably good modern hotel, with decent if unexciting rooms & attached restaurant with good food. Wi-Fi. **$$**

New Star Hotel 3 Ruelle Belle Ville, Av des Dattes; 3466 4262/3799 2844; www.newstarhotelgonaives.com. Find spacious rooms with fridge & couch here, & breakfast brought to your room. Also popular for weddings, so check for late weekend parties. Signed off the main road. Wi-Fi. **$$**

Polo Hotel 482 Bigot, Route National 1; 3649 3393. Red-&-white hotel on the southern limits of Gonaïves near the transport station. Good-quality rooms, restaurant on site. Wi-Fi. **$$**

Union des Frères Hotel 21 Gatreau, Route Nationale 1; 2941 5056/3803 4614; e solene101@yahoo.fr. Reasonable accommodation on the north side of town, some rooms a bit tatty but basically unexcitingly sound. **$$**

Shoestring

Romy Family Hotel 28 Detour Laborde, Av des Dattes; 3745 8194. A pretty basic cheapie – decent value & clean for the price, but absolutely no frills. Handy restaurant below. **$**

WHERE TO EAT

Mid range

BS Resto Gatereau 3, Route National 1; 10.00–22.00 daily. Cheery yellow restaurant above the handy Gonaibo Supermarket. Good & generous servings of Haitian food in clean café surroundings. **$$$**

Carlomina Av Admiral Killick:; 11.00–22.00 daily. Mint-green dining salon serving all things Haitian. Lifeless during the day; come in the evenings. **$$$**

Cheap and cheerful

Reference 2000 Rue Christophe; 10.00–21.00 daily. Bright & clean diner-style restaurant, with chilly AC. Sandwiches, Creole dishes, some pasta & pizza, plus excellent fruit juices. **$$**

Saveur Tropicales 117 Av des Dattes; 11.00–23.00 daily. Small fast-food place, with fried chicken, burgers & ice cream. **$$**

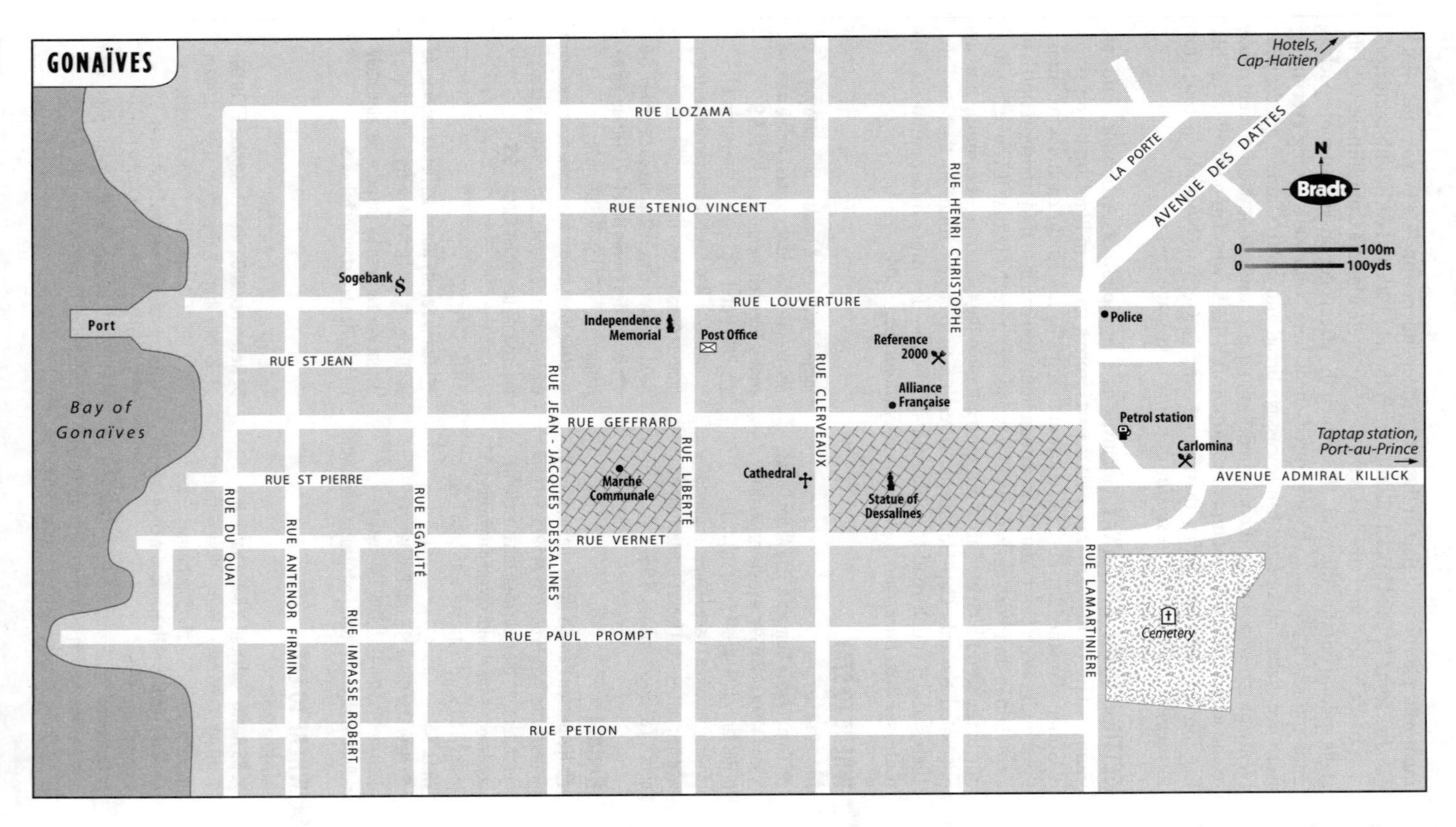
GONAÏVES
Hotels, Cap-Haïtien
RUE LOZAMA
LA PORTE
AVENUE DES DATTES
N
Bradt
0 100m
0 100yds
RUE STENIO VINCENT
Sogebank
RUE LOUVERTURE
Port
Independence Memorial
Post Office
Police
Reference 2000
RUE HENRI CHRISTOPHE
RUE ST JEAN
Alliance Française
Bay of Gonaïves
RUE GEFFRARD
Petrol station
Taptap station, Port-au-Prince
Carlomina
RUE ST PIERRE
Marché Communale
Cathedral
RUE CLERVEAUX
Statue of Dessalines
AVENUE ADMIRAL KILLICK
RUE JEAN - JACQUES DESSALINES
RUE LIBERTÉ
RUE VERNET
RUE DU QUAI
RUE ANTENOR FIRMIN
RUE EGALITÉ
RUE LAMARTINIÈRE
Cemetery
RUE PAUL PROMPT
RUE IMPASSE ROBERT
RUE PETION

OTHER PRACTICALITIES There was no ATM in Gonaïves at the time of research, but **Sogebank** (*corner of rues Louverture & Egalité*) is likely to get one in the near future. Opposite the cathedral, the **Alliance Française** (*Pl de la Cathédrale; ☎ 2943 4815; e alliancefr1_gonaives@yahoo.fr; www.alliancefrancaisedesgonaives.com*) has a pretty lively programme of arts events.

SAINT-MARC

The port of Saint-Marc is the main town of the Artibonite Valley. Although the town itself is bounded by dry hills, it sits on the edge of a green and fertile plain, which stretches inland to the Chaîne des Matheux and Montagnes Noires mountain ranges – a landscape crossed by irrigation canals and fields of rice.

Saint-Marc itself is a trading town, and still has an important port bringing in goods from Miami. In 1779, the port was the embarkation point for one of Saint-Marc's most celebrated moments, when a regiment of 500 free men of colour set sail to America to fight in the revolutionary war against the British. They saw action at the six-week Battle of Savannah in Georgia, where they distinguished themselves with great bravery.

Although there's no compelling reason to stop in Saint-Marc, it's an interesting town to base yourself in to explore the historical sites of the Artibonite Valley. The

THE *KHIAN SEA* INCIDENT

The 2008 floods were far from the first environmental disaster to hit Gonaïves. Twenty years earlier it was the site of illegal toxic waste dumping, in a case so notorious it helped prompt a change in international law.

In 1986 the city of Philadelphia was having problems disposing of its rubbish. With its landfill sites full it hit upon the idea of burning its waste and shipping it overseas. A barge named the *Khian Sea* was contracted to take 15,000 tonnes of ash to the Bahamas but on arrival, the Bahamian government pronounced the waste toxic and refused to accept it. Six further Caribbean countries refused to allow the ship to dump its waste before the *Khian Sea* arrived in Haiti. Port officials were persuaded to take possession after being told the cargo was actually topsoil fertiliser rather than toxic ash, and over 4,000 tonnes were dumped on a beach on the edge of Gonaïves before the Haitian government got wise. The captain was ordered to remove the waste, but fled the scene instead. The *Khian Sea* spent the next two years being refused harbour in African and southeast Asian ports, before arriving empty in Singapore – the remaining 10,000 tonnes of waste having been finally been dumped at sea.

Two executives of the shipping company were jailed, but Gonaïves remained saddled with the ash, which locals complained was affecting their health. In 1996, a deal between the Haitian and US governments agreed that the waste be shipped back to America, but it took until 2000 – 14 years after the dumping – that the ash was removed. It was eventually buried in a landfill just 120 miles from Philadelphia.

The case became a *cause célèbre* for environmental groups and helped lead to the Basel Convention in 1992, an international treaty regulating the export of hazardous waste to the developing world. Signed by 175 countries, Haiti and the United States have yet to ratify it into law.

town has two forts itself: **Fort Blockus** and **Fort Diamant**. Fort Blockus is the more accessible, on a hill in the neighbourhood of Blockus in the east of Saint-Marc. It's sadly dilapidated. Fort Diamant overlooks the north of the town. It's a stiff 20-minute climb from the outskirts, but is worth it for the great views along the coast. Below it is **Plage Grosse Roche**, a small beach area next to Portail Guepes. It's a place for live music in the summer.

The centre of Saint-Marc is Place Philippe Guerrier, named for one of Haiti's short-lived presidents, who served for just 11 months in 1845 (unusually, he died in office of natural causes). Two blocks behind the square is the fine stone **Catholic Cathedral**, reputedly an early-20th-century gift from the Americans during their occupation, in thanks for Saint-Marc's contribution to the Battle of Savannah.

GETTING THERE AND AWAY Route National 1 bisects Saint-Marc. *Taptaps* leave from a confused mess of side-streets a few blocks south of the square, including good new minibuses to Port-au-Prince (125HTG, 90 minutes), which terminate at Carrefour Aviation. There are plenty of motos, in the main pretty weedy scooters – flag down something a bit more powerful if you want to get to Pont Sondé 15 minutes northeast of Saint-Marc, for bikes to Marchand Dessalines or Petite Rivière de l'Artibonite.

SOUVENANCE

The festival of Souvenance, held every Easter, is one of the big events of the Vodou calendar. It celebrates the *lwa* of Dahomey, the ancestral Africa that is the mainspring of Vodou, and takes place just north of Gonaïves. Ogue Ferray is also especially commemorated here.

Souvenance officially begins on the Saturday of the Easter weekend, but events start on Good Friday, when *rara* bands from all over the region converge on the *lakou* for processions and a big party – a loud, raucous affair. Prayers kick off the Vodou side of things on the following day, but the best day for visitors is considered to be Easter Sunday. Vodouisants dressed in white gather, pray in and around the bounds of the peristyle, and bathe in a sacred pool. A bull and several goats are sacrificed. Proceedings start around dawn, pick up pace mid morning and continue late into the night. There are many dance ceremonies, and later in the day the adherents switch into bright clothes to continue the celebrations. All the while, there is the constant thundering of the drums, beating out rhythms from ancestral Dahomey.

On the Monday, the dancing and feeding of the lwa is done in the grove of giant *mapou* trees in the lakou. It's a riotously colourful scene, but after the rituals the procession to take the ceremony back to the peristyle is a sombre affair, representing the middle passage that took the slaves from Africa.

The festival is purposely designed to welcome people into the community – visitors come from across Haiti, and foreigners are happily accepted. To visit, head for Lakou Souvanans, about 30 minutes north of Gonaïves on the road to Cap-Haïtien. If you don't have your own vehicle, grab a moto-taxi or ask a *taptap* to drop you at the turning on Route National 1. The site is a large walled compound about the size of a football field. If you want to stay for the whole event rather than visit for the day, there's simple accommodation on site (*$ for the week*), with basic shared bathroom facilities.

WHERE TO STAY AND EAT

Kiss Inn Hotel 6 Av Gabard, Portail Guèpes; 3794 5271/3879 2491. Just off Route National 1 at the northern end of town. Dependable option with rooms in a variety of sizes, well-turned out for the most part. Restaurant, Wi-Fi. **$$**

Le Gou-T Hotel Portail Guèpes; 3882 0917/2813 8866; info@hotelgou-t.com; www.hotelegou-t.com. Good-value hotel with friendly service. Rooms are sizeable if occasionally spartan (avoid those facing the noisy main road if possible). Tasty food at the informal poolside. Wi-Fi. **$$**

Kay Foun 8 bis, Rue Pivert; open daily. Popular restaurant hangout, with excellent Creole dishes, seafood, burgers, steak & barbecued options. Icy-cold beer, occasional live music & humming atmosphere. **$$$**

Villannemarie 23 Rue Pivert; daily. Open-air bar-resto known for its seafood (the fish bouillon served on Fri is worth detouring for). Opposite Kay Foun. **$$$**

Delimart Route National 1, corner Rue Chavannes. A good supermarket with upstairs eating, the 'Bon Jean' Restaurant. An Epi d'Or franchise, with pizzas, pasta, sandwiches, pastries, crêpes & the like.

Between the main square and the cathedral, **Référence Bar-Resto** (*Rue Armand Thoby*) is a fair option, along with the very simple **La Cayenne** (*Rue Chavanne*), which is good for seafood.

OTHER PRACTICALITIES There's a Sogebank **ATM** on Route National 1 on the corner of Place Philippe Guerrier. Saint-Marc Expo (*23 Rue Pivert; www.saintmarc-expo.com*) is a good artisans' co-operative. As well as many of the traditional handicrafts you see in most places, it sells Carnival-style papier-mâché masks and locally designed clothes. It also hosts occasional cultural events.

MARCHAND DESSALINES

A chain of hilltop forts are just visible from Route National 1 as you travel between Saint-Marc and Gonaïves. These are the guardians of Marchand Dessalines, a small market town sitting amid the well-watered Artibonite Valley. Often overlooked by visitors, it's a piece of the patchwork of Haitian history well worth the diversion.

At independence, Dessalines decided to move the centre of political power away from the seemingly vulnerable ports of Cap-Haïtien and Port-au-Prince, and founded his own capital on this spot, then known as L'Habitation Marchand. He modestly named it Dessalinesville, but it was something of a folly as it was simply too far from the political mainstream to make any lasting impact. It quickly reverted to a quiet backwater after his death.

A smooth asphalt road leads off Route Nationale 1 to Marchand Dessalines just north of L'Estere – also the best place to get a moto-taxi or occasional *taptap*. It's about 20 minutes either way. At Marchand, the good unsealed road continues to St-Michel de l'Attalaye – buses trundle through en route to Port-au-Prince. You can also cut across country to the Artibonite Valley, emerging at Petite Rivière de l'Artibonite.

WHAT TO SEE AND DO Marchand contains a good number of old houses, dating from the revolutionary period. They differ slightly from contemporary rural houses, having verandas running the length of the house, shaded by long stone-tiled roofs. Most famous is the **House of Claire Heureuse**, Dessalines's wife, who was born here. Walk past the town square towards the hills and you'll find it.

If you continue in this direction – the road leading to St-Michel de l'Attalaye – you'll come to the first of the town's six forts. At independence, Dessalines ordered practically the entire country to be fortified, and Marchand has the highest concentration in the country. **Fort La Source** (also called Fort Culbuté) guards the town's water supply. It had a bastion surrounding a courtyard, a separate powder magazine and water channels running through a sizeable pool. It's one of the liveliest historical sites you might visit in Haiti, as the pool (called Bassin Felicité) is a popular spot for doing laundry and swimming. As you explore, watch out for clothes drying on old cannon barrels. The open space outside the magazine is regularly used for Vodou services.

A footpath leads uphill from here to **Fort Decidé**, a 20-minute climb. The fort is a classic military design – square with extending diamond-shaped bastions at each corner. The only entrance is an airlock pierced with defensive loopholes, although to get inside now it's easier to climb through one of the opened window spaces. In the centre is an old water reservoir and powder magazine, as well as stairs down to the collapsed basement of the southwest bastion. The views are gorgeous – over the town and its rice fields, and further up the chain of hills to the other forts.

Next is **Fort Innocent**. There's no proper path to this or the remainder of the forts, so you have to pick your way carefully through the scrub. It's a good hour; if you plan on attempting the whole chain you'll need to be in Marchand with the dawn chorus. The fort is in rough shape, with a polygonal design that's initially hard to get hold of, and the ruins of a central building with thick arcaded walls. It's named for Dessalines's son, Innocent.

Fort Madame is next. It has the largest footprint of the forts, and was big enough to have its own parade ground. **Fort Doko** – the smallest fort but very similar to Fort Decidé – is the next rise, and has a small number of abandoned cannon. Finally, congratulate yourself if you reach the last in the chain. It's a stocky irregular pentagon, with a magazine and the barest traces of the barracks building. The builders obviously relished the joke of its remote location, dubbing it **Fort Fin du Monde**.

PETITE RIVIERE DE L'ARTIBONITE AND DESCHAPELLES

At Pont Sondé, just north of Saint-Marc where Route National 1 crosses the Artibonite River, it's possible to turn off and follow the road up the Artibonite Valley to Mirebalais and the Central Plateau. It's rich farming country, threaded with irrigation canals, electric-green fields of rice and traditional wooden houses.

The road is unpaved but has a pretty good surface. While it's possible to reach Mirebalais in about 90 minutes, there are a couple of towns en route worth diverting for. *Taptaps* run from Saint-Marc and Pont Sondé along this road to Mirebalais.

The first town after leaving Route National 1 is Liancourt. Soon after passing through, take the next major left turn for **Petite Rivière de l'Artibonite** (Petite Rivière for short) on the opposite side of the river. This quiet farming town, with mounds of rice drying in the streets, was the location of one of the most hard-fought battles of the Haitian Revolution, the siege of **Fort Crête-à-Pierrot**, the site of which can be found on a low hill on the outskirts of the town.

The fort, built by the British during their brief occupation of the region, is a long rectangle with extending bastions at each corner. The views south along the Artibonite River and the Chaîne des Matheux Mountains show its strategic importance. There are several cannons scattered about behind the ramparts, and at the centre of the fort, the large square powder magazine – the only remaining original building. Given the gusto with which revolutionary sites in Haiti are expropriated by followers of Vodou, there's also a large cross dedicated to Baron Samedi.

In the centre of town is the **Palais de 365 Portes** (Palace of 365 Doors), the southernmost monument to Henri Christophe's rule, built in 1816. Despite the hyperbolic name, don't expect another version of Sans Souci – this is a much more modest affair, a low one-storey building that looks more like a warehouse than a palace. It was restored in the 1930s but is currently in a poor state of affairs.

The next major town is **Deschapelles**, which is home to the renowned **Albert Schweitzer Hospital** (*www.hashaiti.org*). Established in 1956 by Larry and Gwen Mellon, it serves nearly 350,000 people in the Artibonite Valley. Near the hospital is an interesting crafts shop, **Galerie d'Art Deschapelles** (*3782 2075; 08.00–17.00, but call ahead*). It offers something different from the standard handicrafts, including local pottery and home-spun cotton – cultivation of which is an income-generating project originally set up by the Mellons.

There's a new guesthouse in town, **Kay Ayiti** (*3709 0327; e luquecebelizaire@aol.com;* **$$**), with nice en-suite rooms, good electricity and a garden with pavilion. Meals are available on request. It makes Deschapelles a potentially good place to base yourself – there's a good hike along the irrigation canals to Petite Rivière, as well as the **Cascade Fondeau** waterfall in the hills above town.

MIREBALAIS

After Hinche, Mirebalais is the Central Plateau's second town. It's an important junction, linking the plateau with Port-au-Prince as well as the Artibonite Valley. Since the inauguration of the newly resurfaced Route National 3, it's little more than an hour from the capital.

The plateau consists of mountains interspersed with high grassy plains. There are relatively few trees, although the palmiste palm is common, and houses in rural villages split its logs for planking – look out for the grain stores raised on stilts that are common in the area. There's plenty of quarrying too, and the landscape en route from Port-au-Prince has plenty of big creamy chunks bitten out of it – the clearly visible balding layer of earth and grass shows exactly what Haiti is made of, and how exposed the landscape is once cleared of trees.

The main draw to Mirebalais for visitors is the nearby waterfalls of **Saut d'Eau**, a major centre of pilgrimage for Catholics and Vodouisants alike.

Mirebalais is home to an impressive new hospital built and run by the pioneering medical NGO **Partners In Health** (*www.pih.org*), in conjunction with the Ministry of Health. Many years in the making, following the 2010 earthquake it was redesigned to also serve as a teaching hospital – a deliberate move to decentralise from Port-au-Prince. The hospital opened in 2012, and is the largest in the region. It's on the western outskirts of Mirebalais, on the road to Verettes.

Half an hour north of Mirebalais is **Lac Peligré**, the artificial lake created in the late 1950s by the construction of the hydro-electric Peligré Dam across the Artibonite River. The highway skirts high above it, giving pretty views across its mountainous shores; if you have your own vehicle it's worth making the short detour to the dam itself.

GETTING THERE AND AWAY Route National 3 bypasses the eastern edge of Mirebalais. You enter via one of two traffic circles – from Port-au-Prince onto Boulevard Jean-Jacques Dessalines in the south, or from Hinche onto Rue Claire Heureuse. Both roads converge on the main square; Rue Claire Heureuse then continues west towards Verettes and the Artibonite Valley. *Taptaps* to Port-au-Prince and Hinche congregate at the two roundabouts, as do moto-taxis. There's

THE SIEGE OF CRETE-À-PIERROT

In March 1802, the small fort of Crête-à-Pierrot was identified by Toussaint Louverture as a place where the tide of the war might be swung. He put Dessalines in charge of a garrison there to entice a French attack, drawing their forces away from Port-au-Prince. If successful, the French would be pulled north into a running guerrilla campaign. For their part, the French general Lacroix thought that a crushing victory here might nip the rebellion in the bud once and for all.

The initial French attacks didn't go quite to plan. They were lured into trenches surrounding the fort and subjected to a withering fire. Dessalines inspired his troops through the risky laying of a gunpowder trail around the main gate, threatening to blow up the fort himself if his men did not defend it.

The French threw numbers of soldiers at the fort, but were always beaten back, and even retreated at one point. When they returned with reinforcements and artillery, Dessalines had already slipped out of the fort to try to raise local levies against the French. Instructing the remaining garrison, he promised for the first time that the war would end with an independent nation, free of whites.

The French army, now 12,000 strong, bombarded Crête-à-Pierrot but never broke through. After nearly three weeks the defenders ran out of food and water. Incredibly, the remaining troops managed to fight their way out and break through the French lines to rejoin Dessalines in the mountains. When the French finally entered the fort, they found only a few white prisoners remaining, all for the cost of 1,500 dead.

also a good (unpaved) road east through Lascahobas and Belladère, the border town with the Dominican Republic.

SAUT D'EAU The sacred waterfalls at Saut d'Eau sit above the village of Ville-Bonheur, half an hour west of Mirebalais on the road through the Artibonite Valley. While beautiful at any time of year, every 16 July they become the focus for an important Catholic and Vodou pilgrimage.

The falls are set in a lush grove and topple 30m to the rocks and pools below, their spray sending up rainbows in the sunshine. They were created by the diversion of a local river by the great earthquake of 1842, and a local guide told me that they split again after the 2010 earthquake. Immediately after their creation, they became associated with the Vodou *lwa* Damballah (the snake) and his wife Ayido Weda (the rainbow). A third strand to the devotions was added in 1847, when the splendidly named Fortune Morose had a vision here of the Virgin Mary, who left her image in a palm leaf. The site was made famous by the emperor Faustin Soulouque, who visited the site and ordered a church to be erected here, dedicated to Our Lady of Mount Carmel (in the Vodou pantheon, associated with Ezili Danto). It's her *fête patronale* every 16 July that draws thousands of visitors.

The pilgrimage is a perfect example of the syncretic nature of Haitian religious life. In Ville-Bonheur there is a Mass, and the church's statue of the Virgin is paraded around town; while at the falls there are Vodou baptisms and ceremonies. It's a quite incredible scene of communal bathing, *rara* bands and prayer, as people gather in their devotions. Ville-Bonheur throngs with people, who happily attend both religious gatherings.

Entrance to the site is via a gate and ticket stand (50HTG), which also sells a few religious pamphlets and bottles of curative water taken from the falls. Steps lead down to the falls. If you wish, you're free to join the locals who bathe in the pools at the bottom.

Where to stay and eat

Wozo Plaza Hotel Route National 3; 3455 7730/3454 6967; e wozoplazahotel@yahoo.fr. About 4km north of Mirebalais on the road to Hinche. A series of pink bungalows with good rooms set in pleasantly leafy grounds. Bar, restaurant & pool, Wi-Fi. **$$$**

Le Mirage Hotel 86 Rue Louverture; 3444 6521. Small, bright hotel facing the main square. Simple throughout but decent value for money. Restaurant. **$$**

Pelerin Hotel Ville-Bonheur; 3110 4767/3792 9603. Pretty basic hotel with attached bar-resto. Uninspiring, but the only option if you want to sleep near the waterfalls. **$**

Le Toit Blanc Ville-Bonheur; 2947 0134; 11.00–18.00 Fri–Sun. Really charming restaurant in a gingerbread-style house with large terrace; worth detouring for. Creole food, but with regular diversions into other cuisines. Friendly hosts, small craft shop attached. **$$$**

In Mirebalais, there are plenty of bar-restos around the main square, including **Moto**, **Fierté** (*both Bd Jean-Jacques Dessalines*) and **Bueno** (*Rue Claire Heureuse*).

HINCHE

Hinche is the departmental capital of the Central Plateau. It's a large, neatly paved market town bound on two sides by the curve of the Guayamoue River. Farming is the main occupation, especially maize, cassava, beans and peanuts. Hinche is also famous for its *rapadou*, a sticky sweet made from molasses.

Hinche has a **colonial-era cathedral** on Place Charlemagne Péralte. Built in the 16th century, it's one of the oldest churches in the Americas. It's a low structure in white and blue with a pitched roof; the bell tower next to it is a more modern addition. A few streets over on Rue Claire Heureuse is its modern replacement, a shining white rotunda flanked by two domed towers.

Churches aside, the main attraction in Hinche is the scenery. Most people visit to go to Bassin Zim, but the enterprising and adventurous will take one look at the hills and want to pull on their hiking boots; a few expats have also extolled the virtues of mountain biking in the region. It's also possible to arrange birdwatching tours in English from nearby Pignon, through **Zwazo Yo** (e *naturesphoto@hotmail.com; http://zwazoyo.blogspot.com; from US$10 for a 2hr tour*), who teach ecology in the Central Plateau.

GETTING THERE AND AWAY

By air The quickest way to get to Hinche is to fly with **Mission Aviation Fellowship** (MAF; *+1 208 498 0800 (USA); e flyhaiti@maf.org; www.mafhaiti.org*), who have a daily flight to nearby Pignon.

By road The fine tarmac highway that has led here from Port-au-Prince stops abruptly in Hinche, and if you're continuing north the road gets pretty rough in places as it heads towards Cap-Haïtien. It passes through Pignon (the slowest part of the road – two hours), Saint-Raphaël and Dondon before popping out at Milot. There are ultimate plans to extend the sealed road as far as Cap-Haïtien, at which point it will probably become very busy, as it will offer a faster alternative to the north than travelling via Gonaïves. For now, it's a dusty and very bumpy

CHARLEMAGNE PERALTE

Hinche's proudest son is Charlemagne Péralte, who led the armed uprising against the US occupation of Haiti in the early 20th century.

Péralte was an officer in the Haitian army, which was disarmed by the US marines during the early months of the occupation in 1915. Based in Léogâne, he refused to surrender his weapon, proclaiming he could only accept a direct order from the Haitian president. He was dismissed, and returned to his home in Hinche, but soon after was arrested for allegedly attacking the *gendarmie* building in the town. Péralte was sentenced to hard labour; his brother was executed. After serving three years, he escaped and set about organised armed insurrections.

There had already been armed resistance against the Americans – the rebels were dubbed the Cacos, the traditional name for peasant fighters – but Péralte was the first to give them shape. Gathering men and arms he led an attack on Hinche that was quickly beaten back, but then settled into a prolonged guerrilla campaign. An educated suit-wearing man, he was equally at home writing impassioned manifestoes invoking the names of Dessalines and Pétion, as he was leading his troops by carrying a crucifix-topped banner to the accompaniment of Vodou drums. The Cacos carried out raids across the country, and within a year, Péralte claimed to have 40,000 men under arms.

Péralte was killed aged 33 on 31 October 1919 – a double agent smuggled two American soldiers wearing blackface into his camp, where they shot him at point-blank range. In order to proclaim victory, they displayed his body in public, and then distributed a photo of his corpse tied to a plank as if he had been crucified. In doing so they unwittingly created the perfect image of a martyr, one famously re-imagined by the artist Philomé Obin in his painting *The Crucifixion of Charlemagne Péralte for Liberty*. When Haiti regained her sovereignty in 1934, his remains were given a state funeral in Cap-Haïtien.

route (except during the rains, when it's a muddy and very bumpy route) through increasingly green and hilly territory. At Saint-Raphaël, it's possible to turn east to St-Michel de l'Attalaye and continue through to Marchand Dessalines and the Artibonite Valley.

There are plentiful minibuses travelling every day between Hinche and Port-au-Prince, and somewhat fewer rough *taptaps* heading north.

WHERE TO STAY AND EAT The majority of good sleeping options are actually outside Hinche proper – transport is required.

Centre Emmaus Route de Bassin Zim; 3946 6956/6958; e centreemmaus@hotmail.com. Ostensibly a religious retreat, this place 5km north of Hinche has rooms in lovely grounds for NGO staff (proof of organisation needed). Comfy rooms & excellent food. Half-board, Wi-Fi. **$$**

Haiti Outreach Guest House Pignon; e Guesthouse@haitioutreach.org. Some way from Hinche, but a good & welcoming Central Plateau option. Modern & comfortable, full-board & 24hr solar electricity. Advance booking only. Wi-Fi. **$$**

Hotel Maguana 2 Rue Rivage; 3690 1662. The only decent option in town. Set in a large green yard with a few pecking fowl; average rooms but plenty of space. **$$**

L'Ermitage De Pandiassou Maissade; 3472 5934/3474 1599; e lermitagedepandiassou@yahoo.com; http://lermitagedepandiassou.com. On a turning 5km from Hinche when arriving from Mirebalais. Delightful airy guesthouse surrounded by greenery & bordering its own lake. Restaurant & bar. Wi-Fi. **$$**

If you're staying outside Hinche, your meal options are covered, but in Hinche itself you can get big plates of Haitian food at **Sainteté de Dieu Bar-Resto** (*Rue Toussaint Louverture*) and **Eben-Ezer Bar-Resto** (*Rue Paul Eugène Magloire*), which also has a small supermarket.

BASSIN ZIM The Bassin Zim waterfall is the big draw for those travelling as far as Hinche. It's yet another example of Haiti's unerring ability to conjure sites of breathtaking beauty seemingly out of nowhere. The falls are located in wooded country and run in white water down a rocky chute into a turquoise pool over

TAÍNO ROCK ART

Haiti could be a spelunker's paradise. The soft limestone that makes up much of the country is highly permeable and easily eroded by water, leaving a landscape riddled with caves. They were important in the cosmology of the original Taíno inhabitants of the islands, and accounts contemporary to Columbus record their use as ritual spaces, frequently covered with art – either pictographs painted onto the rocks, or petroglyphs scratched into the surface. Although the Taínos have long vanished, it's still possible to find tantalising traces of their culture in these caves, the best of which can be found dotted around the Central Plateau.

The large cave at Bassin Zim (see page 219) is the most readily accessible, and has a good number of petroglyphs, but there are better examples if you travel a little further afield. There are a series of caves around Dondon that have superb carvings, although to reach them you'll need to find a guide in town, and prepare for a hike (one cave I visited was half an hour from the road, and involved fording a river multiple times). Inside, the walls are festooned with cartoon-like faces, stick figures, spiders and a host of images of unknown meaning. The natural shapes of the walls are often used to great effect – in one cave a stalactite near the entrance stands like a ghostly sentinel with a frightening face carved onto its ridges. You can also find some quite wonderful carvings at the caves at St Michel de l'Attalaye.

Although the Taíno petroglyphs in the Dominican Republic are increasingly well described by archaeologists, those in Haiti remain largely undiscovered by the outside world. Their nature makes them incredibly difficult to date, although over the centuries the carvings slowly acquire a patina of bacterial or fungal growth, indicating their great age. Many exist in a precarious state – many caves are used for Vodou rituals, attesting to the continual ritual significance of such sites, but this has frequently led them to remain dangerously exposed, as shown by the large amounts of graffiti found in caves like that at Bassin Zim.

Long-term Port-au-Prince resident and speleologist Brian Oakes has been exploring Haiti's caves and rock art for years, and runs informal tours by 4x4 to some of the more accessible sites – he can be contacted via email at e haitianspeleosurvey@gmail.com.

50m wide. You'll regret it if you don't bring a swimming costume, as the basin makes the perfect spot for a dip. The water is chest-deep, so you can wade right out to the falls. Bring a picnic too, as the whole spot seems designed to idle away an afternoon.

To the right of the falls, a rough path leads uphill through the trees. If you follow this as it climbs and bears around to the left, you'll find yourself at the mouth of a large cave, out of which the river that forms the waterfall pours. It's a brilliant scene, and entering the cave (you'll need to skip over a few potentially slippery rocks), you can find evidence of the island's original inhabitants. Several of the walls have Taíno petroglyphs carved into the walls. Unfortunately there's a fair degree of graffiti as well, but thankfully the power of the carvings still manages to overcome the vandalism. During the wet season, the flow of water is strong enough to prevent access to the cave altogether.

The waterfall is a 12km drive north of Hinche (about 30 minutes). On leaving the town, turn right off the main road as soon as you've crossed the bridge over the Guayamoue River and then left after crossing another small tributary. The road quality isn't great and there are certainly no signs, so check en route that you're heading in the right direction for the *cascades*.

Appendix 1

LANGUAGE

Haiti has two official languages: Creole and French. The latter is the language of government, law and education, but it's actually a minority language. For 90% of the population, the language of discourse is Creole. Luckily, Creole is relatively easy to pick up, and if you already have some French, you'll find a great deal of common vocabulary.

There are a couple of worthwhile Creole phrasebooks on the market: *Haitian Creole Phrasebook: Essential Expressions for Communicating in Haiti* by C Laguerre and Cecile Accilien (McGraw-Hill, 2010) and *Haitian Creole Dictionary and Phrasebook* by Charmant Theodore (Hippocrene, 2008). If you want to really get your Creole up and running, go for the excellent *Creole Made Easy Workbook* by Betty Turnbull (Light Messages, 2005), which you can also find for sale in Haiti. *Byki Haitian Creole* (Transparent Language, Inc) is a good app to get smartphone users started.

PRONUNCIATION Creole is pronounced phonetically, with every letter being sounded out. Consonants are hard ('k' instead of 'c') and vowels are never silent. The letter 'e' is pronounced as an acute, unless it carries a grave, when it is flat. For instance, *kafe* (coffee) is pronounced 'ka-fay', while *frèt* (cold) rhymes with 'get'. Note the personal pronouns *m* (me, pronounced as a short 'mm' or 'um') and *w* (you, pronounced 'ou' to rhyme with 'do').

WORDS AND PHRASES

Essentials

Good morning	*bonjou*
Good afternoon/evening	*bonswa*
Good night (departing)	*bonnwit*
Goodbye	*orevwa*
See you later	*na we pita*
Sir	*msye*
Madam	*madam*
My name is …	*m rele …*
What is your name?	*ki jan ou rele?*
I am from England/America/Haiti	*mwen soti Anglete/Amerik/Ayiti*
I am English/American/Haitian	*mwen se Angle/Ameriken/Ayisyen*
How are you?	*koman w ye?*
Fine thanks	*m pa pli mal*
I'm OK	*m'ap kenbe*
Please	*silvouple*
Thank you	*mesi*
Thank you very much	*mesi anpil*
Sorry/excuse me	*padon/eskize m*

OK	*dakò*
Yes	*wi*
No	*non*
I	*m/mwen*
You	*w/ou*
He/she/it	*li*
We	*nou*
Do you speak English/French?	*eske ou pale Angle/Franse?*
I don't understand	*m pa konprann*

Questions

How?	*kouman?*	Who?	*ki?*
What?	*ki?*	How much?	*konbyen?*
What is it?	*ki sa?*	Do you have … ?	*eske ou gen … ?*
Where?	*ki kote?*	Can you … ?	*ou kapab … ?*
Which?	*ki?*	Can I … ?	*m kapab … ?*
When?	*lè?*	I want/need …	*m bezwen …*
Why?	*poukisa?*		

Numbers

0	*zewo*	16	*sèz*
1	*yon*	17	*disèt*
2	*de*	18	*dizuit*
3	*twa*	19	*diznèf*
4	*kat*	20	*ven*
5	*senk*	21	*venteen*
6	*sis*	22	*vennde*
7	*sèt*	30	*trant*
8	*uit*	40	*karant*
9	*nèf*	50	*senkant*
10	*dis*	60	*swasant*
11	*onz*	70	*swasann dis*
12	*douz*	80	*katreven*
13	*trèz*	90	*katrevan dis*
14	*katòz*	100	*san*
15	*kinz*	1,000	*mil*

Time and dates

What time is it?	*kilè li ye?*	Today	*jodiya*
Second	*segonn*	Tomorrow	*demen*
Minute	*minit*	Yesterday	*ayè*
Hour	*è*	Morning	*lematen*
Day	*jou*	Evening	*sware*
Week	*semenn*	Night	*lannwit*
Month	*mwa*	Now	*kounye-a*
Year	*ane*	Later	*pita*

Monday	*lendi*	Friday	*vandredi*
Tuesday	*madi*	Saturday	*samdi*
Wednesday	*mèkredi*	Sunday	*dimanche*
Thursday	*jedi*		

January	*janvye*
February	*fevriye*
March	*mas*
April	*avril*
May	*me*
June	*jen*
July	*jiyè*
August	*out*
September	*septanm*
October	*oktob*
November	*novanm*
December	*desanm*

Getting around

I want to go to …	*m vle ale …*
What time does it leave?	*ki lè li kite?*
From	*apati*
To	*a*
Here	*isit*
There	*isit la*
Bus station	*estasyon*
Airport	*ayewopò*
Car	*mashin, oto*
Bus	*otobis*
Minibus	*minibuss*
Taxi	*taxi*
Motorbike	*moto*
Bicycle	*bisiklèt*
Boat	*bato*
Is this the road to … ?	*se wout sa a pou … ?*
Where is it?	*ki kote?*
I'm lost	*m pèdi*
Left/right	*goch/dwat*
Crossroads/intersection	*kafou*
Near	*toupre*
Opposite	*anfas*
Where is the petrol station?	*ki kote ponp gazolin?*
Diesel	*dizèl*
Petrol (gas)	*gazolin*

Accommodation

I'm looking for a hotel	*m'ap chache pou yon otel*
Do you have a room?	*eske ou gen yon chanm?*
I'd like …	*m vle …*
… a single room	*… yon chanm simple*
… a double room	*… yon chanm double*
… a room with air conditioning	*… yon chanm ak klime*
How much is it per night?	*se konbyen chak lannwit?*
Is there hot water?	*ki gen dlo cho?*
Is there electricity?	*ki gen elektrisite/kouran?*
Is there breakfast included?	*ki gen dejene?*

Eating

For Haitian dishes, see *Chapter 2, Eating and drinking*, page 74.

What do you have?	*ki sa ou gen?*
I'd like to eat …	*m vle manje …*
I'd like to drink …	*m vle bwè …*
I'm a vegetarian	*m se vejetaryen*
Meat	*vyann*
Chicken	*poul*
Beef	*bèf*
Goat	*kabrit*
Pork	*vyann cochon*
Fish	*pwason*
Conch	*lambi*
Lobster	*woma*
Rice	*diri*
Avocado	*zaboka*
Banana	*fig*
Beans	*pwa*
Breadfruit	*lam veritab*
Cabbage	*chou*
Cauliflower	*chouflè*
Coconut	*kokoye*
Fruit	*fwi*
Grapefruit	*panplemous*
Lemon	*limon*
Lime	*sitwon*

EMERGENCY

Help!	*ede!*	Ambulance	*anbilans*
Police	*polis*	Thief	*vole*
Fire	*dife*	Hospital	*lopital*

Mango	*mango*	Vegetables	*legim*
Onion	*zonyon*	Yam	*yanm*
Orange	*zoranj*	Bread	*pen*
Papaya	*papay*	Egg	*ze*
Peanut	*pistach*	Drink	*bwason*
Pepper	*piman*	Water	*dlo*
Pineapple	*zannanna*	Ice	*glas*
Plantain	*bannan*	Milk	*lèt*
Potato	*pomdetè*	Coffee	*kafe*
Spinach	*zepina*	Juice	*ji*
Sweet potato	*patat*	Beer	*byè*
Tomato	*tomat*	Rum	*wonm*

Shopping

Do you sell … ?	*eske ou vann … ?*	More	*plis*
I'd like to buy …	*m vle achte …*	Less	*mwens*
I want …	*m bezwen …*	Bigger	*pi gwo*
How much is it?	*konbyen?*	Smaller	*pi piti*
It's too expensive	*li two chè*	I want to change money	*mven ta vle chanje lajan*
Is it Haitian dollars or American dollars?	*eske se dola ayisyen ou dola ameriken?*		

Health

Where is the hospital?	*kote lopital la?*	… headache	*… tèt fè mal*
		… malaria	*… palidis*
Pharmacy	*famasi*	… vomiting	*… vomi*
Doctor	*doktè*	I am allergic	*m se allejik*
Toilet	*twalèt*	diabetic	*dyabetik*
I have …	*m gen …*	asthma	*opresyon*
… diarrhoea	*… dyare/vant fè mal*	tampons	*tanpon ijyenik*
… nausea	*… vomisman*	condoms	*pwotèj/kapòt*
… fever	*… fyèv*	sun block	*solèy losyon*

Places

Bank	*labank*	House	*kay*
Church	*legliz*	Beach	*plaj*
Office	*biwo*	Mountain	*mòn*
Embassy	*anbasad*	Road	*wout*
Post office	*lapòs*	River	*rivye*
Shop	*magazen*	Sea	*lamè*
Market	*mache*		

Appendix 2

FURTHER INFORMATION

HISTORY AND BACKGROUND

Alexis, Gérald *Haitian Painters* Éditions Cercle d'Art, 2000. Richly illustrated and researched coffee-table guide to Haitian painting.

Arthur, Charles and Dash, Michael (editors) *Libète: A Haiti Anthology* Latin America Bureau, 1999. Useful anthology of writing from and about Haiti, from history and politics to culture and religion.

Consentino, Donald (editor) *Sacred Arts of Haitian Vodou* UCLA Fowler, 1995. Lavishly illustrated collection of essays examining the cultural and artistic roots and fruits of the Vodou religion.

Danticat, Edwidge *After the Dance* Crown Journeys, 2002. History and travelogue wrapped together in an account of the novelist's first trip to Carnival in Jacmel. Short but lively.

Danticat, Edwidge *Brother, I'm Dying* Knopf, 2007. Powerful family biography by the Haitian-American novelist, centred on her uncle and his tragic flight to the USA after the 2004 coup. Heart-wrenching.

Danticat, Edwidge *Create Dangerously* Princeton University Press, 2010. A beautifully written and thought-provoking series of essays about the role of the Haitian artist in society, by the acclaimed novelist.

Danticat, Edwidge (editor) *The Butterfly's Way* Soho, 2001. Collection of essays from the Haitian diaspora, on identity and their relationship with their mother country.

Deibert, Michael *Notes from the Last Testament* Seven Stories Press, 2005. Blow-by-blow account of the run-up to the 2004 Aristide coup by a journalist on the ground.

Deren, Maya *Divine Horsemen: The Voodoo Gods of Haiti* Vanguard Press, 1953. Classic work on Vodou culture by experimental film-maker and anthropologist Deren (the accompanying DVD of the same name is a fascinating window into traditional practices).

Dubois, Laurent *Avengers of the New World* Harvard University Press, 2004. Hard-to-beat history of the Haitian Revolution, neatly distilling this complex period into a single narrative.

Dubois, Laurent *Haiti – The Aftershocks of History* Metropolitan Books, 2012. Possibly the best history of Haiti out there – lucid and engagingly written. Note that it stops just short of the Aristide period, otherwise hard to beat.

Dupuy, Alex *The Prophet and The Power* Rowan & Littlefield, 2006. Powerfully argued account and analysis of the two complicated and sometime contentious presidencies of Jean-Bertrand Aristide.

Farmer, Paul *Haiti After the Earthquake* Public Affairs, 2011. Powerful eyewitness account of the 2010 earthquake and its aftermath, from the rubble all the way to the international donor conferences, by Partners In Heath co-founder Paul Farmer.

Farmer, Paul *The Uses of Haiti* Common Courage Press, 1994 (updated 2003). Analysis of the long and complicated relationship between Haiti and the USA, argued with urgency and frustration.

Girard, Philippe *Haiti – The Tumultuous History* Palgrave Macmillan, 2010. Handy one-volume history of Haiti, from Columbus in 1492 to the 2010 earthquake.

Gordon, Leah *Kanaval: Vodou, Politics and Revolution on the Streets of Haiti* Soul Jazz, 2010. Gorgeous photography book examining Jacmel's Carnival traditions through portraiture and accompanying essays.

Hallward, Peter *Damming the Flood* Verso, 2008. Impassioned and detailed account of the 2004 coup against Aristide, with its sympathies firmly with the ousted president.

Heinl, Robert and Heinl, Nancy *Written In Blood – The Story of the Haitian People 1492-1995* UPA, 2005 (revised edition). A wrist-cracker of a history book – voluminous and dense with detail. Better for reference than narrative reading.

Hurbo, Laënec *Voodoo – Truth and Fantasy* Thames and Hudson, 1995. Handy pocket-sized and well-illustrated primer to Vodou, and its history and function in Haiti.

James, C L R *The Black Jacobins* Penguin, 1938. The first major historical work on the Haitian Revolution. A thrilling account – some of the research is now a little dated, but still an essential read.

Katz, Jonathan *The Big Truck That Went By: How the World Came to Save Haiti and Left Behind a Disaster* Palgrave Macmillan, 2013. Gripping and finely written account of the 2010 earthquake and what followed it, written from the ground up by the Associated Press's Haiti correspondent.

Kidder, Tracy *Mountains Beyond Mountains* Random House, 2003. Biography of Paul Farmer and the story of his medical NGO Partners In Health, with a strong focus on its activities in Haiti.

Nicholls, David *From Dessalines to Duvalier* Rutgers University Press, 1996 (revised edition). Excellent academic history of post-independence history, seen mostly through the contentious lens of race in Haitian society.

Popkin, Jeremy *You Are All Free: The Haitian Revolution and the Abolition of Slavery* Cambridge University Press, 2010. Detailed academic account of the causes and progress of the Haitian Revolution; reveals many new facts and ideas.

Schuller, Mark and Morales, Pablo (editors) *Tectonic Shifts* Kumarian Press, 2012. Anthology of essays tackling the 2010 earthquake and the struggle to rebuild. Brilliant and angry.

Schwartz, Timothy *Travesty In Haiti* Book Surge, 2008. Angry and cynical take by one aid worker on the aid and missionary 'industries' in Haiti.

Shacochis, Bob *The Immaculate Invasion* Viking, 1999. A graphic journalist's-eye-view of the chaotic US military mission to Haiti in 1994, following the return to power of Aristide.

Thomson, Ian *Bonjour Blanc – A Journey Through Haiti* Vintage, 2004. Still the only major modern travelogue written about Haiti. The erudite and bemused author travels through the country just before Aristide's first election victory. Fascinating, although much has changed since publication.

Wilentz, Amy *The Rainy Season* Simon & Schuster, 1989. Gripping reportage from the last days of Jean-Claude Duvalier and the rise of Aristide from priest to presidential candidate. Superb.

FICTION

Bell, Madison Smartt *All Souls' Rising* Pantheon, 1996. First in Bell's epic and densely written trilogy about the Haitian Revolution, with the emergence of Toussaint Louverture as its key figure.

Bell, Madison Smartt *Master Of The Crossroads* Pantheon, 2000. The second of the sweeping revolutionary trilogy.
Bell, Madison Smartt *The Stone That The Builder Refused*, 2004. The close of Bell's masterwork, cutting between the bloody war and Toussaint Louverture's lonely death in a French prison.
Danticat, Edwidge *Breath, Eyes, Memory* Soho Press, 1994. A novel of female relationships and family secrets, with a young girl travelling from her home in rural Haiti to the USA.
Danticat, Edwidge (editor) *Haiti Noir* Akashic, 2007. Unexpectedly satisfying anthology of loosely noir-themed fiction in and around Haiti.
Danticat, Edwidge *Krik? Krak!* Soho Press, 1991. Collection of nine short stories about Haiti that first announced the author as a major new voice. A perfect introductory volume.
Danticat, Edwidge *The Dew Breaker* Abacus, 2004. Flitting between 1960s Haiti and present-day New York, a tragic story of one of Duvalier's prison guards and the possibility of redemption.
Danticat, Edwidge *The Farming of Bones* Soho Press, 1998. Dramatic and moving novel of two lovers who are immigrants to the Dominican Republic, swept up in the 1937 anti-Haitian massacres.
Greene, Graham *The Comedians* Penguin, 1965. Greene's untouchable satire about life under Papa Doc Duvalier and his Tontons Macoutes that seems to be in the luggage of every other visitor to Haiti. Razor-sharp.
Laferrière, Dany *Heading South* Douglas & McIntyre, 2009. A sharp take on race, culture and power politics in 1970s Haiti, refracted through the lens of the decadent tourist industry. Rich and satisfying.
Roumain, Jacques *Masters of the Dew*, Heinemann, 1978. Translated by Langston Hughes, Roumain's classic novel of rural struggle in Haiti. An unreserved masterpiece.
Vieux-Chauvet, Marie *Love, Anger, Madness* Modern Library, 2009. Only recently translated into English, the shocking trilogy of novels about life under an unnamed dictatorship, that drove its author into exile from the Duvalier regime.
Wolkstein, Diane *The Magic Orange Tree* Schocken, 1997. Charming anthology of Haitian folktales, with each accompanied by insightful accounts of their collection in Haiti by the professional storyteller author.

WEBSITES

http://dloc.com Digital Library of the Caribbean. Fascinating online archive.

http://haitianbloggers.collected.info Site bringing together Haitian bloggers living in Haiti or abroad.

http://haitimemoryproject.org Haiti Memory Project. Oral history project about the earthquake and its aftermath.

http://haitirewired.wired.com Haiti Rewired. Resource and networking website from Wired, focusing on technology, news and rebuilding.

http://thelouvertureproject.org The Louverture Project. Wiki-style guide to the Haitian Revolution.

www.haiticherie.ht Association Touristique d'Haiti. Website of Haiti's tourism association.

www.lenouvelliste.com *Le Nouvelliste.* Website of Haiti's largest newspaper.

www.bostonhaitian.com Boston Haitian. US-based diaspora-led reporting on Haiti.

www.haitilibre.com Haiti Libre. Haitian news website.

www.kreyolicious.com Kreyolicious. Fun and informative website on Haitian culture, arts and lifestyle.

www.lematinhaiti.com *Le Matin.* Online version of the print newspaper.

www.mappinghaitianhistory.com Mapping Haitian History. Visual mapping of Haiti's historical sites.

www.visithaiti.gouv.ht Ministry of Tourism. Official tourism website for Haiti.

Index

Page numbers in **bold** refer to major entries; those in *italics* indicate maps

INDEX TO ADVERTISERS